CHRISTIAN ZIONISM

To Joanna,
Rachel, Katie, Louise & Michael

CHRISTIAN ZIONISM

Road-map to Armageddon?

Stephen Sizer

ivp

Inter-Varsity Press

Inter-Varsity Press
38 De Montfort Street, Leicester LE1 7GP, England
Email: ivp@uccf.org.uk
Website: www.ivpbooks.com

Unless otherwise stated, Scripture quotations are taken from the Holy Bible, New International Version. Copyright © 1973, 1978, 1984 by International Bible Society. Used by permission of Hodder & Stoughton, a division of Hodder Headline Ltd. All rights reserved. 'NIV' is a trademark of International Bible Society. UK trademark number 1448790.

Preface is adapted from Stephen R. Sizer, 'The Premised Land: Palestine and Israel', in Michael Prior (ed.), *They Came and They Saw* (London: Melisende, 2000). Used by permission.

Song on p. 264, 'Ten Measures of Beauty' by Garth Hewitt, is copyright © Chain of Love Music/Admin. by Daybreak Music Ltd, PO Box 2848, Eastborne, East Sussex, BN20 7XP. Used by permission.

First published 2004

British Library Cataloguing in Publication Data
A catalogue record for this book is available from the British Library.

ISBN 1-84474-050-1

Set in Monotype Garamond 11/13pt
Typeset in Great Britain by Servis Filmsetting Ltd, Manchester
Printed in Great Britain by Creative Print & Design (Wales), Ebbw Vale

Inter-Varsity Press is the publishing division of the Universities and Colleges Christian Fellowship (formerly the Inter-Varsity Fellowship), a student movement linking Christian Unions in universities and colleges throughout Great Britain, and a member movement of the International Fellowship of Evangelical Students. For more information about local and national activities write to UCCF, 38 De Montfort Street, Leicester LE1 7GP, email us at email@uccf.org.uk, or visit the UCCF website at www.uccf.org.uk.

CONTENTS

FOREWORD

Evangelical Christians are sometimes accused of not being sufficiently interested in politics and not contributing to the great debates about social welfare in our world today. 'Too heavenly minded to be of any earthly use', is the charge. While there may often be truth in this accusation, Stephen Sizer's challenging study of Christian Zionism demonstrates that there is at least one area in contemporary politics where this is decidedly not so. But is the influence of Christian Zionism valid and helpful? Is the theological basis of this political stance misguided and the outcome contrary to God's will?

Stephen's careful survey of this movement demonstrates that theology really matters and, if the theology is wrong, the consequences are disastrous. Prior to examining the theological position of the various strands of Christian Zionism, Stephen devotes his first chapter to an historical exploration of the development of this movement. He traces the transition of Christian Zionism from early nineteenth-century rural England to mainstream American evangelicalism in the twentieth century. He notes the historical and interpretative reasons why Christian Zionism evolved into different schools of thought. Then he launches into a theological analysis and critique of those positions in his second chapter.

Seven basic theological tenets are accepted in varying degrees by evangelical Christian Zionists. The foundation upon which the other tenets are based is a literalist hermeneutic and a consistently futurist reading of prophecy. Quite apart from the political outcome of this way of reading the Bible, there are serious implications for the church and the gospel. At heart of the problem, he claims, there is actually a devaluing of the significance of the Lord Jesus Christ and his atoning work for Israel and the nations.

The third chapter of this book shows how the belief that the Jews remain

God's chosen people (apart from Christ and his church) leads Christian Zionists to endorse and justify many of the current policies of the Israeli government, including the annexation and settlement of Palestinian-owned land. The return of Jews to Israel is actively encouraged and facilitated. Western governments are pressured to relocate their embassies to Jerusalem and to recognize this as the eternal and exclusive capital of the Jews. Those who believe that Scripture predicts the rebuilding of the temple in Jerusalem and a reinstitution of the priesthood and sacrificial system offer varying degrees of support to Jewish Temple Mount organizations committed to achieving this end. Moreover, as Stephen concludes,

> since Christian Zionists are convinced there will be an apocalyptic war between good and evil in the near future, there is no prospect for lasting peace between Jews and Arabs. Indeed, to advocate that Israel compromise with Islam or coexist with Palestinians is to identify with those destined to oppose God and Israel in the imminent battle of Armageddon (p. 252).

Stephen shows that the New Testament must be our guide in understanding how the Old Testament has been fulfilled for us in Christ and in judging what remains to be worked out in history. Every Christian needs to be clear about the way the Bible fits together, observing the way the inspired writers of the New Testament reveal this. But especially those who presume to tell us how the future will unfold need to be sure that they are not misusing the Bible and, in their misguided zeal, dishonouring God. I hope that Christian Zionists who read this book will recognize that it is written by someone who believes in the inspiration and authority of Scripture as they do, and will consider carefully the challenge he brings to their particular line of interpretation.

David Peterson
Oak Hill College, London

PREFACE

The seeds of this book were sown over thirty years ago when, as a young Christian, I remember devouring Hal Lindsey's best-selling book, *The Late Great Planet Earth*, and hearing in person his lectures on eschatology and the book of Revelation. It seemed as if the Bible was literally coming true in our generation.

The Jews, the 'chosen people', had been brought back to their promised land in 1948. Apparently, the prophetic clock was now ticking. God had miraculously delivered them again in 1967 giving victory over their Arab enemies. Jerusalem, their eternal capital, was now at last, once again, under Jewish sovereignty. The temple would soon be rebuilt. The prophetic signs were being fulfilled on the front pages of our newspapers. The world seemed to be rushing towards a cataclysmic end in the great battle of Armageddon.

The threat of nuclear war, the fear of world domination by atheistic communism, as well as Palestinian terrorism, were futile attempts to annihilate the Jewish people and destroy the State of Israel. The moral responsibility of evangelical, Bible-believing Christians was clear – stand with God's 'chosen' people, because God was on the side of those who 'blessed' Israel.

Alongside these Zionist convictions there was also a strong desire to visit the Holy Land to see for myself where Jesus walked. It never occurred to me that there might be an indigenous church, except for the small but growing assemblies of Messianic believers spoken of in revered but hushed tones.

Christian Zionist friends helped me plan my first pilgrimage to the Holy Land in 1990. On their advice, a Messianic guide called Zvi led our group. With the *intifada* at its height it did not appear strange that he was unwilling to meet us at our hotel in Arab East Jerusalem. The sight of heavily armed Israeli soldiers, encounters with occasional stone-throwing Palestinian children, and Zvi's advice that some of the archaeological sites on the West Bank were 'unsafe' for tourists fuelled my latent prejudice against Palestinians.

Our memorable tour began with a visit to Yad Vashem, the *Shoah* museum. This helped explain the Israeli preoccupation with security. They could not rely on the West any more now than they had done in the 1930s. During the week,

Zvi enthusiastically showed us how the new State of Israel was turning a barren and deserted wilderness into a land flowing with milk and honey. We visited the Kibbutz at En Gev in the Golan with its armour-plated tractors, and to Masada to see where the heroic Zealots took their last stand against the Roman invaders in AD 73. It is here that Israeli soldiers take an oath: 'Masada shall not fall again.' Apart from Jerusalem, it has become the most popular location for Jewish tourists and Christian Zionists visiting Israel. It is ironic that a place where 960 Jews committed suicide 2,000 years ago has become a modern symbol of Zionism.

Two encounters that week led me to the beginning of a radical change of perspective. The first came on the Via Dolorosa, at the Lithostrotos, the Roman pavement below street-level at the Sisters of Zion convent. A member of the party asked Zvi an innocuous question about the Palestinians. He responded by giving us all a piece of paper with the heading, 'Who are the Palestinians?' Ignoring the significance of the archaeological site before us, he proceeded to 'prove' that there was no such thing as a Palestinian. They had no unique history, culture or language. They were Arabs who had entered Israel in the early twentieth century to threaten the fledgling State of Israel. Zvi was adamant; the Arabs should return to Arabia. The Jews had a divine right to *Eretz Yisrael* which extended from the River of Egypt to the Euphrates.

The second encounter came in a meeting later that week with Riah Abu El Assal, then Archdeacon of Nazareth. In a simple presentation, and with great humility, he explained how he was a Christian Arab Palestinian Israeli. He spoke of the historic presence of an indigenous church in Palestine long before the founding of the young State of Israel. He shared with us his joy at just receiving back his Israeli passport. He had been banned from travel abroad for four years without explanation or charges ever having been made. At the end of his presentation Riah warmly shook hands with Zvi and we left Nazareth. But my bubble had burst. We had met a real-life Christian Palestinian. They did exist. And so began the stream of questions that would not go away.

Back in Britain I began my search to make sense of the historical and theological issues behind the Palestinian–Israeli conflict. Discovering our common interest in Palestine, Garth Hewitt invited me to join him on a concert-tour of Jerusalem and West Bank churches in early 1991. Garth has written many songs about the search for peace between Jews and Palestinians. He has a rare talent for empathizing with people and being able to express in song their pain and suffering, their faith and hope. Conditions for travel were difficult, with tensions high due to the *intifada* and Israeli security measures.

On this and subsequent tours, my convictions were further shaped by deepening friendships with Naim Ateek of Sabeel (the Palestinian Liberation

Theology Centre in Jerusalem), Jonathan Kuttab, a human-rights lawyer, Edmund Shehadeh of the Arab Bethlehem Centre for Rehabilitation in nearby Beit Jala, Zougbi Zougbi of Wi'am, a conflict resolution centre in Bethlehem, the late Audeh Rantisi of the Evangelical Boys Home in Ramallah, Elias Chacour of the Prophet Elias School in Ibillin, Bishara Awad of Bethlehem Bible College, Salim Munayer of Musalaha, a reconciliation project in Bethlehem, Cedar Duyabis of the YWCA, East Jerusalem, and Tom Getman of World Vision. Though a small and diminishing presence in the Holy Land, the Palestinian church has been blessed by God with some courageous and outspoken leaders.

In 1992, at the request of the Anglican bishop Samir Kafity, a three-month visit to our diocese was arranged for the Revd Zahi Nassir from Nazareth. During his stay in our home, three notable events stand out which helped me understand what it felt like to be a Palestinian.

At a clergy gathering Zahi had the opportunity to meet the mayor of Guildford. Attempting no doubt to be welcoming, the mayor explained that she had 'once met your Prime Minister, Golda Meir'. Zahi politely informed her that Golda Meir was not his Prime Minister: 'She had been a good Prime Minister to her own people but not for the Palestinians.' There was incomprehension in the mayor's face and an embarrassing silence ensued until someone moved the conversation on to less controversial matters.

At another event intended to give Zahi an opportunity to speak about Palestine to Christians in Guildford, a senior member of a large evangelical church stood up and asked if Zahi could answer a basic question: 'What is a Palestinian?' Zahi handled the insult with dignity, inviting the Zionist to answer it himself. Nevertheless, the public embarrassment of having to justify the existence of his own people cast a shadow over Zahi's stay.

On another occasion Zahi travelled to Wales by train and borrowed a book of mine to read on the way. He chose *Israel: An Apartheid State* by Uri Davis. Nervous at being seen reading the book, he made a brown paper dust-cover to hide the title. It had never occurred to me that reading a book on a train in Britain might be perceived as a threat to the security of Israel, and could therefore be a hazardous pursuit for a Palestinian.

Between 1993 and 1997, growing interest in pilgrimages gave the impetus for some postgraduate research into the impact of pilgrimages on the Christian community of the Holy Land. The results revealed deep-seated prejudices and stereotyped caricatures of Palestinians and a lamentable lack of contact between pilgrims and the indigenous Christians. The presence of tens of thousands of Western Christian tourists and pilgrims in the Holy Land at any one time has great potential for good. Ironically, for the most part, it does great harm. That is because most Western Christians visiting the Holy Land follow a predetermined itinerary purposely designed to bring them into contact with a Jewish Israel perpetuating a myth of the Zionist dream being fulfilled.

In 1995, Garth Hewitt and I made a second concert-tour of churches in Israel and the Occupied Territories. This also provided the inspiration for Garth's book *Pilgrims and Peacemakers*, based on interviews with Jewish and Palestinian peacemakers. One episode in the book highlights an unusual personal application of the Parable of the Good Samaritan. After a rather tense visit to Gaza when I had naïvely accepted a lift in a yellow-plated Israeli car into the heart of Gaza city to speak at an Anglican service, we decided a short break would be good, and I offered to show Garth the beautiful scenery of northern Galilee. It was February, and by mid-afternoon the light was fading as I drove a borrowed minibus up the winding road past Mount Hermon and into the snowy slopes of the occupied Syrian Golan Heights.

Above the snow-line we encountered a group of young Israeli army conscripts. They were cold, wet and tired and wanted a lift. We nervously avoided stopping and carried on driving up into the darkness. With hopes of showing Garth the isolated UN post at Qunaytirah fading, we turned round and headed home. As we turned a corner our headlights caught the shape of one of the young soldiers lying in the road and his companions attempting to revive him. Wet and cold, he appeared to have hypothermia. Garth helped them lift the semi-conscious soldier into the minibus and we continued to descend before being met by an army vehicle that took the unknown soldier to hospital. Despite my anger at the arrogant Israeli settlers and soldiers I had encountered in Gaza the day before, I realized that these young conscripts, just seventeen years old, were as vulnerable, needy and human as my Palestinian friends. It reminded me of Elias Chacour's profound statement that forms part of the presentation he gives to groups visiting his university which brings together Jewish, Christian and Muslim faculty and students: we are not born Jews, Arabs or British; first of all, God makes us babies in his image.

Beginning in 1995, I began to write a series of articles about the political and theological issues surrounding the involvement of Western Christians in the peace process. The flak received from some readers gave an indication of the depth of feeling within British evangelicalism on the Arab–Israeli issue. Despite further criticism, and even the occasional anonymous threat, the articles began to flow, and more importantly, were published.

From 1997 the haunting images from my journeys to Israel/Palestine and the many unanswered questions became the stimulus for doctoral research into the historical involvement of Christians in the Palestinian–Israeli conflict. It included an examination of the biblical and theological basis for the justification of Zionism, and also an analysis of the political consequences of such partisan support. The fruits of that research have been distilled into this book and I welcome the dialogue that may now ensue as you read on and engage with some of these controversial and deeply divisive issues.

My motivation for this book lies in the conviction, deeply held, that for Western Christians, especially evangelicals, to ignore or stereotype their Palestinian brothers and sisters, now threatened with extinction, is not only deeply offensive, it is surely a contradiction of our faith, and ultimately immoral before God. It is nothing less than to perpetuate the evil of the Levite in the Parable of the Good Samaritan who walked by on the other side.

Stephen R. Sizer
Virginia Water
January 2004

The following additional resources on Christian Zionism are available from the author.

Zion's Christian Soldiers (CD)
An audio book read by the author, summarizing the history, theology and politics of Christian Zionism.

Christian Zionism and the Last Days Temple (CD)
A more detailed examination of the most controversial aspect of the Christian Zionist agenda.

Christian Zionism (DVD)
A graphic six-part series featuring the author in which he explores the historical roots, theological basis and political consequences of contemporary Christian Zionism.

Christian Zionism: The Definitive Document Collection (CD)
This text CD contains the author's PhD thesis in Adobe format, all his published articles and PowerPoint presentations.

To obtain any of these resources please contact Stephen Sizer by email at stephen@sizers.org. For further information as well as details of other books and resources visit <http://www.sizers.org>.

ACKNOWLEDGMENTS

I want to express my deep gratitude to many people who have made this book possible.

The inspiration for the research that has led to this book has come, in part, from the writings of John Stott, Donald Wagner, Colin Chapman, Garth Hewitt, Peter Walker, Naim Ateek, Gary Burge and Michael Prior. They introduced me to the sufferings of the Living Stones of the Holy Land. They are members of a small band of Christ's followers unafraid to question whether Christianity and Zionism are compatible.

For seven long years Michael Butterworth, Martin Davie and Alan Storkey patiently coached me through the doctoral research that provided the basis for this book.

I want to thank Philip Duce and the staff at IVP for patiently and gently helping me turn an unwieldy thesis into a readable manuscript. I am also thankful for their courage in publishing this book. I can count on one hand the number of authors willing to speak out on the subject, and even fewer publishers, it seems, willing to print.

I am very grateful to Colin Chapman, Andrew Walker, Stephen Travis and Donald Wagner who have read the manuscript in various editions and offered wise and perceptive advice.

I also wish to express my appreciation to the Right Revd Riah Abu El Assal, Episcopal Bishop of Jerusalem, the Right Revd Kenneth Cragg, former Assistant Bishop of Jerusalem and the Right Revd John Gladwin, Bishop of Chelmsford, for their gracious support, guidance and blessing.

Lastly, I thank my patient and understanding wife, Joanna, and four enthusiastic children for journeying with me, often literally, on visits to Israel/Palestine. It is, therefore, to Joanna, Rachel, Katie, Louise and Michael that I dedicate this book.

Stephen R. Sizer

LIST OF FIGURES

INTRODUCTION

Underneath the beautiful Sea of Galilee lies a hidden fault-line that runs down from Mount Hermon through the Jordon Valley to the Red Sea, the Arabian peninsula and on to the heart of East Africa. Over thousands of years, earthquakes along this fault-line have devastated countless civilizations. Today there is a human fault-line running through the same land – a fault-line that is largely hidden from view until it erupts in violence. The cause of these volcanic eruptions has to do with the pressure of two peoples, like two tectonic plates, trying to occupy the same land – one the military occupier, the other the occupied. The media present this as a clash between two cultures, Palestinian and Israeli or Oriental and Western. As I hope to show, the convictions of Christian Zionists have made a significant contribution to the Israeli–Palestinian conflict.

Zionism defined

In general terms, Zionism may be defined as 'the national movement for the return of the Jewish people to their homeland and the resumption of Jewish sovereignty in the Land of Israel'.[1] The term 'Zionism' was first coined in

---

1. *A Definition of Zionism* (2004) [Internet], Jewish Virtual Library, a division of the

1892 by Nathan Birnbaum, then a student in Vienna. A year later in 1893, he published a booklet entitled, *The National Rebirth of the Jewish People in Its Homeland as a Means of Solving the Jewish Problem*, in which he advocated Jewish nationalistic ideas that Theodor Herzl was to later expound in *A Jewish State*, published in 1896.[2]

At the First World Zionist Congress, which Herzl convened in Basle a year later, in 1897, he and Birnbaum articulated the deep longings of many Jewish people for their own homeland. Various strands of Zionism emerged in the early twentieth century including practical, socialist and communist.[3] The most recent and probably most destructive form to appear is known as Messianic Zionism. Distinct from much more traditional and less extreme expressions of Zionism, this is associated with individuals like Rabbi Kahne and Gershon Salomon, together with the Gush Emunim movement and the Temple Mount Faithful. Messianic Zionism was spawned from within the ultra-Orthodox subcultures of the 'Charedi Bible-belt' around Jerusalem following the 1967 'Six Day War'. The Charedim (ultra-Orthodox Jews) were, according to Sachar, 'the first to embrace the territorialist mysticism inherent in the 1967 triumph'[4] and came to be a decisive factor in Likud's electoral victory in 1997.

Equating Arabs with the ancient Amalekites, and convinced they have a divinely ordained mandate to carry out ethnic cleansing of the Palestinians from Israel, religious Zionists have been in the forefront of the illegal occupation of Palestinian land, attacks on Muslims and mosques and the systematic expansion of the West Bank settlements, especially in places like Arab East Jerusalem and Hebron.

American-Israeli Cooperative Enterprise, <http://www.us-israel.org/jsource/Zionism/zionism.html>. [Accessed May 2004.]

   For a comprehensive appraisal of Jewish Zionism, see also, Gary Smith, *Zionism, The Dream and the Reality – A Jewish Critique* (Newton Abbot: David & Charles, 1974); Bernard Avishai, *The Tragedy of Zionism: Revolution and Democracy in the Land of Israel* (New York: Farrar Straus Giroux, 1985); Claude Duvernoy, *The Zionism of God* (Jerusalem: Ahva Press, 1985).

2. Herzl, *Jewish State*.

3. David Vital, *The Origins of Zionism* (Oxford: Oxford University Press, 1975); *Zionism: The Formative Years* (Oxford: Oxford University Press, 1982); *Zionism: The Crucial Phase* (Oxford: Oxford University Press, 1987).

4. Howard M. Sachar, *A History of Israel from the Rise of Zionism to our Time*, 2nd edn (New York: Alfred Knopf, 1998) p. 923.

Ironically, the Zionist vision which initially called simply for a 'publicly secured and legally assured homeland for the Jews in Palestine',[5] was largely nurtured and shaped by Christians long before it was able to inspire widespread Jewish support. As will be shown in chapter one, proto-Christian Zionism predated and nurtured Jewish Zionism, while the contemporary Christian Zionist movement emerged only after 1967, alongside Messianic Zionism, in part in reaction to the widespread criticism Israel has endured over the last thirty-five years.

Christian Zionism defined

At its simplest, Christian Zionism is a political form of philo-Semitism, and can be defined as 'Christian support for Zionism'.[6] The term 'Christian Zionist' first appears to have been used by Theodor Herzl to describe Henri Dunant, the Swiss philanthropist and founder of the Red Cross. Dunant was one of only a handful of Gentiles to be invited to the First World Zionist Congress. Walter Riggans interprets the term in an overtly political sense as 'any Christian who supports the Zionist aim of the sovereign State of Israel, its army, government, education etc., but it can describe a Christian who claims to support the State of Israel for any reason'.[7]

Evangelicals, in particular, are increasingly polarized as to whether Christian Zionism is biblical and orthodox or heretical and cultic. Two mutually exclusive positions have emerged – that of covenantalism and dispensationalism. A detailed examination of both is available elsewhere.[8] Colin Chapman observes, 'It is hard to think of another situation anywhere in the world where politics have come to be so closely bound up with religion, and where scriptures have such a profound effect on political action.'[9]

Walter Riggans, for example, elaborates on the relationship between theology and politics in Zionism:

> A biblical Zionism, which is surely the desire of every Christian, will be fundamentally about God and His purposes. Thus Zionism, when seen in a proper Christian perspective, will be understood as a branch of theology, not of politics . . . The State

---

5. Cited in Sharif, *Non-Jewish Zionism,* p. 1.

6. Chapman, *Whose Promised Land?*, p. 274.

7. Riggans, *Israel and Zionism,* p. 19.

8. Holwerda, *Jesus and Israel;* O. P. Robertson, *Israel of God;* Venema, *Promise of the Future.*

9. Chapman, *Whose Promised Land?*, p. 304.

of Israel is only the beginning of what God is doing for and through the Jewish people.[10]

He goes on to suggest that Christians should not only support the idea of a Jewish State, but also support its policies: '. . . in the most modest of ways I would suggest that Christians . . . must give support in principle to the State of Israel as a sign of God's mercy and faithfulness, and as a biblical mark that God is very much at work in the world'.[11]

While not specifying the geographical extent of Zion, the Israel branch of the Lausanne Consultation on Jewish Evangelism, which draws together most evangelical and charismatic denominations, as well as Messianic and evangelical mission agencies, made the following commitment in 1989:

> We affirm our belief that, as part of the fulfillment of God's promises in the Bible, the Jewish people have a right to the land of Israel. We further affirm the legitimacy of the Jewish national political entity in the land within safe and secure borders.[12]

Advocates argue, therefore, that Christian Zionism is born out of the conviction that God has a continuing special relationship with, and covenantal purpose for, the Jewish people, apart from the church, and that the Jewish people have a divine right to possess the land of Palestine. This is based on a literal and futurist interpretation of the Bible and the conviction that Old Testament prophecies concerning the Jewish people are being fulfilled in the contemporary State of Israel.

For Christian Zionists, God's promise to Abraham remains unconditional and eternal:

> 'To your descendants I give this land, from the river of Egypt to the great river, the Euphrates . . . The whole land of Canaan, where you are now an alien, I will give as an everlasting possession to you and your descendants after you; and I will be their God.' (Gen. 15:18; 17:8)

Invariably, Christian Zionists are therefore also defenders of, and apologists for, the State of Israel. This support consistently involves opposing those

---

10. Walter Riggans, *The Covenant with the Jews* (Tunbridge Wells: Monarch, 1992), pp. 91, 93.
11. Riggans, *Israel and Zionism*, p. 21.
12. Baruch Maoz, 'A Statement on Christian Zionism', *Mishkan* 1, 12 (1990), p. 6.

deemed to be critical of, or hostile towards Israel, but also leads to the justification of Israel's occupation and settlement of the West Bank, Golan and Gaza on biblical grounds.

Whether consciously or otherwise, Christian Zionists subscribe to a religious Jewish agenda best expressed by Rabbi Shlomo Aviner, who claims: 'We should not forget . . . that the supreme purpose of the ingathering of exiles and the establishment of our State is the building of the Temple. The Temple is at the very top of the pyramid.'[13] Another rabbi, Yisrael Meida, explains the link between politics and theology within Jewish Zionism: 'It is all a matter of sovereignty. He who controls the Temple Mount, controls Jerusalem. And he who controls Jerusalem, controls the land of Israel.'[14] This paradigm may be illustrated by way of three concentric rings. The land represents the outer ring, Jerusalem the middle ring and the temple is the centre ring. The three rings comprise the Zionist agenda by which the land was claimed in 1948, the Old City of Jerusalem was occupied in 1967 and the temple site is being contested. For the religious Zionist, Jewish or Christian, the three are inextricably linked. The Christian Zionist vision, therefore, is to work to see all three under exclusive Jewish control since this will lead to blessing for the entire world as nations recognize and respond to what God is seen to be doing in and through Israel.

As tensions simmer in the Middle East, so the stakes are raised to gain the moral high-ground, and the Bible is used both to silence Israel's critics as well as to castigate her. In such a polarized culture, anti-Zionism is equated with anti-Semitism and the *Shoah*[15] exploited by what Norman Finkelstein describes as 'holocaustology' to immunize Israel from censure.[16]

Grace Halsell, who regards the movement as a cult, asks: 'What is the message of the Christian Zionist? Simply stated it is this: every act taken by Israel is orchestrated by God, and should be condoned, supported, and even praised by the rest of us.'[17] Dale Crowley, a Washington-based religious broadcaster, similarly describes dispensational Christian Zionism as the 'fastest growing cult in America':

---

13. Rabbi Shlomo Chaim Hacohen Aviner, cited in Halsell, *Forcing God's Hand*, p. 71.

14. Yisrael Meida, cited in Halsell, *Forcing God's Hand*, p. 68.

15. *Shoah* is the Hebrew word for 'holocaust' and is preferred among Jews. See <www.yahoodi.com/peace/holocaust.html>.

16. Finkelstein, *Holocaust Industry*; see also, Sam Schulman, 'Did Six Million Die for This?', *Jewish World Review* (Jan. 2000).

17. Grace Halsell, 'Israeli Extremists and Christian Fundamentalists: The Alliance', *Washington Report* (Dec. 1988), p. 31.

It's not composed of 'crazies' so much as mainstream, middle to upper-middle class Americans. They give millions of dollars each week – to the TV evangelists who expound the fundamentals of the cult. They read Hal Lindsey and Tim LaHaye. They have one goal: to facilitate God's hand to waft them up to heaven free from all the trouble, from where they will watch Armageddon and the destruction of planet earth.[18]

The Middle East Council of Churches (MECC), drawing together the historic as well as evangelical churches of the Holy Land, rejects Christian Zionism 'as representing a heretical interpretation of Holy Scripture',[19] while John Stott has described it as 'biblically anathema'.[20]

The significance of the Christian Zionist movement

Christian Zionism as a movement is very diverse, ranging from individual Christian leaders whose denominations have no stated position on Zionism, to major international evangelical organizations that are unapologetically Zionist. Some have an explicit political agenda, such as Bridges for Peace (BFP) and the International Christian Embassy Jerusalem (ICEJ), which also enjoys diplomatic status in several Central American countries.[21] Both have disavowed or redefined evangelism and identify with right-wing Israeli opinion, lobbying the United States government to continue to finance Israel's expansionist agenda. Other organizations such as Jews for Jesus (JFJ) and Church's Ministry Among Jewish People (CMJ)[22] are primarily evangelistic or

---

18. Dale Crowley, 'Errors and Deceptions of Dispensational Teachings', *Capitol Hill Voice* (1996–1997), cited in Halsell, 'Israeli Extremists and Christian Fundamentalists', p. 5.

19. Middle East Council of Churches, *What is Western Fundamentalist Christian Zionism?*, Preface; see also, Peter Makari, 'Abrahamic Heritage', *MECC News Report*, 10:2/3 (Summer 1998).

20. John Stott, cited in Wagner, *Anxious for Armageddon*, p. 80.

21. ICEJ have diplomatic status in Honduras and Guatemala and have been implicated in facilitating the funding of the US-backed Contras during the 1980s; Wagner, *Anxious for Armageddon*, p. 109.

22. In this book various ex-staff members of CMJ are quoted. Tony Higton, the current general director, writes: 'CMJ will continue its historic ministry to the Jewish people, its stand against anti-Semitism and its concern for the welfare and

Messianic but also espouse Zionism on biblical grounds. Exobus and the Ebenezer Trust are representative of smaller organizations specializing in facilitating the transportation of Jews to Israel from Russia and Eastern Europe, while Christian Friends of Israel Communities encourages churches to adopt Jewish settlements in the Occupied Territories.[23]

Contemporary British and American Christian Zionist leaders have achieved considerable influence in popularizing an apocalyptic premillennial and largely dispensational eschatology legitimizing Zionism among Western Christians. That their teaching also warrants the description 'Armageddon theology' is evident from the provocative titles of many of their recent books.[24]

Dispensational Christian Zionism, which is the dominant form of Christian Zionism in America, with its teaching on the rapture of the church, the rebuilding of the temple and imminent battle of Armageddon, is pervasive within mainline evangelical, charismatic and independent denominations including the Assemblies of God, Pentecostal and Southern Baptists, as well as many of the independent mega-churches. George Marsden concedes that:

> Even most of those neo-evangelicals who abandoned the details of Dispensationalism still retained a firm belief in Israel's God-ordained role. This belief is immensely popular in America, though rarely mentioned in proportion to its influence.[25]

Estimates as to the size of the movement as a whole vary considerably. While advocates such as Pat Robertson and Jerry Falwell claim the support of 100 million Americans with whom they communicate weekly, Halsell estimates there are more likely between 25 and 30 million Zionist Christians in America. She claims they are led by 80,000 fundamentalist pastors, their views

---

safety of Jewish people everywhere, including in Israel. We recognize the suffering of the Palestinian people. Many of them have lost their ancestral homes and continue to experience military occupation. Sometimes they suffer unjustified oppression, humiliation, violence and the destruction of their homes. They also experience economic disaster and lack of infrastructure, partly through Israeli policies and partly through the failures of the Palestinian Authority. We seek to implement biblical teaching on reconciliation' (unpublished letter from Tony Higton, 17 May 2004).

23. See Sarah Honig, 'Adopt-a-Settlement Program', *Jerusalem Post*, 2 Oct. 1995.

24. Notably, Lindsey, *1980's: Countdown*; Walvoord, *Armageddon*; Rosen, *Overture to Armageddon?*; Hunt, *Peace, Prosperity and the Coming Holocaust*.

25. Marsden, *Understanding Fundamentalism and Evangelicalism*, p. 77.

disseminated by 1,000 Christian radio stations and 100 Christian TV stations.[26] She cites Doug Kreiger who lists over 250 pro-Israeli organizations founded in the early 1980s alone.[27]

Robert Boston, in his biography of Pat Robertson, argues that his Christian Coalition, with an annual budget of $25 million and over 1.7 million members, is probably the most influential political organization in the United States today.[28] However, the National Unity Coalition for Israel (recently renamed the Unity Coalition for Israel), founded in 1994, which brings together 200 different Jewish and Christian Zionist organizations, including the International Christian Embassy Jerusalem, Christian Friends of Israel, and Bridges for Peace, claims a support-base of 40 million active members.[29]

These organizations, in varying degrees and for a variety of reasons, some contradictory, make up a broad coalition that is shaping not only the peace negotiations between Israelis and Palestinians, but also the perception of Christianity among Jews and Muslims and thereby Christian witness in the wider world.

A critique of Christian Zionism

In this investigation of evangelical Christian Zionism, chapter 1 will trace the historical development of the movement since 1800 and its transition from British sectarianism to mainstream American evangelicalism. Chapter 2 will assess, from a covenantal perspective, seven basic theological tenets that distinguish the various strands within the Christian Zionist movement: an ultra-literal and futurist hermeneutic; a belief that the Jews remain God's chosen people; restorationism and the return of the Jews to Palestine; the justification of Eretz or Greater Israel; the centrality of Jerusalem as the Jewish capital; the expectation that the temple will be rebuilt; and a pessimistic premillennial apocalyptic eschatology. Chapter 3 will focus on the political consequences of this theology and the way in which Christian Zionists bolster the pro-Israeli lobby; facilitate *aliyah*, that is the return of Jews to the land; sustain the West

---

26. Halsell, *Forcing God's Hand*, p. 50.
27. Halsell, *Prophecy and Politics*, p. 178.
28. Boston, *Most Dangerous Man in America?*
29. See the website of the Unity Coalition for Israel: <http://www.israelunitycoalition. org>. The reference to their 40 million members can be found on <http://www. israelunitycoalition.org/events/events/php>. [Accessed May 2004.]

Bank settlements; lobby for international recognition for Jerusalem; promote the rebuilding of the temple; and oppose a peaceful settlement of the Palestinian–Israeli conflict. The concluding chapter will delineate the variant forms of Christian Zionism from the more benign to the most destructive and will offer an alternative. There is also a glossary providing definitions of some of the theological terms used (see pp. 265–269).

Clearly not all evangelicals identify with or support Christian Zionism, the author included, although the two are synonymous in the minds of many Jews and Muslims. In Europe, a larger proportion of evangelicalism would identify with a covenantal perspective than in the United States. But just as British evangelicals exported dispensational Christian Zionism to the United States in the nineteenth century, so now, through the popular writings of Tim LaHaye and Jerry Jenkins, for example, evangelicals in the United States are exporting their apocalyptic dispensational pro-Zionism to the rest of the world, with devastating consequences in the Middle East. It is intended that this book will expose the historical origins, the theological basis and political consequences of this movement. It is hoped that this book will contribute not only to greater dialogue between advocates and critics, but also to the wider search for peace between the children of Abraham, physical and spiritual. Jesus Christ said 'Blessed are the peacemakers, for they will be called children of God' (Matt. 5:9 TNIV).

1. THE HISTORICAL ROOTS OF CHRISTIAN ZIONISM

As the navel is set in the centre of the human body,
so is the land of Israel the navel of the world . . .
situated in the centre of the world,
and Jerusalem in the centre of the land of Israel,
and the sanctuary in the centre of Jerusalem,
and the holy place in the centre of the sanctuary,
and the ark in the centre of the holy place,
and the foundation stone before the holy place,
because from it the world was founded.[1]

This quotation from the Talmud, called the 'Midrash Tanchuma', and written around the ninth century AD, epitomizes the deep resonance many Jewish people have felt for the land of Israel, the city of Jerusalem and the temple from their exile in AD 70 to the present day. It also helps explain the emotional attachment many evangelical Christians feel for the Holy Land which undergirds their solidarity with Zionism in particular.

This chapter will focus on the historical events, socio-cultural factors and

---

1. Midrash Tanchuma, Qedoshim. This part of the oral Torah was probably written in the ninth century.

theological developments that have been most determinative in the rise of evangelical Christian Zionism within British and American religious and political circles, from the early nineteenth century until the present day. It will highlight the influence of a relatively small group of British evangelical Christian leaders who were instrumental in providing the theological grounds as well as political connections which enabled Zionism to become a reality.

The early intimations: proto-Christian Zionism

While advocates claim that Christian Zionism is entirely biblical in origin,[2] its genesis as a theological doctrine and religious movement lies within the Protestant Reformation which brought about a renewed interest in the Old Testament and God's dealings with the Jewish people. The translation, publication and free access to the Bible among the laity created a major paradigm-shift in popular thinking. Interpretation was no longer the exclusive prerogative of an ecclesiastical hierarchy.

The emergence of biblical literalism

From Protestant pulpits right across Europe, the Bible was now taught within its historical context and given its plain literal sense rather than the allegorical interpretations offered for centuries within Roman Catholicism. A new assessment of the place of the Jews within the purposes of God emerged, especially through the writings of Theodore Beza, who succeeded John Calvin in Geneva, and Martin Bucer in Strasbourg. In his *Institutes of the Christian Religion*, Calvin stressed that divine blessing was associated with and dependent upon covenantal obedience. Furthermore, he insisted that there was only one covenant in which both old- and new-covenant believers shared: 'For, even now, the only kingdom of heaven which our Lord Jesus Christ promises to his followers, is one in which they may sit down with Abraham, and Isaac and Jacob (Matthew 8:11).'[3]

While Calvin and Luther understood the word 'Israel' in Romans 11:25 to refer to the church of Jewish and Gentile believers, as had the Roman Catholic Church, Theodore Beza and Martin Bucer preferred to apply the word to unbelieving Jews and Judaism. The various editors of the Geneva Bible,

---

2. Stearns, *Biblical Zionism*; Fruchtenbaum, *Israelology*, 1st edn.

3. John Calvin, *Institutes of the Christian Religion* (electronic edition), 4.16.14 (Garland, TX: Galaxie Software, 1999).

influenced both by Calvin and Beza, increasingly favoured this interpretation. In the 1557 and 1560 editions, a short note on Romans 11 defined 'Israel' as 'the nation of the Jews'. In later editions, this was amplified to suggest a future conversion of the Jewish nation to Christ: 'He sheweth that the time shall come that the whole nation of the Jews, though not everyone particularly, shall be joined to the church of Christ.'[4] Through the notes accompanying this translation, which became the most widely read translation in England and Scotland prior to the Authorized Version of 1611, together with the writings of Puritans such as William Perkins and Hugh Broughton, the idea of the conversion of the Jewish people spread in Britain and the American Colonies.[5]

The conversion and restoration of the Jews

Puritan eschatology was essentially postmillennial and, based on Romans 9–11, believed the conversion of the Jews would lead to future blessing for the entire world: 'Puritan England and covenanting Scotland knew much of spiritual blessing and it was the prayerful longing for wider blessing, not a mere interest in unfulfilled prophecy, which led them to give such place to Israel.'[6] Thomas Brightman (1562–1607), who has been described as the father of the doctrine of the 'restoration of the Jews', also predicted the imminent conversion of the Jewish people. In his *Apocalypsis Apocalypseos* (meaning, 'A Revelation of the Revelation'),[7] he speculated that the seven vials began with Elizabeth's accession to the throne in 1558 and that the seventh trumpet of Revelation 10 had been sounded in 1588 with the destruction of the Spanish Armada. He argued that the Turkish Empire (the false prophet), having formed an unholy alliance with the Roman Church (the Antichrist), would be destroyed followed by 'the calling of the Jews to be a Christian nation', leading to 'a most happy tranquillity from thence to the end of the world'.[8] Brightman's commentary on Daniel 11 – 12, first

---

4. Murray, *Puritan Hope*, p. 41.

5. Peter Toon, 'The Latter-Day Glory', in Toon (ed.), *Puritans, the Millennium and the Future of Israel*, p. 24.

6. Murray, *Puritan Hope*, pp. 59–60.

7. First published in Frankfurt in 1609; English translation (1615), *A Revelation of the Revelation*, published in Amsterdam.

8. Cited in Edward E. Hindson (2001), *Medieval and Reformation Backgrounds of Dispensationalism* [Internet], the Conservative Theological Society, <http://www.conservativeonline.org/journals/01_03_journal/1997v1n3_id01. htm>. [Accessed May 2004.]

published in 1614, was subtitled *The restoring of the Jewes and their callinge to the faith of Christ after the utter overthrow of their three enemies is set forth in livelie colours.* Brightman was also convinced that 'the rebirth of a Christian Israelite nation' would become 'the centre of a Christian world'. Brightman's preaching and writings attracted considerable attention and his views were influential even in English government circles. In 1621, for example, Sir Henry Finch, an eminent lawyer and Member of Parliament, developed Brightman's views further, publishing a book entitled *The World's Great Restauration* (sic) or *Calling of the Jews, (and with them) all the Nations and Kingdoms of the Earth, to the Faith of Christ.* In it he argued:

> Where Israel, Judah, Zion and Jerusalem are named [in the Bible] the Holy Ghost
> meant not the spiritual Israel, or the Church of God collected of the Gentiles or of
> the Jews and Gentiles both . . . but Israel properly descended out of Jacob's loynes.
> The same judgement is to be made of their returning to their land and ancient seats,
> the conquest of their foes . . . The glorious church they shall erect in the land itself of
> Judah . . . These and such like are not allegories, set forth in terrene similitudes or
> deliverance through Christ (whereof those were types and figures), but meant really
> and literally the Jews.[9]

Other Reformers such as Richard Sibbes, Samuel Rutherford and John Owen, also postmillennialists, were equally convinced that one day the Jews would be brought to faith in Jesus Christ and become part of the church, for which they prayed earnestly. This belief in the conversion of the Jews was so universally embraced that it was written into the *Westminster Larger Confession* and the Congregationalist 'Savoy Declaration' of 1658.

By the late seventeenth century and right through the eighteenth century, especially during the period of the Great Awakening, postmillennial eschatology continued to dominate European and American Protestantism. The writings and preaching of Jonathan Edwards and George Whitefield were influential in the spread of the belief that the millennium had arrived, that the gospel would soon triumph against evil throughout the world and God's blessings of peace and prosperity would follow the conversion of entire nations, including Israel, prior to the glorious return of Christ. Edwards wrote:

---

9. Henry Finch, *The World's Great Restauration* (sic) or *Calling of the Jewes* (London: Edward Griffin for William Braden, 1621), cited in Wagner, *Anxious for Armageddon*, p. 87.

> Though we do not know the time in which this conversion of Israel will come to
> pass, yet this much we may determine by Scripture, that it will be before the glory of
> the Gentile part of the Church shall be established . . . Jewish infidelity will be
> overthrown. Jews will cast away their old infidelity. They shall flow together to the
> blessed Jesus . . . Nothing is more certainly foretold that this national conversion of
> the Jews in Romans XI . . . They shall then be gathered into one fold together with
> the Gentiles.[10]

Based on his interpretation of Revelation 16:1, Edwards speculated that the
vials of God's wrath had been poured out during the Reformation, that the
papacy might expire in 1866, Islam would be destroyed, the Jews converted,
and the heathen of America, Africa and India soon brought to faith in
Jesus.[11] In the context of such a renewed and Christianized world, Palestine
gradually came to be seen as the rightful Jewish homeland. Under the protection of the Protestant Church, a proto-Zionist movement emerged, convinced the Bible promised that the Jewish people, once 'converted' to
Christianity, would then return to Palestine and enjoy a national existence
alongside other Christian nations prior to the second advent. If the proto-
Zionist era of the seventeenth and eighteenth centuries might be character-
ized by the relationship between the Puritans and the 'Israelites', in the
nineteenth century this shifted to the bond between evangelicals and the
Jews.[12]

The socio-political context for the rise of Christian Zionism

The late eighteenth and early nineteenth centuries saw a dramatic movement
away from the optimism of postmillennialism following a sustained period of
turmoil on both sides of the Atlantic. This was associated with the American
War of Independence (1775–1784), the French Revolution (1789–1793) and
the Napoleonic Wars (1809–1815).

With the fall of several European monarchies between 1804 and 1830,

---

10. Jonathan Edwards, *The Complete Works of Jonathan Edwards*, vol.1 (Edinburgh:
    Banner of Truth, 1974), p. 607.
11. Cited in Clouse, Hosack & Pierard, *New Millennium Manual*, pp. 90–91.
12. Jan Nederveen Pieterse, 'The History of a Metaphor: Christian Zionism and
    the Politics of Apocalypse', *Archives de Sciences des Religions* 75 (1991),
    pp. 75–104.

coupled with widespread unrest in England, Napoleon's menacing words, 'Remember that I march followed by the god of fortune and the god of war',[13] seemed an ominous sign of the end of the world.

In 1804, Napoleon had been crowned Emperor of the Gauls in the reluctant presence of the Pope. In 1807 he agreed to divide Europe with the Tsar of Russia and blockaded British goods in Europe. In 1809 he had arrested the Pope and annexed the Papal States. By 1815, Napoleon's armies had fought, invaded or subjugated much of Europe and the Middle East, including Italy, Austria, Germany, Poland, Russia, parts of Palestine and Egypt. Napoleon set his brothers on the thrones of Holland, Naples, Spain and Westphalia, as well as giving his son the title 'King of Rome'. His intention was to create a confederated Europe, each ruled by a vassal monarch, subject to himself as 'supreme King of Kings and Sovereign of the Roman Empire'.[14] Numerous preachers and commentators, including Robert Jamieson and George Stanley Faber, speculated on whether Napoleon represented the Antichrist.[15] Others predicted that, in fulfilment of Daniel 2, ten European kingdoms including England, France, Spain and Austria were about to revive the Holy Roman Empire and form a United States of Europe in partnership with the Antichrist.[16] For example, Jamieson speculated:

> The First Napoleon's Edict published at Rome in 1809, confiscating the papal dominion and joining them to France, and later the severance of large portions of the Pope's territory from his sway and the union of them to the dominions of the king of Italy, virtually through Louis Napoleon, are the first instalment of the full realization of this prophecy of the whore's destruction.[17]

Napoleon's destruction of the Roman Catholic Church in France, his seizure of church assets, execution of priests and the exile of the Pope from Rome all

13. Cited in John Abbott, *The History of Napoleon Bonaparte*, 2 vols. (New York: Harper & Brothers, 1883), p. 121.

14. G. H. Pember, *The Great Prophecies of the Centuries concerning Israel and the Gentiles* (London: Hodder, 1902), pp. 236–241.

15. Darby, 'Remarks on a tract circulated by the Irvingites', in *Collected Writings*, vol. 15, Doctrinal 4, p. 2; Janet M. Hartley, 'Napoleon in Russia: Saviour or anti-Christ?' *History Today* 41 (1991).

16. Fromow (ed.), *B. W. Newton and Dr. S. P. Tregelles*, pp. 120–127.

17. Robert Jamieson, *Commentary, Critical and Explanatory on the Whole Bible* (London: Oliphants, 1934).

appeared to corroborate this. Some even believed they were witnessing the 'deadly wound' inflicted on the 'Beast' predicted in Revelation 13.

These tensions and upheavals fuelled the second Great Awakening, the revivals associated with Charles Finney, the Adventism of Joseph Miller and the founding of the Jehovah's Witnesses by Charles Taze Russell. They also brought about a renewal of interest in prophecy which eventually led to a revival of premillennialism within mainstream and sectarian evangelicalism.

George Stanley Faber (1773–1854), for example, was one of the earliest to write speculative treatises on prophecy in the nineteenth century. He also identified Napoleon, the head of the revived Roman Empire, as the Antichrist. He predicted Napoleon would be destroyed in Palestine by a Western alliance of England and Russia. Faber recognized England as the 'Isles of the Sea' referred to in Isaiah 24:15 and the 'ships of Tarshish' mentioned in Isaiah 60:9, since England was 'the great maritime sea power'. As England's ally in the Napoleonic Wars, Russia's prophetic involvement as the 'king of the North' in Daniel 11 would, he argued, be benevolent.[18]

Several nineteenth-century Christian leaders in America predicted the imminent end of the world. In 1835, for example, Charles Finney speculated that 'If the church will do all her duty, the Millennium may come in this country in three years.'[19] Joseph Miller narrowed the return of Christ down to 21 March 1843, while Charles Russell more prudently predicted that Christ would set up his spiritual kingdom in the heavenlies in 1914. Russell's success was in part due to the launch of a magazine in 1879, entitled *Zion's Watchtower*. It had an initial print run of 6,000 copies. Within a century, this had increased to 15 million copies. For many years, Russell's popular sermons linking biblical prophecy with contemporary events were reproduced in over 1,500 newspapers in the USA and Canada.

At the same time, in America and Europe there was renewed interest in both the Orient as well as the Jewish people, in part shaped by a growing literary romanticism infatuated with the Hebrew world. Authors included Robert Byron, Walter Scott, William Wordsworth, Robert Browning and George Eliot. Eliot, for example, not only attended synagogue services regularly but also held dialogues with Jewish rabbis. In 1874 she began working on *Daniel Deronda*, described by Regina Sharif as, 'the first truly Zionist novel in the history of non-Jewish fiction', and 'the apex of non-Jewish Zionism in

---

18. Faber, *A General and Connected View*, p. 4.

19. Charles Finney, *Lectures on Revival* (Cambridge, MA: Harvard University Press, 1960), p. 306.

the literary field'.[20] Sharif observes how Eliot dispensed with the idea of Jewish emancipation being linked to or dependent on their conversion and integration within the church: 'Restoration had instead become identified with a return to the Hebrew heritage.'[21]

Interest in the land of Palestine itself was largely due to a succession of archaeological discoveries, military adventurism and the growing number of travelogues published which fired the popular imagination. Between 1800 and 1875, over 2,000 authors wrote about the Holy Land. Arthur P. Stanley's guidebook, *Sinai & Palestine*, for example, went through four editions within a year of its publication in 1856.[22] Other popular authors included William Thackeray, Gertrude Bell, Robert Byron, Robert Graves, Alexander Kinglake, Rudyard Kipling, T. E. Lawrence and Freya Stark. As early as the 1830s, a visit to the Near East formed part of the grand tour taken by most young European gentlemen.

The Palestine Exploration Fund (PEF) was founded in 1865 by a group of distinguished British academics and clergymen, most notably James Finn, the British consul in Jerusalem, Lord Shaftesbury, Arthur P. Stanley, the dean of Westminster Abbey, and Sir George Grove. The object of the PEF remains to promote research into the history, geology, archaeology, topography and natural sciences of biblical Palestine and the Levant. However, Finn and Shaftesbury, both avid restorationists, saw the PEF primarily as a vehicle for achieving the return of the Jews to Palestine.[23] The PEF was also associated with many of the outstanding names in Middle East exploration, including Major General Sir Charles Wilson, General Sir Charles Warren, Claude Regnier Condor, Lt Horatio Kitchener of Khartoum and T. E. Lawrence. The survey of Western Palestine undertaken between 1871 and 1878 by Condor and Kitchener, together with soldiers of the Royal Engineers, was the first cartographic survey ever conducted of Palestine and provided the Zionist movement with invaluable information on natural resources and locations for settlement.

In 1869, the Suez Canal was opened and, coincidentally, in the same year Thomas Cook led his first tour-group to Jerusalem made up of sixteen ladies, thirty-three gentlemen and two assistants. By the end of the nineteenth

20. Sharif, *Non-Jewish Zionism*, p. 46.

21. Ibid., p. 46.

22. Arthur Penrhyn Stanley, *Sinai & Palestine* (London: Murray, 1871).

23. Cited in Derek White, *Christian Zionism* (n. d.) [Internet], Saltshakers Messianic Community, <http://www.saltshakers.com/midnight/chrzion1.htm>. [Accessed May 2004.]

century, his company had arranged for 12,000 tourists to visit the Holy Land. It is not an exaggeration to say that Cook probably did more than any other person to facilitate and shape evangelical contact with the Holy Land. His reputation as an organizer of pilgrimages grew after he was invited in 1882 to arrange the visit by Prince Edward, later King Edward VII, and his son Prince George, later King George V.

These political, literary, geographical and educational factors provided the context for a growing interest among evangelical Christians in a futurist interpretation of Old Testament prophecy, in the rediscovery of the land of Palestine and in the conversion and restoration of the Jewish people.

As the postmillennialism of the Reformation and Puritanism gave way to a more pessimistic premillennialism of the early nineteenth century, two differing views regarding the relationship of the church to the Jewish people emerged at the same time and developed in parallel. Historic or covenantal premillennialism believed that Jewish people would be incorporated within the church and return to Palestine a converted nation alongside other Christian nations. Dispensational premillennialism, however, came to believe the Jewish people would return to the land before or after their conversion but would remain distinctly separate from the church. The former view became the driving force behind the restorationist movement and British Christian Zionism, while the latter view came to dominate in the United States. Both perspectives were present in embryonic form within what became known as the Albury Circle, and each will be considered in turn.

The origins of covenantal premillennial restorationism in Britain

As has been shown, the beginning of the nineteenth century was a time of great turmoil right across Europe. One of the first to contribute to the renaissance in premillennialism and to link it to Jewish restoration was George Stanley Faber. In 1809, he wrote a work entitled *A General and Connected View of the Prophecies relative to the Conversion, Restoration, Union and Future Glory of the Houses of Judah and Israel. The Progress and Final Overthrow of the Antichristian Confederacy in the Land of Palestine and the Ultimate General Diffusion of Christianity.*

In May of the same year, the London Society for Promoting Christianity amongst the Jews was formed. The less accurate description of London Jews' Society (LJS) eventually proved more popular.[24] Their earliest objective was

---

24. Stevens, *Go, Tell My Brethren*, p. 13.

essentially philo-Semitic, 'for the purpose of visiting and relieving the sick and distressed, and instructing the ignorant, especially such as are of the Jewish nation'. This charitable endeavour soon also came to embrace Jewish restoration.[25] It was the combination of these twin objectives, evangelism and restorationism, within the LJS that gave Christian Zionism its first distinct identity as an embryonic movement, and its earliest location within British evangelicalism.

A small number of influential Christian leaders helped determine the emergence, priorities and future direction of the LJS as well as other philo-Semitic missionary societies formed in nineteenth century Britain.[26] They were driven by a literal hermeneutic, a covenantal premillennial eschatology and shared a strong commitment to evangelize the Jewish people. Four of the most significant leaders were Lewis Way, Charles Simeon, Joseph Wolff and Charles Spurgeon.

Lewis Way (1772–1840): the financial benefactor

Way may be regarded as the founder of the LJS as well as the foremost exponent of nineteenth-century restorationism and Christian Zionism. A barrister and Fellow of Merton College, Oxford, in 1804, he purchased Stanstead Park, an impressive Georgian mansion at Emsworth in Hampshire, and set up a college to convert Jews to Christianity. He then rescued the London Jews' Society from a £20,000 debt, on condition that it became an Anglican society. With the end of the Napoleonic Wars in 1815, he began to promote the cause of Jewish emancipation and settlement in Palestine by lobbying the European heads of state to support the provision of a Jewish homeland. Way found an ally in Tsar Alexander I of Russia, who shared an interest in Jewish restorationism. Way's efforts culminated in October 1818 when he spoke at the Congress of Aix la Chapelle before the leaders of Great Britain, Prussia, Russia, Austria and France, urging them to support Zionism. Influenced by his association with Edward Irving and Joseph Wolff, and using the pseudonym 'Basilicus', between 1820 and 1822 Way wrote a series of speculations on the restoration of the Jews and the imminent return of Christ in the LJS journal, *The Jewish Expositor*. In 1821, Way published a pamphlet entitled

---

25. See Kelvin Crombie, *For the Love of Zion: Christian Witness and the Restoration of Israel* (London: Hodder & Stoughton, 1991), pp. 13, 15.

26. The British Society for the Propagation of the Gospel Among the Jews (1842), the Mildmay Mission to the Jews (1876) and the Barbican Mission to the Jews (1879), for example. By 1910 there were 99 missions to the Jews worldwide with 914 known missionaries. See William Bjoraker, 'The Beginning of Modern Jewish Missions in the English Speaking World', *Mishkan* 16.1 (1992), p. 62.

The Latter Rain, in which he called Christians to pray for the Jews based on the conviction that Old Testament prophecies have a 'primary and literal reference to the Jews'. Way galvanized evangelical support for Zionism by promoting a futurist eschatology which anticipated that the exiled Jewish people would soon return to their promised homeland. Kelvin Crombie claims that Way and the LJS provided the leadership within the evangelical movement that was calling for the restoration of national Israel.[27] Far from being an eccentric or fringe phenomenon, through Way's efforts restorationism came to be embraced by the evangelical establishment and even enjoyed the support of a significant proportion of the English episcopacy. Way was aided in this most notably by Charles Simeon who helped found several 'Religious Societies for Diffusing the Knowledge of the Gospel', such as the Church Missionary Society, the British and Foreign Bible Society, the Simeon Trust and the Prayer-Book and Homily Society.

Charles Simeon (1759–1836): the optimistic evangelist

The growth of Christian Zionism within Anglican evangelical circles was undoubtedly shaped to a large degree by the initiatives of Charles Simeon. Simeon became consumed with a passion for the conversion of Jews and the work of the London Jews' Society, looking also for 'a full and imminent restoration of God's chosen people'.[28] He conducted preaching tours on behalf of the LJS and spoke on Jewish evangelism and restorationism right across the UK. His notes were even distributed as far away as India and the United States. Simeon was convinced, based on his reading of the Bible, that the Jews would soon return to Palestine, but, significantly, only as Christians. He claimed, 'The future restoration of the Jews, and their union with the Gentiles in one universal Church . . . both of these events will take place together, or in the nearest connexion with each other.'[29] Unlike Irving and Darby, Simeon remained a postmillennialist and believed the millennium had already begun. For this reason, he was energetic in promoting evangelism among the Jews, confident that through their conversion and dispersion throughout the world they would act as evangelists so that, 'God will shortly interpose to bring all nations

---

27. Crombie, *For the Love of Zion*, p. 15.

28. Arthur Pollard, 'The Influence and Significance of Simeon's Work', in Arthur Pollard and Michael Hennell (eds.), *Charles Simeon, 1759–1836* (London: SPCK, 1964), p. 180.

29. Simeon, 'Conversion of the Jews and Gentiles', *Horae Homileticae* 10, p. 240; 'Conversion of the Jews Gradual', *Horae Homileticae* 8, pp. 10–14.

to such a unity in religious faith and practice as has never been seen upon earth'.[30]

Though he supported restorationism, Simeon did not regard the physical restoration of the Jews to Palestine to be as significant as their spiritual restoration to God:

> So rapid will their conversion be, that they will flock to Christ even as doves to their windows, and a nation will be born in a day . . . If you desire only the conversion of the Gentile world, you should begin with the Jews; because it is the fulness of the Jews that is to operate on the Gentiles.[31]

While others such as Irving and Darby were beginning to distinguish between God's purposes for the Jews and those of the church, Simeon held to a reformed covenantal position, understanding Old Testament prophetic terms such as 'Zion' to have been fulfilled in the church. In a sermon concerning the future of Israel, Simeon insisted, 'We are God's Israel, as much as ever they were; and heirs of all these blessings no less than they; for "if we be Christ's, then are we Abraham's seed, and heirs according to the promise".'[32] According to his biographer, Arthur Pollard, Simeon acted 'as a kind of one-man general staff, preaching for the Society, recruiting workers, spreading propaganda, collecting funds, advising on overall strategy. He did so with even more than his usual sense of urgency.'[33] Simeon's patronage of the LJS undoubtedly ensured that its restorationist agenda, advocated more strongly by others such as Way, nevertheless gained increasingly widespread support not only among Anglicans but also among other evangelicals around the world.

Joseph Wolff (1795–1862): the pioneer missiologist

Wolff was a German Jew, converted first to Roman Catholicism and then subsequently to Anglicanism. He became known as the first great pioneer missionary of the LJS.[34] Wolff also played an influential role at the Albury 'unfulfilled prophecy' conference of 1826 (see below pp. 45–47). Irving describes his impact: 'No appeal was allowed but to the Scriptures, of which the originals lay before us; in the interpretation of which, if any question arose,

---

30. Simeon, 'The Millennial Period Fast Approaching', *Horae Homileticae* 8, p. 24.

31. Ibid., pp. 416, 419.

32. Simeon, 'The Future Prosperity of Israel', *Horae Homileticae* 10, p. 240.

33. Pollard, 'The Influence and Significance of Simeon's Work', p. 180.

34. See Palmer, *Joseph Wolff*.

we had the most learned Eastern scholar perhaps in the world to appeal to, and a native Hebrew. I mean Joseph Wolff.'[35] This disregard for traditional inter-pretation or scholastic helps at Albury marks a radical discontinuity with the presuppositions of mainstream reformed theology, and prepared the ground for Irving and Darby's sectarian futurist premillennial dispensationalism.

Like Hugh McNeile, another Anglican member of the Albury Circle, Wolff was preoccupied with the discovery of the lost tribes of Israel, so indispens-able to any future restoration of the Jews. A report about their possible dis-covery was received at the LJS annual conference of 1822. Another report given by Henry Drummond at the 1828 Albury Conference claimed that traders from the lost Jewish tribes had been discovered in Leipzig:

> The Tribes have been discovered, twenty millions in number, inhabiting the region
> north of Cashmere and towards Bokhara, in the great central plain of Asia. It would
> seem that there came men from them to Leipsic fair . . . They were trading in
> Cashmere shawls.[36]

Wolff, fluent in Arabic, Hebrew, Chaldean, Persian and Syriac, set out that same year to find the lost tribes, travelling as far as India, Armenia and Abyssinia. He spent much of the rest of his life speaking on behalf of the LJS, travelling in search of, and ministering to, oriental Jews.

Charles Haddon Spurgeon (1834–1892): the baptist restorationist

Spurgeon was probably England's most influential nineteenth-century Non-conformist preacher. With sixty-seven volumes of his sermons published, this is more than any other author in English history. Indeed, more of his works are in print today than of any other Christian author in history. Spurgeon enjoyed a photographic memory and accumulated one of the largest personal theological libraries in the entire British Empire. Although Iain Murray considers Spurgeon to have had a 'fundamental uncertainty' in his mind on eschatological matters, and Hulse classifies him as a postmillennialist,[37] Spurgeon actually affirmed a historical or covenantal premillennial position, and 'added his considerable voice to the question of Jewish restoration to the Promised Land'.[38] Spurgeon's

---

35. Margaret Oliphant, *The Life of Edward Irving* (3rd edn, London: Hurst & Blackett, 1864), p. 205.

36. Cited in ibid., p. 243.

37. Murray, *Puritan Hope*, p. 363; Hulse, *Restoration of Israel*, p. 154.

38. Cited in Dennis M. Swanson, 'Charles H. Spurgeon and the Nation of Israel,

premillennial views are found in several of his sermons, for example: 'I conceive that the advent will be premillennial; that he will come first; and then will come the millennium as the result of his personal reign upon earth.'[39]

During the Down-Grade Controversy[40] that led to his withdrawal from the Baptist Union over the rise of liberalism within the denomination, Spurgeon contributed to a statement of faith clarifying his doctrinal views. The final point reads, 'Our hope is the Personal Pre-Millennial Return of the Lord Jesus in Glory.'[41] Spurgeon was a premillennialist because he held to a literal herme- neutic. This is why he rejected an amillennial position: 'We expect a reigning Christ on earth; that seems to us to be very plain, and put so literally that we dare not spiritualise it.'[42] Spurgeon also repudiated dispensational premillenni- alism which was emerging at the same time. He rejected any suggestion that God had separate purposes for the Jews apart from the church. Not without a little sarcasm he observed:

> Distinctions have been drawn by certain exceedingly wise men (measured by their
> own estimate of themselves), between the people of God who lived before the
> coming of Christ, and those who lived afterwards. We have even heard it asserted
> that those who lived before the coming of Christ do not belong to the church of
> God! We never know what we shall hear next, and perhaps it is a mercy that these
> absurdities are revealed at one time, in order that we may be able to endure their
> stupidity without dying of amazement. Why, every child of God in every place
> stands on the same footing; the Lord has not some children best loved, some
> second-rate offspring, and others whom he hardly cares about . . . Before the first

A Non-Dispensational Perspective on a Literal National Restoration' (unpublished
paper delivered at the Evangelical Theological Society Conference in Nashville,
November 2000), p. 2.

39. C. H. Spurgeon, 'Justification and Glory', *Metropolitan Tabernacle Pulpit* 11 (London:
Passmore & Alabaster, 1862–1917), p. 249.

40. The term 'down-grade' was first used by Spurgeon in the *Sword and Trowel* (March
1887) to describe the decline into liberalism occurring within the Baptist
denomination. Later that year he withdrew from the Baptist Union. See John F.
MacArthur, Jr, *Spurgeon and the Down-Grade Controversy* (1992) [Internet], The Spurgeon
Archive, <http: www.spurgeon.org/downgrd.htm>. [Accessed May 2004.]

41. 'Mr. Spurgeon's Confession of Faith', in *Sword and Trowel*, 26 (August 1891), pp.
446–448.

42. C. H. Spurgeon, 'Things to Come', *Metropolitan Tabernacle Pulpit* 15 (London:
Passmore & Alabaster, 1862–1917), p. 329.

advent, all the types and shadows all pointed one way – they pointed to Christ, and to him all the saints looked with hope. Those who lived before Christ were not saved with a different salvation to which shall come to us. They exercised faith as we must; that faith struggled as ours struggles, and that faith obtained its reward as ours shall.[43]

Spurgeon saw the church and Israel one day united spiritually; the church, not Israel, as the recipient of the kingdom promises; the church and Israel facing the tribulation together; and the millennial kingdom on earth the culmination of God's purposes for both Jewish and Gentile believers in one church of which Jesus is the head.[44]

As a covenantal premillennialist, Spurgeon not only believed in the restoration of Israel but, from its inception, supported the work of the British Society for the Propagation of the Gospel Amongst the Jews. Although similar in name and objectives, it was a Nonconformist equivalent of the London Society for Promoting Christianity Amongst the Jews, which was by then Anglican. The new society was formed in November 1842, ironically in Irving's former church, known as the 'National Scotch Church' in Regent's Square, London. With the support of Robert Murray M'Cheyne and Andrew Bonar, the new society worked in partnership with the Church of Scotland's Mission to the Jews.[45] In an address based on Ezekiel 37:1–10, delivered to the Society in 1864, entitled 'The Restoration and Conversion of the Jews', Spurgeon spoke of his expectation of a Messianic kingdom in Israel:

'I will place you in your own land' is God's promise to them . . . They are to have a national prosperity which shall make them famous . . . If there be anything clear and plain, the literal sense and meaning of this passage – a meaning not to be spirited or spiritualised away – must be evident that both the two and the ten tribes of Israel are to be restored to their own land, and that a king is to rule over them.[46]

---

43. C. H. Spurgeon, 'Jesus Christ Immutable', *Metropolitan Tabernacle Pulpit* 15 (London: Passmore & Alabaster, 1862–1917), p. 8.

44. C. H. Spurgeon, 'There be Some That Trouble You', *Sword and Trowel* (March 1867), p. 120. See also, Swanson, 'Charles H. Spurgeon and the Nation of Israel', p. 9.

45. The agency is now known as Christian Witness to Israel, an interdenominational evangelistic society which has also enjoyed the support of Martyn Lloyd-Jones and Francis Schaeffer. For more information, see <http://www.cwi.org.uk>.

46. C. H. Spurgeon, 'The Restoration and Conversion of the Jews', *Metropolitan Tabernacle Pulpit* 10 (London: Passmore & Alabaster, 1862–1917), p. 426.

Spurgeon preached on the same subject on several other occasions linking three great themes: a national Jewish repentance when they will come to faith in Jesus Christ, a restoration to the land and the return of Jesus, in that order.

Spurgeon even envisaged that, 'if the temple itself be not restored, yet on Zion's hill shall be raised some Christian building, where the chants of solemn praise shall be heard as erst of the old Psalms of David were sung in the Tabernacle'.[47] Spurgeon, therefore, held to a covenantal premillennial view of Israel, neither spiritualizing the Old Testament promises nor replacing the church. Swanson comments: 'He would neither make the millennium the exclusive domain of Israel without the church, nor would he exclude the national Israel from the glorious church of the millennium.'[48] In light of the way dispensational premillennialism was evolving at the same time, with its particular focus on prophetic speculation, Spurgeon held the line on the gospel priority with both wit and precision:

> Your guess at the number of the beast, your Napoleonic speculations, your conjectures concerning a personal Antichrist – forgive me, I count them but mere bones for dogs; while men are dying, and hell is filling, it seems to me the veriest drivel to be muttering about an Armageddon at Sebastopol or Sadowa or Sedan, and peeping between the folded leaves of destiny to discover the fate of Germany.[49]

Spanning the nineteenth century, Lewis Way, Charles Simeon, Joseph Wolff and Charles Spurgeon shared a common passion to see Jewish people come to faith in Jesus Christ. Their literal reading of the Bible and premillennial eschatology gave them confidence that the Jewish people as a nation would soon turn to Christ and be restored to the land of Palestine, after which Jesus would return to set up his millennial kingdom. Support for restorationism was a personal matter and secondary to the priority of gospel ministry among the Jews.

From the same premillennial roots, a very different form of Christian Zionism was emerging in parallel in Britain during the nineteenth century. Known as dispensationalism, it gradually reversed those priorities, giving greater emphasis to political restoration than evangelism as it became increasingly preoccupied with interpreting biblical prophecy from a futurist perspective and publicizing what it saw as its contemporary fulfilment.

---

47. Ibid., p. 426.
48. Swanson, 'Charles H. Spurgeon and the Nation of Israel', p. 17.
49. C. H. Spurgeon, *Lectures to My Students* (1st series, London: Passmore and Alabaster, 1877), p. 83.

The origins of dispensational Christian Zionism in Britain

The development of dispensationalism in the nineteenth century and the revolution in futurist prophetic speculation concerning the church and Israel can
be largely attributed to Edward Irving, John Nelson Darby, Benjamin Newton
and others associated with the Albury and Powerscourt prophetic conferences
held between 1826 and 1833.

Edward Irving (1792–1834) and the Albury prophetic conferences

Born at Annan in Scotland in 1792, Irving was licensed as a minister of the
Church of Scotland in 1815. Having accepted a call in 1822 to pastor the Church
of Scotland congregation at the Caledonian Chapel in Hatton Gardens, London,
Irving soon became a popular if controversial and eccentric speaker. Thomas
De Quincey described him as 'the greatest orator of our times'.[50] The chapel
became too small and a larger church was built in Regent Square in 1827. Because
of his growing popularity, Irving was invited to preach at the annual service of
the London Missionary Society in 1824, and a year later to the Continental
Society, in both of which Henry Drummond was influential. On each occasion,
Irving provoked a furore. Irving's address in 1825 was entitled 'Babylon and
Infidelity Foredoomed'. In reaction to the prevailing optimistic postmillennial
drive towards missionary expansion, Irving predicted that the world was about
to experience a 'series of thick-coming judgements and fearful perplexities'
before the imminent return of Jesus Christ.[51] He insisted that missionary work,
especially in Southern Europe, where the Continental Society concentrated its
ministry, was futile because God's judgment was about to fall on the lands of the
former Roman Empire who would align themselves with the Antichrist. Some
walked out of the meeting in protest while the leaders of the society accused
Irving of undermining their ministry.[52] When Irving's address was later published as *Babylon and Infidelity Foredoomed*, it was dedicated to James Hatley Frere,
a premillennial layman.[53] Irving's biographer, Margaret Oliphant explains why:

> Several years before, Mr. Hatley Frere, one of the most sedulous of those prophetical
> students who were beginning to make themselves known here and there over the

---

50. Cited in Murray, *Puritan Hope*, p. 188.
51. Cited in ibid., p. 189.
52. Dallimore, *Life of Edward Irving*, p. 62.
53. In the foreword to *Babylon and Infidelity Foredoomed*, Irving acknowledged his
    indebtedness to Hatley Frere.

country, had propounded a new scheme of interpretation, for which, up to this time, he had been unable to secure the ear of the religious public. Not less confident in the truth of his scheme that nobody shared his belief in it, Mr. Frere cherished the conviction that if he could but meet some man of candid and open mind, of popularity sufficient to gain a hearing, to whom he could privately explain and open up his system, its success was certain. When Irving, all ingenuous and ready to be taught, was suddenly brought into contact with him, the student of prophecy identified him by an instant intuition. Here is the man![54]

Frere insisted that the prophetic portions of Scripture 'must be understood either literally throughout or figuratively throughout otherwise it will be utterly impossible to ascertain the meaning designed to be conveyed'.[55] This led him to interpret the book of Revelation as describing God's impending judgment on the Western and Eastern Roman Empires and upon 'Paganism, Popery and Infidelity'.[56]

Irving clearly resonated with Frere's futurist premillennial scheme and it seems Frere came to influence others within Irving's circle at one or more of the Albury conferences he attended in the years that followed. Like Frere and Faber, Irving became increasingly preoccupied with the interpretation of the apocalyptic writings of Daniel and Revelation. He calculated, for example, that the church had suffered for 1,260 years under papal rule from 533, when Justinian recognized the Bishop of Rome as head of the church, until 1793.[57] He also saw the French Revolution and Industrial Revolution as evidence of the 'signs of the times' and the imminent return of Christ. As Brightman had predicted some two hundred years earlier, Irving speculated that the first six vials of the book of Revelation had already been poured out and claimed the seventh vial could be dated to the 1820s. Through the pages of the *Morning Watch* (see p. 49), Irving's colleague John Tudor explained the significance of 1793 and reasons for believing it signified the end of the Christian era:

> This is that spirit of infidelity which, gaining the upper hand in France in May 1793, abolished public worship, declared the scriptures to be fable, treated them with utmost contempt, changed weeks for decades; substituted the year of the Republic for the Christian era; and did, as far as the influence of infidelity extended, overcome

---

54. Oliphant, *Life of Edward Irving*, p. 189.

55. Frere, *Brief Interpretation of the Apocalypse*, p. 2.

56. Ibid., p. 2.

57. Cited in Columba Graham Flegg, *Gathered under Apostles*, p. 325.

and kill these two witnesses, by suppressing their prophesying in which alone their life and power consisted.[58]

In 1826, Irving was also introduced to the views of Manuel Lacunza, a Spanish Jesuit, who, disaffected by the corruption of Rome, had written a book under the pseudonym of Juan Josafat Ben-Ezra, first published in Spanish in 1812. Claiming to be the work of a converted Jew, the book was entitled *The Coming of the Messiah in Glory and Majesty*. In it, Lacunza interpreted all but the first three chapters of the book of Revelation as predicting imminent apocalyptic events. Irving was so excited by Lacunza's futurist speculations (which mirrored his own), that he mastered Spanish in order to translate and publish the work in English. Irving added a 194-page preface to the translation, in which he presented, with great conviction, his own prophetic speculations about the end of the world, predicting the apostasy of Christendom, the subsequent restoration of the Jews and imminent return of Christ. The publication in English attracted widespread interest, not least because of the association with Irving.

At the time, Irving was very much aware that he was virtually alone in proclaiming views that went well beyond even those of traditional premillennialism which itself had not been popular within evangelical circles for over a century. Irving did not appear intimidated by the knowledge that the evangelical establishment regarded his views as eccentric. Indeed, he seemed to enjoy the notoriety:

> These three points of doctrine concerning the Gentile church, the future Jewish and universal church, and the personal advent of the Lord to destroy the one and to build up the other, I opened and defended out of the scriptures from Sabbath to Sabbath, with all boldness, yet with fear and trembling . . . at that time I did not know of one brother in the ministry who held with me in these matters . . . so novel and strange a doctrine . . . such uncivil and implacable language, concerning overwhelming judgements upon the very eve of the millennial blessedness . . . but the more I examined, the more I was convinced, and resolved, though alone and single-handed, to maintain these three great heads of doctrine from the holy scriptures, against all who should undertake to uphold the commonly-received notion, that the present Gentile dispensation was about to burst forth with the

---

58. John Tudor, *Morning Watch* 1 (December 1829), p. 563.3, cited in Mark R. Patterson, *Designing the Last Days: Edward Irving, the Albury Circle and the Theology of the Morning Watch* (PhD thesis, Kings College, London, 2001), p. 118.

millennial blessedness, after which, to wind up and consume all, the Lord would come in the latter end.[59]

Irving was in no doubt that the Gentile church was finished. His pessimism predated and inevitably influenced Darby's similar denunciations of a 'failing church' and expectation of a future Jewish 'dispensation'. Referring to the predictions Jesus had made concerning the destruction of Jerusalem in Matthew 24, Irving insisted these were a type and foreshadowing of the impending destruction of the church. He wrote, 'And the reason why the destruction of Jerusalem can typify and foreshow the destruction of Gentile Christendom is, that they are both the acts of God's vengeance upon a back-sliding and incorrigible Church.'[60] Irving insisted that even evangelical churches had 'set aside' the Bible and were more aligned to Paine's *Age of Reason* than the gospel. He wrote: 'The intellect hath become all sufficient . . . the Church is in the Laodicean state.'[61] On this issue Irving increasingly showed what his biographer Arnold Dallimore describes as 'sectarian bitterness and reckless dogmatism'.[62] Many saw him as a prophet, while others 'a visionary quack'.[63]

On the first day of Advent in 1826, the same year Irving was translating Lacunza's work, Henry Drummond (1786–1860), a city banker, politician and High Sheriff of Surrey, opened his home at Albury Park to a select group of some twenty invited guests to discuss matters concerning 'the immediate fulfilment of prophecy'. Earlier in 1826, Irving, along with Lewis Way and James Hatley Frere, had founded the Society for the Investigation of Prophecy. At Drummond's suggestion, however, their meetings were eventually subsumed within those taking place at Albury.

In 1828, Drummond published his own work, *Dialogues on Prophecy*, in which he asserted, like Irving, that God was about to judge the visible church and return the Jewish people to Palestine. He predicted, 'during the time that these judgements are falling upon Christendom, the Jews will be restored to the land'.[64]

---

59. Edward Irving, *The Rev. Edward Irving's Preliminary Discourse to the Work of Ben Ezra entitled the Coming of Messiah in Glory and Majesty* (1859 reprint), pp. 7–8.

60. Irving, *Last Days*, p. 11.

61. A. Drummond, *Edward Irving and His Circle*, p. 130.

62. Ibid., p. 130.

63. Murray, *Puritan Hope*, p. 188.

64. Henry Drummond, *Dialogues on Prophecy* (London: James Nisbet, 1828), pp. ii-iii.

Edward Miller describes how the Albury Circle 'met to deliberate on the great prophetic questions which at present do instantly concern Christianity'.[65] Columba Flegg elaborates on their purpose:

> The Albury conferences were called for the purpose of examining the scriptures – and especially the prophetic writings – with a view to interpreting the political and social events of the day, and also determining the extent to which biblical prophecies had already been fulfilled in the life of Christ and the history of the Christian church, thus making it possible to identify those still awaiting fulfilment in the future.[66]

Those present at Albury for these conferences, held each year during Advent, included Lewis Way and Joseph Wolff of the London Jews' Society, James Hatley Frere and Hugh McNeile, who, in 1830, published *The Prophecies Relative to the Jewish Nation*.[67] Like Irving and Drummond, McNeile advocated a separate status for the Jews apart from the church, within their own 'dispensations'. He also predicted the imminent repentance and then restoration of the Jews, and finally their pre-eminence on earth, a blessing to the whole world.[68] Miller confirms the influence of Lewis Way's literalism on Irving and the Albury Circle:

> The meetings of those people who were interested in the question of the immediate fulfilment of prophecy and were anxious to work out the application, according to the special mode of interpretation then adopted by Irving and his friends, owed their origin to a suggestion made by Mr Lewis Way to Mr Drummond.[69]

Further conferences were held annually during Advent at Albury between 1826 and 1830. About two thirds of those who attended were, like Lewis Way, convinced Anglicans, one of whom, Daniel Wilson, later became Bishop of Calcutta. Others of the Moravian, Church of Scotland and Nonconformist churches also participated, as well as Lady Powerscourt, S. Percival, the son of the Prime Minister, and E. Simon, Director of the Jews' Asylum in London.

---

65. Edward Miller, *The History and Doctrines of Irvingism*, vol. 1 (London: Kegan Paul, 1878), p. 36.

66. Flegg, *Gathered under Apostles*, p. 36.

67. Hugh McNeile, *The Collected Works*, vol. 2: *The Prophecies Relative to the Jewish Nation* (London: The Christian Book Society, [1830] 1878).

68. McNeile, *Collected Works*, vol. 2, pp. 431–433.

69. Miller, *History and Doctrines of Irvingism*, vol. 1, p. 36.

Irving described the atmosphere of the first conference thus: 'the six days we spent under the holy and hospitable roof of Albury House . . . no council, from that first which convened at Jerusalem until this time, seemed more governed, and conducted, and inspired by a spirit of holy communion'.[70] Irving called the Albury conferences a 'Prophetic Parliament' and a 'School of the Prophets'. His notes reveal the distinction he was already beginning to make between God's continuing purposes for the Jews in a restored land apart from those which applied to the church:

> Perfect unanimity:
>
> That the present Christian dispensation is not to pass insensibly into the millennial state by gradual increase of the preaching of the gospel; but that it is to be terminated by judgements, ending in the destruction of this visible Church and polity, in the same manner as the Jewish dispensation has been terminated.
>
> That during the time that these judgements are falling upon Christendom, the Jews will be restored to their own land . . .[71]

At the conference in 1827, the interpretation of prophecy became more speculative, moving from general discussions concerning the return of the Jews to Jerusalem to more detailed predictions as to the 'times and seasons' and imminent return of Jesus. Miller notes, 'The Apocalyptic vial was supposed to have been poured out on Rome in 1798 and it was concluded that the coming of our Lord would take place in 1847.'[72] Somewhat charitably, he goes on to say, in this 'method of precise interpretation they had ventured on unsafe ground'. He describes, for example, how news arrived during the conference of the death of the Duke of Reichstadt, the son of Napoleon. '"That cannot be true", said one of them, springing from his seat, "for it would overturn this whole interpretation," for young Napoleon had been taken for the Beast of the Apocalypse.'[73] The conference of 1827 also deplored the unwillingness of other well-known evangelical leaders of the Clapham Sect such as William Wilberforce to participate.

The conference held in 1828 focused more specifically on speculation concerning the imminent restoration of the Jews. McNeile offered corroborating evidence provided in a report given by a Mr Sargon to the LJS in 1822, which

---

70. Irving, *Preliminary Discourse*, pp. 197–202.

71. Cited in Miller, *History and Doctrines of Irvingism*, vol. 1, pp. 44–45.

72. Cited in ibid., vol. 1, p. 42.

73. Cited in ibid.

claimed that the lost tribes had been discovered in India and China, calling themselves Beni-Israel, and longing for their restoration:

> . . . bearing, almost uniformly, Jewish names, but with Persian terminations . . . They circumcise their own children . . . they observe the Kippoor . . . they call themselves Gorah Jehudi, or White Jews . . . they speak of the Arabian Jews as their brethren . . . they expect the Messiah, and that they will one day return to Jerusalem.[74]

In the same year, Irving published another book of over 500 pages, entitled *The Last Days: A Discourse on the Evil Character of These Our Times, Proving Them to be the 'Perilous Times' and the 'Last Days'*. The first chapter's title was 'Introductory, to prove that the Last Times and Last Days of Holy Scripture are the Conclusion of the Jewish Captivity and the Gentile Dispersion.' Irving was emphatic – the Lord would return within the next few years and certainly within his lifetime. Irving also believed he would live to see the final battle of Armageddon, the second advent and the beginning of the millennium.[75] On one occasion, he wrote:

> there can be little doubt that the one thousand two hundred and sixty days concluded in the year 1792, and the thirty additional days in the year 1823, we are already entered upon the last days, and the ordinary life of a man will carry many of us to the end of them. If this be so, it gives to the subject with which we have introduced this year's ministry a very great importance indeed.[76]

Irving went on to speculate that the second advent would occur in 1868, 'being fixed seventy-five years after 1793'.[77] The *Christian Observer* noted the controversy Irving's eschatology was causing among the majority of evangelicals who in 1828 still held to a postmillennial approach to mission:

> Mr Irving and Mr McNeile, speak in the strongest terms of the deteriorated and deteriorating state of the world; they view Christendom as verging to its downfall; they consider our Bible and missionary societies, not as instruments for ushering in the latter day glory, not as harbingers of mercy to the wide world, but only as

---

74. McNeile, *The Collected Works*, vol. 2, pp. 433–434.
75. See P. E. Shaw, *The Catholic Apostolic Church* (New York: King's Crown Press, 1946), p. 18.
76. Ibid.
77. A. Drummond, *Edward Irving and His Circle*, p. 130.

messengers to gather out a few elect vessels, and to fill up the measure of the wicked, till God in his wrath shall consume the world of the ungodly, and bring in a whole new dispensation, even the Millennium of Christ's personal reign with his saints.[78]

The proceedings of the Albury conferences from 1828 gained a wider audience through a short-lived but highly influential quarterly journal on prophecy published by Drummond, entitled *Morning Watch*.[79] The majority of the articles dealt with aspects of eschatology and were unsigned, although Drummond, Tudor and Thomas Carlyle (author and close friend of Irving) are known to have contributed. As will be shown in the next chapter, Darby's embryonic and rather rambling dispensational outline, published in 1836, was preceded by a much more developed scheme arising out of the Albury conference of 1830 and published in the *Morning Watch* in 1831. According to Mark Patterson, 'None compare, in breadth and intricacy, to that developed by Albury and disseminated in the pages of the *Morning Watch*.'[80]

The journal came to an abrupt end, however, in June 1833 when its benefactor, Henry Drummond, as well as John Tudor, its editor, became Apostles in the new Catholic Apostolic Church (CAC) founded at Albury. Patterson gives this helpful assessment of the legacy of Irving and the Albury Circle:

> The Albury Circle was a product of its own age and thus a theology shaped by romanticism's love for grand all-inclusive systems, the enlightenment's rational methodology and their own subjective polemic. These coalesced to form a system that was tacitly understood to be God's final revelation . . . Its self-fulfilling character affirmed its validity that in turn locked the Circle into a system and perspective beyond which they could see nothing else.[81]

Irving's premature death in 1834 while on a preaching tour of Scotland left a void in millennial Pentecostal speculations, the reins of the CAC in Drummond's hands, the hope of the restoration of Israel to men like Lewis Way and the LJS, and the cause of dispensational premillennialism to be shaped by Darby and his Brethren colleagues.

---

78. *Christian Observer* (June 1828), pp. 398–399, cited in Michael Hennell, *Sons of the Prophets* (London: SPCK, 1979), p. 11.

79. See Dallimore, *Life of Edward Irving*, p. 93.

80. 'The Seven Dispensations', *Morning Watch* 4 (September 1831), p. 134. 9f., cited in Patterson, *Designing the Last Days*, p. 138.

81. Patterson, *Designing the Last Days*, p. 166.

John Nelson Darby (1800–1882) and the rise of dispensationalism

Darby is regarded by many as the father of dispensationalism and the most influential figure in the development of its progeny, Christian Zionism.[82] Darby was initially ordained in the Church of Ireland in 1825 but, like Irving, came to renounce both Anglican and Dissenting churches as apostate. In Darby's case, it followed a disagreement with his bishop over the expectation that Catholic converts had to swear allegiance to the English King. His analysis of the contemporary ecclesiastical scene was to become increasingly pessimistic, judgmental and sectarian. His repeated response was to declare, 'The Church is in ruins.'[83] He went on to insist that this was not merely the result of denominational division but that 'the entire nature and purpose of the church has become so perverted that it is diametrically opposed to the fundamental reason for which it is instituted'.[84] Following Irving's lead, Darby opposed the prevailing postmillennial optimism. In 1840, he insisted:

> We are to expect evil, until it becomes so flagrant that it will be necessary for the Lord to judge it . . . I am afraid that many a cherished feeling, dear to the children of God, has been shocked this evening; I mean, their hope that the gospel will spread by itself over the whole earth during the actual dispensation.[85]

Darby's distinctive premillennial views were also inevitably influenced by those of a similar persuasion whom he met at the prophetic conferences held near Dublin under the sponsorship of Lady Powerscourt from 1830 to 1833, which followed a similar pattern to those held in Albury.[86] Increasingly, however, the Powerscourt conferences came to be shaped by Darby's own

---

82. Wagner, *Anxious for Armageddon*, pp. 81, 88. This is disputed by Charles Ryrie who attempts unconvincingly to place the origin of dispensationalism some 150 years earlier, allegedly finding evidence in the writings of the French mystic Pierre Poiret (1646–1719) and John Edwards (1639–1716), an amillennial Calvinist, as well as Isaac Watts (1674–1748). See Ryrie, *Dispensationalism*, pp. 65–71.

83. Darby, 'On the Formation of Churches, Further Developments', in *Collected Writings*, vol. 1, Ecclesiastical 1, p. 303.

84. Darby, 'What is the Unity of the Church?', in *Collected Writings*, vol. 20, Ecclesiastical 4, p. 456.

85. Darby, 'Progress of Evil on the Earth', in *Collected Writings*, vol. 2, Prophetic 1, pp. 471, 483.

86. Lady Powerscourt, for example, attended one or more of the Albury conferences and Edward Irving visited her in Ireland. See Murray, *Puritan Hope*, p. 191.

dominating and charismatic leadership.[87] These exclusive prophetic gatherings, which focused on a pessimistic interpretation of world events and the imminent return of Christ, confirmed Darby's own denunciation of the established churches. Roy Coad insists, 'He felt himself an instrument of God, burdened with an urgent call to His people to come out of associations doomed to judgement.'[88]

Whereas the five annual Albury conferences drew together no more than forty individuals, the Powerscourt conference of 1831 attracted some four-hundred 'elite' evangelicals drawn from all over Britain and Ireland. Subjects considered included speculation on the timing and signs of the Antichrist, and, significantly, 'By what covenant did the Jews, and shall the Jews, hold the land? . . . What light does Scripture throw on present events, and their moral character?'[89]

Despite compelling evidence of Irving's influence in these ideas of a failing church and future Jewish dispensation, Darby rarely acknowledged anyone else in the development of his own theological views. There is, for example, just one reference to Irving in Darby's entire thirty-four volumes. Even then, Darby does so to disassociate himself from the fanciful prophecies of the Irvingites and the Catholic Apostolic Church.[90]

Darby was a charismatic figure with a dominant personality. He was a persuasive speaker and zealous missionary for his dispensationalist beliefs. He personally founded Brethren churches as far away as Germany, Switzerland, France and the United States, and translated the entire Scriptures. The churches Darby and his colleagues planted with the seeds of premillennial dispensationalism in turn sent missionaries to Africa, the West Indies, Australia, New Zealand and, ironically, to work among the Arabs of Palestine. By the time of his death in 1885, around 1,500 Plymouth Brethren churches had already been founded worldwide.

From 1862 onwards, his controlling influence over the Brethren in Britain waned due, in particular, to the split between Open and Exclusive Brethren in

---

87. Bass, *Backgrounds to Dispensationalism*, p. 146.
88. Coad, *History of the Brethren Movement*, p. 111.
89. J. N. Darby, *Letters of John Nelson Darby, Vol. 1: 1832–1868* (London: Stow Hill and Bible Trace Depot, n.d.), pp. 6–7.
90. J. N. Darby, 'Remarks on a tract circulated by the Irvingites', in *Collected Writings*, vol. 15, Doctrinal 4, p. 34. According to Scofield, 'Irving was excluded, not for heresy in doctrine, but for his view on church order', see Gaebelein, *History of the Scofield Reference Bible*, p. 43.

1848. Darby consequently spent more and more time in North America, making seven journeys in the next twenty years. Sandeen estimates that Darby spent 40% of his time in the United States. During these visits, he came to have an increasing influence over evangelical leaders such as James H. Brookes, D. L. Moody, William E. Blackstone and C. I. Scofield. His ideas helped shape the emerging evangelical Bible schools and also the prophecy conferences, which came to dominate both evangelicalism and fundamentalism in the United States between 1875 and 1920.

Clarence Bass, in his definitive history of dispensationalism, describes Darby's abiding influence on American evangelicalism:

> Suffice it to say that he stamped his movement with his own personality. Much of its spiritual atmosphere undoubtedly belongs to his influence; and certainly its interpretative principles, its divisive compartmentalization of the redemptive plan of God, its literalness as to prophetic interpretation, and its separatist spirit may be traced to this personality.[91]

One of Darby's early associates in Plymouth, Benjamin Newton, also became a prolific writer on prophetic subjects, fuelling speculation on the timing of the Lord's return.

Benjamin Newton (1807–1899) and the impact of prophetic speculation

Newton was one of the earliest Brethren leaders. His books on speculative prophecy were reprinted on numerous occasions between the 1850s and 1900s.[92] He specialized in interpreting the contemporary European political scene in the light of biblical prophecy. He saw, for example, great significance in the fact that one of the Rothschilds was negotiating with the Sultan for the construction of a railway from Constantinople to Baghdad. He believed this to be one of many signs of the impending merger of the revived Eastern and Western halves of the Roman Empire, a 'Roman world, from England to the Euphrates' centred on Rome. Writing in 1859, Newton commented: 'The interests of France, Great Britain and Austria are more and more felt to be identical as respects the aggression of Russia; and this feeling Spain, Italy and Greece will soon thoroughly share.'[93] His colourful predictive map of the ten kingdoms making up a revived Roman Empire, published in 1863, comprised

91. Bass, *Backgrounds to Dispensationalism*, p. 176.

92. Newton, *Antichrist*; *Babylon*.

93. Newton, *Antichrist*, p. 143.

of France, Spain, Northern Italy, the Neapolitan States, Austria, Turkey, Greece, Syria and Egypt, together with the British Isles.[94] Ironically, in his *Prophetic Forecasts and Present Events re America and Russia* (also published in 1863), Newton discounted growing speculation that America and Russia featured in biblical prophecy: 'Until recently many entertained the expectation that American Republicanism and Russian Despotism would ultimately divide the world between them. The slightest knowledge of Dan. 2 dispels all these illusions.'[95]

While Newton identified with Darby's dispensational system and millennial distinction between God's heavenly church and earthly Jewish people, he rejected the idea of a secret rapture or belief that the Jews and the church would be eternally separate.

In 1865, Newton's *Propositions for Christian Consideration* gained the endorsement of Horatius Bonar for their strong premillennial emphasis. Indeed, even Charles Spurgeon invited Newton to lecture at his college and 'maintained warm and cordial relations' with Newton and other Open Brethren including George Muller and Samuel Tregelles. Newton eventually came to recognize Darby's elevation of Israel above the church as heresy, and repudiated the idea that the Jews could be blessed apart from faith in Jesus Christ. It was 'virtually to say there are two kinds of Christianity, two Gospels, two ways, and two ends of salvation'.[96]

Another former colleague of Darby, F. W. Newman, describes the effect of his pessimistic dispensational preoccupation with the second advent on missionary work: 'The importance of this doctrine is, that it totally forbids all working for earthly objects distant in time.'[97] Newman illustrates this with the story of a young man with an aptitude for mathematics who had sought advice of Darby on whether he should pursue the subject. Darby's reply was this: 'Such a purpose was very proper, if entertained by a worldly man. Let the dead bury their dead; and let the world study the things of the world . . . such studies cannot be eagerly followed by the Christian, except when he yields to unbelief.'[98] This world-denying dispensational attitude came to eclipse the optimism of the postmillennialism of a century earlier as well as distance itself

---

94. Newton, *Map of Ten Kingdoms*.

95. B. W. Newton, *Prophetic Forecasts and Present Events Re America and Russia* (1863), reprinted in Fromow (ed.), *B. W. Newton and Dr S. P. Tregelles*, pp. 128–133.

96. Fromow (ed.), *B. W. Newton and Dr S. P. Tregelles*, p. 75.

97. Ibid., p. 40.

98. Ibid.

from covenant premillennialists who remained passionately committed to Jewish evangelism and to restorationism. Social involvement associated with the Reformation, the Puritans and, more recently, William Wilberforce, the Clapham Sect and Lord Shaftesbury were, Murray argues, 'no longer regarded as legitimate political activity'.[99]

An indication of the influence that the Albury and Powerscourt conferences had upon other clergy in the United Kingdom is given by E. B. Elliott, who wrote his own four-volume, 2,500-page treatise on the Apocalypse, which went through five editions in eighteen years:

> In the year 1844, the date of the first publication of my own work on the Apocalypse, so rapid has been the progress of these views in England, that instead of its appearing a thing strange and half-heretical to hold them, as when Irving published his translation of Ben Ezra, the leaven had evidently now deeply penetrated the religious mind; and from the ineffectiveness of the opposition hitherto formally made to them, they seemed gradually advancing foward to triumph.[100]

Similarly, in 1866, McNeile could look back to an earlier generation when the views of Irving and the others of the Albury Circle concerning a failing church and Jewish restoration were regarded as an eccentric novelty by those he termed 'anti-restorationists':

> When these lectures were first published in 1830, the subject was comparatively new to the Church in this country. It had no place in the battle-field of the Reformation. It had not been discussed by any of the theological lights of the last Century. It was just beginning to be ventilated in consequence of the labours of Mr. Lewis Way and Mr. Hawtrey; and more especially in consequence of the writings of Mr. Faber, and the zealous advocacy of Mr. Simeon.[101]

In the second half of the nineteenth century, that number increased significantly so that by 1873 a prophetical conference held in London had the support of senior evangelical Anglicans such as Lord Shaftesbury, Lord Radstock and the Earl of Cavan.[102]

---

99. Murray, *Puritan Hope*, p. 202.
100. E. B. Elliott, *Horae Apocalypticae: A Commentary on the Apocalypse*, 4 vols. (4th edn, 1851), vol. 4, p. 522.
101. McNeile, *Collected Works*, vol. 2, preface to new edition 1866.
102. Murray, *Puritan Hope*, p. 197.

A summary of the rise of British dispensationalism

The family tree of Christian Zionism clearly had its roots deep in the Reformation and Puritan era, but its visible origins as a movement lie in the preaching, writings and missionary endeavours of British evangelical leaders such as Lewis Way, Charles Simeon, Joseph Wolff, Charles Spurgeon, Edward Irving, John Nelson Darby and Benjamin Newton. Two distinct branches emerged, one based on covenantal premillennialism emphasizing evangelism, the other on dispensational premillennialism which stressed restorationism.

In Britain, Anglicans associated with the London Jews' Society, as well as Nonconformists who identified with the British Society for the Propagation of the Gospel among the Jews, continued to promote evangelism and humanitarian work among the Jews of Europe and Palestine as well as work towards their restoration. By 1845, it is estimated that over 700 Anglican clergy now held to a premillennial restorationist eschatology, including Edward Bickersteth, secretary of the Church Missionary Society, who came to have a dominant influence in Lord Shaftesbury's life, as well as others who were to become Anglican evangelical leaders, such as J. C. Ryle, the Bishop of Liverpool. At the same time, with the break up of the ecumenical fellowship at Powerscourt over whether the church had failed and whether Christians should separate from their denominations, Irving and Darby's influence in Britain waned.

Through Darby's Brethren missionaries and his American visits, however, the seeds of his innovative dispensational Christian Zionism, distinguishing between God's purposes for the Jews and the church, received increasingly enthusiastic endorsement from contemporaries including William E. Blackstone, D. L. Moody, James H. Brookes, Arno C. Gaebelein and C. I. Scofield. Their influence over these two branches, covenantal premillennial and dispensational premillennial, extended well beyond pulpit and journal and had an impact not only on American fundamentalism but, more significantly, on British foreign policy in the late nineteenth and early twentieth centuries and indeed, to inspire the birth of the Jewish Zionist movement itself.

Lord Shaftesbury and the influence of restorationism upon British foreign policy

Zionism would have remained simply a religious ideal were it not for the intervention of a handful of influential aristocratic politicians who came to share the theological convictions of Way, Irving and Darby and translated them into political reality. One in particular, Lord Shaftesbury (1801–1885), became convinced that the restoration of the Jews to Palestine was not only predicted in the Bible, but also coincided with the strategic interests of British foreign policy. Others who shared this perspective, in varying degrees and for different reasons, included Lord Palmerston, David Lloyd George and Lord Balfour. Ironically, this conviction was precipitated by the actions of an atheist, Napoleon, in the spring of 1799.

During the Syrian campaign of Napoleon's oriental expedition, in which he had sought to defeat the Ottoman rulers, cut off Britain from its empire and recreate the empire of Alexander from France to India, he became the first political leader to propose a sovereign Jewish State in Palestine:

> Bonaparte, Commander-in-Chief of the Armies of the French Republic in Africa and Asia, to the Rightful Heirs of Palestine. Israelites, unique nation, whom, in thousands of years, lust of conquest and tyranny were able to deprive of the ancestral lands only, but not of name and national existence . . . She [France] offers to you at this very time, and contrary to all expectations, Israel's patrimony . . . Rightful heirs of Palestine . . . hasten! Now is the moment which may not return for thousands of years, to claim the restoration of your rights among the population of the universe which had shamefully withheld from you for thousands of years, your political existence as a nation among the nations, and the unlimited natural right to worship Yehovah in accordance with your faith, publicly and in likelihood for ever (Joel 4:20).[103]

Napoleon believed that with sympathetic Jews controlling the territory between Acre, Lower Egypt and the Red Sea, French imperial and commercial interests as far as India, Arabia and Africa could be secured. Neither Napoleon nor the Jews were able to deliver. Nevertheless, his proclamation 'is a barometer of the extent to which the European atmosphere was charged with these messianic expectations'.[104] The European powers became increasingly preoccupied with the 'Eastern Question'. Britain and Prussia sided with the Sultan of Turkey against Napoleon and his vassal, Mehemet Ali. The necessity of preventing French control had led not only to the battles of the Nile and Acre, but also to a British military expedition in Palestine. With the defeat of Napoleon, Britain's main concern was with restraining Russia and this required supporting Turkish sovereignty. The race was on to control Palestine.

Stirred by memories of the Napoleonic expedition, Shaftesbury argued for

---

103. Cited in Franz Kobler, *Napoleon and the Jews* (New York: Schocken, 1976), pp. 55–57.
104. Salo W. Baron, *A Social and Religious History of the Jews*, 2 vols. (New York: Columbia University Press, 1937), vol. 2, p. 327.

a greater British presence in Palestine and saw this could be achieved by the sponsorship of a Jewish homeland on both religious and political grounds. British protection of the Jews, he argued, would give a colonial advantage over France for the control of the Middle East; provide better access to India via a direct land route; and open up new commercial markets for British products.

In 1839, Shaftesbury wrote an anonymous thirty-page article for the *Quarterly Review*, entitled 'State and Restauration (sic) of the Jews.' In it he advocated a Jewish national homeland, with Jerusalem the capital, but remaining under Turkish rule with British protection.[105] Shaftesbury predicted a new era for the Jews in terms similar to those Charles Simeon had used in 1836:

> the Jews must be encouraged to return in yet greater numbers and become once more the husbandman of Judea and Galilee . . . though admittedly a stiff-necked, dark hearted people, and sunk in moral degradation, obduracy, and ignorance of the Gospel . . . [They are] not only worthy of salvation but also vital to Christianity's hope of salvation.[106]

Shaftesbury appeared to share Simeon's optimistic postmillennial eschatology, seeing the conversion of the Jews as a means to bringing the whole world to faith before Christ returned.

When Palmerston, the Foreign Secretary, married Shaftesbury's widowed mother-in-law, Shaftesbury seized the opportunity to lobby for this cause. In his diary for 1 August 1840, Shaftesbury wrote:

> Dined with Palmerston. After dinner left alone with him. Propounded my scheme which seems to strike his fancy. He asked questions and readily promised to consider it. How singular is the order of Providence. Singular, if estimated by man's ways. Palmerston had already been chosen by God to be an instrument of good to His ancient people, to do homage to their inheritance, and to recognize their rights without believing their destiny. It seems he will yet do more. Though the motive be kind, it is not sound . . . he weeps not, like his Master, over Jerusalem, nor prays that now, at last, she may put on her beautiful garments.[107]

---

105. Cited in John Pollock, *Shaftesbury* (London: Hodder & Stoughton, 1985), p. 54.

106. Earl of Shaftesbury, 'State and Prospects of the Jews', *Quarterly Review* 63 (January/March 1839), pp. 166–192.

107. Anthony Ashley, Earl of Shaftesbury. Diary entries as quoted by Edwin Hodder, *The Life and Work of the Seventh Earl of Shaftesbury* (London, 1886), vol. 1, pp. 310–311.

Although Shaftesbury lamented Palmerston's unbelief, nevertheless he saw him as God's appointed man to bring about the restoration of the Jews. As a first step, Shaftesbury persuaded Palmerston to appoint the fellow-restorationist William Young as the first European vice-consul in Jerusalem. He subsequently wrote in his diary, 'What a wonderful event it is! The ancient City of the people of God is about to resume a place among the nations; and England is the first of the Gentile kingdoms that ceases to "tread her down".'[108] His gentle lobbying of Palmerston proved successful.

Fuelling speculation about an imminent restoration, on 4 November 1840, Shaftesbury placed an advertisement in *The Times* to give greater visibility to his vision. The advertisement included the following:

RESTORATION OF THE JEWS. A memorandum has been addressed to
the Protestant monarchs of Europe on the subject of the restoration of the
Jewish people to the land of Palestine. The document in question, dictated by a
peculiar conjunction of affairs in the East, and other striking 'signs of the times',
reverts to the original covenant which secures that land to the descendants of
Abraham.[109]

Back in 1818 Lewis Way had made such an appeal at the Congress of Aix la Chapelle. Now it was being revived on the grounds of political expediency as well as biblical mandate. Having helped achieve the former by securing the appointment of Young as vice-consul, and later consul, in Jerusalem, Shaftesbury now turned to the latter and advocated the founding of an Anglican bishopric in Jerusalem. This would, he argued, be a means by which God would continue to bless England as well as facilitate the return of the Jewish people to Palestine. The bishopric would, he said, be both 'political and religious . . . a combination of Protestant thrones, bound by temporal interests and eternal principles, to plant under the banner of the Cross, God's people on the mountains of Jerusalem'.[110]

At the beginning of the nineteenth century, the sole representatives of Western Christianity in Jerusalem had been the Franciscans, and only the Orthodox and Armenian traditions were resident in significant numbers. A Protestant bishopric under joint British and Prussian auspices was founded in 1841 and an Anglican church, Christ Church, near the Jaffa Gate in the

---

108. Cited in Pragai, *Faith and Fulfilment*, p. 45.

109. Cited in Wagner, *Anxious for Armageddon*, p. 91.

110. Merkley, *Politics of Christian Zionism*, p. 14.

Old City, was dedicated in 1845. Despite great expectations, Solomon Alexander, the first bishop and a former Jewish rabbi, did not survive long in the post. He was succeeded by Samuel Gobat, a Swiss Lutheran. The arrangement with Germany then lapsed and the bishopric became solely Anglican from 1881.

Having secured a sympathetic British consul as well as an Anglican bishop in Jerusalem, the next step in the restorationist agenda was to survey and map Palestine. To this end, Shaftesbury became the founding President of the Palestine Exploration Fund (PEF) in 1865. In his inaugural speech at the launch of the PEF, he declared their motives openly:

> Let us not delay to send out the best agents . . . to search the length and breadth
> of Palestine, to survey the land, and if possible to go over every corner of it, drain
> it, measure it and, if you will, prepare it for the return of its ancient possessors,
> for I believe that the time cannot be far off before that great event will come
> to pass.[111]

Shaftesbury's influence, therefore, in promoting the Zionist cause within the political, diplomatic and ecclesiastical establishment in Britain was immense. Donald Wagner claims,

> He single-handedly translated the theological positions of Brightman, Henry Finch,
> and John Nelson Darby into a political strategy. His high political connections,
> matched by his uncanny instincts, combined to advance the Christian Zionist
> vision.[112]

Indeed, it was probably Shaftesbury who inspired Israel Zangwell and Theodore Herzl to coin the phrase: 'A land of no people for a people with no land.' Shaftesbury, a generation earlier, imagining Palestine to be empty, had come up with the slogan, 'A country without a nation for a nation without a country.'[113] Shaftesbury had probably adapted the phrase of James Finn, his

---

111. Cited by Derek White, *Christian Zionism* (n.d.) [Internet], Saltshakers Messianic
     Community website, <http://www.saltshakers.com/midnight/chrzion1.htm>.
     [Accessed May 2004.]

112. Wagner, *Anxious for Armageddon*, p. 92.

113. Cited in ibid., p. 92; also Albert H. Hyamson, *Palestine under the Mandate, 1920–1940*
     (Westport, CT: Greenwood Press, 1976), p. 10, cited in Sharif, *Non-Jewish Zionism*,
     p. 42.

colleague in the PEF, who in 1857, while British consul in Jerusalem, had reported, 'The country is in a considerable degree empty of inhabitants and therefore its greatest need is that of a body of population.'[114]

Like Moses, Shaftesbury did not live to see his 'promised land' realized. However, through his lobbying, writings and public speaking, he did more than any other British politician to inspire a generation of Joshuas to translate his religious vision into a political reality.

British Christian political support for the Jewish Zionist movement

Of those Christian political leaders to take up the mantle of Shaftesbury and achieve the Zionist dream, a small number stand out. These include Laurence Oliphant (1829–1888), William Hechler (1845–1931), David Lloyd George (1863–1945) and, probably most significant of all, Arthur Balfour (1848–1930).

By 1897, when the First World Zionist Congress met in Basle, Switzerland, Jewish leaders who favoured a Zionist State already had sympathetic support from many more senior British political figures. This was largely due to the efforts of one man, William Hechler. The son of LJS missionaries in France and Germany, Hechler was an Anglican priest and became chaplain to the British Embassy in Vienna in 1885, a position of strategic significance for the Zionist movement. As with Shaftesbury's slogan, so Hechler's booklet, *The Restoration of the Jews to Palestine* (1894), pre-dated Herzl's *Der Judenstaat* by two years, and spoke of the need for 'restoring the Jews to Palestine according to Old Testament prophecies'.[115] Hechler became Herzl's chief Christian ally in realizing his vision of a Zionist State, one of only three Christians invited to attend the World Congress of Zionists. Herzl was not religious but he was superstitious and records a meeting with Hechler on 10 March 1896 in his diary:

> The Reverend William Hechler, Chaplain of the English Embassy here, came to see me. A sympathetic, gentle fellow, with the long grey beard of a prophet. He is enthusiastic about my solution of the Jewish Question. He also considers my movement a 'prophetic turning-point' – which he had foretold two years before. From a prophecy in the time of Omar (637CE) he had reckoned that at the end of

---

114. James Finn to the Earl of Clarendon, Jerusalem (15 September 1857), Public Record Office, FO 78/1294 (Pol. No. 36).
115. Sharif, *Non-Jewish Zionism*, p. 71.

forty-two prophetic months (total 1260 years) the Jews would get Palestine back. This figure he arrived at was 1897–98.[116]

In March 1897, the year Hechler expected the Jews to begin returning to Palestine, Herzl described their second meeting at Hechler's apartment. Herzl was amazed to find books from floor to ceiling, 'Nothing but Bibles', and a large military staff map of Palestine made up of four sheets covering the entire floor of the study:

> He showed me where, according to his calculations, our new Temple must be located: in Bethel! Because that is the centre of the country. He also showed me models of the ancient Temple. 'We have prepared the ground for you!' Hechler said triumphantly ... I take him for a naïve visionary ... However, there is something charming about his enthusiasm ... He gives me excellent advice, full of unmistakable genuine good will. He is at once clever and mystical, cunning and naïve.[117]

Despite Herzl's initial scepticism, Hechler kept his word and gained access to the German Kaiser William II, the Grand Duke of Baden, as well as the British political establishment for Herzl and his Zionist delegation. Although sympathetic to the evangelistic ministry of the LJS, Hechler's advocacy and diplomacy highlighted a progressive and radical shift in Christian Zionist thinking away from the views of Way and Simeon, who saw evangelism as a priority and restoration to the land as a consequence of Jewish people coming to faith in Jesus Christ. Now, Hechler was insisting instead that it was the destiny of Christians simply to help restore the Jews to Palestine. This is clear in a letter he wrote to a missionary in Jerusalem in 1898:

> Of course, dear colleague, you look for the conversion of the Jews, but the times are changing rapidly, and it is important for us to look further and higher. We are now entering, thanks to the Zionist Movement, into Israel's Messianic age ... All of this, dear colleague, is messianic work; all of this the breath of the Holy Spirit announces. But first the dry bones must come to life, and draw together.[118]

Hechler's arguments appear to prefigure those of political dispensational

---

116. Herzl, *Diaries of Theodore Herzl*, entry for 26 March 1896.

117. Cited in Merkley, *Politics of Christian Zionism*, pp. 16–17; see also, Pileggi, 'Hechler, CMJ and Zionism', *Shalom* 3(1998).

118. Cited in Merkley, *Politics of Christian Zionism*, pp. 15–16.

Christian Zionists who, having disavowed evangelism, believe they are fulfill-ing their Christian mandate by bringing blessing to Israel. When Hechler even-tually resigned from his chaplaincy in Vienna in 1910, the Zionist Organization in London provided a pension for his 'loyal' support of Zionism in accordance with Herzl's instructions. In 1922 Hechler was present when the British Parliament ratified the Palestine Mandate, convinced this event was itself, if somewhat belated, the fulfilment of biblical prophecy.

David Lloyd George, who became Prime Minister in 1916, was another self-confessed Zionist, sharing similar views to those of Shaftesbury. In his own words, he was Chaim Weizmann's proselyte, 'Acetone converted me to Zionism.'[119] Weizmann had assisted the British government in the develop-ment of explosives and, in part, Palestine appears to have been the reward. In the same speech given before the Jewish Historical Society in 1925, Lloyd George reminisced on his inherited Nonconformist conscience:

> I was brought up in a school where I was taught far more about the history of the Jews than about the history of my own land. I could tell you all the kings of Israel. But I doubt whether I could have named half a dozen of the kings of England, and not more of the kings of Wales . . . We were thoroughly imbued with the history of your race in the days of its greatest glory.[120]

Christopher Sykes, whose father Sir Mark Sykes had co-authored the secret Sykes-Picot Agreement of 1916, which dismembered the Ottoman Empire between Britain, France and Russia, was also one of Lloyd George's biographers. Sykes observes how, prior to the Paris Peace Accord signed in 1919, various advisors had tried unsuccessfully to brief Lloyd George on the issues relating to the Palestine settlement, but that he was unable to grasp the issues. Sykes claims this was,

> largely because he could not move beyond the Christian Zionist worldview of his youth. When briefed repeatedly on the contemporary geography of Palestine, Lloyd George insisted on reciting from his memory of childhood Sunday school lessons the Biblical cities and lands of Bible times, some of which no longer existed.[121]

---

119. Weizmann had discovered how to synthesize acetone, a solvent used in the manufacture of explosives, which became of great benefit to the British war-effort.

120. David Lloyd George, *Memoirs of the Peace Conference* (New Haven: Yale University Press, 1939), vol. 2, p. 720. See also, Chaim Weizmann, *Trial and Error: An Autobiography* (London: Hamish Hamilton, 1949), p. 194.

121. Cited in Wagner, *Anxious for Armageddon*, pp. 94–95.

Oliphant, Hechler and Lloyd George all nurtured the fledgling Jewish Zionist movement, in part from religious conviction but also because it served the purposes of British foreign policy. It is ironic that the Jewish Zionist movement led by Herzl was essentially secular, and yet it relied heavily on Christian Zionists such as William Hechler who had a deep reverence for the Hebrew Scriptures and a passionate certainty that Eretz Israel was the Jewish destiny.

The Balfour Declaration and the implementation of the Zionist vision

Probably the most significant British politician of all, however, was Arthur James Balfour (1848–1930), who pioneered the Balfour Declaration in 1917. Like Lloyd George, Balfour had been brought up in an evangelical home and was sympathetic to Zionism because of the influence of dispensational teaching. He regarded history as 'an instrument for carrying out a Divine purpose'.[122] From 1905 Chaim Weizmann, then a professor of chemistry at Manchester University, began to meet regularly with Balfour to discuss the implementation of that goal. Following a meeting with Weizmann on 9 January 1906, Balfour wrote to his neice saying that he could see 'no political difficulty about obtaining Palestine, only economic ones'.[123] Weizmann convinced Balfour that none of the other Jewish homeland 'solutions' offered, such as Uganda or Argentina, were tenable. According to his niece, shortly before his death Balfour remarked that 'the Jewish form of patriotism was unique . . . Their love of their country refused to be satisfied by the Uganda scheme. It was Weizmann's absolute refusal even to look at it that impressed me.'[124]

Negotiations over a British declaration of support for the Zionists began in early 1917 between Balfour (then British Foreign Secretary) other members of the British government and representatives of the Zionist Organization. Mark Sykes (the Assistant Secretary to the War Cabinet) had been given responsibility for Middle Eastern affairs and set about extricating the British from the Sykes-Picot Agreement of 1916 which envisaged Anglo-French administration of Palestine. In October 1917, Balfour learned that Germany

---

122. See Sharif, *Non-Jewish Zionism*, p. 78.
123. Cited in Kenneth Young, *Arthur James Balfour* (London: G. Bell & Sons, 1963), p. 256.
124. Young, *Arthur James Balfour*, p. 256.

was about to issue its own declaration of sympathy with Zionism and therefore recommended that the British Cabinet pre-empt them.[125] After several
drafts written by the Zionist Organization, on 2 November 1917, Balfour
made public the final version of the letter written to Lord Rothschild on 31
October. This became known as the Balfour Declaration:

> His Majesty's Government views with favour the establishment in Palestine of a
> National Home for the Jewish people, and will use their best endeavours to facilitate
> the achievement of that object, it being clearly understood that nothing shall be done,
> which may prejudice the civil and religious rights of the existing non-Jewish
> Communities in Palestine, or the rights and political status enjoyed by Jews in any
> other country.[126]

Not only had the Zionist Organization written the initial draft for Balfour, the
British government's response was also drafted by a Jew – Leopold Amery.
Amery was a covert Jew whose mother, Elisabeth Joanna Saphir, was
Hungarian. Amery had changed his middle name from Moritz to Maurice in
order to disguise his origins. As Assistant Secretary to the British War Cabinet,
Amery not only wrote the final version of the Balfour Declaration, but was
also responsible for establishing the Jewish Legion, the first organized Jewish
army for 2,000 years and forerunner to the Israeli Defence Force. According
to the historian William Rubinstein, Amery misled British officials as to his
sympathy for the Jews. Indeed, he claims Amery's deception was 'possibly the
most remarkable example of concealment of identity in 20th Century British
political history'.[127]

Balfour was in fact already committed to the Zionist programme out of
theological conviction and had no intention of consulting with the indigenous
Arab population, as he had promised in his declaration. In a letter to Lord
Curzon, written in 1919, Balfour insisted somewhat cynically:

> For in Palestine we do not propose even to go through the form of consulting the
> wishes of the present inhabitants of the country . . . the Four Great Powers are
> committed to Zionism. And Zionism, be it right or wrong, good or bad, is rooted in

125. *The Balfour Declaration* (n.d.) [Internet], World Zionist Organization website,
         <http://www.wzo.org.il/home/politic/balfour.htm>. [Accessed May 2004.]
126. Ibid.
127. William Rubinstein, 'The Secret of Leopold Amery – Conservative Politician',
         History Today 49 (2 February 1999), pp. 17–23.

age-long traditions, in present needs, in future hopes, of far profounder import than
the desires or prejudices of the 700,000 Arabs who now inhabit that ancient land . . .
I do not think that Zionism will hurt the Arabs . . . in short, so far as Palestine is
concerned, the Powers have made no statement of fact which is not admittedly
wrong, and no declaration of policy which, at least in the letter, they have not always
intended to violate.[128]

What the Balfour Declaration left intentionally ambiguous was the meaning of
a 'national home'. Balfour's draft of August 1917 read 'Palestine should be
reconstituted as the national home of the Jewish people.' In the final version
in October 'the' had become 'a' and it now read, 'the establishment in Palestine
of a national home for the Jewish people'. Was this synonymous with sovereignty or statehood and, if so, what were to be the borders? Would it occupy
all of Palestine or just a portion? What was to be the status of Jerusalem?
Furthermore, while it stated that 'the civil and religious rights of the existing
population' were to be safeguarded and the territory was designated 'Palestine',
there was no reference to Palestinians. Kenneth Cragg acknowledges: 'They
were an actual, but awkward non-identity.'[129] Clearly Balfour did not believe
that 'the present inhabitants' need be consulted, either before or afterwards.
That 90% of the indigenous population of Palestine were Arabs, of whom
around 10% were Christian, seemed irrelevant to the politicians and Zionists
who had another agenda. So the awkward questions were left unanswered and
it is these ambiguities that have plagued Middle East peace negotiations and
divided Christians ever since. However, this momentous declaration by the
British government for the first time gave Zionism a measure of 'political
legitimacy' and provided the impetus for the colonization of Palestine.

Just a month after publishing the Balfour Declaration, on 9 December 1917,
British troops occupied Jerusalem. Anglo-French diplomacy and strategic self-
interest in the possession of territory gained from the Turks led to duplicity
over the Balfour Declaration in promising the same land to both the Jews and
Arabs. Thus Balfour and Lloyd George, probably two of the most influential
British political leaders of the First-World-War years, like Shaftesbury and
Palmerston a generation earlier, were both committed to a Christian Zionist
agenda. Their support for the World Zionist movement was a direct result of
their evangelical upbringing and the influence of clergy like Way, Simeon and

---

128. Cited in Doreen Ingrams, *Palestine Papers 1917–1922: Seeds of Conflict* (London: John
Murray, 1972), p. 73.
129. Cragg, *Arab Christian*, p. 234.

Darby, as much as from their desire to dismember the Ottoman Empire and ensure British dominance in the Middle East.

From the mid-nineteenth century, a similar marriage between religious dogmatism and political expediency in the United States was to lead theologians and politicians alike to support the Zionist cause. While dispensationalism became marginalized in Britain, limited to the sectarian fragmentation of the Brethren, in the United States it was to become a dominant influence within mainstream evangelicalism. The link between British and American dispensational Christian Zionism was first brokered by J. N. Darby.

Dispensationalism and the birth of Christian Zionism in America (1859–1945)

During the Colonial period and even beyond the Civil War (1861–1865), American Christianity, as in Britain at the beginning of the nineteenth century, was essentially postmillennial in outlook. Strengthened by the Wesleyan Holiness movement, there was a strong focus on evangelism, personal morality and civil responsibility. The Revolutionary War provided a stimulus to popular apocalyptic speculation and, by 1773, King George III was being portrayed as the Antichrist and the war as a 'holy crusade' that would usher in the millennium. In parallel with Britain, the late eighteenth and early nineteenth centuries also saw an explosion of millennial sects including the Shakers, Mormons and Millerites. Influenced by the French Revolution and the destruction of the papacy in France, historic premillennialism gradually became more popular.

Between 1859 and 1872, resulting from his extensive tours throughout America, and reinforced by the trauma of the Civil War, Darby's premillennial dispensational views about a failing church and revived Israel came to have a profound and increasing influence upon American evangelicalism. It resulted not only in the birth of American dispensationalism but also influenced the millenarianism associated with the prophecy-conference movement and, later, fundamentalism.[130] Darby's influence on end-time thinking in North America was both profound and pivotal, more so perhaps than any other Christian leader for the last 200 years. In the absence of a strong Jewish Zionist movement,

---

130. Sandeen, *Roots of Fundamentalism*; R. A. Torrey, *The Fundamental Doctrines of the Christian Faith* (New York: Doren, 1918); *The Fundamentals: A Testimony to the Truth* (Chicago: Testimony Publishing Co., 1910–1915).

American Christian Zionism arose from the confluence of these complex associations, evangelical, premillennial, dispensational, millenarian and proto-fundamentalist. Those most closely influenced by Darby who contributed to the development of Christian Zionism in America were James H. Brookes, Arno C. Gaebelein, D. L. Moody, William E. Blackstone and C. I. Scofield.

James H. Brookes (1830–1897): restoration to Zion

Brookes, the minister of Walnut Street Presbyterian Church, St Louis, Missouri, has been described as 'The father of American Dispensationalism'.[131] He was also an important leader in the proto-fundamentalist movement. Brookes not only sympathized with Darby's dispensational views of a failing church, corrupt and beyond hope, but also met Darby during five visits he made to St Louis between 1864–1865. They also met again between 1872 and 1877 when Darby preached in Brookes's church. While American evangelicals were less inclined to accept Darby's notion of a failing church and remained committed to their own denominations, they increasingly endorsed his futurist premillennialism and his distinction between the church and Israel. Mindful though of the notoriety with which the Brethren, and in particular Darby, were regarded within traditional denominational circles, Brookes insisted, like Darby, that he had reached his particular premillennial views through his own study of the Scriptures and not from anyone else.

Brookes was nevertheless instrumental in bringing Moody to St Louis for the 1879–1880 campaign and for introducing Scofield, and probably also Darby, to Moody. Brookes became the most influential lobbyist for dispensationalism for several reasons. Through his Bible classes, he was responsible for nurturing many young Christian leaders, notably Scofield who became his close friend and disciple. He also published many books and pamphlets including a Christian magazine called *The Truth*. This magazine was published for twenty-three years from 1874 until his death. Probably most significantly of all, however, Brookes helped organize the New York prophecy conference of 1878. He then served as the principal speaker and president of the annual Niagara Bible conference from 1878 until his death in 1897. He was therefore pivotal in ensuring that the futurist dispensational views associated with the Albury and Powerscourt conferences in England and Ireland came to take root in Middle America.

Following Darby's dispensational distinction between Israel and the church, Brookes went on to write *Israel and the Church*. In it, he challenged the notion

---

131. See Gerstner, *Wrongly Dividing the Word of Truth* (Brentwood, TN: Wolgemuth & Hyatt, 1991), p. 38.

that God's purpose was for Jews to be converted and incorporated in the church, insisting that history had shown this approach largely to have failed. Furthermore, he insisted, Old Testament promises concerning Israel could not be spiritualized nor had they been fulfilled in the church. Interestingly, Moody's publishing company printed the book.

In 1891, Brookes then wrote *Till He Come*, in which he presented a futurist premillennial scheme through which 'the Jews will be literally restored to their land'.[132] In his journal, *The Truth*, he urged Christians to show love and compassion towards the Jews, referring to the pogroms of Russia and Romania and restrictions placed upon them in Germany. He called upon Christians to support the return of Jews to Palestine and repudiated the anti-Semitism prevalent in Europe and in America:

> All Jews, except those who have become utter infidels, confidently expect to be restored to the land of their fathers, and it is most important to show them that their hope is founded upon Jehovah's immutable covenant, and that it shall be fulfilled by the coming of Messiah.[133]

Committed not only to a literal return to the land but also to a literal return to the Lord, Brookes supported independent missionary work among the Jewish people, notably with Arno Gaebelein and Ernst Stroeter who founded the Hope of Israel Mission in Chicago in 1894.

Dwight L. Moody (1837–1899): respectability for Zionism

Moody was first and foremost an evangelist and shared with Brookes a passion to reach the Jews for Christ. However, his theology was not particularly systematic and perhaps by default he came to share the dispensational premillennial presuppositions of those who became his friends and confidants. Darby's influence over Moody came about principally through one of Darby's disciples, a young evangelist called Henry Moorehouse, who impressed Moody with his 'extraordinary' preaching. According to his son, Moody's message and style were revolutionized by Moorehouse: 'Mr Moorehouse taught Moody to draw his sword full length, to fling the scabbard away, and to enter the battle with the naked blade.'[134]

Albert Newman confirms the strong influence Darby had over Moody's

---

132. Brookes, *Till He Come*, pp. 1–2.
133. James H. Brookes, 'How to Reach the Jews', *The Truth*, pp. 135–136, cited in Rausch, *Zionism*, p. 224.
134. Moody, *Life of Dwight L. Moody*, p. 140.

circle: 'The large class of evangelists, of whom Dwight L. Moody was the most eminent, have drawn their inspiration and their Scripture interpretation largely from the writings and the personal influence of the Brethren.'[135] Gaebelein, Scofield's biographer, also describes how Scofield kept Moody conformed to a dispensational prophetic framework: 'Moody himself needed at times a better knowledge of prophecy, and Scofield was the man to lead him into it.'[136]

There are several references in Moody's writings that indicate his sympathy for the Jewish people and restorationism. In a sermon entitled 'Christ in the Old Testament', delivered in Boston in 1877, Moody explored the meaning of God's promise to Abraham in Genesis 22 to make him a great nation:

> Now, let me ask you, hasn't that prophecy been fulfilled? Hasn't God made that a great and mighty nation? Where is there any nation that has ever produced such men as have come from the seed of Abraham? There is no nation that has or can produce such men . . . That promise was made 4000 years ago . . . When I meet a Jew I can't help having a profound respect for them, for they are God's people.[137]

In the same sermon, he gave evidence of his dispensational conviction that the Jews will be converted at the return of Christ and remain a separate people apart from the church: 'I have an idea that they are a nation that are to be born in a day, and when they are converted and brought back to Christ, what a mighty power they will be in the land, what missionaries to carry the glad tidings around the world.'[138] Moody did, however, distance himself from those who speculated that specific signs had to be fulfilled before Christ's return. On one occasion he preached:

> Now there is no place in the Scripture where we are told to watch for signs – the rebuilding of Babylon, or the returning of the Jews to Jerusalem; but all through Scripture we are told what to do – just to watch for Him; just to be waiting for our Lord's return from Heaven.[139]

---

135. Albert Henry Newman, *Manual of Church History*, vol. 2: *Modern Church History 1517–1902* (Philadelphia: American Baptist Society, 1904), p. 713.

136. Gaebelein, *History of the Scofield Reference Bible*, p. 25.

137. D. L. Moody, *To All People: Comprising Sermons, Bible Readings, Temperence Addresses, and Prayer-Meeting Talks* (Boston: The Globe Publishing Company, 1877), p. 354, cited in Rausch, *Zionism*, p. 155.

138. Ibid.

139. Moody, *To All People*, p. 508, cited in Rausch, *Zionism*, p. 155.

Moody's name is particularly associated with the popular Northfield conferences which he founded in 1880. Apparently, none of Moody's biographers have noted how at these conferences dispensational speakers dominated the platform, especially in the 1880s and 1890s.[140]

Moody's greatest service to Darby and dispensationalism, however, came through the Bible Institute for Home and Foreign Missions of the Chicago Evangelization Society, which he founded in 1886. The Moody Bible Institute, as it was later renamed, became the 'West Point' of the fundamentalist movement giving respectability to dispensationalism and training many of its future leaders. Rausch highlights the fact that many of the dispensational prophecy-conference speakers were also regular instructors at the Moody Bible Institute (MBI).[141] These included Dr W. G. Moorehead of Xenia, Ohio, who also became one of the consulting editors for the *Scofield Reference Bible*. The MBI became a prototype for many other colleges and institutions that facilitated the spread of dispensational theology across America, the most prominent of which were the Bible Institute of Los Angeles (Biola), and the Northwestern Bible Training School of Minneapolis. By 1956, a further forty Bible schools were teaching dispensationalism, training some 10,000 pastors and missionaries annually.[142]

William Eugene Blackstone (1841–1935): recognition of Zionism

Another of Darby's disciples and a friend of Brookes was William Blackstone, an influential evangelist and lay-worker for the Methodist Episcopal Church, as well as a financier and benefactor. After the Civil War he married and settled in Chicago. In 1887, on the advice of Brookes, he wrote a book on biblical prophecy entitled *Jesus is Coming*, which by 1916 had been translated into twenty-five languages, and by 1927 into thirty-six. His book took a premillennial dispensational view of the second coming, emphasizing that the Jews had a biblical right to Palestine and would soon be restored there. In this, Blackstone was one of the first Christian Zionists in America, like Hechler in Britain, to lobby actively for the Zionist cause. Blackstone took the Zionist movement to be a sign of the imminent return of Christ even though its leadership, like Herzl, were agnostic. Like Gaebelein, he could distinguish between the worldly means and divine ends:

---

140. Ernest R. Sandeen, 'Towards a Historical Interpretation of the Origins of Fundamentalism', *Church History* 36 (1967), p. 76.

141. Rausch, *Zionism*, p. 159.

142. Gerstner, *Wrongly Dividing the Word of Truth*, p. 51.

> The Zionists have seized the reins and eschewing the help of Abraham's God they have accepted agnostics as leaders and are plunging madly into this scheme for the erection of a godless state. But the Bible student will surely say, this godless national gathering of Israel is not the fulfilment of all the glorious restoration, so glowingly described by the prophets. No, indeed.[143]

Nevertheless, he argued, based on his reading of Zephaniah 2:1–2, this was precisely what the Scriptures predicted: 'Could this prophecy be more literally fulfilled than in this present Zionist movement?'[144]

Blackstone, like Hal Lindsey a century later, interpreted Scripture in the light of unfolding contemporary events, something which Spurgeon had described as 'exegesis by current events'.[145] No longer were Christian Zionists expecting Jewish national repentance to precede restoration; it could wait until after Jesus returned. Although popular with proto-fundamentalists, Blackstone's book *Jesus is Coming* became more widely known in 1908, when a presentation edition was sent to several hundred-thousand ministers and Christian workers, and again in 1917, when the Moody Bible Institute printed 'presentation copies' and sent them to ministers, missionaries and theological students. *Jesus is Coming* was the most widely read book on the return of Christ published in the twentieth century until the publication of Hal Lindsey's *The Late Great Planet Earth*, which in turn was superseded only by Tim LaHaye's fictional twelve-volume *Left Behind* series.[146] By the time of Blackstone's death in 1935 over a million copies had been printed.

In 1887, Blackstone founded the Chicago Hebrew Mission, which later became the American Messianic Fellowship International (AMFI). In 1888, Blackstone travelled to London for the General Missionary Conference and then journeyed through Europe to Palestine and Egypt. On his return in 1890, he organized and chaired the first conference between prominent Christian leaders and Reform rabbis in Chicago, entitled 'The Past, Present and Future of Israel'.[147] To his surprise, Blackstone discovered that it was only the Christians who favoured Zionism. The Reform rabbis had no desire to return to Palestine and he faced strong opposition from them. Rabbi Emil Hirsh

---

143. Blackstone, *Jesus is Coming*, p. 240.

144. Ibid.

145. C. H. Spurgeon, *Lectures to My Students* (London: Passmore & Alabaster, 1893), p. 100.

146. See W. M. Smith, 'Signs of the Times', *Moody Monthly* (August 1966), p. 5.

147. See William E. Currie, *God's Little Errand Boy: 100 Years of Blessing* (Lansing, IL: American Messianic Fellowship International, 1987).

insisted, 'We modern Jews do not wish to be restored to Palestine . . . the country wherein we live is our Palestine . . . we will not go back . . . to form a nationality of our own.'[148] Without agreement, the conference issued somewhat diluted 'resolutions of sympathy' for the oppressed Jews of Russia which were then sent to the Tsar and other leaders. Blackstone felt these were inadequate and so in the following year, in March 1891, he lobbied the President of the United States, Benjamin Harrison, and his Secretary of State, James G. Blaine, with a petition signed by no less than 413 prominent Jewish and Christian leaders, including John and William Rockefeller. The petition called for an international conference on the restoration of the Jews to Palestine. The petition became known as the Blackstone Memorial. Conveniently ignoring the fact that Palestine was inhabited by Palestinians it offered this solution:

> Why not give Palestine back to them [the Jews] again? According to God's distribution of nations, it is their home, an inalienable possession from which they were expelled by force. Under their cultivation, it was a remarkably fruitful land, sustaining millions of Israelites, who industriously tilled its hillsides and valleys. They were agriculturalists and producers as well as a nation of great commercial importance – the centre of civilization and religion. Why shall not the powers which under the treaty of Berlin, in 1878, gave Bulgaria to the Bulgarians and Servia to the Servians now give Palestine back to the Jews?[149]

Although President Harrison did not act upon the petition, it was nevertheless pivotal in galvanizing Christian and Jewish Zionist activists in the United States for the next sixty years. Justice Louis Brandeis, the first Jewish Justice of the Supreme Court, who led the Jewish Zionist movement in the United States from 1914, became a close friend of Blackstone and they laboured for twenty years to convince the American people and successive presidents, in particular, to support the Zionist agenda. During that time, Blackstone sent Brandeis large sums of money to support the Zionist cause. Responsible for disbursing millions of dollars of dispensational funds entrusted to him for missionary work, Blackstone promised Brandeis that if he should not be raptured with Blackstone, he was to use the funds for the relief of Jews who would come to believe in Christ and need supporting as missionaries throughout the world during the millennium.

---

148. Cited in Lindberg, *A God-Filled Life*, pp. 7–9.

149. Reuben Fink, *America and Palestine* (New York: American Zionist Emergency Council, 1945), pp. 20–21, cited in Sharif, *Non-Jewish Zionism*, p. 92.

In 1917, Blackstone was excited by the developments in Palestine following the defeat of the Turks and the triumphal entry of the Allies into Jerusalem. They were 'welcomed as deliverers by the people, and a Jewish Commission, authorized by the Allied governments already taking charge of the development of Jewish interests in Palestine – all of this does indeed thrill my heart'.[150] In January 1918, Blackstone spoke at a large Jewish Zionist meeting in Los Angeles and declared that he had been committed to Zionism for thirty years: 'This is because I believe that true Zionism is founded on the plan, purpose, and fiat of the everlasting and omnipotent God, as prophetically recorded in His Holy Word, the Bible.' He then went on to explain to the Jews present that they had three options: the first was to become Christians, although he conceded few would choose this option; the second was to become a 'true' Zionist and 'thus hold fast to the ancient hopes of the fathers, and the assured deliverance of Israel, through the coming of their Messiah, and complete national restoration and permanent settlement in the land which God has given them'; and the third option was to assimilate within American society and be neither Christian or Zionist. Blackstone then challenged his audience to choose the second option: 'Oh, my Jewish friends, which of these paths shall be yours? . . . study this wonderful Word of God . . . and see how plainly God Himself has revealed Israel's pathway unto the perfect day.'[151] Blackstone's appeal reveals, perhaps more clearly than any other statement made by a contemporary dispensationalist, the logical consequences of the distinction made between God's separate purposes for Israel and the church, and the way in which this affected their approach to Jewish 'mission'. To Blackstone, evangelism and restoration were not mutually exclusive but equal means to fulfilling God's purposes among the Jews. In Blackstone's mind, to choose 'Jesus' might be the Christian answer and was acknowledged, albeit half-heartedly; but to choose Zionism was to be a 'true Jew' and certainly preferable to their assimilation into secular Western society.

During his lifetime, Jewish Zionists honoured Blackstone more times than any other Christian leader. On one occasion, Brandeis wrote, 'You are the Father of Zionism as your work antedates Herzl.'[152] In 1918, Elisha Friedman, Secretary of the University Zionist Society of New York, similarly declared, 'A well-known Christian layman, William E. Blackstone, antedated Theodor

150. Lindberg, *A God-Filled Life*, pp. 12–13.

151. Cited in Rausch, *Zionism*, pp. 268–269.

152. Cited in Currie, *God's Little Errand Boy*, available online at <http://www.amfi.org/errandboy/htm>.

Herzl by five years in his advocacy of the re-establishment of a Jewish State.'[153] What Blackstone expressed in his speeches, books and petitions, Scofield was to systematize and canonize through his thoroughly dispensational reference Bible.

Cyrus Ingerson Scofield (1843–1921): the canonizing of Zionism

Scofield may be regarded as the most influential exponent of dispensationalism, following the publication of his *Scofield Reference Bible* by the Oxford University Press. Ernest Sandeen insists: 'in the calendar of Fundamentalist saints no name is better known or more revered'.[154] Yet while writings abound on the early Brethren, such as J. N. Darby, and American dispensationalists, such as D. L. Moody, Scofield remains an elusive and enigmatic figure. Only two biographies have been published; one by a fellow dispensationalist eulogizes Scofield, and the other portrays him as a charlatan, accused of perjury, fraud and embezzlement. He also deserted his wife and children, failed to pay maintenance and married again only three months after his divorce became final.[155]

As a young and largely illiterate Christian, Scofield was profoundly influenced and schooled by James H. Brookes, who, in turn, introduced him to Darby. Serving as Brookes's assistant, Scofield popularized Darby's distinctive futurist dispensationalism, basing his reference notes on Darby's own distinctive translation of the Bible. Clarence Bass notes: 'the parallel between Scofield's notes and Darby's works only too clearly reveals that Scofield was not only a student of Darby's works, but that he copiously borrowed ideas,

---

153. Cutler B. Whitwell, 'The Life Story of W.E.B. – and of "Jesus is coming"', *Sunday School Times* (11 January 1936), p. 19, cited in Rausch, *Zionism*, p. 265.

154. Sandeen, *Roots of Fundamentalism*, p. 222.

155. Charles G. Trumball, *The Life Story of C. I. Scofield* (New York: Oxford University Press, 1920); Canfield, *Incredible Scofield*. Scofield's wife Leontine divorced him in 1881 while he was pastor of Hyde Park Congregational Church, St Louis. Her divorce papers charged Scofield with 'gross neglect of duty', having 'failed to support this plaintiff or her said children, or to contribute thereto, and has made no provision for them for food, clothing or a home . . .' The court decided in favour of Leontine after some delay in 1883 and issued a decree of divorce in December of that year, describing Scofield as, '. . . not a fit person to have custody of the children' (from the papers in case number 2161, supplied by the Atchison County Court, cited in Canfield, *Incredible Scofield*, p. 89). Scofield married Hettie Van Wark just three months later on 11 March 1884 (Canfield, *Incredible Scofield*, p. 100).

words and phrases'.[156] Essentially, Scofield plagiarized Darby's works, never acknowledging his sources or indebtedness to Darby.

Scofield's first work, entitled *Rightly Dividing the Word of Truth*, was published in 1888 and presented the dispensational hermeneutic principles he had allegedly been teaching in his Bible classes for many years. These became the basis for the notes contained in his *Scofield Reference Bible*. Not surprisingly, it was the publishing house of the Plymouth Brethren, Loizeaux Brothers of New York, who printed the first edition and continue to publish the work a century later. The dispensational views later popularized by Scofield were shaped by a series of Bible and prophetic conferences held across North America beginning in 1868. These followed the pattern of Bible readings and discussion of prophetic subjects established in the 1830s by Darby and Irving at Albury and Powerscourt. For example, one of the resolutions adopted by the 1878 Niagara Bible conference gives clear evidence of Darby's pessimistic dispensational language, of which Scofield was becoming an eager proselyte:

> We believe that the world will not be converted during the present dispensation, but is fast ripening for judgement, while there will be fearful apostasy in the professing Christian body; and hence that the Lord Jesus will come in person to introduce the millennial age, when Israel shall be restored to their own land, and the earth shall be full of the knowledge of the Lord.[157]

Scofield first attended the Niagara Bible conference in 1887, completing his book *Rightly Dividing the Word of Truth* during the 1888 conference. It was at these conferences that, in discussion with other Brethren leaders, the idea for his reference Bible took shape and found sponsors. The combination of an attractive format, illustrative notes and cross references has led both critics and advocates to acknowledge the *Scofield Reference Bible* to have been the most influential book among evangelicals during the first half of the twentieth century. James Barr claims that half of all conservative evangelical student groups in the 1950s were using the *Scofield Reference Bible*, and that it was '... the most important single document of all Fundamentalism'.[158] Craig Blaising, professor of systematic theology at Dallas Theological Seminary and a dispensationalist, similarly acknowledges that, 'The *Scofield Reference Bible* became the

---

156. Bass, *Backgrounds to Dispensationalism*, p. 18. See also, Boettner, *Millennium*, p. 369.
157. Resolution included as Appendix A, in Sandeen, *Roots of Fundamentalism*.
158. James Barr, *Escaping from Fundamentalism* (London: SCM, 1984), p. 6.

Bible of Fundamentalism, and the theology of the notes approached confessional status in many Bible schools, institutes and seminaries established in the early decades of this Century.'[159] Sandeen observes:

> The book has thus been subtly but powerfully influential in spreading those views among hundreds of thousands who have regularly read that Bible and who often have been unaware of the distinction between the ancient text and the Scofield interpretation.'[160]

Scofield's reference Bible has, nevertheless, undergone significant revision since it was first published in 1909. Scofield completed the first revision in 1917, apparently with the help of seven consulting editors, several of whom were colleagues of D. L. Moody.[161] Their names appear to have been added, together with their academic qualifications, to give greater credibility to the work.[162] Sandeen goes further, arguing that Scofield 'only meant to gain support for his publication from both sides of the millenarian movement with this device'.[163] Subsequent revisions have continued to adapt, sanitize and elaborate Scofield's dispensational package.[164] William E. Cox offers this appraisal of his abiding influence:

> Scofield's footnotes and his systematized schemes of hermeneutics have been memorized by many as religiously as have verses of the Bible. It is not at all uncommon to hear devout men recite these footnotes prefaced by the words: 'The Bible says . . .' Many a pastor has lost all influence with members of his congregation and has been branded a liberal for no other reason than failure to concur with all the footnotes of Dr. Scofield. Even many ministers use the teachings of Scofield as tests of orthodoxy![165]

Scofield's influence extended well beyond his published writings. In the

---

159. Craig A. Blaising, 'Dispensationalism, The Search for Definition', in Blaising and Bock (eds.), *Dispensationalism*, p. 21.

160. Sandeen, *Roots of Fundamentalism*, p. 222.

161. James M. Gray, President of Moody Bible Institute, and William J. Erdman.

162. See Canfield, *Incredible Scofield*, p. 204.

163. Sandeen, *Roots of Fundamentalism*, p. 224.

164. For examples of this, see Schuyler English (ed.), *The New Scofield Study Bible* (New York: Oxford University Press, 1984) and Charles Ryrie, *Ryrie Study Bible* (Chicago: Moody Bible Institute, 1994).

165. Cox, *Examination of Dispensationalism*, pp. 55–56.

1890s, during Scofield's pastorate in Dallas, he was also head of the Southwestern School of the Bible, a forerunner to Dallas Theological Seminary, which became dispensationalism's most influential and academic institution. The seminary was founded in 1924 by one of Scofield's disciples, Lewis Sperry Chafer, who in turn became Scofield's most influential exponent. Chafer wrote the first systematic pro-Zionist dispensational theology, running to eight large volumes. Shortly before his death, Chafer described his greatest academic achievement: 'It goes on record that the Dallas Theological Seminary uses, recommends, and defends the Scofield Bible.'[166] So it is perhaps not surprising that, since then, Dallas Theological Seminary has continued to be the foremost apologist for, and proponent of, Scofield's classical dispensational views and of Christian Zionism through the writings of Charles Ryrie, Charles Dyer, Hal Lindsey and John Walvoord.

Arno C. Gaebelein (1861–1945): anti-Semitic Christian Zionism

Gaebelein is probably the most complex and controversial of the early dispensational Christian Zionists, principally for his views on prophecy, the Jews and Zionism. Gaebelein is distinguished for being the source of the prophetic notes in the *Scofield Reference Bible*. He was also a regular speaker at the Niagara Bible conferences, and, at the invitation of Lewis Sperry Chafer, lectured for a month each year at the Evangelical Theological College in Dallas, which later became Dallas Theological Seminary. In 1893, Gaebelein began publishing a periodical in Yiddish, *Tiqweth Israel – The Hope of Israel Monthly*. A year later, he began to publish an English version, *Our Hope*, specifically to acquaint Christians with the Zionist movement and the imminent return of Christ. Like Scofield, Gaebelein was also discipled by Brookes who, he admitted, 'took me literally under his wings'.[167] Scofield wrote the foreword to Gaebelein's *The Harmony of the Prophetic Word*, which he admitted to devouring. In a letter to Gaebelein, written in September 1905, Scofield acknowledged:

> My beloved brother: By all means follow your own views of prophetic analysis. I sit at your feet when it comes to prophecy, and congratulate in advance the future readers of my Bible on having in their hands a safe, clear, sane guide through what to most is a labyrinth. Yours lovingly in Christ, Scofield.[168]

---

166. Cited in Gerstner, *Wrongly Dividing the Word of Truth*, p. 46.
167. Arno C. Gaebelein, *Half A Century* (New York: Publication Office of Our Hope, 1930), p. 20, cited in Gerstner, *Wrongly Dividing the Word of Truth*, p. 44.
168. See Gaebelein, *History of the Scofield Reference Bible*, p. 33.

Gaebelein's speculative prophetic interpretations, for example, led him to deduce that NATO represented the ten kings of the revived Roman Empire.

Gaebelein has also been accused of anti-Semitism.[169] Wilson claims that in Gaebelein's book, *The Conflict of the Ages*, he appears to provide legitimacy for Nazism.[170] In response to the publication of *Protocols of the Elders of Zion*, a spurious work alleging to be the secret plans of a worldwide Jewish conspiracy to undermine civil authority, destroy Christianity and take over the international economy, Gaebelein accepted it as the work of a Jew, agreeing:

> . . . they certainly laid out a path for the revolutionary Jews that has been strictly and literally followed. That the Jew has been a prominent factor in the revolutionary movements of the day, wherever they may have occurred, cannot truthfully be denied, any more than that it was a Jew who assassinated, with all his family, the former Autocrat of all the Russians; or than that a very large majority (said to be over 80%) of the present Bolshevist government in Moscow, are Jews: while along other lines, in the assembly of the League of Nations, the Jew's voice is heard, and it is by no means a plaintive, timid, or uninfluential one.[171]

Gaebelein distinguished them from 'the God-fearing, law-abiding, peace-loving kind . . . the very opposite of the law and order-loving portion of the Jewish people'. According to Rausch, 'that they were hindering the Zionist movement was a crucial prophetic sign to Gaebelein'. In another article, entitled 'Aspects of Jewish Power in the United States', Gaebelein referred in rather disparaging terms to secular Jews who did not acknowledge their faith: '. . . there is nothing so vile on earth as an apostate Jew, who denies God and His Word. It is predicted in the Word of God that a large part of the Jews will become apostate, along with the Gentile masses. But not all Jews are liquor fiends, apostates and immoral.'[172]

Nevertheless, at other times, Gaebelein distanced himself from those who were overtly anti-Semitic. Following a visit to Germany in 1895, he wrote: 'It is only too true that Protestant Germany is Jew-hating, and we fear, from what we have seen and heard, that sooner or later there will come another disgraceful

169. See Weber, *Living in the Shadow*, p. 154.
170. See Wilson, *Armageddon Now!*, p. 97.
171. Arno C. Gaebelein in *Our Hope* 27 (April 1921), p. 601, cited in D. Rausch, 'Fundamentalism and the Jew: An Interpretive Essay', *Journal of the Evangelical Theological Society* 23/2 (June 1980), p. 108.
172. Cited in Rausch, 'Fundamentalism and the Jew', pp. 107–112.

outbreak.'[173] Weber describes this apparent contradiction as 'ironic ambivalence', suggesting that premillennial prophetic views, like those of Gaebelein, 'enabled them to give credence to the Protocols (and thereby sound anti-Semitic) even though they had been and remained staunch opponents of anti-Semitism'.[174]

Gaebelein clearly had no illusions as to the origin or motives of the Zionist movement, which he regarded as 'apostate', yet he could also write about the slow return of Jews to Palestine in these terms:

> The wonderful development year after year, the ever-increasing enthusiasm, the wise and far-seeing schemes . . . are surely amazing . . . the return of the Jews to Palestine in unbelief is before us in modern Zionism, therefore it is the most startling sign of all the signs of our times.[175]

Furthermore, in the pages of *Our Hope*, Gaebelein frequently reported with enthusiasm the development of the various Zionist colonization societies in Palestine, supported the efforts of Herzl and informed a still largely ignorant and complacent American Christian community how prophecy was indeed being fulfilled in Palestine. Dispensationalists like Gaebelein may not necessarily have offered unconditional support for Zionism in the same way that Falwell and Robertson do today, but this did not make him any less a Christian Zionist.

Like other classical dispensationalists, Gaebelein distinguished between God's purposes for the Jews in this church dispensation from those of the millennium to follow, keeping them in separate watertight compartments chronologically as well as eternally. He could, therefore, promote evangelism, which theoretically could lead to the disappearance of the Jews as a separate race altogether, while supporting Jewish nationalism; he could describe 'apostate' Jews as in league with the devil, yet defend them from anti-Semitism; he could malign Zionism, while supporting Jewish restoration to Israel; he could show compassion for the Jews, yet believe most would be destroyed in the battle of Armageddon – simply because all these were 'signs' foretold in the Bible.

---

173. *Our Hope* (2 October 1895), p. 78, cited in Rausch, 'Fundamentalism and the Jew', p. 108.

174. Timothy P. Weber, 'A Reply To David Rausch's "Fundamentalism and the Jew"', *Journal of the Evangelical Theological Society* 24/1 (March 1981) pp. 68–77.

175. Gaebelein, 'The Fourth Zionistic Congress: The Most Striking Sign of Our Times', *Our Hope* 6 (September 1900), p. 72, cited in Rausch, *Zionism*, p. 247.

Therefore, in many ways Gaebelein sums up the contradictions inherent within the proto-fundamentalist movement.

Dispensational Christian Zionism, with its commitment to biblical literalism, increasingly came to recognize that restoration was indeed being achieved, but in 'unbelief', and, therefore, biblical predictions were found to confirm it. While dispensationalists remained committed to Jewish evangelism, there was no imperative or necessity to share the gospel with Jews, since their national repentance would occur only after their restoration and Jesus' return. Offering practical and financial support to bring about their restoration became the principal means of its fulfilment.[176]

Although dispensationalists in the early twentieth century continued to see evidence of the imminent return of Christ in such events as the rise of communism, the Balfour Declaration and anti-Semitism, there was a gradual decline in the 'intellectual prestige of Fundamentalism'.[177] In the period from 1918 right up to 1948, increasingly secular arguments were being made for the Zionist cause. American foreign policy progressively came to be shaped by the need to maintain good relations with the strategic oil-rich Arab nations, while at the very same time counter Soviet hegemony in the Middle East.

As the American political establishment began to show less enthusiasm for Blackstone's memorial, the Jewish Zionist movement discovered more influential friends among liberal church leaders who had greater leverage with the presidency and were more interested in Jewish rights than in converting Jews or fulfilling biblical prophecy.

Anti-Semitism and American liberal Christian Zionism (1918–1967)

Following the devastating toll of the First World War and then the Great Depression, fundamentalism in America became more and more preoccupied with refuting liberal theology, the social gospel and Darwinian evolution, rather than with prophetic speculation. Between 1910 and 1915 a series of twelve booklets, called *The Fundamentals*, was published in which sixty-four different authors wrote some ninety articles in defence of a conservative evangelical position on various doctrinal and moral issues.[178] Gaebelein contributed an article addressing the place of the Jews in prophecy, in defence

---

176. See Rausch, *Zionism*, pp. 213–216; also, Merkley, *Politics of Christian Zionism*, p. 92.
177. Merkley, *Politics of Christian Zionism*, pp. 72–74.
178. *The Fundamentals*, 12 vols. (Chicago: Testimony Publishing Company, 1910–1915).

of the Bible's inerrancy.[179] Conservative evangelicals, while initially suspicious of the 'new' premillennialists and resistant of their 'secret rapture' doctrine, gradually welcomed the support of dispensationalists against a
common liberal enemy. This *rapprochement* did much to legitimize and spread
the acceptance of dispensational eschatology. By 1901, Norman Kraus
argues, 'the dispensationalists had won the day so completely that for the
next fifty years friend and foe alike largely identified Dispensationalism with
Premillennialism'.[180]

In his detailed history of the rise of twentieth-century American fundamentalism prior to 1970, entitled *The Politics of Doomsday*, Erling Jorstad traces the
emergence of the Christian right with its anti-Communist and xenophobic
agenda, yet surprisingly there is not a single reference to Israel. Similarly,
George Marsden in his historical overview of the rise of fundamentalism and
evangelicalism in America, *Fundamentalism and American Culture*, observes that,
despite some evidence of anti-Semitism in the early twentieth century, there
was little interest in Zionism or Israel among conservative evangelicals.

During the same period, there is evidence of a growing anti-Semitism
within Christian fundamentalism.[181] For example, in 1919, aware that the
British and French were undermining his goal of self-determination in Syria,
Woodrow Wilson sent Charles Crane, a wealthy American Arabist, as head of
the King-Crane Commission to investigate the wishes of the indigenous
people. Reservations expressed by Arab leaders and expatriate Americans led
Crane's commission to recommend the abandonment of American support
for a Jewish homeland, that further Jewish immigration be severely restricted
and that America or Britain should govern Palestine instead. Crane went on to
help finance the first explorations for oil in Saudi Arabia and the Yemen. At
that time, his admiration for Hitler's Germany, which he described as 'the real
political bulwark of Christian culture', and also of Stalin's anti-Jewish purges
in Soviet Russia, led his biographer to describe his later life as dominated by 'a
most pronounced prejudice . . . [and] unbridled dislike of Jews'.[182] Crane even

---

179. Arno C. Gaebelein, 'Fulfilled Prophecy, A Potent Argument for the Bible',
    The Fundamentals 11, pp. 55–86.

180. Kraus, *Dispensationalism in America*, p. 104.

181. For a detailed analysis of how Christian teaching has shaped American attitudes
    towards the Jews, see Glock and Stark, *Christian Beliefs and Anti-Semitism*; Rausch,
    Fundamentalists, Evangelicals and Anti-Semitism.

182. See Leo J. Bocage, *The Public Career of Charles R. Crane* (unpublished PhD thesis,
    Fordham University), cited in Kaplan, *Arabists*, p. 71.

tried to persuade President Franklin D. Roosevelt to shun the counsels of Felix Frankfurter, the son of a Jewish merchant, who gave legal advice to Roosevelt both during his time as Governor of New York (1929–1932) and also later when he become President. Crane also put pressure on Roosevelt to avoid appointing other Jews to government posts. Crane 'envisioned a world-wide attempt on the part of the Jews to stamp out all religious life and felt that only a coalition of Muslims and Roman Catholics would be strong enough to defeat such designs'.[183] In 1933, he even proposed to Haj Amin Husseini, the Grand Mufti of Jerusalem, that the Mufti open talks with the Vatican to plan an anti-Jewish campaign.[184]

The reasoning behind opposition to the founding of the State of Israel among American missionaries in the Middle East, is very complex. In 1948, weeks before the State of Israel was declared, Bayard Dodge, who had founded the American University in Beirut, retired to Princeton in New Jersey. In April 1948, he wrote a watershed article for *The Readers Digest* entitled 'Must There Be War in the Middle East?' Robert Kaplan describes it as the 'definitive statement' of American Arabists on the birth of the State of Israel.

While Dodge was not anti-Semitic and acknowledged that 'Not all Jews are Zionist and not all Zionists are extremists', nevertheless he regarded the Zionist movement as a 'tragedy'. He opposed Zionism primarily because the Arabs were opposed to it and it would harm American interests in the Middle East. In the article he wrote:

> All the work done by our philanthropic non-profit American agencies in the Arab
> world – our Near East Foundation, our missions, our YMCA and YWCA, our
> Boston Jesuit College in Baghdad, our colleges in Cairo, Beirut, Damascus – would be
> threatened with complete frustration and collapse . . . so would our oil concessions.[185]

This was something Dodge insisted would serve to strengthen the Communists who 'intend to get many thousands of Russian Communist Jews into the Palestinian Jewish State'. Therefore, he urged Jews to 'lay down their arms and talk to the Arabs'.[186]

Dodge's views reflected those of the wider expatriate and missionary community of Beirut who believed the United States, Britain and Russia morally

---

183. Cited in Kaplan, *Arabists*, p. 71.
184. See ibid., p. 71.
185. Ibid., p. 80.
186. Ibid.

and politically wrong to railroad the partition of Palestine through the United Nations. Richard Crossman, a member of the Anglo-American team investigating the Palestine crisis in 1947, observed that the American Protestant missionaries 'challenged the Zionist case with all the arguments of the most violently pro-Arab British Middle Eastern officials'.[187] Kaplan concludes, 'the American community in Lebanon was almost, to a man, psychologically opposed to the State of Israel'.[188] In his memoirs, Harry Truman also claims that his post-war State Department specialists were opposed to the idea of a Jewish State because they either wanted to appease the Arabs or because they were anti-Semitic.[189]

During the 1930s and 1940s, both prior to and after the founding of the State of Israel, the principal allies of Zionism were liberal Protestant Christians, such as Paul Tillich, William F. Albright and Reinhold Niebuhr, who founded the Christian Council on Palestine in 1942. Niebuhr, as professor of social ethics at Union Theological Seminary, defended his Zionism on pragmatic rather than religious grounds. Jewish persecution in Europe, combined with restrictive immigration laws in America, led Niebuhr to recognize the Jews' 'moral right' to Palestine in order for them to survive as a nation.[190] In 1946, he testified before the Anglo-American Committee of Inquiry in Washington on behalf of the Christian Council on Palestine. While acknowledging the conflicting rights of Arabs and Jews in Palestine, he argued:

> The fact, however, that the Arabs have a vast hinterland in the Middle East, and the fact that the Jews have nowhere to go, establishes the relative justice of their claims and of their cause . . . Arab sovereignty over a portion of the debated territory must undoubtedly be sacrificed for the sake of establishing a world Jewish homeland.[191]

In 1958, by which time he was at odds with most other liberal Protestant leaders, Niebuhr continued to insist on a wider definition of Christian Zionism. In an article entitled 'The Relation of Christians and Jews in Western Civilization', Niebuhr wrote:

---

187. Ibid., p. 81.
188. Ibid., p. 185.
189. See ibid.
190. Reinhold Niebuhr, in *The Nation* (21 February 1942), pp. 214–216; (28 February 1942), pp. 253–255.
191. US Department of State, 'Hearings of the Anglo-American Committee of Inquiry' (14 January 1946), p. 147.

> Many Christians are pro-Zionist in the sense that they believe that a homeless people require a homeland; but we feel as embarrassed as anti-Zionist religious Jews when messianic claims are used to substantiate the right of the Jews to the particular homeland in Palestine.[192]

Apart from wishing to see Arabs 'otherwise compensated', Niebuhr did not appear to support the view that homeless Palestinians also 'require a homeland'.

The 1967 'Six Day War' marked a significant watershed for evangelical Christian interest in Israel and Zionism. With the annexation of the West Bank, liberal Protestants and organizations such as the World Council of Churches increasingly distanced themselves from Zionism, whereas the same events fuelled a resurgence of enthusiasm for Eretz Israel among fundamentalists and evangelicals.

Contemporary American evangelical Christian Zionism (1967–2002)

During the first half of the twentieth century, some notable dispensational leaders, including Harry Ironside, M. R. DeHaan and Reuben A. Torrey,[193] maintained a vocal commitment to a 'biblical' basis for the imminent realization of a Jewish restoration to Palestine. A. B. Simpson, who founded the Christian and Missionary Alliance, apparently sobbed as he read to his church congregation the text of the Balfour Declaration.[194] Others saw the Nazi-Soviet non-aggression pact of 1939, Chinese Communism and the rise of Japanese Imperialism as 'electrifying' signs of the coming battle of Armageddon.[195]

---

192. Reinhold Niebuhr, 'The Relation of Christians and Jews in Western Civilization', in R. Niebuhr, *Pious and Secular America* (New York: Scribner's, 1958), pp. 86–112.

193. M. R. DeHaan, *The Jew and Palestine in Prophecy* (Grand Rapids: Zondervan, 1950); R. A. Torrey, *The Return of the Lord Jesus* (Los Angeles: Bible Institute of Los Angeles, 1913), p. 89.

194. See *Weekly Evangel*, 19 May 1917, p. 17, cited in Kyle, *Last Days are Here Again*, p. 109. The Balfour Declaration was not actually released until November 1917, so the dating of this response is suspect.

195. Louis S. Bauman, 'Russia and Armageddon', *King's Business* (29 September 1938), p. 286; H. A. Ironside, 'The Kings of the East', *King's Business* (29 January 1938), p. 9; Louis T. Talbot, 'The Army of 200 Million', *King's Business* (23 October 1932), p. 424; Kyle, *Last Days are Here Again*, p. 111.

Dr M. R. DeHaan, founder of the Radio Bible Class Worldwide Gospel Broadcast, was regularly heard on more than 600 radio stations worldwide. In 1947, in his published studies on the book of Daniel, he interpreted the events before and after the Balfour Declaration in the light of the Abrahamic covenant and Belshazzar's 'Handwriting on the Wall'. He also described the failure of Balfour to set aside the whole of Palestine for the Jewish people as probably 'the greatest mistake in all history'.[196] Like many Zionists, DeHaan lamented British intransigence over the creation of a Jewish State and failure to 'clear the land of its unlawful possessors':

> If only the nations had been able to see their way clear to keep their promise to set aside the Holy Land as a national refuge and return it again to their rightful possessors to whom God had promised it, God might have raised many, many more of the seed of Jacob like Dr. Weizman (sic) to bring blessing and help to the nations of the world.[197]

It is not clear how DeHaan intended his readers to regard as a blessing to the world Weizmann's discovery of a synthetic method for acetone production, used in the manufacture of high explosives.

The founding of the State of Israel in 1948 came to be seen, perhaps not surprisingly, as the most significant fulfilment of biblical prophecy and 'the greatest piece of prophetic news that we have had in the 20th Century'.[198]

Following the war of 1967, Nelson Bell, father-in-law to Billy Graham and editor of the prestigious and authoritative mouthpiece of conservative evangelicalism, *Christianity Today*, expressed the sentiments of many American evangelicals when, in an editorial for the magazine, he wrote: 'That for the first time in more than 2,000 years Jerusalem is now completely in the hands of the Jews gives a student of the Bible a thrill and a renewed faith in the accuracy and validity of the Bible.'[199] From 1967 onwards, a succession of American Christian and political leaders, including several presidents, identified with this

---

196. DeHaan, *Jew and Palestine in Prophecy*, p. 61.

197. M. R. DeHaan, *Daniel the Prophet: 35 Simple Studies in the Book of Daniel* (Grand Rapids: Zondervan, 1947), pp. 169–172.

198. Louis T. Talbot and William W. Orr, *The Nation of Israel and the Word of God!* (Los Angeles: Bible Institute of Los Angeles, 1948), p. 8. See Grenz, *Millennial Maze*, p. 92; Lindsey, *Late Great Planet Earth*, pp. 43, 53–58.

199. Cited in Donald Wagner, 'Evangelicals and Israel: Theological Roots of a Political Alliance', *The Christian Century* (4 November 1998), pp. 1020–1026.

perspective. In 1968, for example, in much the same way that Lloyd George had described the influence of his own upbringing, Lyndon B. Johnson explained the origin of his sympathy for Zionism:

> Most, if not all of you, have very deep ties with the land and with the people of Israel, as I do; for my Christian faith sprang from yours. The Bible stories are woven into my childhood memories as the gallant struggle of modern Jews to be free of persecution is also woven into our souls.[200]

Beginning in 1976, a series of events brought Christian Zionism to the forefront of US mainstream politics. Jimmy Carter was elected as the 'born-again' president, drawing the support of the evangelical right. In Israel, Menachem Begin and the Likud Party came to power in 1977. A powerful tripartite coalition emerged between the political right, evangelicals and the US Israeli lobby. In 1978, Jimmy Carter acknowledged how his own pro-Zionist beliefs had influenced his Middle East policy. In a speech, he described the State of Israel as, 'a return at last, to the biblical land from which the Jews were driven so many hundreds of years ago . . . The establishment of the nation of Israel is the fulfilment of biblical prophecy and the very essence of its fulfilment.'[201] However, when Carter vacillated over the aggressive Likud settlement-programme and proposed the creation of a Palestinian homeland, he alienated the pro-Israeli coalition of Jews and evangelicals who switched their support to Ronald Reagan in the 1980 elections.

Ronald Reagan: president of Christian Zionism

While the popular perception of Ronald Reagan is of someone driven by political expediency, he was nevertheless raised on premillennial dispensational theology, influenced not only by his mother Nelle, but also by leaders such as Billy Graham, Pat Boone and George Otis. Grace Halsell traces their influence on Reagan's study of biblical prophecy and views of the end times.[202] In 1971, for example, Reagan read Hal Lindsey's *The Late Great Planet Earth* and many

---

200. Lyndon B. Johnson, speech delivered on 10 September 1968; see *President Johnson: 'A Just and Dignified Peace ... Is Possible'* (2004) [Internet], Jewish Virtual Library, a division of the American-Israeli Cooperative Enterprise, <http://www.us-israel.org/jsource/US-Israel/lbjpeace1.html>. [Accessed May 2004.]
201. Speech by President Jimmy Carter on 1 May 1978, *Department of State Bulletin*, Vol. 78, No. 2015 (1978), p. 4. See also Carter, *Blood of Abraham*.
202. Halsell, *Prophecy and Politics*, p. 42.

other popular books about Armageddon. Reagan's legal secretary, Herb Ellingwood, whom Halsell describes as 'one of the most fervent believers in the cult of Israel' and the imminent battle of Armageddon, described how they would often discuss the fulfilment of biblical prophecy.[203]

In 1971, while a governor in California, Reagan discussed at length with a close colleague, James Mills, his understanding of how contemporary geo-political events were the fulfilment of biblical prophecy. Mills made copious notes of their conversation, later published in the *San Diego Magazine*. Based on his reading of Ezekiel 38, Reagan insisted that Israel would soon come under attack from ungodly nations like Libya and Ethiopia:

> Do you understand the significance of that? Libya has now gone communist, and that's a sign that the day of Armageddon isn't far off . . . It's necessary to fulfill the prophecy that Ethiopia will be one of the ungodly nations that go against Israel . . . For the first time ever, everything is in place for the battle of Armageddon and the Second Coming of Christ . . . Ezekiel tells us that Gog, the nation that will lead all of the other powers of darkness against Israel, will come out of the north. Biblical scholars have been saying for generations that Gog must be Russia . . . now that Russia has become communist and atheistic, now that Russia has set itself against God. Now it fits the description of Gog perfectly.[204]

Mills described how Reagan spoke about impending nuclear holocaust, 'like a preacher to a sceptical college student'.[205] In another conversation recorded by the evangelist Harald Bredesen of California, Reagan described how he was convinced God was bringing the Jews back to Israel. Bredesen was impressed by Reagan's grasp of a dispensational view of Israel, even down to his memorizing of the very day in 1948 when Israel was 'reconstituted as a nation'.[206]

George Otis, a former electronics manufacturer of components for nuclear weapons, who later operated four Christian radio stations in southern Lebanon, was influential in securing Reagan's election as President. Otis was also honorary chairman of 'Christians for Reagan'. In a 1976 TV interview, Otis discussed with Reagan their views on how 'dramatic Bible prophecy' was being fulfilled in the 're-emergence of Israel as a nation'. Otis then asked Reagan, 'What do you feel America should do if ever in the future, Israel were

203. Ibid., p. 43.
204. Cited in ibid., pp. 5, 45.
205. Cited in ibid.
206. Ibid., pp. 46–47.

about to be destroyed by attacking enemy nations?' Reagan replied, 'We have a pledge to Israel to the preservation of that nation . . . we have an obligation, a responsibility, and a destiny.'[207]

During the 1980 presidential campaign, on numerous occasions, Reagan was recorded as saying, 'We could be the generation that sees Armageddon.'[208] In the same year, William Saffire, a columnist for the *New York Times*, quoted Reagan as saying to a group of Jewish leaders, 'Israel is the only stable democracy we can rely on as a spot where Armageddon could come.'[209] In a personal conversation reported in the *Washington Post* two years later in April 1984, Reagan elaborated on his own personal convictions to Tom Dine, one of Israel's chief lobbyists working for the American Israel Public Affairs Committee:

> You know, I turn back to the ancient prophets in the Old Testament and the signs foretelling Armageddon, and I find myself wondering if – if we're the generation that is going to see that come about. I don't know if you've noted any of these prophecies lately, but believe me they certainly describe the times we're going through.[210]

In 1986, when tensions grew between the US and Libya, James Mills, by then President *pro tem* of the California State Senate, claimed Reagan expressed strong animosity towards Libya because he saw it as 'one of the prophesied enemies of Israel and therefore an enemy of God's'.[211] Mills noted the logical consequences of Reagan's pessimistic and deterministic dispensational presuppositions for American politics:

> Certainly his attitudes relative to military spending, and his coolness to all proposals for nuclear disarmament, are consistent with such apocalyptic views . . .
> Armageddon, as foreseen in the books of Ezekiel and Revelation, cannot take place in a world that has been disarmed . . . It is contrary to God's plan as set forth in his word . . . The President's domestic and monetary policies, too, are in harmony with a

---

207. Larry Jones and Gerald T. Sheppard, 'Ronald Reagan's "Theology" of Armageddon' in Haddad and Wagner (eds.), *All in the Name of the Bible*, pp. 32–33.
208. Halsell, *Prophecy and Politics,* p. 5. See also, Kenneth Woodward, 'Arguing Armageddon', *Newsweek*, 5 November 1984.
209. Cited in Halsell, *Prophecy and Politics*, p. 47.
210. Ronnie Dugger, 'Does Reagan Expect a Nuclear Armageddon?' *Washington Post*, 18 April 1984.
211. Cited in Halsell, *Prophecy and Politics*, p. 5.

literal interpretation of biblical prophecies. There is no room to get wrought up
about the national debt if God is soon going to foreclose on the whole world . . .
Why be concerned about conservation? Why waste time and money preserving things
for future generations when everything is going to come to a fiery end with this one?
. . . It follows that all domestic programs, especially those that entail capital outlay, can
and should be curtailed to free up money to finance the development of nuclear
weapons in order to rain fiery destruction upon the evil enemies of God and His
people.[212]

Halsell claims Reagan was convinced he had 'a mandate to spend trillions of
dollars preparing for a nuclear Gog and Magog war'.[213]

While George Bush, Sr, Bill Clinton and George Bush, Jr have not appeared
to share the same dispensational presuppositions of either Jimmy Carter or
Ronald Reagan, they have maintained, however reluctantly, the strong pro-
Zionist position of their predecessors.[214] Politicians tend to reflect the views
of their electorate, or at least of lobby groups, and the Zionist lobby is
regarded as one of the most powerful in the United States today.[215] In the last
forty years, three Christian leaders, each first given a White House platform by
Reagan, have probably done more than any others in ensuring American
foreign policy remains resolutely pro-Zionist. They are Jerry Falwell, Pat
Robertson and Hal Lindsey. Each has also made a unique contribution to the
development of Christian Zionism.

Jerry Falwell: ambassador of Christian Zionism
Falwell is pastor of Thomas Road Baptist Church and founder and Chancellor
of the 10,000-student independent Baptist Liberty University, Lynchburg,
Virginia. Jerry Falwell Ministries sponsor the Liberty Broadcasting Network
TV channel and syndicated *Old Time Gospel Hour* programme which is shown
on more than 350 stations in the US.

In his early ministry, Falwell shunned politics. In 1964, he wrote:

---

212. Ibid., pp. 49–50.

213. Ibid.

214. E.g. George Bush, speech to the American Jewish Committee (3 May 2001); cited
in *U.S. Presidents on Israel* (2004) [Internet], Jewish Virtual Library, a division of the
American-Israeli Cooperative Enterprise, <http://www.us-israel.org/jsource/
US-Israel/presquote.html>. [Accessed May 2004.]

215. Michael Lind, 'The Israel Lobby and American Power', *Prospect* (April 2002),
pp. 22–29.

Believing the Bible as I do, I would find it impossible to stop preaching the pure saving gospel of Jesus Christ and begin doing anything else, including fighting communism, or participating in civil rights reform. Preachers are not called to be politicians but to be soul winners. Nowhere are we commissioned to reform the externals.[216]

Falwell's change of mind came in 1967 after Israel's 'Six Day War'. He entered politics and became an avid supporter of the Zionist State. At a time when America was bogged down in the Vietnam War, Israel's lightning victory over the Palestinian forces in just six days had a profound effect. Grace Halsell writes:

Many Americans, including Falwell, turned worshipful glances toward Israel, which they viewed as militarily strong and invincible. They gave their unstinting approval to the Israeli take-over of Arab lands because they perceived this conquest as power and righteousness . . . Macho or muscular Christians such as Falwell credited Israeli General Moshe Dayan with this victory over Arab forces and termed him the Miracle Man of the Age, and the Pentagon invited him to visit Vietnam and tell us how to win that war.[217]

In 1979, Falwell founded Moral Majority, a political action group composed of conservative, fundamentalist Christians, and the Israeli government gave him a Lear jet to assist him in his advocacy of Israel. A year later in 1980, Falwell also became the first Gentile to be awarded the Vladimir Ze'ev Jabotinsky Medal for Zionist excellence by Israel's Prime Minister, Menachem Begin. Jabotinsky was the founder of revisionist Zionism and held that Jews had a divine mandate to occupy and settle 'on both sides of the Jordan River' and were not accountable to international law.[218] When Israel bombed Iraq's nuclear plant in 1981, Begin phoned Falwell before he called Reagan. He also asked Falwell to 'explain to the Christian public the reasons for the bombing'.[219] During the 1982 invasion of Lebanon and the massacres in Sabra and Shatilla, Falwell similarly defended Israel's actions, claiming, 'The Israelis

216. James Price and William Goodman, *Jerry Falwell: An Unauthorized Profile*, cited in Halsell, *Prophecy and Politics*, pp. 72–73.

217. Halsell, *Prophecy and Politics*, pp. 72–73.

218. See Allan C. Brownfeld, 'Fundamentalists and the Millennium: A Potential Threat to Middle Eastern Peace', *Washington Report* (June 1999), pp. 82–84.

219. Cited in Donald Wagner, 'Evangelicals and Israel: Theological Roots of a Political Alliance', *Christian Century* (4 November 1998), pp. 1020–1026.

were not involved.' When the *New York Times* suggested otherwise, publishing eyewitness accounts of Israeli forces outside the refugee camps sending flares at night to enable the Phalangists[220] to continue their operations, Falwell described the reports as 'propaganda'.[221]

In March 1985, Falwell spoke to the conservative Rabbinical Assembly in Miami pledging to 'mobilize 70 million conservative Christians for Israel and against anti-Semitism'.[222] In January 1998, when Israeli Prime Minister Binyamin Netanyahu visited Washington, his first meeting was with Jerry Falwell and with the National Unity Coalition for Israel, rather than with President Clinton. According to Donald Wagner, the crowd hailed Netanyahu as 'the Ronald Reagan of Israel'. This time, Falwell promised to contact 200,000 pastors and church leaders who received his *National Liberty Journal* and ask them to 'tell President Clinton to refrain from putting pressure on Israel' to comply with the Oslo Accords.[223]

In an interview with the *Washington Post* in 1999, Falwell described the West Bank as 'an integral part of Israel'. Pressing Israel to withdraw, he added, 'would be like asking America to give Texas to Mexico, to bring about a good relationship. It's ridiculous.'[224]

In 2000, Falwell revived Moral Majority under the name People of Faith 2000, 'a movement to reclaim America as one nation under God' and which also takes a strong pro-Israeli stance.[225] Falwell has succeeded, probably better

---

220. The name 'Phalangists' ('Phalange' and 'Phalange Party' are variations on the same) comes from the word 'phalanx'. Also known as the Lebanese Kataeb Social Democratic Party, the Phalange attracted Christian youths from the mountains northeast of Beirut as well as Christian students in Beirut. The politics of the Phalange Party was pro-Western, and they opposed any pan-Arabism.

221. Cited in Brownfeld, 'Fundamentalists and the Millennium', pp. 82–84.

222. Wagner, 'Evangelicals and Israel', pp. 1020–1026.

223. Cited in ibid., pp. 1020–1026. The Oslo Accords (1993) is the name given to The Declaration of Principles on Interim Self-Government Arrangements, signed by both Israel and the Palestine Liberation Organization. Deteriorating relationships mean that many Israelis and Palestinians now consider this process to be dead. See *Declaration of Principles* (1993) [Internet], Islamic Association for Palestine, <http://www.iap.org/oslo.htm>. [Accessed May 2004.]

224. Brownfeld, 'Fundamentalists and the Millennium', pp. 82–84.

225. Associated Press report, *Falwell Launches Campaign to Mobilize Religious Right* (2000) [Internet], Cable News Network, <http://cnn.com/2000/ALLPOLITICS/ stories/04/14/falwell.voters/>. [Accessed May 2004.]

than any other American Christian leader, in ensuring his followers recognize that their Christian duty to God involves providing unconditional support for the State of Israel.

Pat Robertson: politician of Christian Zionism

Along with Falwell, Robertson is one of the most powerful men in US political and religious circles today.[226] His Christian Broadcasting Network (CBN), founded in 1960, was the first and remains the most influential Christian satellite-TV network in the world. He is also a writer and the founder and Chancellor of Regent University in Virginia, as well as founder of numerous other educational, entertainment, political and humanitarian organizations, including the Christian Coalition which has around 2 million members. The goal of the Christian Coalition, founded by Robertson in 1989, is 'to take working control of the Republican party' and elect 'Christian candidates' to public office.[227] While claiming to be a 'pro-family citizen action organization', the Christian Coalition nevertheless regularly lobbies the US government on pro-Israeli issues. In April 2002, for example, it called upon the US Congress to continue supporting Israel's right to 'self-defense against Palestinian terrorists and pressure from Yasser Arafat'.[228]

In 1990, Robertson founded International Family Entertainment Inc. (IFE) and The Family Channel, a satellite-delivered cable-TV network with 63 million US subscribers. In 1997, Robertson sold IFE to Fox Worldwide Inc. for $1.9 billion. With such significant investment, CBN is now one of the world's largest television ministries and produces programmes seen in 180 countries and heard in 71 languages including Russian, Arabic, Spanish, French and Chinese. CBN's most popular programme, the *700 Club*, which Robertson hosts, is one of the longest-running religious television programmes and reaches a weekly audience of 7 million American viewers. Robertson explains CBN's role in the fulfilment of end-time prophecy:

I will never forget the time, April 29, 1977, when we had built the first earth station

---

226. See Straub, *Salvation for Sale*, passim.
227. *Right Wing Organizations: Christian Coalition of America* (n.d.) [Internet], People for the American Way, <http://www.pfaw.org/pfaw/general/default.aspx?oid= 4307>. [Accessed May 2004.]
228. *Christian Coalition Defends Israel Against Arafat* (n.d.) [Internet], Christian Coalition of America, <http://www.cc.org/becomeinformed/pressrelease040502.html>. [Accessed May 2003.]

ever to be owned by a Christian ministry in the history of the world, and we were the first ever to take a full-time transponder on a satellite . . . so we were pioneers in this area. I remember it was ten o'clock in the morning when we went on with the broadcast. We then cut to the Mount of Olives in Jerusalem . . . There were some clouds forming over the Temple Mount . . . And when I saw the Mount of Olives, and I saw where my Savior is going to put His foot down when He comes back to earth, I was thinking, 'I'm transmitting it!' The Bible says every eye is going to behold Him, and here it is happening! We see how it is going to be fulfilled right in front of our eyes![229]

Not surprisingly, events in the Middle East dominate CBN's news pro-grammes, which show a clear bias in favour of Israel. In 2002, CBN formed its own dedicated Israel news channel with links to the Israeli embassy, International Christian Embassy Jerusalem, Bridges for Peace and Christian Friends of Israel. Robertson is quite outspoken about his personal views on Israel and the occupation of the Palestinian West Bank. His powerful media network ensures that a strongly pro-Israel perspective is presented to millions of Americans daily. His hope is clearly to televize the second coming.

With the high-profile support of fundamentalist Christian leaders like Falwell and Robertson, by the end of the 1970s, Christian Zionism had become syn-onymous with American evangelicalism. Since then, the relationship between Christians and Zionism has been sustained with increasing effectiveness to the point that it is rare to find a single elected politician or senator in Congress willing to express public criticism of the Israeli government. The coalition of religious and political support for Israel in America has received its most explicit and popular grounding in the prophetic speculations of Hal Lindsey.

Hal Lindsey: prophet of Christian Zionism
Lindsey is undoubtedly the most influential of all twentieth-century Christian Zionists. Although rarely quoted by others, he has nevertheless been described by *Time* as, 'The Jeremiah for this Generation', and, in 1980, by the *New York Times* as, 'The best-selling author of the decade.'[230] He is one of very few authors to have had three books on the *New York Times* best-seller list simultaneously. His current publisher describes him as 'The Father of the

---

229. Cited in Skipp Porteous, *Road to Armageddon* (1998) [Internet], Institute for First Ammendment Studies, Inc., <http://www.buildingequality.us/ifas/fw/9512/robertson.html>. [Accessed August 2004.]

230. Cited in Lindsey, *1980's: Countdown*, p. 179.

Modern-Day Bible Prophecy Movement', and 'The best-known prophecy teacher in the world.'[231] Lindsey is a prolific writer, the author of at least twenty books spanning twenty-seven years, most of which deal explicitly or implicitly with a dispensational interpretation of the future, biblical prophecy and Christian Zionism. He hosts his own radio and television programmes, leads regular pro-Israeli Holy Land tours and, by subscription, makes available a monthly Christian 'intelligence journal' called *Countdown*. Along with Grant Jeffrey, Lindsey also hosts a weekly news programme, *International Intelligence Briefing*, on the Trinity Broadcasting Network television station.

Lindsey's most famous book, *The Late Great Planet Earth*, was described by the *New York Times* as the '#1 Non-fiction Bestseller of the Decade'. It has gone through more than 108 printings, with sales of more than 18 million copies in English by 1993, with estimates varying between 18 to 20 million further copies in fifty-four other languages. Despite dramatic changes in the world since its publication in 1970, Lindsey maintains that the prophetic and apocalyptic scenario depicted is biblically accurate and the book remains in print in its original unrevised form.

Lindsey's popularity may be attributed to a combination of factors. These include his readable, journalistic style of writing, his imaginative (if rather dogmatic) insistence, like Darby and Scofield, that contemporary geopolitical events are the fulfilment of biblical prophecy and his repeated assertions that the end of the world is imminent: for example, 'This book describes in more detail and explicitness than any other just what will happen to humanity and to the Earth, not a thousand years from now, but in our lifetime – indeed in this very generation.'[232] Readers are reassured:

> Hal will be your guide on a chilling tour of the world's future battlefields as the Great Tribulation, foretold more than two thousand years ago by Old and New Testament prophets, begins to unfold. You'll meet the world leaders who will bring man to the very edge of extinction and examine the causes of the current global situation – what it all means, what will shortly come to pass, and how it will all turn out.[233]

Like Darby, Scofield and Brookes before him, Lindsey fails to acknowledge the influence of anyone else on his ideas. Instead, he claims his interpretation of the Bible has been revealed directly and personally by God:

---

231. Lindsey, *Final Battle*, back cover; *Apocalypse Code*, back cover.
232. Lindsey, *Final Battle*, p. xiii.
233. Lindsey, *Planet Earth 2000 AD*, back cover.

I believe that the Spirit of God gave me a special insight, not only into how John described what he actually experienced, but also into how this whole phenomenon encoded the prophecies so that they could be fully understood only when their fulfilment drew near.[234]

Lindsey's success is probably due in part to the way he revises his predictions in the light of changing world events. So, for example, *The Final Battle* (1994) is essentially an unacknowledged revision of *The Late Great Planet Earth* (1970); *The Apocalypse Code* (1997) is a revision of *There's a New World Coming* (1973); and the two editions of *Planet Earth 2000 AD* (1994 and 1996) both recycle material from *The 1980's: Countdown to Armageddon* (1981). In keeping pace with history, Lindsey shows, for example, that the demise of the Soviet Union, the rise of militant Islam, the success of the Allies in the Gulf War, the Palestinian–Israeli conflict and even the terrorist attack on the World Trade Center were all the fulfilment of biblical prophecy and signs of the imminent return of Christ.

Lindsey's apocalyptic scenarios are highly speculative yet continue to enjoy popular support, especially among dispensationalists in the United States. As will be shown in the following chapter, his particular reading of history, coloured by a literal exegesis of highly selective Scriptures, is essentially polarized, dualistic and confrontational. For example, he justifies the demonization of Russia and China as well as of Islam and the Arab nations; he encourages the continued military and economic funding of Israel by the United States; urges Israelis to resist negotiating land for peace and, instead, settle and annexe the Occupied Territories. In so doing, Lindsey identifies unconditionally with the political and religious far right, both in the United States and Israel. Ironically, his attempts to defend Israel and to refute anti-Semitism may actually be leading to the very holocaust he abhors but repeatedly predicts.[235]

These three high-profile individuals, Pat Robertson, Jerry Falwell and Hal Lindsey, are merely figureheads for a much wider and growing alliance of more than 150 influential fundamentalist Christian leaders, including Oral Roberts, Mike Evans, Tim LaHaye, Kenneth Copeland, Paul Crouch, David Wilkerson, Peter Wagner, James Dobson, Ed McAteer, Jim Bakker, Chuck Missler and Jimmy Swaggart.

Regular meetings between these Christian Zionist leaders and Israeli

---

234. Lindsey, *Apocalypse Code*, p. 37. Compare with Darby, *Collected Writings*, vol. 2 Prophetic 1, pp. 6–7, 108.

235. See DeMar and Leithart, *Legacy of Hatred*; Russell, *Prophecy and the Apocalyptic Dream*, p. 86.

officials take place at venues such as the Harvard Business School. At one held in early 2002, participants included Avigdor Itzchaki, the Director General of the Israeli Cabinet, James Watt, former Secretary of the Interior, Mike Evans and Richard Hellman of Christian Israel Public Action Campaign (CIPAC).[236]

Together, these leaders reach an audience of over 100 million Americans weekly through radio and television, enjoy direct personal access to the Israeli and American political establishment, and provide virtually unconditional support for Israel today. Just as Shaftesbury and Hechler used the Bible to help underwrite the Zionist ambitions of a secular Herzl in the nineteenth century, so the American religious right of Falwell and Robertson has helped galvanize the expansionist Zionist agenda of secular Israel in the twentieth century.

The proliferation and diversification of Christian Zionist organizations

The earliest proto-Christian Zionist organizations were the London Jews' Society (1809) and the British Society for the Propagation of the Gospel among the Jews (1842). Although now known as the Church's Ministry Among Jewish People (CMJ) and Christian Witness to Israel (CWI), respectively, they remain primarily covenantal premillennial in emphasis and evangelistic in purpose. As a result of the influence of J. N. Darby and the growing dispensational network in the USA, William E. Blackstone founded the Chicago Hebrew Mission in 1887. This is now known as the American Messianic Fellowship International (AMFI). AMFI is, according to its own literature, a 'conservative evangelical ministry committed to seeing the Lord's purposes fulfilled by building bridges of understanding between Christian and Jewish Communities'.[237] The Messianic Jewish Alliance of America (MJAA), founded in 1915, claims to be the largest association of Messianic Jewish believers in the world. MJAA now has affiliations in fifteen countries, 250 Messianic synagogues and 350,000 Messianic Jews worldwide. They insist they are 'the leading representative organisation for American Jews who believe in Messiah Yeshua'.[238] Their simple

---

236. Others invited included Tony Campolo, James Dobson, Kenneth Copeland, Robert Schuller, Chuck Smith, Joyce Meyer, E. V. Hill and Marlin Maddoux.

237. *What is AMF?* (n.d.) [Internet], American Messianic Fellowship International, <http://www.amfi.org/faqs.htm>.

238. *What is the MJAA?* (2004) [Internet], Messianic Jewish Alliance of America (MJAA), <http://www.mjaa.org/mjaa.html>. [Accessed May 2004.]

statement of belief is made up of four short paragraphs. The fourth states: 'We believe in G-d's eternal covenant with Abraham, Isaac, and Jacob. We therefore stand with and support the Jewish people and the State of Israel and hold fast to the Biblical heritage of our forefathers.'[239] In 1992, a MJAA position paper was published in the Israeli newspaper *Ha'aretz* entitled 'Messianic Jews Say: "The Land Belongs to Israel."'[240] In it, MJAA expressed its conviction that Eretz Israel has been given to the Jews by God and that they will 'repossess the regions of Judea, Samaria, Gaza and the Golan Heights'.[241] Like the AMFI, MJAA is dispensational in origin. Both are committed to Jewish evangelism as well as political activism. Jews for Jesus, founded in 1973, is the most overtly evangelistic expression of this form of Messianic dispensationalism.

Since 1970, influenced by the apocalyptic dispensationalism of Walvoord, Lindsey and LaHaye, Christian Zionism has become more politicized and identified with campaign lobbying on various pro-Israeli issues such as over the status of Jerusalem. Some of the largest and most influential Christian Zionist agencies have related their Christian message to that of 'blessing Israel'. They have disavowed evangelism in order to gain recognition from the Israeli government, set up headquarters in Jerusalem and collaborate with Jewish Zionist organizations.

Contemporary Christian Zionism may therefore be classified not only in terms of whether it is covenantal or dispensational, but also as to whether it is primarily evangelistic or political. Since 1980 there has been a significant proliferation of such organizations. It is estimated, for example, that over 250 pro-Israeli evangelical organizations operating in America were founded between 1980 and 1985 alone.[242] Christian Zionism as a movement today is, nevertheless, dominated by the activities of a small number of para-church, non-denominational organizations which have successfully harnessed grass-roots evangelical political support for Israel. This summary will seek to place the most influential Christian Zionist organizations within their wider historical context.

---

239. *What does MJAA believe?* (2004) [Internet], MJAA, <http://www.mjaa.org/ believe.html>. [Accessed May 2004.] Orthodox Jews and some Messianic Christian Zionists refuse to write the full name of God in deference to Deuteronomy 12:3–4.

240. 'Messianic Jews Say: "The Land Belongs to Israel!"' (MJAA Position Paper), *Ha'aretz* (20 March 1992), cited on <http://66.70.185.249/ biblicaljudaism/LandBelongsIsrael.html>. [Accessed May 2004.]

241. MJAA Position Paper, 'Messianic Jews Say'.

242. Halsell, *Prophecy and Politics*, p. 178.

London Jews' Society (1809): covenantal premillennialism

The London Jews' Society, founded in 1809, was renamed several times in the twentieth century and is now known as the Church's Ministry Among Jewish People (CMJ). To avoid criticism, in Israel it operates as the Israel Trust of the Anglican Church (ITAC). Besides being the first, it remains the only denominational Christian Zionist organization of significance today. Originally an interdenominational body, it was reconstituted in 1815 as an Anglican missionary society under the influence of Charles Simeon. The primary aim was the conversion of Jews to Protestant Christianity. The LJS reached its zenith in 1914 when it had a staff of 280 working in sixty cities, a third of whom were of Jewish origin. Following the Napoleonic Wars, and beginning in 1817, LJS appointed staff among Jewish communities in places as diverse as Morocco, Algeria, Egypt, Tunisia, Ethiopia, Iraq, Holland, Germany, Austria, Romania, India and Canada, as well as in Britain and Palestine. LJS withdrew most of their European staff during the Second World War, when they claim 250,000 Jewish Christians died in the Holocaust.

CMJ remains committed 'to be workers with God in his continuing purpose for the Jewish people' which includes evangelism, humanitarian work and defending Jews from anti-Semitism.[243] It has also retained a commitment to restorationism. In his eulogy of the CMJ, Kelvin Crombie equates biblical literalism with restorationism:

> For if the Bible is true, literally, then Israel would be restored, first physically, then spiritually. The CMJ work in Israel was founded during the last century upon such a belief. The establishment of the State of Israel in 1948 was surely an indication that such beliefs were correct.[244]

While never an 'official' position of CMJ, several of its staff have in the past advocated that the birth of the State of Israel and restorationism are the fulfilment of Old Testament prophecy and should be supported.[245] Some within CMJ continue to see the return of the Jewish people to the land (but not the political State of Israel) as the beginning of a fulfilment of prophecy. Whereas the Society supports the existence of a homeland for the

---

243. CMJ, *Shalom* 3 (1999), p. 1.
244. Crombie, *For the Love of Zion*, pp. 257–258.
245. Richards, *Has God Finished with Israel?*, pp. 209–210; 'Welcome to CMJ', *Shalom* (February 1990), p. 2; CMJ, *The State of Israel: Why should we support it?* (St Albans: CMJ, 1996).

Jewish people after almost 2,000 years of anti-Semitism, Tony Higton has stated that CMJ does not feel obliged to support the political State of Israel any more than it would any other secular state.[246] Theologically, CMJ remains convinced that God continues to have an ongoing covenant relationship with the Jews who remain God's 'chosen people'.[247] CMJ requires no specific eschatological view of its staff, however its publications still broadly reflect the historic or covenantal premillennialism of its founders, although some leaders, such as E. L. Langston, General Secretary in 1914, advocated dispensationalism.[248]

Jews for Jesus (1973): Messianic dispensationalism

Jews for Jesus (JFJ) was founded in 1973 by Moishe Rosen, an ordained Jewish Baptist minister, and arose out of the Jesus People movement of the 1960s and early 1970s. In the Haight-Ashbury district of San Francisco, from where Jews for Jesus was born, *Time* magazine estimated that 30% of hippies were Jewish, while Rosen believes 20% of the Jesus People were also.[249] JFJ claims to be '. . . the largest and best-known of the non-denominational Jewish evangelistic agencies'. While identifying itself as 'evangelical fundamentalist', JFJ enjoys the support of conservative evangelicals such as Dr J. I. Packer. In addition to their fifteen branches and sixty chapters, JFJ sends out evangelistic teams such as the emotively named 'Liberated Wailing Wall'. Their founder Rosen, Executive Director David Brickner, and scholar-in-residence Louis Goldberg are all classic dispensationalists. Their doctrinal statement reflects this, asserting belief in the continuing existence of two parallel but separate covenants for Israel and the church: 'We believe Israel exists as a covenant people through whom God continues to accomplish His purposes and that the Church is an elect people in accordance with the New Covenant, comprising both Jews and Gentiles.' Sharing a similar ministry philosophy to that of Campus Crusade for Christ, Young Life and the Navigators, Jews for Jesus represents a robustly evangelistic form of dispensational premillennialism. As an organization of Messianic Christians committed to both evangelism among

---

246. Tony Higton (unpublished letter, 17 May 2004).

247. Tony Higton, 'Meet the new management team', *Shalom* 2 (1999), p. 3.

248. E. L. Langston, *Ominous Days! Or the Signs of the Times* (London: Chas. J. Thynne, 1914), pp. 1–30; see also, Patricia Higton, 'Return of the King of Kings', *Shalom* Overview Edition (2001), in which David Brickner's *Future Hope* is recommended. Brickner is director of Jews for Jesus and a dispensationalist.

249. See Tucker, *Not Ashamed*, p. 78.

Jews and restorationism, JFJ is unique, having, in its own words, 'Out-Zioned the Zionists'.[250]

Bridges For Peace (1976): political dispensationalism

Bridges for Peace (BFP) was founded in 1976 by G. Douglas Young. Young had worked in Israel since the 1950s, founding the Israel-American Institute of Biblical Studies in Jerusalem in 1957. In 1976, he also began to publish his 'Dispatch from Jerusalem', a monthly newsletter distributed by an organization called Christians for Israel, based in Dallas. After Young's death, Clarence H. Wagner became the President and first Executive Director of BFP in 1980. BFP affirms: 'Through programs both in Israel and world-wide, we are giving Christians the opportunity to actively express our biblical responsibility before God to be faithful to Israel and the Jewish community.'[251] This 'biblical responsibility' does not include Jewish evangelism since they claim the promises made to Israel were both prior to and independent of the church: 'The Church does not exist independently from the covenant God made with the Jewish people and Israel.'[252]

BFP also holds to the dispensational view that 'God's covenant promises between the land and His people Israel were everlasting and unconditional.'[253] Most commentators understand Ephesians 2:14–18 as describing how Jesus broke down the wall of hostility between Jews and Gentiles by his death and so made 'the two one'. Wagner, however, claims this passage describes the ministry of BFP in bringing reconciliation between the State of Israel and the church.[254] BFP is in fact one of the more politicized Christian Zionist organizations. Having disavowed evangelism, it is active instead through 'Operation Rescue', encouraging Jews from the former Soviet

---

250. See Louis Goldberg, 'Whose Land Is It?', *Issues* 4.2.

251. C. H. Wagner, *Who are we?* (1996) [Internet], Bridges for Peace, Jerusalem, <http://www.bridgesforpeace.com>. [Accessed May 2004.]

252. See C. H. Wagner, *Israel and the Church at the Dawn of the New Millennium* (n. d.) [Internet], Bridges for Peace, Jerusalem, <http://www.bridgesforpeace.com/ publications/teaching/Article-33.html>. [Accessed May 2004.]

253. See C. H. Wagner, *Did God break his covenant with the Jews?* (n. d.) [Internet], Bridges for Peace, Jerusalem, <http://www.bridgesforpeace.com/publications/teaching/ Article-34.html>. [Accessed May 2004.]

254. See C. H. Wagner, *Israel, God's covenants, and the Church* (n. d.) [Internet], Bridges for Peace, Jerusalem, <http://www.bridgesforpeace.com/publications/teaching/ Article-51.html>. [Accessed May 2004.]

Union to emigrate to Israel. BFP works in partnership with the International Christian Embassy, Jerusalem, and forms part of the Unity Coalition for Israel.

International Christian Embassy Jerusalem (1980): political dispensationalism

Of all Christian Zionist organizations, ICEJ is probably the most influential and controversial, with 'ambassadors' in 140 countries and a membership of over 100,000.[255] In 1980, the Israeli Knesset unilaterally declared Jerusalem to be the eternal and undivided capital of Israel. As a result, the Dutch embassy and the twelve remaining Latin American governments finally vacated their premises in Jerusalem. Whether responding to the threat of an oil embargo, or from a desire to uphold international law, they joined the diplomatic staff of the other foreign embassies, which had all relocated to Tel Aviv in 1967. In response to worldwide condemnation of Israel's unilateral action, Christian Zionists meeting in Jerusalem in 1980 founded the International Christian Embassy, to demonstrate solidarity with Israel at a time when they felt the rest of the world had abandoned her. Jan Willem van der Hoeven explained their decision as 'a direct response to the world's cowardice and shameful rejection of Israel's right to her unified city'.[256]

ICEJ is strongest in the USA, Canada and South Africa, with offices in other European, Asian and Central American countries. It draws its support almost exclusively from independent charismatic and fundamentalist churches. Its main priority is to 'bring comfort' to Israel. ICEJ achieves this by encouraging Jews from the former Soviet Union and Eastern Europe to emigrate to Israel. Through a social assistance programme, it also facilitates the integration of Jewish immigrants into Israeli life, sponsors an annual Christian Zionist Feast of Tabernacles celebration in Jerusalem and holds diplomatic banquets and receptions through which church leaders and government officials around the world are lobbied on behalf of the State of Israel.

ICEJ has also developed a sophisticated news service which produces weekly radio and video programmes broadcast on four continents, together with newsletters, e-news and periodicals such as the *Middle East Intelligence Digest*, a pro-Israeli summary of Israeli and Arab newspapers and journals. These are aimed at countering what Felix Corley has described as 'increasingly warped and twisted' coverage, which has a 'marked bias against

---

255. See <http://www.icej.org/>.
256. Van der Hoeven, *Babylon or Jerusalem?*, pp. 151–152, 158.

Israel'.[257] In the USA, ICEJ works closely with political lobbyists such as the Christian Israel Public Action Campaign (CIPAC) to which ICEJ is affiliated, as well as with Pat Robertson's Christian Broadcasting Network and the National Unity Coalition for Israel.

It is claimed that funds from ICEJ have been used to support illegal Jewish settlements[258] as well as the Jerusalem Temple Foundation (JTF) founded by Terry Reisenhoover and Stanley Goldfoot, a former member of the Stern Gang.[259] The JTF is also committed to the destruction of the Dome of the Rock and rebuilding of the Jewish temple.[260]

ICEJ appears to have reinterpreted the Christian message and made the teachings of Jesus subservient to a political Zionist ideology.[261] It is also a self-appointed and self-regulated organization entirely unaccountable to the wider Christian community.[262]

In May 1998, because of tensions between the board of ICEJ and its Director Johann Luckhoff, Jan Willem van der Hoeven left ICEJ to set up a rival organization, the International Christian Zionist Center in Jerusalem.[263] Similar disagreements during the First International Christian Zionist Congress held in Basle in 1985 led to the founding of Christian Friends of Israel.

Christian Friends of Israel (1985): humanitarian Christian Zionism

CFI was founded by Derek White and other disaffected members of ICEJ

---

257. Felix Corley, 'Is Radical Zionism an Option for Christians?' *Church of England Newspaper*, 7 February 1997, p. 7.

258. See Wagner, *Dying in the Land of Promise*, p. 23.

259. Called the 'Stern Gang' by critics, Fighters for the Freedom of Israel was founded by Avraham Stern in 1940 together with a majority of disillusioned members of the Irgun, another Jewish terror organization. Members of the Stern Gang were responsible for the assassinations of Lord Moyne and Count Bernadotte, and the massacre of residents of the Palestinian village of Deir Yassin.

260. See Louis Rapoport, 'Slouching towards Armageddon: Links with evangelicals', *Jerusalem Post International Edition* (17–24 June 1984); and Halsell, *Prophecy and Politics*, pp. 96–116.

261. Wagner, *Anxious for Armageddon*, pp. 96–113.

262. Ibid., pp. 109–113.

263. For information about this organization, see *Israel My Beloved: God's Banner for the Nations* (n. d.) [Internet], International Christian Zionist Center, <http://www.israelmybeloved.com/about/organization.htm>. [Accessed May 2004.]

from the UK, USA, France and Israel in December 1985. Other leading Christian Zionists associated with CFI include Lance Lambert, Derek Prince, Barry Segal and Dave Dolan who produces CFI's monthly *Middle East Digest*. CFI likewise insists on the unconditional necessity of 'standing with Israel' and bringing blessing to her as a nation, though CFI claims it does this primarily through prayer and humanitarian projects rather than by evangelism or political action. CFI sees itself as first and foremost 'a humanitarian organisation', in contrast to ICEJ which it regards as 'a religious-political organisation'.[264] Nevertheless, CFI's monthly newsletter and website make strong political statements in support of Israel. For example, in 'Myths and Facts' published in April 2000, Derek White argues:

> The propaganda line that Judea, Samaria, and Gaza are 'Occupied Arab lands' or 'Palestinian lands occupied in 1967' is just one of the myths requiring clarification for the sake of those that remain confused regarding the history of the region.[265]

CFI, though international in scope, is probably the most politically active and influential Christian Zionist organization in Britain.

These Christian leaders and their organizations have regular access to over 100 million American Christians and more than 100,000 church leaders. With a combined budget of well in excess of $300 million per annum they are shaping the Christian Zionist agenda today.

The historical roots of Christian Zionism: conclusions

This chapter has traced the emergence of Christian Zionism as a movement from early nineteenth-century rural England to twenty-first-century Capitol Hill, and its transition from British sectarianism to mainstream American evangelicalism.

British evangelicalism and restorationism
Five key factors led to the rise of the Christian Zionist movement in Britain:

---

264. Hannelle Sorensen, director of CFI on the East Coast of the USA, cited in Merkley, *Christian Attitudes Towards the State of Israel*, p. 180.
265. Derek White, 'Myths and Facts', Christian Friends of Israel, Newsletter 113 (April–May 2002).

1. With war and revolution consuming much of Europe and America, the optimistic eschatology of eighteenth-century postmillennialism was severely undermined.

2. A resurgence of premillennialism based on a literalist hermeneutic and futurist eschatology emerged through the influence of Lewis Way, Edward Irving and J. N. Darby and those associated with the Albury and Powerscourt prophecy conferences.

3. Several evangelical missionary societies, such as the LJS, were formed to provide education and humanitarian assistance, as well as to share the gospel with Jewish people. Through the efforts of leaders such as Charles Simeon and Charles Spurgeon, the idea of active British involvement in the restoration of the Jews to Palestine also took shape.

4. Their theological ideas were translated into political reality through the zealous efforts of British politicians such as Lord Shaftesbury, Lord Palmerston, David Lloyd George and Lord Balfour who saw the strategic value of a Jewish State in Palestine.

5. The Jewish Zionist movement itself grew in no small measure due to the involvement of Christian restorationists such as William Hechler. Zionism eventually gained international recognition through the Balfour Declaration, which, in 1917, finally guaranteed a Jewish homeland in Palestine.

American evangelicalism and Christian Zionism

Christian Zionism has become a dominant factor within American evangelicalism as a result of five additional factors:

1. Following frequent visits by J. N. Darby from the 1850s, his radical dispensational ideas about a failing church and revived Israel, as well as rigid separation between them in eternity, began to gain ground within the American evangelical establishment.

2. It was principally through the influence of James Brookes, D. L. Moody, C. I. Scofield and William Blackstone, together with the prophecy conferences and Bible schools which they founded, that Christian Zionism became indigenous to American evangelicalism during the latter half of the nineteenth century.

3. The *Scofield Reference Bible* became the standard text of Christian Zionism by systematizing and legitimizing the hermeneutics of dispensationalism as well as the futurist application of ancient biblical prophecies to the contemporary Jewish people.

4. The theological justification of Christian Zionism was provided by Lewis Sperry Chafer, Charles Ryrie, John Walvoord and the faculty of other dispensational institutions such as Dallas Theological Seminary and the Moody Bible Institute.

5. Contemporary Christian Zionism has evolved into three discrete strands through the apocalyptic writings of Hal Lindsey and Tim LaHaye, Messianic agencies such as Jews for Jesus and pro-Israeli political organizations such as the International Christian Embassy Jerusalem, and those associated with Pat Robertson and Jerry Falwell.

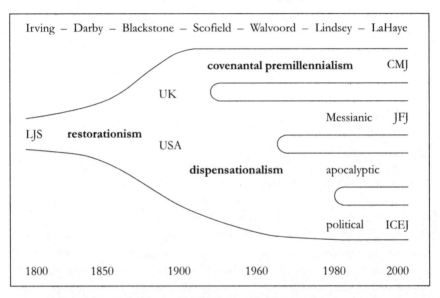

Figure 1. The historical development of Christian Zionism since 1860

In varying degrees, and for a variety of reasons, some contradictory, these individuals and organizations comprise what is probably the most powerful lobby in the United States today, influencing not only American foreign policy but also the chances of a peaceful resolution of the Palestinian–Israeli conflict.

Figure 1 provides a simplified illustration of the historical development of Christian Zionism from 1800. The next two chapters will appraise the distinctive theological emphasis of Christian Zionism and then assess its political agenda and consequences.

2. THE THEOLOGICAL EMPHASES OF CHRISTIAN ZIONISM

It has been shown that Christian Zionism, as a contemporary phenomenon, arose through the revival of historic or covenantal premillennialism in the nineteenth century, out of which emerged the novel theological system known as dispensationalism. While both are based on a literal and futurist hermeneutic and favour Jewish restoration, covenantal premillennialism teaches that God's future purposes for a restored Israel depend on faith in Jesus Christ and involve a close relationship with the worldwide church, both enjoying God's blessing together during the millennium.[1] Dispensationalists, however, distinguish between God's eternal purposes for Israel and the church in separate dispensations: the former seen as God's earthly people, the latter his heavenly people. In this regard, dispensationalism was profoundly sectarian in origin, preceding and inspiring the development of both Christian and Jewish Zionism. While still marginal in the UK, it has, however, become normative within American evangelical, Pentecostal, charismatic and independent

---

1. This view was propounded by Charles Haddon Spurgeon, Benjamin Newton, Samuel Tregelles, J. C. Ryle, Andrew and Horatius Bonar, Francis Schaeffer and Martyn Lloyd-Jones, among others. Christian Witness to Israel and many serving with the Church's Ministry among Jewish People identify with this position. See Hulse, *Restoration of Israel*, pp. 154–158.

churches, and pervasive among para-church institutions, Christian TV and radio stations and mission agencies. While classic dispensationalism has remained predominantly evangelistic, since 1970 especially, new forms of dispensational Christian Zionism have emerged in America, distinguished by very different emphases. Three, in particular, have influenced the development of Christian Zionism: apocalyptic dispensationalism is preoccupied with the 'signs of the times'; Messianic dispensationalism with evangelizing Jews for Jesus; and political dispensationalism with defending and 'blessing' Israel. These different and sometimes contradictory strands of evangelical Christian Zionism share three basic tenets: a commitment to biblical literalism, a futurist eschatology[2] and the restoration of the Jews to Palestine.

This chapter will assess seven essential doctrines that form the theological basis of evangelical Christian Zionism. Christian Zionism is founded first of all upon a literal and futurist interpretation of the Bible which leads proponents to distinguish between references to Israel and the church. Injunctions and promises concerning the ancient Jews are applied to the contemporary State of Israel rather than to the church. From this hermeneutic flows the conviction that the Jews remain God's 'chosen people', distinct from the church, whether until the end of the millennium, as held by covenant premillennialists, or into eternity, as affirmed by most dispensationalists. God's end-time purpose for the Jews is expressed in restorationism. The destiny of the Jewish people is to return to the land of Israel and reclaim the inheritance promised to Abraham and his descendants for ever. The role of the church is to assist in this 'end-time' event. This inheritance extends from the River of Egypt to the Euphrates. Within their land, Jerusalem is recognized to be their exclusive, undivided and eternal capital, and therefore it cannot be shared or divided. At the heart of Jerusalem will be the rebuilt Jewish temple to which all the nations will come to worship God. Just prior to the return of Jesus, there will be seven years of calamities and war, known as the tribulation, which will culminate in a great battle called Armageddon, during which the godless forces opposed to both God and Israel will be defeated. Jesus will then return as the Jewish Messiah and king to reign in Jerusalem for a thousand years and the Jewish people will enjoy a privileged status and role in the world. Each of these seven doctrines will be considered in turn.

---

2. Most dispensationalists (but not covenant premillennialists) also believe in the rapture when Christians will be removed from the earth either prior to, during or after the tribulation – hence three sub-divisions within dispensationalism – pre-tribulationists, mid-tribulationists and post-tribulationists. See Marvin Rosenthal, *The Pre-Wrath Rapture of the Church* (Nashville, TN: Thomas Nelson, 1990).

The Bible: a literal futurist hermeneutic

Christian Zionism is constructed upon a novel hermeneutic in which all Scripture is interpreted in an ultra-literal sense; the prophetic parts of Scripture are seen as pre-written history; and eschatology fulfilled in the interpreter's generation. This type of hermeneutic has been described as *pesher*, from the Aramaic for 'interpretation'. This differs from a traditional Protestant or covenant hermeneutic which, while also based on literalism, nevertheless begins with the setting of the author as well as recipients and is also shaped by the historical, cultural, grammatical and theological contexts.[3]

As has already been shown, the origin of this ultra-literal and futurist hermeneutic can be traced to the early nineteenth century and in particular to the writings of James Hatley Frere, George Stanley Faber, Lewis Way, Edward Irving and those who attended the Albury conferences from 1826. David Bebbington argues:

> There is a tight logical connection between high hopes for the Jews and a new
> estimate of scripture . . . The beginning of the innovatory interpretation can be
> located precisely . . . innovations in the fields of prophecy and understanding of
> scripture went hand in hand.[4]

Mark Patterson describes how Albury's premillennial system redefined revelation in historicist terms, 'from the self giving of God in history to an interpretation of history':

> The French Revolution became the key to understanding God's revelation, not only
> as a point of temporal triangulation, but as an unveiling of the very spiritual issues at
> work in the Last Days. The French Revolution unveiled the fact that prophecy and
> history were inextricably and beautifully interlaced . . . Thus Albury looked to history
> to discern this principle and history again to see it manifested . . . The malleable
> character of prophecy allowed the scriptures and history to assume the very shape
> determined by the Albury presuppositions and literal typical hermeneutic . . . a self
> perpetuating system in which theory, scripture and history combined in ever

---

3. For an appraisal of developments within Protestant biblical interpretation, see
   D. A. Carson and John D. Woodbridge (eds.), *Scripture and Truth* (Leicester: IVP,
   1983); Carson and Woodbridge (eds.), *Hermeneutics, Authority and Canon*; Goldingay,
   Models for the Interpretation of Scripture. See also, Packer, *'Fundamentalism'*.
4. Bebbington, *Evangelicalism in Modern Britain*, p. 88.

tightening symmetry, to form a system that explained each constituent part in terms of a single narrative and teleology.[5]

J. N. Darby, who subsequently pioneered this hermeneutic in a more explicitly futurist and dispensational form, summed it up in one sentence when he admitted, 'I prefer quoting many passages than enlarging upon them.'[6] Based on his own form of literalism, Darby developed his doctrine of dispensationalism with its rigid distinction between Israel and the church which forms the basis of much contemporary Christian Zionism. Following Darby closely, it was C. I. Scofield who first distilled and codified this literalist hermeneutic. An analysis of Scofield's distinctive understanding of literalism will lead to an examination of the ways in which others have developed and applied this hermeneutic. An appraisal of dispensational literalism will then show how it has evolved, how it utilizes symbolism, is on occasion self-contradictory, relies on enhancements of the biblical text, and leads to arbitrary conclusions.

Darby's innovative dispensationalism
Central to dispensationalism is the assumption that seven dispensations are self-evident in biblical history, if a literal hermeneutic is applied consistently. Darby was not the first to discover dispensations within biblical history, nor, as will be shown, was his own scheme necessarily the clearest, or universally accepted even within Brethren circles. However, with the death of Irving, the break up of the Albury Circle and the cessation of the *Morning Watch*, Darby's scheme, with its rigid distinction between Israel and the church, came to dominate dispensational thinking. Prior to the rise of dispensationalism it was common to divide history into two or three dispensations. Jonathan Edwards, for example, had acknowledged the lack of unanimity even on the distinction between the Old and New Testaments: 'There is, perhaps, no part of divinity attended with so much intricacy, and wherein orthodox divines so much differ, as in stating the precise agreement and difference between the two dispensations, of Moses

---

5. Mark R. Patterson, *Designing the Last Days: Edward Irving, the Albury Circle and the Theology of the Morning Watch* (PhD thesis, Kings College, London, 2001), pp. 117, 166.

6. Darby, 'The Hopes of the Church of God in Connection with the Destiny of the Jews and the Nations as Revealed in Prophecy', in *Collected Writings*, vol. 2, Prophetic 1, p. 363.

and Christ.'[7] In his principal work on the dispensations, published in 1823, George Faber distinguished three stages in God's gracious dealing with mankind: Patriarchal, Levitical and Christian. However, unlike Darby, he did not regard them as necessarily consecutive nor was each a remedy for the failure of the previous. Instead, he argued,

> From the time of the fall down to the termination of the world, man lives under one and the same system of divine grace, a system, which was rendered necessary for him by the very circumstances of the fall, and which therefore at no one period can differ essentially from itself.[8]

Irving was also using the term 'dispensation' as early as 1828 to contrast God's contemporary dealings with Israel and the church.[9] Edward Miller quotes Irving's notes of the first Albury conference: 'perfect unanimity on the following . . . that the Christian Dispensation was to be terminated, ending in the destruction of the visible Church, like the Jewish; during which "judgements" the Jews were to be restored to Palestine'.[10]

The first and clearest expression of Darby's thinking on the dispensations is to be found in 'The Apostasy of the Successive Dispensations', published in the *Christian Witness* in October 1836. Darby introduces his dispensational framework in these terms:

> The detail of the history connected with these dispensations brings out many most interesting displays . . . But the dispensations themselves all declare some leading principle or interference of God, some condition in which He has placed man, principles which in themselves are everlastingly sanctioned of God, but in the course of these dispensations placed responsibly in the hands of man for the display and discovery of what he was, and the bringing in their infallible establishment in Him to whom the glory of them all rightly belonged . . . In every instance, there was a total and immediate failure as regarded man, however the patience of God might tolerate

7. Jonathan Edwards, 'On Full Communion', *The Complete Works of Jonathan Edwards*, vol. 1 (Edinburgh: Banner of Truth, 1974), p. 160.

8. George Stanley Faber, 'On the peculiar genius of the three dispensations, Patriarchal, Levitical, and Christian', in *A Treatise on the Genius and Object of the Patriarchal, the Levitical and the Christian Dispensations* (London: F. C. and J. Rivington, 1823), p. 2.

9. Edward Irving, *The Last Days: A Discourse on the Evil Character of These Our Times, Proving Them to be The 'Perilous Times' and the 'Last Days'* (London: James Nisbit, 1850), p. 10.

10. Edward Miller, *The History and Doctrines of Irvingism* (London, 1878).

and carry on by grace the dispensation in which man has thus failed in the outset; and further, that there is no instance of the restoration of a dispensation afforded us, though there might be partial revivals of it through faith.[11]

His actual chronological delineation of these so called dispensations is rambling and can only be described as embryonic compared with later attempts to impose a dispensational scheme on Scripture:

The paradisaical state cannot properly perhaps be called a dispensation . . . until the Lord destroyed the first world created . . . Here dispensations, properly speaking, begin. *On the first, Noah* I shall be very brief . . . of faithful Abraham which as a minuter circumstance I also pass briefly over . . . But to take up the point of the dispensation – *obedience under the law* by which life was to be: this obedience they undertook; and Moses returned to receive the various orderings of divine appointment as under it, and the two tables of testimony . . . The ordinance or *dispensation of priesthood* failed in like manner . . . The *kingly dispensation* failed in the same way as did the nation under the previous ordering which made way for the king . . . till the provocation's of Manasseh set aside all hope of recovery or way of mercy in that dispensation. The same is true of universal rule transferred to the Gentiles . . . The rejection of our blessed Lord proved that no present mercy or grace, no present interference of God in goodness here would meet the wilful and persevering enmity of the human heart, but only showed it in its true light. But this never being set up as a dispensation but only the manifestation of His Person (by faith), I pass by. *The last* we have to notice, in a humbled sense of sin in us, *is the present*, where we are apt to take our ease in the world . . . the *dispensation of the Spirit*. Much has been said, with strong objection to it, as to the apostasy or failure of this dispensation. The results are but too plain . . . The attempt to set this dispensation on another footing, as to its continuance, than those dispensations which have failed already, not only shows ignorance of the principles of God's dealings . . .

And the close of all dispensation, and the end of all question and title of authority shall come, and all be finished, God shall be all in all without question and without failure . . . In fact the *Gentile dispensation*, as a distinct thing, took its rise at the death of Stephen, the witness that the Jews resisted the Holy Ghost: as their fathers did, so did they.[12]

---

11. Darby, 'The Apostasy of the Successive Dispensations', in *Collected Writings*, vol. 2, Ecclesiastical No. 1, p. 124.

12. Ibid., pp. 124–130 (emphasis added). See Figure 2 on p. 113 for a comparison with the *Morning Watch* and Scofield.

It may be shown, however, by a comparison with an article on the dispensations that appeared in 1831 in Henry Drummond's journal, the *Morning Watch*, that the Albury Circle had an earlier, much clearer and more logical dispensational framework than Darby. The *Morning Watch* article is both succinct and logical, basing its scheme on the seven days of creation:

> As he created all things in six days, and rested on the seventh, hallowing it, so has he ordained in six successive ages to work out the work of all new creation, and added a seventh age as an eternal one, the age of rest and sanctified glory. These seven ages are, 1: the age before the fall, or Adam age; 2. the age until the flood, or Noah age; 3. the age until the deliverance of the church, or Patriarchal age; 4. the age of the Jewish church; 5. the age of the Gentile church; 6. the age of the Millennial church; and 7. the age of the resurrection church.[13]

It may be argued that Darby was not attempting to devise a scheme of seven dispensations but rather, as his title implies, merely showing how all attempts by mankind to find acceptance with God so far had failed. It was only later in the writings of Scofield that seven dispensations became fixed within dispensational thinking, long after any association with Irving and the Albury Circle had been ignored or forgotten. Charles Ryrie's later interpretation of Darby's dispensations is significantly at variance with Darby's own writings but more consistent with Scofield and closer, in fact, to that of the *Morning Watch*. Therefore, it is an understatement for Ryrie to claim that Darby's scheme is 'not always easily discerned from his writings'.[14] Ryrie appears to have read back into Darby's mind, like Scofield, a scheme that suited his own purposes. From Darby's own pen we may attempt to reconstruct his dispensational chronology and compare it with the *Morning Watch*, Scofield's 1909 version and Ryrie's version of Darby. (See Figure 2 on p. 113.)

Nevertheless, Darby defended his own innovative dispensational hermeneutic on two grounds: 'The covenant is a word common in the language of a large class of Christian professors . . . but in its development and detail, as to its unfolded principles, much obscurity appears to me to have arisen from a want of simple attention to scripture.'[15]

---

13. 'The Seven Dispensations', *Morning Watch*, 4.134.9f. (September 1831), cited in Patterson, *Designing the Last Days*, p. 138.
14. Ryrie, *Dispensationalism*, p. 68.
15. Darby, 'The Covenants', in *Collected Writings*, vol. 3, Doctrine 1, p. 68.

The *Morning Watch*[16]	Darby's dispensations[17]	Ryrie's version of Darby[18]	Scofield's dispensations[19]
1. Adam		1. Paradisaical state	1. Innocency (Gen. 1:28)
2. Noah	1. Noah (Government)	2. Noah	2. Conscience (Gen. 3:23)
3. Patriarchs		3. Abraham	3. Human government (Gen. 8:20)
4. Jewish	2. Moses (Law) 3. Aaron (Priesthood) 4. Kingly (Manasseh)	4. Israel – under law under priesthood under kings	4. Promise (Gen. 12:1) 5. Law (Exod. 19:8)
5. Gentiles	5. Spirit (Gentile)	5. Gentiles	6. Grace (John 1:17)
6. Millennium		6. Spirit	
7. Resurrection		7. Millennium	7. Kingdom (Eph. 1:10)

Figure 2. A comparison of the dispensational schemes of the *Morning Watch*, J. N. Darby, Charles Ryrie and C. I. Scofield

16. Patterson, *Designing the Last Days*.
17. Darby, 'The Apostasy of the Successive Dispensations', in *Collected Writings*, vol. 2, Ecclesiastical No. 1, pp. 124–130.
18. Ryrie, *Dispensationalism*, pp. 68, 71.
19. Scofield, 'Introduction', *Scofield Reference Bible*, p. 5.

A little later he claimed, '. . . because it was in this the Lord was pleased, without man's teaching, first to open my eyes on this subject, that I might learn His will concerning it throughout'.[20] Darby, therefore, justified his own dispensational scheme on the basis that others had not studied the Scriptures correctly and that his interpretation was correct because the Lord had revealed it to him personally. Darby's views were to gain far wider acceptance through the influence of one of his disciples, C. I. Scofield.

Scofield's contribution to a dispensational literal hermeneutic

Scofield's own dispensational scheme clearly draws upon Darby's writings, although no credit is given. Nevertheless, he insisted that his dispensational scheme recovers for the Bible 'a clear and coherent harmony of the predictive portions':

> The Dispensations are distinguished, exhibiting the majestic, progressive order of the divine dealings of God with humanity, the 'increasing purpose' which runs through and links together the ages, from the beginning of the life of man to the end in eternity. Augustine said: 'Distinguish the ages, and the scriptures harmonize.'[21]

Whether Augustine understood 'ages' in terms of Scofield's dispensations is highly questionable. Nevertheless, Scofield claimed his own scheme was natural and self-evident:

> . . . there is a beautiful system in this gradualness of unfolding. The past is seen to fall into periods, marked off by distinct limits, and distinguishable period from period by something peculiar to each. Thus it comes to be understood that there is a doctrine of Ages or Dispensations in the Bible.[22]

A comparison between these 'distinct limits' as they appear in the *Scofield Reference Bible* and in its subsequent revised versions, in which the dispensations have been moved or renamed, would suggest that they are not as clear as Scofield claimed.

---

20. Darby, 'Evidence from Scripture for the passing away of the present dispensations', in *Collected Writings*, vol. 2, Prophetic 1, p. 108.
21. Scofield, 'Introduction', *Scofield Reference Bible*, p. 3.
22. C. I. Scofield, *Addresses on Prophecy* (New York: Chas. C. Cook, 1914), p. 13.

Scofield Reference Bible (1917)[23]	The New Scofield Study Bible (1984)[24]
1. Innocency (Gen. 1:28)	1. Innocence (Gen. 1:28)
2. Conscience (Gen. 3:23)	2. Conscience or moral responsibility (Gen. 3:7)
3. Human government (Gen. 8:20)	3. Human government (Gen. 8:15)
4. Promise (Gen. 12:1)	4. Promise (Gen. 12:1)
5. Law (Exod. 19:8)	5. Law (Exod. 19:1)
6. Grace (John 1:17)	6. Church (Acts 2:1)
7. Kingdom or fulness of times (Eph. 1:10)[25]	7. Kingdom (Rev. 20:4)

Figure 3. A comparison of the dispensations in the *Scofield Reference Bible* and *The New Scofield Study Bible*

Scofield's rigid adherence to his dispensations also required him to make some rather unusual if not speculative assertions to ensure consistency. So, for example, in describing the transition between his fourth dispensation of promise and his fifth dispensation of law, Scofield argued that Abraham's descendants need do no more than 'abide in their own land to inherit every blessing'. He went on to claim:

> The Dispensation of Promise ended when Israel rashly accepted the law (Ex. 19:8). Grace had prepared a deliverer (Moses), provided a sacrifice for the guilty and by divine power brought them out of bondage (Ex. 19:4); but at Sinai they exchanged grace for law.[26]

---

23. Scofield, 'Introduction', *Scofield Reference Bible*, fn. 4, p. 5.
24. *The New Scofield Study Bible* (New York: Oxford University Press, 1984), p. 3.
25. *Scofield Reference Bible*, fn. 3, p. 1250.
26. Ibid., fn. 1, p. 20.

In doing so, Scofield reduces the giving of the law by Moses from being God's gracious initiative to the 'rashness' of the Jewish people.

Similarly, in his introduction to the Gospels, Scofield artificially imposes stark divisions before and after Calvary which lead him to make a surprising assertion: 'The mission of Jesus was, primarily, to the Jews ... The Sermon on the Mount is law, not grace ... the doctrines of grace are to be sought in the Epistles not in the Gospels.'[27] Surprisingly, Scofield ignores the one division that is self-evident between the old and new covenants: Mark 1:1 categorically states, 'The beginning of the gospel about Jesus Christ', while Matthew 11:13 further informs us, 'For all the Prophets and the Law prophesied until John.' However, Scofield places the life and ministry of Jesus within the dispensation of law along with John the Baptist and the Old Testament prophets, arguing that the sixth dispensation of grace only 'begins with the death and resurrection of Christ'.[28] So, for example, he claims the Lord's Prayer, and in particular the petition, 'Forgive us our debts, as we also have forgiven our debtors' (Matt. 6:12), is not applicable to the church, since it is 'legal ground'.[29] This is because Scofield believed the Gospels were essentially for the Jews and therefore not relevant for the church. So, in the note attached to Ephesians 3 he states: 'In his (Paul's) writings alone we find the doctrine, position, walk, and destiny of the church.'[30] Scofield has imposed divisions that do not exist in Scripture and ignored those that do.

Scofield was the first to formalize the methodology of literalism promoted within early dispensationalism in his book, *Rightly Dividing the Word of Truth*, published in 1888. Scofield based his thesis on the Authorized Version's rendering of 2 Timothy 2:15 in which Paul instructed Timothy to, 'rightly divide the word of truth'. Scofield explains:

> The Word of Truth, then, has right divisions, and it must be evident that, as one cannot be 'a workman that needeth not to be ashamed' without observing them, so any study of that Word which ignores these divisions must be in large measure profitless and confusing. The purpose of this pamphlet is to indicate the more important divisions of the Word of Truth.[31]

---

27. Ibid., p. 989.
28. Ibid., fn. 2, p. 1115.
29. Ibid., p. 1002. Many other dispensationalists take the same view. See Chafer, *Systematic Theology*, vol. 4, p. 221.
30. *Scofield Reference Bible*, p. 1252.
31. Scofield, *Rightly Dividing the Word of Truth*, p. 3.

Ironically, the foundation of Scofield's hermeneutic is based on an over-literalized misreading of the verse. The United Bible Societies' textual commentary, which is the standard work used by translators worldwide, clarifies the meaning of the verse:

> 'Rightly handling' translates a Greek verb that occurs only here in the New Testament. Literally it refers to the act of cutting something in a straight way; figuratively it refers to expounding something rightly, or teaching something correctly. Here, what needs to be handled correctly is the word of truth.[32]

Scofield took the verb literally to say that the Bible must be cut up into divisions. Non-dispensational commentators, however, recognize that Paul is using the term figuratively to mean 'correctly handle' the Bible.

The first chapter of Scofield's book, entitled 'The Jew, the Gentile and the Church of God', sets the tone for all future dispensational teaching in which Israel is distinguished from the church. It is also based on an over- literal interpretation of another verse, 1 Corinthians 10:32, where Paul urges Christians to 'Give none offence, neither to the Jews, nor to the Gentiles, nor to the church of God' (AV). On the basis of this verse, Scofield divided the world into three classes of people: Jews, Gentiles and the church, an idea which is now the 'warp and woof of dispensational teaching'.[33] Other commentators suggest, however, that the verse is actually delineating two groups of people, Christians and non-Christians, whether Jews or Gentiles.[34] Nevertheless, beginning with these passages, Scofield insisted that promises made to the Jews in the Old Testament were not fulfilled in the New Testament church but continue to apply to Israel. So, for example, he insists that, 'Not one instance exists of a "spiritual" or figurative fulfilment of prophecy . . . Jerusalem is always Jerusalem, Israel is always Israel, Zion is always Zion . . . Prophecies may never be spiritualised, but are always literal.'[35] Scofield's literalism

---

32. An alternative translation for this verse is: 'You must try as hard as you can to cause God to fully approve of you as a worker who is not ashamed of his work and correctly teaches the true message', *UBS New Testament Handbook* (New York: United Bible Societies, 1997; online version available at <www.biblesoft.com>).

33. Canfield, *Incredible Scofield*, p. 166.

34. 'In the present verse it simply means "not causing (moral or spiritual) damage to anyone else"', *UBS New Testament Handbook*.

35. C. I. Scofield, *Scofield Bible Correspondence Course* (Chicago: Moody Bible Institute, n.d.), pp. 45–46.

extended to exact verbal phraseology. This led him to claim, for example, that there are seven dispensations, eight covenants and eleven great mysteries.

In the introduction to his reference Bible, Scofield explained that over the previous fifty years there had been an 'unprecedented' degree of interest in Bible study 'free from merely controversial motive'. He claimed that from this 'new and vast exegetical and expository' body of literature, which was 'inaccessible for bulk, cost, and time to the average reader', Scofield had taken the 'winnowed and attested results' of this study and these were now 'embodied in the notes, summaries, and definitions of this edition'. He insisted that 'expository novelties, and merely personal views and interpretations, have been rejected'.[36] He distinguished his own from previous Bible reference systems, which he regarded as 'unscientific and often misleading'. Instead, Scofield insisted that in his new system:

> all the greater truths of the divine revelation are so traced through the entire Bible, from the place of first mention to the last, that the reader may himself follow the gradual unfolding of these, by many inspired writers through many ages, to their culmination in Jesus Christ and the New Testament scriptures. This method imparts to Bible study an interest and vital reality which are wholly lacking in fragmented and disconnected study.[37]

The footnotes which appear in the *Scofield Reference Bible* are actually highly selective, appearing on less than half the pages of the Bible.[38] Indeed, Scofield goes much further than other Bible commentators, such as Albert Barnes or Matthew Henry, in also providing comprehensive headings embedded within the biblical text. These not only include chapter and paragraph titles but also, in many cases, verse by verse headings in chapters deemed significant to dispensationalists that would otherwise prove obscure were it not for such 'helps'. For example, in Isaiah 11 under the heading 'The Davidic kingdom set up', in the space of ten verses additional headings guide readers carefully through the chapter to ensure a dispensational reading:

1. The King's ancestry (11:1);
2. The source of the King's power, the sevenfold Spirit (11:2);

---

36. Scofield, *Scofield Bible Correspondence Course*, 'Introduction', p. iii.

37. Ibid.

38. Footnotes appear on only 327 out of a total of 970 pages of the Old Testament, and on only 214 out of 352 pages in the New Testament.

3. The character of his reign (11:3–5);
4. The quality of the kingdom (11:6–8);
5. The extent of the kingdom (11:9);
6. How the kingdom will be set up (11:10–16).[39]

Had Scofield's notes been published as a separate commentary, in all probability his views would have eventually been forgotten or superseded. The difference, however, according to one of Scofield's biographers, is that 'neither Henry nor Barnes had the temerity, guile or gall to get their notes accepted as scripture itself'.[40] Within a few years of publication the *Scofield Reference Bible* achieved confessional status for the notes which appeared alongside the biblical text. Charles G. Trumball, editor of the *Sunday School Times*, described Scofield's Bible as nothing less than a 'God-planned, God-guided, God-energized work'.[41]

Scofield's reference Bible has, however, undergone significant revision since it was first published in 1909. Scofield completed the first revision in 1917 himself, apparently with the help of seven consulting editors, several of whom were D. L. Moody's colleagues.[42] Further revisions continued to adapt, modify and elaborate Scofield's dispensational package after his death. *The New Scofield Reference Bible* was published in 1967 by Oxford University Press, and edited by Dr E. Schuyler English. In 1984 a further revision based on the New International Version of the Bible was undertaken by three of the faculty from Philadelphia College of Bible: Clarence Mason, Sherrill Babb and Paul Karleen. Also published by Oxford University Press, its title is *The New Scofield Study Bible*.

Dallas Theological Seminary, founded in 1924 by Lewis Sperry Chafer, one of Scofield's students, has probably accomplished more for the cause of dispensationalism and Christian Zionism than any other institution in the world. For nearly eighty years, through its faculty and students, Dallas has contributed to a proliferation of dispensational thinking, from the classic dispensationalism of Scofield and Chafer to the revised dispensationalism of Ryrie and Walvoord; the apocalyptic dispensationalism of Lindsey and LaHaye; the Messianic dispensationalism of Moishe Rosen and Arnold Fruchtenbaum; and the progressive dispensationalism of Craig Blaising and Darrel Bock.

---

39. *Scofield Reference Bible*, p. 723.
40. Canfield, *Incredible Scofield*, p. 209.
41. Cited in Cox, *Examination of Dispensationalism*, pp. 55–56.
42. E.g. Revd Henry G. Weston, DD, LLD, President of Crozer Theological Seminary; Revd W. G. Moorehead, DD, President of Xenia (U.I.) Theological Seminary; Revd James M. Gray, DD, President of Moody Bible Institute.

Blaising and Bock represent a new generation of younger dispensational-ists among the faculty of Dallas Theological Seminary who have attempted to redefine their movement and engaged in constructive dialogue with covenan-tal theologians on the relationship of the church to Israel.[43] They distance themselves from what they regard as the 'naïveté' of the founder's vision, dis-tinguishing the traditional dispensationalism of Chafer and Ryrie from 'Scofieldism', as well as from the popular apocalypticism of 'Lindseyism'. They regard themselves as less land-centred and less future-centred.

Ryrie, however, is sceptical, unwilling to concede to such revisionism. He prefers to describe the position of Blaising and Bock as 'neo-dispensational-ist' or 'covenant dispensationalist', for holding to what he terms a 'slippery' hermeneutic.[44]

Following Scofield's literalistic hermeneutic and rigid distinction between Israel and the church, most contemporary dispensationalists still regard the founding of the State of Israel as evidence of divine intervention, believe the Jews remain God's 'chosen people', have a divine right to their land in perpe-tuity and that the battle of Armageddon is imminent.

Developments in literalist hermeneutics

In 1936, Chafer defined Scofieldian literalism in the following terms: 'The out-standing characteristic of the dispensationalist is . . . that he believes every state-ment of the Bible and gives to it the plain, natural meaning its words imply.'[45] Like Chafer, Ryrie suggests that it is only dispensationalists who are consistent in applying a literal interpretation: 'To be sure, literal/historical/grammatical interpretation is not the sole possession or practice of dispensationalists, but the consistent use of it in all areas of biblical interpretation is.'[46] In its classic form, Ryrie insists the *sine qua non* of dispensationalism to be:

1. A dispensationalist keeps Israel and the church distinct . . .
2. This distinction between Israel and the church is born out of a system of hermeneutics that is usually called literal interpretation . . .
3. A third aspect . . . concerns the underlying purpose of God in the world . . . namely, the glory of God . . . To the normative dispensationalist, the

---

43. See Fuller, *Gospel and Law*; Blaising and Bock (eds.), *Dispensationalism*; Holwerda, *Jesus and Israel*.
44. Ryrie, *Dispensationalism*, pp. 171, 175, 178.
45. L. S. Chafer, 'Dispensationalism', *Bibliotheca Sacra* 93 (October 1936), pp. 410, 417.
46. Ryrie, *Dispensationalism*, p. 40.

soteriological, or saving, program of God is not the only program but one of the means God is using in the total program of glorifying Himself.[47]

He goes on to claim:

> Dispensationalism is a result of consistent application of the basic hermeneutical principle of literal, normal, or plain interpretation. No other system of theology can claim this . . . The nonliteralist is the nondispensationalist, and the consistent literalist is a dispensationalist.[48]

Chafer included non-dispensational premillennialists within his category of inconsistency because, he claimed, they 'spiritualized' prophetic references to Israel. Louis Goldberg has gone further, claiming that it is those who reject a literalist hermeneutic who are imposing their own theological framework on the Scriptures:

> . . . two established rules of interpretation are as follows: 1) 'When scripture makes common sense use no other sense'; 2) 'Prophecy . . . must be interpreted literally . . . The reason a non-literal method of interpretation is adopted is, almost without exception, because of a desire to avoid the obvious interpretation of the passage. The desire to bring the teaching of scripture into harmony with some predetermined system of doctrine instead of bringing doctrine into harmony with the scriptures has kept this practice alive.' The point is that we have to let the prophetic scriptures speak on their own without reading into them![49]

It is ironic that Goldberg should charge non-dispensationalists with holding a 'predetermined system of doctrine' when dispensationalists themselves cannot agree on the parameters of their own system which they claim is self-evident.

Chafer went as far as to teach that without a dispensational distinction between Israel and the church, a simple literal reading of the Bible would lead to confusion and internal inconsistency. Dwight Pentecost, also of Dallas Theological Seminary, similarly insists that 'scripture is unintelligible until one can distinguish clearly between God's program for his earthly people Israel and

---

47. Ibid., pp. 39–40.
48. Ibid., p. 92.
49. Louis Goldberg, 'Whose Land Is It?', *Issues* 4.2; Goldberg quotes from Pentecost, *Things to Come* (2nd edn, Grand Rapids: Zondervan, 1964), p. 60.

that for the Church'.[50] The premise that the Bible is unintelligible without the dispensational distinction between Israel and the church, however, can be sustained only if one excludes *a priori* all other methods of interpretation.

Patrick Goodenough of the International Christian Embassy Jerusalem (ICEJ) explains the consequence of this literalist approach: 'We simply believe the Bible. And that Bible, which we understand has not been revoked, makes it quite clear that God has given this land as an eternal inheritance to the Jewish people.'[51] Anne Dexter also challenges those who reject this hermeneutic:

> Some Arab believers and expatriate Christians in Israel feel so strongly about these matters that they will not read the parts of the Bible that seem to promise the land to the Jews or in any way uphold their election . . . Large parts of the scriptures are effectively invalidated by this approach.[52]

In the 1980s, the Church's Ministry Among Jewish People (CMJ) went further, locating the origin of what it terms a 'spiritualized' reading of the Bible in the heresy of Marcion who proposed the abandonment of the Old Testament: 'But that was unacceptable to the Church and a better way to de-Judaise the Hebrew scriptures was to "Christianise" the Hebrew scriptures so as to spiritualise the text and read New Testament concepts into the text. That view is still prevalent today.'[53] Hal Lindsey has also attributed the development of erroneous views concerning Israel to an allegorical, non-literal hermeneutic allegedly advocated by Origen.[54]

Others, however, have argued that it was the consistent approach of the Post-Apostolic Fathers, including Origen, to interpret the Hebrew scriptures typologically, that is as 'types' preceding the New Testament realities, just as Jesus and the apostles had done.[55]

---

50. Pentecost, *Things to Come*, 1st edn (1958), p. 529.

51. Cited in Kathy Kern, *Blessing Israel? Christian Embassy Responds* (2 November 1997) [Internet], Christian Peacemakers Team, <http://menno.org.cpt.news@ mennolink.org>. [Accessed May 2004.]

52. Anne Dexter, *View the Land* (South Plainfield, NJ: Bridge Publishing, 1986), pp. 214–215.

53. CMJ, 'Replacement Theology: Is the Church the "Israel of God"?' (St Albans, Herts: CMJ, n.d.).

54. Lindsey, *Road to Holocaust*, pp. 7–8.

55. E.g. the temple and its sacrifices are seen as types or illustrations of Jesus; see Heb. 9 and Matt. 26:61: 'Destroy this Temple and I will rebuild it again in three days.' See

It is clear that Jesus was often misunderstood by those who took his words too literally. John's Gospel contains several instances. For example, after he had cleansed the temple and was asked by the Pharisees for a sign, Jesus replied, 'Destroy this temple, and I will raise it again in three days' (John 2:19). They thought he meant their temple, but Jesus does not correct their error. In the next few chapters, Nicodemus wonders how he can enter his mother's womb again (John 3:4), the Samaritan woman believes Jesus is offering her water on tap (4:15), and the religious leaders fear Jesus is advocating cannibalism by insisting they must eat his body and drink his blood (6:51–52). It is ironic, therefore, that one of the most common mistakes made by people in the Gospels, who erroneously deduced a literal interpretation when Jesus intended a spiritual one, is repeated today.

Because of their commitment to literalism, for example, Lindsey and other dispensationalists do not distinguish between the figurative or typological approaches used by the Reformers and the allegorical methods of interpretation found typically in pre-Reformation Roman Catholicism.[56] The distinction between these two methods of interpretation is significant since the former places particular emphasis on the historical context of passages as well as upon the way Scripture interprets Scripture, whereas an allegorical approach finds eternal truths without reference to any historical setting. A typological approach also highlights the way New Testament writers see Jesus Christ to be the fulfilment of most Old Testament images and types. There is evidence that a typological interpretation of the Old Testament was consistently followed by the church from the first century, and did not arise with Marcion, as the CMJ claims, or with Origen, as Lindsey alleges.[57] On the contrary, it is the dispensational distinction between church and Israel that is without historical precedent.[58] Some, like David Holwerda, have even observed that it came to prominence only in post-Holocaust theology.[59]

Clement, 'First Epistle', in Coxe (ed.), *Ante-Nicene Fathers*, vol. 1, pp. 12–13; *Epistle of Barnabas* 4, in Coxe (ed.), *Ante-Nicene Fathers*, vol. 1, p. 138; Justin, *Dialogue with Trypho*, 11, in Coxe (ed.), *Ante-Nicene Fathers*, vol. 1, pp. 200–267; Irenaeus, *Against Heresies*, 4.21.3, in Coxe (ed.), *Ante-Nicene Fathers*, vol. 1, p. 493.

56. J. N. D. Kelly, *Early Christian Doctrine* (rev. edn, San Francisco: Harper & Row, 1978), pp. 69–75.

57. DeMar and Leithart, *Legacy of Hatred*, p. 37.

58. Ladd, *Blessed Hope*, pp. 35–60, 130–136; Doyle, *Eschatology and the Shape of Christian Belief*, pp. 242–250; Venema, *Promise of the Future*, pp. 205–218; Murray, *Puritan Hope*, pp. 187–206.

59. Holwerda, *Jesus and Israel*, pp. 1–26.

A literal futurist hermeneutic examined

As has been noted, Hal Lindsey is probably the most influential Christian Zionist writer today, with book sales in excess of 40 million, published in over fifty languages. This critique will therefore use Lindsey's writings as illustrative of how other Christian Zionist writers apply a 'literal' hermeneutic.

Changing literalism – what did the apostle John see?

One of the most noticeable aspects of a literal futurist hermeneutic is the way some adherents have adapted their interpretations to fit with changing events.[60] For example, in *There's a New World Coming* (1973), Lindsey was relatively circumspect as to the meaning of the symbols used in the book of Revelation. He speculated that John would have been lost for words trying to describe modern weapons: 'In the case just mentioned, the locusts might symbolize an advanced kind of helicopter.'[61] However, by the time he wrote *The Apocalypse Code* (1997), twenty-four-years later, as new and more destructive military hardware became available, Lindsey became more specific and confident of his interpretation. So, for example, 'might symbolize' now became what John 'actually saw':

> Just exactly how could a first Century prophet describe, much less understand, the incredible advances in science and technology that exist at the end of the 20th and the beginning of the 21st centuries? Yet he testified and God bore witness that he actually saw and heard things like: supersonic jet aircraft with missiles . . . advanced attack helicopters . . . intercontinental ballistic missiles with Multiple Independently Targeted Re-entry Vehicles tipped with thermonuclear warheads . . . biological and chemical weapons, aircraft carriers, missile cruisers, nuclear submarines, laser weapons, space stations and satellites.[62]

Such literalism is problematic when futurists attempt to keep pace with the

---

60. Compare Grant Jeffrey, *Armageddon: Appointment with Destiny* (Toronto: Frontier Research Publications, 1988), pp. 182–187 with Jeffrey, *Messiah*, p. 268. In the former, Jeffrey dates Daniel's seventieth week to the seven years from 1993 to 2000 and the Lord's return and cleansing of a rebuilt temple to the twenty-fourth of the ninth month in AD 2000. In the latter book, Jeffrey appears to contradict himself, claiming, 'We cannot and must not set dates' (p. 276).

61. Lindsey, *There's a New World Coming*, p. 8. See also p. 141 for a reference to Cobra helicopters.

62. Lindsey, *Apocalypse Code*, p. 36.

dramatic geo-political changes as seen in Eastern Europe and the former Soviet Union in the last two decades. Lindsey had insisted in 1981 and again in 1994 that his, by then, apparently contradictory assessments of Russia were, nevertheless, both predicted in the Bible.

The 1980's: Countdown to Armageddon	Planet Earth 2000 AD
'Today, the Soviets are without question the strongest power on the face of the earth. Let's look at recent history to see how the Russians rose to the might predicted for them thousands of years ago.'[63]	'We see Russia as no longer a world threat, but a regional power with a world-class military – exactly what Ezekiel 38 and 39 predicted it would be.'[64]

Figure 4. An illustration of the changing significance of Russia in Hal Lindsey's eschatology

With the gradual demise of Russia as a world power and the disintegration of the Communist bloc, Lindsey began to switch his emphasis on the end-time enemies of Israel from Russian communism in 1970 to Islamic fundamentalism by 1994.[65] In *The Late Great Planet Earth* (1970), the threat comes from 'the Russian force' (p. 160). By 1997 this had become 'the Russian-Muslim force'.[66] In keeping pace with the changing Middle East scene, by 1999 Lindsey was claiming this axis of evil was now led by a 'Muslim-Russian alliance'.[67]

Lindsey's difficulty with finding an accurate and lasting interpretation is nowhere more evident than in his attempts to date the second advent. In Matthew 24:34, Jesus said, 'I tell you the truth, this generation will certainly not pass away until all these things have happened.' In 1970, Lindsey raised the question: 'What generation?' Logically, he suggested, it would be the generation that had seen the signs Jesus had described, but added, 'chief among them the rebirth of Israel'. He then suggested a biblical generation was around forty

63. Lindsey, *1980's: Countdown*, p. 68.

64. Lindsey, *Planet Earth 2000 AD*, p. 216.

65. Lindsey, *Final Battle*, ch. 1 is entitled 'The New Islamic Global Threat', p. 1.

66. Lindsey, *Apocalypse Code*, p. 153.

67. Hal Lindsey, *International Intelligence Briefing* (7 January 1999) [Internet], Hal Lindsey Website Ministries, <http://hallindseyoracle.com/>. [Accessed June 2002.]

years: 'If this is a correct deduction, then within forty years or so of 1948, all these things could take place. Many scholars who have studied Bible prophecy all their lives believe that this is so.'[68] Lindsey was not the only writer to suggest that the Messiah would return in 1988.[69] When Jesus did not return that year, however, Lindsey revised his timescale by suggesting that a biblical generation could be anything from forty to 100 years and that perhaps Daniel's prophetic clock had started ticking again not in 1948 but in 1967 when Israel captured Jerusalem.[70] Undaunted, in 1988 Grant Jeffrey calculated that Daniel's last 'week' would begin in 1993, the tribulation would occur in 1997 and the cleansing of the temple and millennium would begin in the autumn of 2000.[71] Like Lindsey, his subsequent books have avoided being so specific.[72]

Symbolic literalism – the Apocalypse code revealed
Although Christian Zionists insist Scripture must be interpreted literally, they have not always been consistent. Indeed, even Scofield conceded, 'It is then permitted – while holding firmly the historical verity – reverently to spiritualize the historical scriptures.'[73] David Brickner's hermeneutic illustrates this tension. In his interpretation of Daniel 9:24–27, he first of all requires a figurative interpretation: 'He is not speaking of literal weeks but of periods of time, each a period of seven years.'[74] However, in order to give a futurist reading to Daniel's prophecy and apply it to today, it is also necessary for dispensationalists to place a 'parenthesis' of 2,000 years between the sixty-ninth and seventieth week, when the prophetic clock was stopped inexplicably in mid-verse.

Daniel 9:26 reads:

> After the sixty-two 'sevens', the Anointed One will be cut off and will have nothing. The people of the ruler who will come will destroy the city and the sanctuary. The end will come like a flood: War will continue until the end, and desolations have been decreed.

---

68. Lindsey, *Late Great Planet Earth*, p. 54.
69. Another classic example was Edgar Whisenant, who predicted the return of Christ some time between 11–13 September 1988 in his book *88 Reasons Why the Rapture Will Be in 1988*, pp. 3, 36, 56. The book sold 2 million copies.
70. Lindsey, *Planet Earth 2000 AD*, p. 6.
71. Jeffrey, *Armageddon*, pp. 171–195.
72. Jeffrey, *Messiah*, pp. 137–154.
73. Scofield, *Scofield Bible Correspondence Course*, pp. 45–46.
74. Brickner, *Future Hope*, p. 17.

Brickner claims that the prophecy has not been completely fulfilled. The first half of the verse was fulfilled in AD 70, but apparently one 'seven' of the seventy still remains, in Brickner's words, 'to be played out'. He argues:

> But there seems to be a break in Daniel's countdown; he indicates a time lapse between the sixty-ninth seven and the final seven . . . the past 2000 years have been a parenthesis in Daniel's prophecy and we await that final seven.

Kenneth Barker offers several reasons for the apparent gap of 2,000 years in Daniel's prophecy. His two strongest arguments are based on literalist presuppositions which crumble if they themselves are questioned. First, he suggests that the seventieth 'week' could not have been fulfilled because the results of the Messiah's work outlined in verse 24 have not yet been realized fully. Secondly, the remaining unfulfilled prophecies would be unintelligible unless the 'present church age is regarded as a distinct period of time of unknown duration in God's prophetic program'.[75] The problem with this interpretation is that it assumes there must be a gap because a literal interpretation becomes 'unintelligible' without one. The arbitrary decision to stop the prophetic clock and place a 2,000-year gap between Daniel's sixty-ninth and seventieth week is probably the most eccentric example of a non-literal and unnatural interpretation imposed on the text by those who insist on a literal hermeneutic. Commentators such as John Goldingay regard as flawed attempts to date Daniel's 'weeks' literally, because they try to read this prophecy as a literal chronology instead of what he terms 'chronography'. He argues that Daniel is using 'a stylized scheme of history used to interpret historical data rather than arising from them'. It is, he claims, 'comparable to cosmology, arithmology, and genealogy'.[76]

Lindsey takes a similar approach to the apocalyptic descriptions in the book of Revelation, suggesting that a first-century person would be unable to comprehend scientific developments some 2,000 years later. He claims that John therefore 'had to illustrate them with phenomena of the first century; for

---

75. Kenneth Barker, 'Premillennialism in the Book of Daniel', *Master's Seminary Journal* 4.1 (Spring 1993), p. 36.

76. John E. Goldingay, *Daniel*, Word Biblical Commentary (Milton Keynes: Word, 1991), p. 257. For a fuller critique, see Edward J. Young, *The Prophecy of Daniel* (Grand Rapids: Eerdmans, 1949), pp. 201–221, and Joyce G. Baldwin, *Daniel: An Introduction and Commentary*, Tyndale Old Testament Commentaries (Leicester: IVP, 1978), pp. 172–178.

instance, a thermonuclear war looked to him like a giant volcanic eruption spewing fire and brimstone'. Lindsey argues that the symbolism found in Revelation was the result of 'a first-century man being catapulted in God's time machine up to the end of the twentieth century', then returning and describing what he saw in ways familiar to his own generation.[77] Capitalizing on the 'Bible code' phenomenon, Lindsey described his own form of interpretation as the 'Apocalypse code'. Using this 'key' Lindsey could claim that John's 'locusts' are helicopters; 'horses prepared for battle' are heavily armed attack helicopters; 'crowns of gold' are the helmets worn by pilots; the 'sound of their wings' is the 'thunderous sound of many attack helicopters flying overhead'; and the 'bow' wielded by the Antichrist in Revelation 6:1–2, is actually 'a code for long range weapons like ICBMs'.[78] Lindsey even claims that the reference to the 'colour of fire and of hyacinth and of brimstone' (his own translation) in Revelation 9:17 refers to the 'Chinese national flag . . . emblazoned on the military vehicles'.[79] Extending the use of this code to the rest of the Bible, Lindsey maintains that while references to 'Israel' always mean Israel, other nations mentioned in prophecy require reinterpretation. So, following Darby and Scofield, Lindsey equates ancient tribes and nations mentioned in Old Testament prophecies with contemporary enemies of Israel in the Middle East. For example: 'In Psalm 83, some 3,000 years ago, God gave a warning of what would happen in the last days . . . In these verses the Philistia or Philistines are the modern Palestinians. Tyre is modern Lebanon. Assyria is modern Syria.'[80] It is not always clear, following Lindsey, on what basis a literal interpretation may become a figurative interpretation, other than when it appears to fit a contemporary application more clearly and reinforces his predetermined eschatology.

Contradictory literalism – 200 million Chinese troops or demons?

Dispensationalists claim to use a consistent plain literal interpretation of Scripture, nevertheless, at times they reach very different, and sometimes contradictory, conclusions. For example, in their interpretation of Revelation 9:13–19 and the identity of the 200 million horsemen, DeHaan and Lindsey contradict one another:

---

77. Lindsey, *Israel and the Last Days*, pp. 32–33. This chapter is reused heavily in *Apocalypse Code*, pp. 30–44.
78. Lindsey, *Apocalypse Code*, pp. 42, 72.
79. Lindsey, *Planet Earth 2000 AD*, p. 247.
80. Cf. Darby, 'The Hopes of the Church of God', in *Collected Writings*, vol. 2, Prophetic 1, p. 380; *Scofield Reference Bible*, fn. 1, p. 883; Lindsey, *Final Battle*, p. 2.

M. R. DeHaan (1946)	Hal Lindsey (1973)
'In Revelation 9:13–21 we have a description of an army of two hundred million horsemen . . . seems to be a supernatural army of horrible beings, probably demons, who are permitted to plague the unrepentant sinners on the earth.'[81]	'The four angels of Revelation 9:14–15 will mobilize an army of 200 million soldiers from east of the Euphrates . . . I believe these 200 million troops are Red Chinese soldiers accompanied by other Eastern allies.'[82]

Figure 5. An example of the contradiction between the literal interpretation of Revelation 9 by DeHaan and Lindsey

For DeHaan and also LaHaye, the 200 million are 'a supernatural horde of 200 million demonic horsemen'[83] while for Lindsey and Schuyler English they are literally Chinese soldiers.[84] Lindsey does, however, suggest their 'horses' are symbolic for mobilized ballistic-missile launchers.[85] Each claims his is a 'literal' interpretation of the text. William Hendrikson raises several pertinent questions about this form of hermeneutics in his own commentary on the book of Revelation:

> Do these symbols refer to specific events, single happenings, dates or persons in history? For if they do, then we may well admit that we cannot interpret them. Because among the thousands of dates and events and persons in history that show certain traits of resemblance to the symbol in question, who is able to select the one and only date, event or person that was forecast by this particular symbol? Confusion results. We get thousands of 'interpretations' but no certainty. And the Apocalypse remains a closed book.[86]

Indeed, this form of literalism has been described as a licence for uninhibited,

---

81. M. R. DeHaan, *Revelation: 35 Simple Studies in the Major Themes of Revelation* (Grand Rapids: Zondervan, 1946), p. 148.

82. Lindsey, *There's a New World Coming*, pp. 142–143.

83. LaHaye and Jenkins, *Are We Living in the End Times?*, pp. 190–192.

84. Schuyler English (ed.), *The New Scofield Reference Bible*, p. 1334.

85. Lindsey, *There's a New World Coming*, p. 143.

86. Hendrikson, *More than Conquerors*, pp. 40–41.

'exegetical exploitation'.[87] LaHaye's 12-volume *Left Behind* series, which provides a fictional account of the seven-year period associated with the dispensational rapture and tribulation, has proved very lucrative financially for the authors and the publishers, selling in excess of 32 million copies since 1995. The books have also spawned several films and a 24-volume *Left Behind* series for children.

Enhanced literalism – Gog and Magog are Russia

To assist readers in their understanding of otherwise obscure passages of Scripture, Lindsey and others add words that, although absent in the original biblical text, nevertheless enhance or amplify the interpretation being made. In *The Road to Holocaust*, for example, where Lindsey takes the promises made in Romans 11 and applies them to the contemporary State of Israel, he adds the word 'national' to the text to reinforce his point (p. 176). Similarly, in a quotation of Matthew 24:15–18, Lindsey assists readers to see that this prophecy refers to some future date which requires the rebuilding of the temple, rather than to AD 70 when the Zealots and Romans both desecrated Herod's temple: 'Therefore when you see the Abomination which was spoken of through Daniel the prophet, standing in the holy place [of the rebuilt temple] (let the reader understand), then let those who are in Judea flee to the mountains.'[88] Lindsey's interpretation of Daniel 11:40–45 is similarly imaginative, claiming this depicts 'the Russian-led Islamic invasion of Israel'.

> At the time of the end the King of the South [the Muslim Confederacy] will engage him [the False Prophet of Israel] in battle, and the King of the North [Russia] will storm out against him with chariots and cavalry and a great fleet of ships. He [the Russian Commander] will invade many countries and sweep through them like a flood. He will also invade the Beautiful Land [Israel]. Many countries will fall, but Edom, Moab and the leaders of Ammon [Jordan] will be delivered from his hand.[89]

Lindsey touches here upon one of the most important prophecies within dispensational eschatology. The claim is that 'Gog', also described as the 'Prince of Rosh' and 'Magog', mentioned in Ezekiel 38:15–16, is an enigmatic refer-

---

87. Boone, *Bible Tells Them So*, p. 44.
88. Lindsey, *Apocalypse Code*, p. 78.
89. Lindsey, *Planet Earth 2000 AD*, pp. 182–183.

ence to Russia. John Cumming had suggested this theory in 1864,[90] but it didn't really gain popular recognition until its inclusion within the notes of the *Scofield Reference Bible*. Scofield was probably relying on Gaebelein when he asserts:

> That the primary reference is to the northern (European) powers, headed up by Russia, all agree . . . 'Gog' is the prince, 'Magog' his land. The reference to Meshech and Tubal (Moscow and Tobolsk) is a clear mark of identification. Russia and the northern powers have been the latest persecutors of dispersed Israel, and it is congruous both with divine justice and with the covenants . . . that destruction should fall at the climax of the last mad attempt to exterminate the remnant of Israel in Jerusalem.[91]

Lindsey and other futurists have simply perpetuated the principle begun by Scofield of adding words like 'Russia' to the text to enhance their interpretation. Lindsey insists, 'And you (Russia) will come from your place out of the remote parts of the north, you and many peoples with you.'[92] The suggestion that 'Gog' and 'Magog' refer to Russia, or that, in Scofield's words, 'all agree', is often repeated by other dispensational writers.[93] Tim LaHaye, for example, insists, 'Etymologically, the Gog and Magog of Ezekiel 38 and 39 can only mean modern-day Russia.'[94]

Nevertheless, this interpretation has been discredited by many biblical scholars and etymologists alike.[95] Further evidence against this futurist interpretation is suggested by Gary DeMar who observes that there is no mention of Gog and

---

90. John Cumming, *Destiny of Nations* (London: Hurst and Blackette, 1864). Ernst Wilhelm Hengstenberg replied: 'the poor Russians have been here very unjustly arraigned among the enemies of God's people. Rosh, as the name of a people, does not occur in all the Old Testament' (*Prophecies of the Prophet Ezekiel*, p. 333).

91. *Scofield Reference Bible*, p. 883.

92. Lindsey, *1980's: Countdown*, p. 65.

93. E.g. Jeffrey, *Armageddon*, pp. 98ff. Unlike later dispensationalists such as Scofield, Walvoord and Lindsey, however, Irving believed the reference to 'Gog' in Ezek. 38 to be 'a confederacy of all the nations of the East, which are left from the destruction of the Roman apostasy, which proceedeth this great congregation of nations against Jerusalem spoken of in all the prophets' (Irving, *Last Days*, p. 25).

94. LaHaye and Jenkins, *Are We Living in the End Times?*, p. 86.

95. Yamauchi, *Foes from the Northern Frontier*, pp. 19–27; Ralph H. Alexander, *Ezekiel*, Expositor's Bible Commentary (Grand Rapids, MI: Zondervan, 1986), p. 930; Hengstenberg, *Prophecies of the Prophet Ezekiel*, p. 333.

Magog in Revelation 4 – 19, which dispensationalists claim describes the period of the tribulation when Russia is supposed to attack Israel.[96]

Arbitrary literalism – Islam and America in the Bible
Some advocates of literalism appear rather arbitrary in the way that they apply passages to contemporary events, peoples or places with neither corroboration or consistency. By circular reasoning, it is assumed that since passages must refer to this generation, contemporary terms or nations may be substituted. So Lindsey can claim, 'The God of Israel has sworn in the prophecies that He will not forsake the Israelis, nor let them be destroyed.'[97]

> I know from my study of the Bible that the final great war includes Turkey as part of the Islamic grouping allied with Russia . . . The great nations that do get biblical reference are the Kings of the East (China, India, Pakistan – all openly nuclear), Russia (Gog and Magog), Libya, Egypt, Iran, Iraq and so on.[98]

Without any substantiation, Lindsey claims that the Bible foretold many other recent events including the rise of Muslim fundamentalism, the collapse of the Middle East peace process and the development of the European Community.[99] Similar assertions have been made by others.[100] For example, David Brickner claims, 'we know that Persia is Iran', and that the destruction of Babylon mentioned in Revelation 18 is 'modern day Iraq'.[101] Surprisingly, Scofield rejected the notion that a 'literal Babylon is to be built on the site of ancient Babylon',[102] identifying Babylon symbolically with Rome. Nevertheless,

---

96. DeMar, *Last Days Madness,* pp. 346–352. He notes that the reference to Gog and Magog in Rev. 20:8 occurs after the millennium. He also notes that 'north' in biblical orientation actually referred to the nations of the east which would attack Jerusalem from the north. He also raises the question that if Rosh does refer to Russia, why do not other nations mentioned in biblical prophecy sound like their modern counterparts? John Walvoord's explanation for the reference to Gog and Magog in Rev. 20 is that Russia will make its appearance at the end of the millennium in yet another battle (Walvoord, *Major Bible Prophecies* [New York: Harper Collins, 1991], p. 480).
97. Lindsey, *1980's: Countdown,* p. 45.
98. Lindsey, *Final Battle,* pp. 183, 213.
99. Lindsey, *International Intelligence Briefing,* 7 January 1999.
100. E.g. Dyer, *Rise of Babylon,* p. 198; Jeffrey, *Armageddon,* pp. 185–187.
101. Brickner, *Future Hope,* pp. 70, 73.
102. *Scofield Reference Bible,* fn. 1, p. 1347.

Charles Dyer has popularized a more consistent literal interpretation, arguing Babylon is indeed Babylon. Dyer, a faculty member of Dallas Theological Seminary, traces the rise of Saddam Hussein in Scripture and concludes that Iraq's invasion of Kuwait was depicted in Isaiah 13 as an attempt to set up a powerbase to attack Israel. However, when Isaiah says 'the day of the Lord is near'(13:6), Dyer and other futurists have to reinterpret this. The word 'near' cannot have a literal meaning of 'soon' as it was said over 2,500 years ago. It must, therefore, they believe, refer to the 'end times'. Dyer also saw Saddam Hussein as the successor to Nebuchadnezzar (the only Arab leader ever to defeat Israel). This was because of his hostility to Israel and intention to rebuild Babylon.[103] Irrespective of Hussein's motives, mimicking the past is hardly synonymous with fulfilling prophecy.

Probably most surprising of all, however, is the claim made by several dispensational authors that the United States is mentioned in the Bible.[104] Lindsey appears to have been the first to make this assertion, based on his reading of Revelation 12:14–17: 'The woman was given the two wings of a great eagle, so that she might fly to the place prepared for her in the desert.' Lindsey suggests that this describes 'some massive airlift' that will transport escaping Jewish believers from the holocaust of Armageddon to the safety of places like Petra. He claims that, 'Since the eagle is the national symbol of the United States, it's possible that the airlift will be made available by aircraft from the US Sixth Fleet in the Mediterranean.'[105] Lindsey does not explain why the symbolism of the eagle should necessarily be applied to the United States rather than to any one of a number of countries like Germany or the Czech Republic who also have an eagle as part of their national emblem. Nor does he explain why in this particular passage in Revelation the eagle is a reference to modern aircraft, but not in other passages such as Exodus 19:4, Deuteronomy 32:11–12 and Isaiah 40:31, which also refer to eagles. Such speculative interpretations hardly corroborate Lindsey's claim to hold to a consistent literal hermeneutic.

However, following Scofield's rigid dispensations, Lindsey has also concluded that Christians are not obligated to keep the Ten Commandments because they were given only to the nation of Israel in a previous dispensation.

---

103. Dyer, *Rise of Babylon*; following his literalist interpretation, references to Babylon in the book of Revelation must logically refer to Babylon, that is, modern day Iraq.

104. Noah Hutchings, *U.S. in Prophecy* (Oklahoma City: Hearthstone Publishing, 2000); Hitchcock, *Is America in Prophecy?*; Hal Lindsey, *Where is America in Prophecy?* (video; Murrieta, CA: Hal Lindsey Ministries, 2001).

105. Lindsey, *There's a New World Coming*, p. 185.

He alleges that the early church made a mistake when it tried to impose the law on Gentile believers: 'Israel's failure under the Law serves as an historical lesson to all of us today that religion of all kinds blinds us to the truth.'[106] It is ironic that Lindsey should charge his critics with anti-Semitism when he arbitrarily nullifies the laws which would, if applied, give protection against such racism.

The Bible: a literal futurist hermeneutic assessed

It has been shown that the development of a literal and futurist reading of Scripture and, in particular, the argument that Old Testament references to Israel apply to contemporary Jews and the State of Israel rather than the church, is directly attributable to Irving, Darby and those who attended the Albury and Powerscourt conferences of the 1820s and 1830s. These were given particular expression in Darby's dispensational scheme and then codified and accorded virtually canonical status in the *Scofield Reference Bible*. Sandeen observes that dispensationalism has 'a frozen biblical text in which every word was supported by the same weight of divine authority'.[107] Clarence Bass goes further, insisting:

> No part of historic Christian doctrine supports this radical distinction between church and kingdom. To be sure they are not identical; but Dispensationalism has added the idea that the kingdom was to be a restoration of Israel, not a consummation of the church.[108]

From Hal Lindsey's writings, in particular, it has been demonstrated that in practice literalism is not necessarily any more consistent or free of bias than any other system of hermeneutics: it is actually flexible enough to be adapted to suit changing events; can contradict other literal interpretations; is often assisted as much by eisegesis as exegesis; and can lead to highly speculative but unsubstantiated claims concerning the contemporary fulfilment of biblical prophecy.

As early as 1871, the Princeton theologian Charles Hodge understood the logical consequences of dispensational literalism. From his perspective:

> The argument from the ancient prophecies is proved to be invalid, because it would prove too much. If those prophecies foretell a literal restoration, they foretell that the

---

106. Lindsey, *Road to Holocaust*, pp. 153–154.

107. Ernest R. Sandeen, 'Toward a Historical Interpretation of the Origins of Fundamentalism', *Church History* 36 (1967), 70; cited in Gerstner, *Wrongly Dividing the Word of Truth*, p. 100.

108. Bass, *Backgrounds to Dispensationalism*, p. 31.

temple is to be rebuilt, the priesthood restored, sacrifices again offered, and that the whole Mosaic ritual is to be observed in all its detail.[109]

This is precisely what many contemporary Messianic and apocalyptic dispensationalists believe is foretold in Scripture. However, covenantalists like Hodge argue that the old covenant should be interpreted in the light of the new covenant, not the other way round. In Colossians, for example, Paul actually uses a typological hermeneutic to explain this:

> Therefore do not let anyone judge you by what you eat or drink, or with regard to a religious festival, a New Moon celebration or a Sabbath day. These are a shadow of the things that were to come; the reality, however, is found in Christ. (Col. 2:16–17)

Therefore, the question is not whether the promises of the covenant are to be understood literally or spiritually;[110] it is instead a question of whether they should be understood in terms of old covenant shadow or new covenant reality. The failure to recognize this principle is the basic hermeneutical error which Christian Zionists make and from which flow the other distinctive doctrines that characterize the movement.

Chosen peoples: the relationship between Israel and the church

Christian Zionists believe that the Jews remain God's 'chosen people', enjoying a unique relationship, status and eternal purpose within their own land, separate from any promises made to the church. Irving was one of the first to suggest this. Based on Lacunza's futurist interpretation, Irving predicted:

> When the Lord shall have finished the taking of witness against the Gentiles . . . He will begin to prepare another ark of testimony . . . and to that end will turn his Holy Spirit unto his ancient people, the Jews, and bring them unto those days of refreshing . . . This outpouring of the Spirit is known in scripture as 'the latter rain'.[111]

---

109. Charles Hodge, *Systematic Theology*, 3 vols. (London: James Clarke, [1871] 1960), vol. 3, p. 808.

110. R. T. Kendall, 'How literally do you read your Bible?', *Israel and Christians Today* (Summer 2001), p. 9.

111. Edward Irving, *The Rev. Edward Irving's Preliminary Discourse to the Work of Ben Ezra entitled the Coming of Messiah in Glory and Majesty* (1859 reprint), pp. 5–6.

The belief that God has two chosen peoples has led some Zionists to suggest that they are accepted on the basis of separate covenants; that the status of Israel is superior to the church; that the role of Israel supersedes that of the church; and that, as a consequence, the primary purpose of the church is to 'bless Israel'.

Two chosen peoples: Israel and the church

Darby developed Irving's ideas and taught not only that national Israel would succeed the church, but that God has two separate but parallel means of working in eternity, one through the church, the other through Israel. Darby insisted that this distinction between Israel and the church has resulted in two separate 'callings', the grounds upon which some today teach that Jews can be saved by the Law and Gentiles by grace:

> There are indeed the called from among the nations (namely the church) but it is for the heavens they are called. The calling of God for the earth is never transferred to the nations; it remains with the Jews. If I want an earthly religion, I ought to be a Jew. From the instant that the church loses sight of its heavenly calling, it loses, humanly speaking, all.[112]

This distinction is borne out of Darby's rigid system of dispensations and led him to believe that there could be no future earthly hope for the church since its dispensation was ending, and that the church was simply a 'parenthesis' soon to be replaced on earth by a revived and restored national Israel:

> The Church has sought to settle itself here, but it has no place on the earth . . . [Though] making a most constructive parenthesis, it forms no part of the regular order of God's earthly plans, but is merely an interruption of them to give a fuller character and meaning to them (the Jews).[113]

Darby's depiction of the church as a 'parenthesis' may also have been plagiarized from the pages of the *Morning Watch*, for in June 1831 an article suggested: 'The Christian dispensation is so sparingly mentioned in the

---

112. Darby, 'The Hopes of the Church of God', in *Collected Writings*, vol. 2, Prophetic 1, p. 378.

113. Darby, 'The Character of Office in The Present Dispensation', in *Collected Writings*, vol. 1, Ecclesiastical 1, p. 94.

prophets, that many have considered it as a kind of parenthesis in their discourse.'[114]

However, Darby was not the first to insist on a radical distinction between Israel and the church. In the second century, Marcion had over-emphasized the discontinuity between Judaism and Christianity claiming the Old Testament God was not the New Testament father of Jesus. However, it was Darby who first insisted that 'The Jewish nation is never to enter the Church.'[115]

Scofield elaborated on Darby's distinction between Israel and the church claiming: 'in origin, calling, promise, worship, principles of conduct and future destiny, all is contrast'.[116] Traditionally, historic Christianity has seen some measure of continuity between the old and new covenants, and in the relationship between Israel and the church. Scofield, however, in his 'Introduction to the Four Gospels' insists:

In approaching the study of the gospels, the mind should be freed, so far as possible, from mere theological concepts and presuppositions. Especially is it necessary to exclude the notion – a legacy in Protestant thought from post-apostolic and Roman Catholic theology – that the Church is the true Israel, and that the Old Testament foreview of the kingdom is fulfilled in the Church.[117]

So, in commenting on Matthew 16:18, which Scofield takes to be part of the dispensation of the law and where Jesus promises to 'build my church', Scofield suggests, 'Israel was the true "church" but not in any sense the N.T. church – the only point of similarity being that both were "called out" and by the same God. All else is contrast.'[118] Again, on Acts 7:38, Scofield explains away Stephen's reference to Israel as the church or assembly in the wilderness. He argues: 'Israel in the land is never called a church. In the wilderness Israel was a true church (Gr. *ekklesia* = called-out assembly), but in striking contrast with the N.T. *ekklesia* (Mt. 16:18).'[119]

Scofield claimed to demonstrate, as Darby had done, that ultimately the

---

114. *Morning Watch*, 3 (June 1831), p. 253.9f.; cited in Patterson, *Designing the Last Days*, p. 144.

115. J. N. Darby, *The Hope of the Church of God* (London: G. Morrish, n.d.), p. 106.

116. C. I. Scofield, *Scofield Bible Correspondence Course*, 19th edn (Chicago: Moody Bible Institute, n. d.), p. 23.

117. *Scofield Reference Bible*, p. 989.

118. Ibid., fn. 2, p. 1021.

119. Ibid., fn. 1, p. 1158.

church age will end in failure and apostasy, to be replaced by a revived national Israel who will enjoy the blessings of the final kingdom dispensation. Based on his literalist hermeneutic, Scofield highlighted the different terms used in Scripture for Israel and the church, distinguishing between Israel as the 'earthly wife' of God while the church is the 'heavenly bride' of Christ:

> The N.T. speaks of the Church as a virgin espoused to one husband (2 Cor. 11.1–2); which could never be said of an adulterous wife, restored in grace. Israel is, then, to be the restored and forgiven wife of Jehovah, the Church the virgin wife of the Lamb (John 3.29; Rev. 19.6–8); Israel Jehovah's earthly wife (Hos. 2.23); the Church the Lamb's heavenly bride (Rev. 19.7).[120]

This led Scofield, following Darby, to insist that Israel's eternal inheritance will be on earth, whereas the destiny of the church lies in heaven. Chafer draws out the implications of Scofield's dichotomy between Israel and the church:

> The dispensationalist believes that throughout the ages God is pursuing two distinct purposes: one related to the earth with earthly people and earthly objectives involved, which is Judaism; while the other is related to heaven with heavenly people and heavenly objectives involved, which is Christianity.[121]

For Chafer, 'Israel is an eternal nation, heir to an eternal land, with an eternal kingdom, on which David rules from an eternal throne', so that, in eternity, 'never the twain, Israel and church, shall meet'.[122] Following Scofield and Chafer, Ryrie claims that the 'basic premise of Dispensationalism is two purposes of God expressed in the formation of two peoples who maintain their distinction throughout eternity'.[123] Ryrie justifies this on the basis that, 'When the Church was introduced God did not abrogate His promises to Israel nor enmesh them into the Church.'[124] He argues that such a distinction is 'built on an inductive study of the two words, not a scheme superimposed on the Bible'.[125]

The historical analysis of the rise of dispensationalism would suggest the exact opposite. Nevertheless, various authors have attempted to find analo-

---

120. Ibid., fn. 1, p. 922.
121. Chafer, *Dispensationalism*, p. 107.
122. Chafer, *Systematic Theology*, vol. 4, pp. 315–323.
123. Ryrie, *Dispensationalism*, pp. 44–45.
124. Ibid., pp. 97–98.
125. Ibid.

gies in the Bible that justify this perpetual distinction between Israel and the church. For example, John Hagee, pastor and founder of the 17,000-member Cornerstone Church in San Antonio, Texas, offers an exposition of Genesis 22:17 to illustrate how God has 'two Israels, one physical and one spiritual'. The verse reads: 'I will surely bless you and make your descendants as numerous as the stars in the sky and as the sand on the seashore.' Departing from a literal hermeneutic, Hagee suggests that since God mentions two separate and distinct elements, the stars in the sky and the sand of the seashore, he is referring in dispensational terms to the heavenly church and the earthly Israel:

> Stars are heavenly, not earthly. They represent the church, spiritual Israel. The 'sand of the shore' on the other hand, is earthly and represents an earthly kingdom with a literal Jerusalem as the capital city. Both stars and sand exist at the same time, and neither ever replaces the other. Just so, the nation of Israel and spiritual Israel, the church, exist at the same time and do not replace each other.[126]

Hagee's exposition is undermined by the fact that around 430 BC Nehemiah looked back and thanked God that the promise made to Abraham had already been fulfilled: 'You made their sons as numerous as the stars in the sky' (Neh. 9:23). It may be assumed that Nehemiah had Jewish sons in mind not Gentiles.

Jews for Jesus also affirms the distinction between Israel and the church, but somewhat more tactfully:

> We believe that Israel exists as a covenant people through whom God continues to accomplish His purposes and that the Church is an elect people in accordance with the New Covenant, comprising both Jews and Gentiles who acknowledge Jesus as Messiah and Redeemer.[127]

Nevertheless, the deduction is that God has two 'chosen peoples', 'two Israels' or two 'covenant people' called out of the world in different dispensations. This also implies that they were chosen on the basis of different criteria as well. The question raised by this ultra-literalist hermeneutic, therefore, is not only whether God has one or two 'chosen people' but also whether there is one covenant or two.[128]

---

126. John Hagee, *Final Dawn over Jerusalem* (Nashville: Thomas Nelson, 1998), pp. 108–109.

127. *Statement of Faith* (n.d.) [Internet], Jews for Jesus website, <http:www.jfjonline.org/about/statementoffaith.htm>. [Accessed August 2004.]

128. For a major treatment of this issue, see Holwerda, *Jesus and Israel*.

Two covenants: law, grace and blessing Israel

Covenant premillennialists, as well as progressive dispensationalists, while accepting that God has two 'chosen people', argue that they share in one covenant through faith in Jesus Christ. However, classic, hyper and political dispensationalists, as well as some others, advocate two covenants and, by implication, two ways to salvation.[129] Scofield, for example, suggested salvation by works, when he contrasts the dispensation of the law with the dispensation of grace:

> As a dispensation, grace begins with the death and resurrection of Christ (Rom. 3.24–26; 4.24, 25). The point of testing is no longer legal obedience as the condition of salvation, but acceptance or rejection of Christ . . . The predicted end of the testing of man under grace is the apostasy of the professing church.[130]

For Scofield, 'legal obedience' was a 'condition of salvation'. Lindsey follows Scofield's position, speculating that had the Jewish people accepted Jesus as their Messiah, the rest of the world would not have been offered the gospel: 'The gospel and the age of grace would not have come to us Gentiles unless Israel had fallen into unbelief.'[131] Hagee put it rather more dramatically: 'If the Jewish people had accepted the suffering Messiah, every Gentile would have been forever lost.'[132] Hagee and Lindsey claim that because Israel has a covenant with God, their national redemption will be achieved when Jesus returns and then they will recognize him as their Messiah. Lindsey explains, 'He redeemed the Church (both Jew and Gentile who trusted in Him) at the Cross. That is an accomplished fact. Israel's national redemption in accordance with the Abrahamic covenant takes place at the Second Advent.'[133] The ICEJ shares this viewpoint, distinguishing between 'the former and latter rains' and between the church and 'His Jewish sons and daughters'.[134] It also claims to

---

129. Margaret Brearley, 'Jerusalem in Judaism and for Christian Zionists', in P. W. L. Walker (ed.), *Jerusalem, Past and Present in the Purposes of God* (Croydon: Deo Gloria Trust, 1992), pp. 99–124.

130. *Scofield Reference Bible*, p. 1115; this footnote is substantially modified in *The New Scofield Study Bible*, to stress that salvation is always through faith (p. 1094).

131. Lindsey, *Road to Holocaust*, p. 208.

132. Hagee, *Final Dawn over Jerusalem*, p. 98.

133. Lindsey, *Planet Earth 2000 AD*, p. 98.

134. Patrick Goodenough, 'Jerusalem journalist hits back for Zionists', *Church of England Newspaper*, 4 May 1997.

have 'received a very clear mandate to be extremely cautious' in proclaiming 'God's Word to Zion', which is why ICEJ staff are forbidden to witness to Jews. When asked by a reporter from the *Jerusalem Post* whether the ICEJ was actually a 'covert' missionary organization in Israel, the director Jan Willem van der Hoeven replied emphatically, 'Not so. The Zionist Christians are different. Our objectives are not as you describe. We don't believe in conversion, we don't want to make the Jews into Christians.' He explained that 'The Jewish religion must modify itself in the course of time – but on one point only, the identity of the Messiah . . . they must make the modification as a collective entity.' As fellow dispensationalists affirm, this will occur after the Messiah returns. For this reason, 'Suborning individuals to secede would serve no purpose.'[135]

The ICEJ therefore understands its 'biblical responsibility toward the Jewish people' in terms of bringing material 'comfort' to Israel. It bases this conviction on Isaiah 40:

'Comfort, comfort my people,
    says your God.
Speak tenderly to Jerusalem,
    and proclaim to her
that her hard service has been completed,
    that her sin has been paid for.'
(Isa. 40:1–2)

The ICEJ interprets this passage as mandating political and practical support for Jews, encouraging them to make *aliyah* and settle the land God promised to Abraham, including the Occupied Territories. According to Isaiah 40:2, however, 'comfort' is brought to Israel by explaining how her sins have been atoned for. In 40:9 more explicitly, it is achieved by proclaiming the good news to Zion: 'Here is your God!' A reductionist and materialistic interpretation of this important passage obscures the ultimate comfort for both Jew and Gentile which has been revealed in the incarnation, atonement and resurrection of the Messiah Jesus. Similarly, the ICEJ narrows and Zionizes Matthew 25:40. Jesus explains that on the day of judgment the King will reply, 'I tell you the truth, whatever you did for one of the least of these brothers of mine, you did for me.' The ICEJ reinterprets this as its mandate

---

135. Cited in John S. Ross, 'Beyond Zionism: Evangelical Responsibility Towards Israel', *Mishkan* 1 (1990), 12, p. 17.

for providing material support rather than evangelistic witness to the State of Israel:

> In the same sense that the first apostles were commissioned by the Lord to be his witnesses from Jerusalem to the uttermost parts of the earth, we also feel compelled to proclaim the word of Israel's restoration, and the Christian's response to it, to every country and in every place where there are believers.[136]

The equation of the 'restoration' ministry of the ICEJ with that of the apostolic commission to preach the gospel to the whole world is simply without precedent. Derek Prince, like the ICEJ, invests biblical terms such as 'message' and 'proclaim' with new meaning, redefining the Christian purpose to that of 'blessing Israel':

> Our obligation is to do everything scripture requires of us to help the Jewish people regain the fulness of their God-appointed inheritance, both natural and spiritual. Our message . . . is this: 'He who scattered Israel will gather them' . . . Today, the regathering of Israel is a banner lifted up by God for all nations to see. It is His preordained purpose at this time that all nations be confronted with this message.[137]

Margaret Brearley explains the theological basis for dissociating from what she terms 'missionizing' the Jewish people:

> Because the Jewish people does in some mysterious way bear God's name and witness to his existence and ethical demand . . . Christianity was clearly not designed to replace Judaism; instead . . . there was a continuing covenant with the Jewish people . . . Christians need to learn from observant Jews. Orthodox Judaism, therefore, can be a helpful reminder of what should be (and often was) orthodox in Christianity . . . The Church, God's Gentile worshippers, vitally needs God's Jewish worshippers; for together we are the 'household of God'.[138]

Her argument appears to be the logical deduction of the dispensational distinction between the church and Israel. However, it is unlikely to be one that Orthodox or indeed Reform Jews share. Her assertion that Paul had Judaism in mind when he described the unity Jews and Gentiles shared in 'God's household' in Ephesians 2:19 is entirely unwarranted given the context. In the

---

136. *International Christian Embassy Jerusalem* (Jerusalem: ICEJ, 1993), p. 22.

137. Prince, *Last Word on the Middle East*, pp. 112, 117–118.

138. Brearley, 'Jerusalem in Judaism and for Christian Zionists', p. 121.

preceding verses, Paul explains that this unity is achieved only through Christ's death. In the following verse, Paul also explains that God's household is built on the foundation of the apostles and 'upon Christ Jesus himself as the chief cornerstone', whom the Orthodox Jews had rejected and crucified. Hagee, however, concurs with a two-covenant perspective, suggesting, 'the idea that the Jews of the world are going to convert and storm the doors of Christian churches is a delusion born of ignorance'.[139] In an interview he speculated:

> I believe that every Jewish person who lives in the light of the Torah, which is the word of God, has a relationship with God and will come to redemption . . . In fact trying to convert Jews is a waste of time . . . Jews already have a covenant with God that has never been replaced by Christianity.[140]

Dispensationalists like Scofield, Lindsey, Hagee and the ICEJ, as well as others such as Brearley, therefore disavow 'missionizing' Jewish people, in part because they believe the Jewish people have a separate covenant relationship with God which makes belief in Jesus as Saviour unnecessary or at least not essential until after he returns. Conveniently, it also ensures they receive favoured status as 'Christian' representatives within the State of Israel.

Ironically, it is Messianic believers, while often also dispensationalists, who are among the strongest critics of this position. Organizations such as Christian Witness to Israel, whose origins lie within covenantal premillennialism, together with Jews for Jesus, whose leaders are dispensational, argue for the vital necessity of Jewish evangelism. John Ross, the deputy director of Christian Witness to Israel and a minister of the Free Church of Scotland, has made this assessment of the ICEJ:

> The ICEJ further contradicts its evangelical claims by forbidding Christians involved in its events from any kind of evangelistic activity. Participants in the annual Christian Celebration of the Feast of Tabernacles organized by the Embassy, are instructed in the printed programmes when visiting Jewish homes: 'Please do not leave tracts or attempt to proselytise. This can cause great offence.'[141]

---

139. Hagee, *Final Dawn over Jerusalem*, p. 112.
140. 'San Antonio Fundamentalist battles anti-Semitism', *Houston Chronicle*, 30 April 1988, cited in G. Richard Fisher, *The Other Gospel of John Hagee: Christian Zionism and Ethnic Salvation* (1999) [Internet], Personal Freedom Outreach, <http://www. pfo.org/jonhagee.htm>. [Accessed May 2004.]
141. Ross, 'Beyond Zionism', p. 17.

Louis Goldberg, scholar-in-residence with Jews for Jesus, has also been highly critical of fellow dispensational organizations, such as Bridges for Peace and the ICEJ, for refusing to engage in evangelism.[142] Brickner argues that the disavowal of evangelism among Jews is an even greater evil than anti-Semitism:

> Some Christian Zionists are so eager to be for Israel that they seem to care little about Jews being for Jesus. They are so in love with the idea of Jewish people being in the Land that they don't think of the implications of those same people being outside of Christ . . . God is no more willing to pass over the sins of disobedient Israel today than He was on that first Passover Eve . . . Without the blood of the Lamb on the doorposts of their hearts, modern Israelites are destined for judgement, too. This means that the majority of the people of Israel are in jeopardy. God will judge the unrighteous of the nations and Israel today, just as He did then. There is no automatic pass. Only in Christ is there assurance of lasting safety and peace for the Jewish nation.[143]

True Christian Zionists are, he says, 'unrepentant evangelists of the Jewish people. The rest are frauds and phonies . . . the blood of Israel will be on their hands.' Although Brickner forcefully repudiates dispensationalists who have dispensed with evangelism, there is a sense in which even he and other Messianic dispensationalists still affirm another way to God for Jewish people. According to Brickner, there remains hope for those unbelievers who miss the rapture but survive Armageddon and are alive when Jesus returns. After the rapture of the church, during the millennium all nations, he claims, will come to worship God in Jerusalem.[144]

Israel has a superior status to the church

By regarding the church as a digression from God's continuing purposes for Israel, it is hard for dispensationalists not to elevate Israel to a superior status above the church. Brickner, for example, following Darby's own dispensational terminology, regards the last two-thousand-year history of the church

---

142. See Louis Goldberg, 'Historical and Political Factors in the Twentieth Century Affecting the Identity of Israel', in House (ed.), *Israel, the Land and the People*, pp. 113–141. Goldberg was formerly professor of theology and Jewish studies at the Moody Bible Institute.

143. David Brickner, 'Don't Pass Over Israel's Jubilee', Jews for Jesus, Newsletter (April 1998.

144. Brickner, *Future Hope*, p. 94.

as merely 'a parenthesis'[145] to God's future plans for the Jews. He concedes that to regard Israel as 'God's chosen people, the apple of his eye – his special one', appears ethnocentric and even arrogant. Nevertheless, his biblical absolutism leads him to insist God is the 'God of Israel' and has his own reasons for using 'a small and seemingly insignificant people to be his light of the world'.[146]

Ironically, while dispensationalists like Brickner follow Darby's differentiation between Israel and the church, and elevate contemporary Israel to a superior status above the church, Darby himself had no desire to do so, believing that, while in this dispensation the church had failed, Israel as a political entity had no significance either, at least until after the rapture. Content with heaven, he wrote dismissively, 'If I want an earthly religion, I ought to be a Jew.'[147] Nevertheless, contemporary dispensationalists and, indeed, many covenant premillennialists believe the promises originally made to Abraham are unconditional, eternal and exclusively reserved for the physical descendants of Isaac, Jacob and Joseph. Therefore, Israel today is truly blessed. Christian Friends of Israel, for example, insists:

> We believe the Lord Jesus is both Messiah of Israel and Saviour of the world; however, our stand alongside Israel is not conditional upon her acceptance of our belief. The Bible teaches that Israel (people, land, nation) has a Divinely ordained and glorious future, and that God has neither rejected nor replaced His Jewish people.[148]

Anne Dexter of the CMJ even suggests that Jewish people who have rejected Jesus are still in a more advantageous position than Gentiles:

> Gentiles never were a covenant people. Talk of a new covenant replacing an old one is meaningless to them. Promises of God's law written upon a renewed heart are, logically, only for those already committed to the Sinai law . . . The Jews never cease to be the covenant people but, by rejecting Jesus, they simply stay in the earlier stage of revelation of the kings and prophets, there to remain until the time when all Israel will be saved.[149]

---

145. Ibid., pp. 18, 130; Darby, 'The Character of Office in The Present Dispensation', in *Collected Writings*, vol. 1, Ecclesiastical 1, p. 94.

146. Brickner, *Future Hope*, p. 96.

147. Darby, 'The Hopes of the Church of God', in *Collected Writings*, vol. 2, Prophetic 1, p. 379.

148. Christian Friends of Israel, *Standing with Israel* (information leaflet, n.d.).

149. Anne Dexter, 'The Eternal Covenant', *Shalom* (February 1990), p. 11.

Dexter argues that since the unconditional covenant with the Jews was made prior to the cross, it was not annulled by it either. Such a view is at variance with the views of Jesus, who drew a distinction between those who had not heard of him and those who had rejected him: 'If you were blind, you would not be guilty of sin; but now that you claim you can see, your guilt remains' (John 9:41). John Fieldsend makes claims similar to Dexter's. In referring to Romans 9 – 11 and the 'mystery' mentioned in Ephesians 3:6, he argues:

> The revealed mystery is NOT that through the gospel Jews and Gentiles become
> heirs together of the grace of God but that, through the gospel 'the Gentiles become
> HEIRS TOGETHER WITH ISRAEL'. If physical Israel is disinherited, then there is
> no inheritance for the Gentiles to share in.[150]

The ICEJ goes further, equating the ancient Hebrew nation with the contemporary State of Israel. The Jewish people, the ICEJ claims, 'remain elect of God, and without the Jewish nation His redemptive purposes for the world will not be completed'.[151] Covenant theologians assert that Gentiles are indeed heirs together with Jewish people in the grace of God, but only in new covenant terms. It is because when Christ died on the cross, he completed the work of redemption and broke down the wall of separation between Jew and Gentile.[152]

Israel will succeed the church

While Christian Zionists generally afford Israel a special status above the church, dispensationalists also believe Israel will succeed the church. So it is ironic that they accuse covenantalists of perpetrating a 'replacement theology' for suggesting the church has replaced Israel.

Hal Lindsey goes further and accuses those who reject dispensationalism of encouraging anti-Semitism for denying a role for the State of Israel in God's future purposes. He claims covenant theology is the basis for 'the same error that founded the legacy of contempt for the Jews and ultimately led to the Holocaust of Nazi Germany'.[153] However, it may be argued that it is dispensa-

---

150. John Fieldsend, 'Prophecy a Dual Dimension', *Shalom* 1 (1992) (*emphasis in the original*).

151. 'International Christian Zionist Congress Proclamation', International Christian Embassy Jerusalem, 25–29 February 1996.

152. Motyer, *Look to the Rock*, pp. 39–62; Holwerda, *Jesus and Israel*, pp. 147–176; this is the entire thesis of the book of Hebrews.

153. Lindsey, *Road to Holocaust*, back page.

tionalists who advocate a replacement theology in that they claim the church is only a parenthesis to God's continuing purposes for national Israel. Many dispensationalists believe that with the founding of the State of Israel in 1948 and the reunification of Jerusalem in 1967 under exclusive Israeli control, the 'church age' or 'dispensation of grace' came to an end or is at least nearly over. They believe Christians will soon be secretly raptured to heaven and the Jewish people will become the centre of divine government in the world during the millennium.[154] Before then the purpose of the church, they claim, is to serve and 'bless Israel'.

Christians are blessed in association with Israel

One of the most frequently misquoted passages in Christian Zionist literature is Genesis 12:3, where God promised Abraham, 'I will bless those who bless you, and whoever curses you will I curse.' Although the context does not suggest that the promise applied to future generations, Scofield nevertheless claims Gentiles today are thereby blessed in association with Israel:[155]

> 'I will bless them that bless thee.' In fulfilment closely related to the next clause, 'And curse him that curseth thee.' Wonderfully fulfilled in the history of the dispersion. It has invariably fared ill with the people who have persecuted the Jew – well with those who have protected him. The future will still more remarkably prove this principle.[156]

Dispensationalists have subsequently insisted that God promises that those who bless his earthly people will themselves be blessed, while those who curse the Jews will be cursed. The notion that Gentiles are 'blessed in association with Israel' is the principal motivation for the ICEJ, which believes Christian Zionists are called to 'comfort Zion' rather than bear witness to Jesus as Messiah. The declaration made at the ICEJ Third International Zionist Congress held in 1996 included the resolution: 'The Lord in His zealous love for Israel and the Jewish People blesses and curses peoples and judges nations based upon their treatment of the Chosen People of Israel.'[157]

Allan MacRae claims that history is full of examples of this: 'The fate of the nations that have injured Israel is a terrible warning that God never goes

---

154. *Scofield Reference Bible*, pp. 724–725.

155. Ibid.

156. Ibid., fn. 3, p. 25.

157. 'International Christian Zionist Congress Proclamation', International Christian Embassy Jerusalem, 25–29 February 1996.

back on His promises. From Haman to Hitler, history shows how dangerous it is to hate His chosen people.'[158] Hagee concurs: 'The man or nation that lifts a voice or hand against Israel invites the wrath of God.' He illustrates this by pointing out that because Great Britain voted against the founding of the State of Israel in 1948, and British officers led the Arab armies that attacked Israel, Britain is 'now a very small kingdom'.[159] Hagee does not comment on the fact that in 1948 the US government was just as opposed to the founding of the State of Israel. Nevertheless, Basilea Schlink pronounces anathemas on those who question Israel's expansionist agenda: 'Anyone who disputes Israel's right to the land of Canaan is actually opposing God and his holy covenant with the Patriarchs. He is striving against sacred, inviolable words and promises of God, which He has sworn to keep.'[160]

There is, however, no indication in the text of Genesis 12 that this promise of blessing and warning of cursing was ever intended to extend beyond Abraham. The promise, when referring to Abraham's descendants speaks of God blessing them, not of entire nations 'blessing' the Hebrew nation, still less the contemporary and secular State of Israel. Furthermore, in Galatians, Christ is portrayed as the 'seed' of Abraham, and the promise of blessing is offered to Gentiles not on the basis of how well they treat the Jews but on whether they have responded to Jesus Christ.[161]

Chosen people: the relationship assessed

In his autobiography, Arno Gaebelein expresses the frustration of many dispensationalists with the covenantal view concerning the relationship between Israel and the church. In so doing, however, he reveals the deep-seated dispensational conviction that for Jews God's plan for them to return to the land is somehow more important than believing Jesus is their Messiah. Speaking of covenantal theology, he laments: 'Israel, that method teaches, is no longer the Israel of old, but it means the Church now. For the natural Israel no hope of a future restoration is left. All their glorious and unfulfilled promises find now their fulfilment in the Church of Jesus Christ.'[162] John Gerstner wryly

158. Allan A. MacRae, 'Hath God Cast Away His People?', in Charles L. Feinberg (ed.), *Prophetic Truth Unfolding Today* (Westwood, NJ: Revell, 1968), p. 95.

159. Hagee, *Final Dawn over Jerusalem*, p. 37.

160. Schlink, *Israel, My Chosen People*, p. 22.

161. Gal. 3:14–16, 24–25.

162. Arno C. Gaebelein, *Half a Century* (New York: Publication Office of Our Hope, 1930), p. 20.

observes: 'This certainly does make it hard on the Jews! When they might have had a glorious piece of real estate on the Mediterranean, all they end up with under this interpretation is Christ.'[163]

The idea that the Jewish people continue to enjoy a special status by virtue of the covenants made with the Patriarchs is in conflict with the clear and unambiguous statements of the New Testament.[164] For example, soon after the Day of Pentecost, Peter warned his Jewish audience that if they persisted in refusing to recognize Jesus as their Messiah, they would cease to be the people of God: 'Anyone who does not listen to him [Christ] will be completely cut off from among his people' (Acts 3:23). The New Testament repudiates the notion that the Jewish people continue to enjoy a special status or relationship with God, apart from faith in Jesus Christ. Christian Zionists also fail to realize that in the Bible 'chosenness' is the gift of God's grace in Jesus Christ to all who trust in him, irrespective of their racial origins.[165]

The term 'chosen' is never used in the New Testament exclusively of the Jewish people, apart from as members of the church of Jesus Christ who are the 'chosen ones'.[166] This is explicitly taught in Galatians 4, where unbelieving Jews are described as the descendants of Hagar and Ishmael:

> Tell me, you who want to be under the law, are you not aware of what the law says? For it is written that Abraham had two sons, one by the slave woman and the other by the free woman. His son by the slave woman was born in the ordinary way; but his son by the free woman was born as the result of a promise.
>
> These things may be taken figuratively, for the women represent two covenants. One covenant is from Mount Sinai and bears children who are to be slaves: This is Hagar. Now Hagar stands for Mount Sinai in Arabia and corresponds to the present city of Jerusalem, because she is in slavery with her children. But the Jerusalem that is above is free, and she is our mother . . . Now you, brothers, like Isaac, are children of promise. (Gal. 4:21–28)

The promises made to Abraham, Isaac, Jacob and Joseph are therefore now to be understood as fulfilled through those who demonstrate the faith of Abraham and follow Jesus Christ, for they alone are designated the true children

---

163. Gerstner, *Wrongly Dividing the Word of Truth,* 2nd edn (Morgan, PA: Soli Deo Gloria, 2000), p. 45.

164. Luke 3:8–9; John 5:39–40; 8:39, 44; 14:6.

165. Eph. 1:11; Col. 3:12; 1 Pet. 2:9–10.

166. See Robertson, *Israel of God.*

of Abraham and Sarah. Jews who reject Jesus Christ are outside the covenant of grace and are, indeed, now to be regarded as children of Hagar. Paul takes Sarah's words of Genesis 21:10 and applies them to the Judaizers who were corrupting the faith of the church in Galatia: 'Get rid of the slave woman and her son, for the slave woman's son will never share in the inheritance with the free woman's son' (Gal. 4:30).

This may be further illustrated by the way Jesus annulled the Levitical food laws: '"Don't you see that nothing that enters a man from the outside can make him 'unclean'? For it doesn't go into his heart but into his stomach, and then out of his body." (In saying this, Jesus declared all foods "clean")' (Mark 7:18–19). A vision of unclean food is specifically used by God to help the apostle Peter realize that in Christ there is now no longer any distinction between Jew and Gentile. Both are accepted as equal in the kingdom of God:

> He saw heaven opened and something like a large sheet being let down to earth by its four corners. It contained all kinds of four-footed animals, as well as reptiles of the earth and birds of the air. Then a voice told him, 'Get up, Peter. Kill and eat.'
>
> 'Surely not, Lord!' Peter replied. 'I have never eaten anything impure or unclean.'
>
> The voice spoke to him a second time, 'Do not call anything impure that God has made clean.' (Acts 10:11–15)

Only when Peter encounters Cornelius does he begin to understand the implications of the vision for the way he should now view Jews and Gentiles: 'I now realise how true it is that God does not show favouritism but accepts men from every nation who fear him and do what is right' (Acts 10:34–35). If, to use Peter's words, 'God does not show favouritism' from a Christian perspective, it cannot logically be presumed that Jews continue to enjoy a favoured or exclusive status. It is therefore no longer appropriate for Christians to designate the Jewish people as God's 'chosen people' since the term has now been universalized to embrace all who trust in Jesus Christ, irrespective of race. The followers of Jesus Christ are Abraham's children according to promise. Bass summarizes the reasons why Darby's dispensational distinction between Israel and the church, so central to Christian Zionism, may be seen as heresy:

> It is not that exegetes prior to his time did not see a covenant between God and Israel, or a future relation of Israel to the millennial reign, but they always viewed the church as a continuation of God's single program of redemption begun in Israel. It is Dispensationalism's rigid insistence on a distinct cleavage between Israel and the

church, and its belief in a later unconditional fulfilment of the Abrahamic covenant, that sets it off from the historic faith of the church.[167]

The dispensational insistence that Israel continues to enjoy a special covenant relationship with God is, however, translated into Christian support for restorationism and the State of Israel.

Restorationism: the return of the Jews to Zion

From the early nineteenth century, Lewis Way, Joseph Wolff, Hugh McNeile and others associated with the London Jews' Society and the prophecy conferences held at Albury and Powerscourt, shared similar convictions concerning the restoration of the Jewish people. Based on their literalist reading of the Bible they held the view that since the Jews remained God's chosen people, God had given them the land of Canaan in perpetuity; that the prophets promised God would restore them to their land, never to disperse them again; and the prophetic signs indicated this would happen imminently. The consensus, prior to 1880, was that restoration to the land would follow restoration to the Lord, and that Israel would be a Christian nation. Hugh McNeile, like Charles Simeon, held this view.[168] Scofield, however, like Hechler, suggested that restoration to the land would occur before Israel's conversion and only after the Lord had returned.[169] From 1881, as waves of Jewish people began to emigrate to Palestine, Christian Zionists began to favour the latter explanation and modified their eschatology to take account of the fact that Jewish people were returning to the land of Palestine in unbelief.

Having established that the Jewish people would eventually return to Palestine in fulfilment of prophecy, there was, however, little agreement as to why they would return, let alone where they would be found, since the ten northern tribes were considered lost following their exile and dispersion throughout the Assyrian Empire. Once these questions had been resolved, a more rigorous theological basis for restorationism emerged, which led Christian Zionists actively to encourage and help facilitate Jewish people in the *diaspora* to make *aliyah* and return to Palestine.

---

167. Bass, *Backgrounds to Dispensationalism*, p. 27.
168. See ibid., p. 67. Charles Simeon also held this view; see Simeon, 'Gentiles blest by the Jews' Restoration', *Horae Homileticae*, vol. 15, pp. 416, 419.
169. *Scofield Reference Bible*, fn. 1, p. 250.

Why the Jewish people would return to Zion

Christian Zionists have, at various times, speculated on a variety of reasons why the Jewish people would return to Palestine. In 1828, for example, Irving suggested that the last days 'will begin to run from the time of God's appearing for his ancient people, and gathering them together to the work of destroying all Antichristian nations, of evangelising the world, and of governing it during the Millennium'. Irving saw the restoration of the Jewish people as a means of God's judging the 'Antichristian' nations. Darby took a rather different approach, believing dispensationally that the Jews would be restored to rule the earth in league with Satan. Darby insisted that after the rapture of the saints:

> Under the influence and direction of the Antichrist . . . the Jews will unite themselves to him, in a state of rebellion, to make war with the Lamb . . . Satan will then be displayed, who will unite the Jews with this apostate prince against heaven . . . a remnant of the Jews is delivered and Antichrist destroyed.[170]

Scofield took a more positive approach, suggesting, 'According to the prophets, Israel, regathered from all nations, restored to her own land, and converted, is yet to have her greatest earthly exaltation and glory.'[171] This is closer to the position taken by Simeon, one of the early leaders of the LJS, who insisted that from a covenantal premillennial position the restoration of the Jews would be related to 'their union with the Gentiles in one universal Church'. He went on to argue that 'both these events will take place together, or in the nearest connection'.[172]

Crombie, in the most recent and comprehensive history of the CMJ, ignores Simeon's view and insists to the contrary, 'From its inception in 1809, the LJS [the original name for the CMJ] had advocated the physical restoration of Israel prior to its spiritual restoration.'[173] While all may have been convinced that the return of the Jewish people to Palestine was imminent and predicted in the Bible, there was clearly no consensus as to why this would happen; what the

---

170. Darby, 'The Hopes of the Church of God', in *Collected Writings*, vol. 2, Prophetic 1, p. 379.
171. *Scofield Reference Bible*, fn. 1, p. 1206.
172. Simeon, 'Conversion of the Jews and Gentiles', *Horae Homileticae*, vol. 10, p. 240; 'Conversion of the Jews Gradual', *Horae Homileticae*, vol. 8, pp. 10–14.
173. Kelvin Crombie, *For the Love of Zion: Christian Witness and the Restoration of Israel* (London: Hodder & Stoughton, 1991), p. 163.

connection was between Israel and the church; between repentance and restoration; or between a secular Jewish State and a remnant of Jewish believers.

Finding the Jewish people to return to Zion

The preoccupation of the later Albury conferences and of Joseph Wolff especially, became the quest to find the 'lost tribes' of Israel, so necessary if a complete restoration to Palestine was to occur. In 1822, George Faber spoke at the annual meeting of the LJS. His talk focused on the dating of the termination of the 'Times of the Gentiles' and on the restoration of the Jewish people.[174] A report was also received that Jews had been discovered in India and China and this caused great interest. Apparently, they longed to return to Palestine. McNeile assured: 'They think that the time of His appearance will soon arrive, at which they much rejoice, believing that at Jerusalem they will see their God, worship Him only, and be despised no more.'[175] After another report was received at the 1828 Albury conference, McNeile assessed its significance:

> The number of scattered members of the tribe of Judah and the half-tribe of Benjamin, rather exceeds than falls short of five millions. Now, if to this number be added the many other millions to be found in the different countries in the East, what an immense power would be brought into action were the spirit of the nationality once aroused.[176]

As travel beyond Europe gradually improved through the nineteenth century, and as anti-Semitic pogroms in Russia and Eastern Europe caused increasing numbers of Jews to flee, the sense of urgency for their restoration to Palestine grew.

The theological basis for restorationism

Like Irving and Darby, Scofield taught that it was God's intention to restore the Jewish people to Palestine. His Bible notes provide the most detailed explanation of the basis for the Jewish restoration. To justify his dispensational scheme and a glorious future for Israel in the 'kingdom age', Scofield claimed that 'the gift of the land is modified by prophecies of three dispossessions and restorations'. He

---

174. See Hugh McNeile, *The Collected Works, Vol. 2: The Prophecies Relative to the Jewish Nation* (London: Christian Book Society, [1830, 1866] 1878), Preface to 1866 edition; see also, George Stanley Faber, *A Treatise on the Genius and Object of the Patriarchal, the Levitical and the Christian Dispensations*, 2 vols. (London: F. C. & J. Rivington, 1823).

175. McNeile, *Collected Works*, vol. 2, p. 434.

176. Ibid., p. 435.

goes on to argue that since two dispossessions and restorations had been accomplished, Israel as a nation was now in a third dispersion, 'from which she will be restored at the return of the Lord as King under the Davidic Covenant'.[177] Scofield's argument for a third return is based on two deductions that follow from his literalist hermeneutic: first, that Israel had never taken all the land promised to Abraham, and secondly, that not all the Messianic promises had been fulfilled during the first advent. In linking these two together, Scofield speculated that the return to the land would follow, not precede, the return of the Messiah.[178] In the note accompanying Deuteronomy 30:1–9, for example, Scofield delineates seven parts to this process under the heading 'The Palestinian Covenant':

(1) Dispersion for disobedience, v. 1 (Deut. 28:63–68; Gen. 15:18).
(2) The future repentance of Israel while in the dispersion, v. 2.
(3) The return of the Lord, v. 3 (Amos 9:9–14; Acts 15:14–17).
(4) Restoration to the land, v. 5 (Isa. 11:11; Jer. 23:3–8; Ezk. 37:21–25).
(5) National conversion, v. 6 (Rom. 11:26, 27; Hos. 2:14–16).
(6) Th(e judgement of Israel's oppressors, v. 7 (Isa. 14:1, 2; Mt. 25:31–46).
(7) National prosperity, v. 9 (Amos 9:11–14).[179]

Schuyler English, in *The New Scofield Reference Bible* revision of 1967, consistently adds to Scofield's original notes to give a more explicit dispensational reading of key texts. In many cases, references to contemporary Israel are appended to verses on which Scofield originally made no comment at all. For example, on Deuteronomy 30:5, Schuyler English adds the following innovative textual note:

No passage of scripture has found fuller confirmation in the events of history than Dt. 28 – 30. In AD 70 the Jewish nation was scattered throughout the world because of disobedience and rejection of Christ. In world-wide dispersion they experienced exactly the punishments foretold by Moses. On the other hand, when the nation walked in conformity with the will of God, it enjoyed the blessing and protection of God. In the twentieth century the exiled people were restored to their homeland.[180]

Inexplicably, Scofield's original chronology in which the Lord returns before

177. *Scofield Reference Bible*, note, p. 25.
178. Ibid., fn. 1, p. 250.
179. Ibid.
180. Schuyler English (ed.), *The New Scofield Reference Bible*, p. 217.

Israel is restored, which is retained by Schuyler English, is nevertheless contradicted by the final sentence he adds to the footnote.[181] No explanation is given for the apparent contradiction between Israel's continued 'disobedience and rejection of Christ' and their restoration 'to their homeland'.

Scofield's claim that Israel never possessed all the land promised to Abraham, contradicts claims made by Joshua and Nehemiah.[182] The compiler of the book of Joshua insists, 'So Joshua took the entire land, just as the LORD had directed Moses' (Josh. 11:23). At the end of the book of Joshua, the same assessment is repeated but more emphatically: 'So the LORD gave Israel all the land he had sworn to give their forefathers, and they took possession of it and settled there . . . Not one of all the LORD's good promises to the house of Israel failed; every one was fulfilled' (21:43–45). It is hard to see how this fulfilment can be reconciled with the ultra-literal futurist claims of dispensationalists. Neither Scofield nor Schuyler English comment on either passage in Joshua.

Scofield, like other dispensationalists since, based his belief in a third restoration on Ezekiel 37 and the vision of the valley of the dry bones.[183] Following the publication of the Balfour Declaration, for example, a CMJ editorial of 1918 was one of the first to assert that a Jewish State would be the fulfilment of Ezekiel's vision:

> We believe we are actually seeing that come to pass which was prophesied by Ezekiel (ch. 37) viz., the movement amongst the 'dry bones' of Israel, bone is uniting with bone . . . The uniting element being the possibility in the very near future of their being allowed to organise a Jewish State in their own God-given country of Palestine.[184]

With the benefit of hindsight, Lindsey elaborates on this, using capitals for emphasis in case his readers miss the plot:

> Ezekiel 37:7–8 . . . is phase one of the prophecy which predicts the PHYSICAL RESTORATION of the Nation without Spiritual life which began May 14, 1948 . . . Ezekiel 37:9–10 . . . is phase two of the prophecy which predicts the SPIRITUAL REBIRTH of the nation AFTER they are physically restored to the land as a nation . . . The Lord identifies the bones in the allegory as representing 'the whole house of

---

181. Ibid., p. 217.
182. Josh. 11:23; 21:43–45; Neh. 9:22–23.
183. *Scofield Reference Bible*, fn. 1, p. 881.
184. Kelvin Crombie, 'CMJ and the Restoration of Israel', *Shalom* 1 (1998).

Israel'. It is crystal clear that this is literally predicting the restoration and rebirth of the whole nation at the time of Messiah's coming [Ezekiel 37:21–27].[185]

It is difficult to conceive how such an entirely futuristic interpretation would have brought comfort to the Jewish exiles in Babylon to whom Ezekiel was sent to minister, yet this and similar passages provide the motivation for the restorationist movement today.

Bridges for Peace and Exobus, for example, both use the term 'fishing' to describe their outreach to Jewish people, based on Jeremiah 16:16, "'But now I will send for many fishermen," declares the LORD, "and they will catch them."'[186] Zionists use this passage as a 'carrot and stick', reminding Jews that the verse goes on to warn how God will also send hunters, 'and they will hunt them down on every mountain and every hill and from the crevices of the rocks'. Jewish people in the *diaspora* are encouraged to return to Israel but also warned that if they delay, further persecution is predicted:

> The time to 'fish' these Jews back to Israel is now! God says that He will send for 'fishers and hunters' (Jeremiah 16:16). These 'fishers' are at work right now in the CIS, calling the Jews home to Israel. We need to assist these laborers wherever possible – through our prayers, our giving, or going ourselves – to urgently summon them back, for we see the anti-Semitic hunters rearing their ugly heads. The time is short! The gates to the CIS could soon slam shut, preventing Jews from leaving.[187]

The context of the verse, however, clearly indicates that Jeremiah is comparing an impending return to the land with the Exodus from Egypt, not with two previous returns. Furthermore both 'fishermen' and 'hunters' are terms used to describe a conquering army. In the next verse, Jeremiah explains why God was going to send them: 'My eyes are on all their ways; they are not hidden from me, nor is their sin concealed from my eyes. I will repay them double for their wickedness and their sin, because they have defiled my land' (Jer. 16:17). In this passage, therefore, the fishermen were not being sent to rescue but to discipline. Only after Israel had repented of their previous sins in the land was there any prospect of a return to it.

---

185. Lindsey, *Road to Holocaust*, p. 180 (*emphasis in the original*).

186. Patricia Golan, 'On Wings of Faith', *Jerusalem Post*, 13 January 2002.

187. *The Aliyah (Immigration) Miracle Continues* (n.d.) [Internet], Bridges for Peace website, <http://www.bridges for peace.com/modules.php?name=News&file=article& sid=1012>. [Accessed August 2004.]

This arbitrary and futurist interpretation is one of many examples in which dispensationalists mishandle biblical texts concerning the exile and restoration in order to maintain their dispensational scheme. The prophets, while warning of judgment and chastisement, also offered the promise of return and this was fulfilled under Zerubbabel, Ezra and Nehemiah. However, Scofield and Lindsey insist promises such as those made by Jeremiah and Ezekiel refer to a third return thousands of years later, on the premise that certain Messianic aspects have not yet been fulfilled literally and completely.

Scofield also claims that two passages in the New Testament speak of this third return: Luke 1:30–33 and Acts 15:13–17. He dwells on the latter in which James simply quotes from Amos to show that Pentecost had been predicted long ago, promising that Gentiles would also seek the Lord along with Jews:

'After this I will return
    and rebuild David's fallen tent.
Its ruins I will rebuild,
    and I will restore it,
that the remnant of men may seek the Lord,
    and all the Gentiles who bear my name,
says the Lord, who does these things'
    that have been known for ages. (Acts 15:16–18)

For Scofield, 'dispensationally, this is the most important passage in the NT', since, he claims, 'It gives the divine purpose for this age, and for the beginning of the next.'[188] However, he reads considerably more into this passage than is there and obscures its most obvious and direct meaning. Scofield interprets the 'after this' not simply as meaning 'after James' or even 'after Pentecost', but after a further 1,900 years. At that time God would 'rebuild the tabernacle of David' in a literal and permanent return of Jewish people to the land. In doing so, Scofield ignores the fact that James is simply appealing to Amos to vindicate the universality of the gospel and the results of the first-century Gentile mission. If this is seen as 'spiritualizing' the Old Testament text, then it must be acknowledged that it is James who does so.[189] Using the passage to teach a predetermined and futuristic plan for national Israel, separate from the church, appears to be the opposite of what James intended. Scofield and Schuyler English thereby undermine the intention of the New Testament to show that

---

188. *Scofield Reference Bible*, fn. 1, pp. 1169–1170.
189. See Fuller, *Gospel and Law*, p. 180.

Jews and Gentiles are now united in Jesus Christ and members together of the one church.

Lindsey takes the same approach with the analogy of the 'fig tree' in Matthew 24. Whereas first-century Christians understood Jesus to be warning them to observe the signs and flee Jerusalem when the city came under Roman siege, Lindsey reverses its meaning. He claims Jesus was predicting the restoration of the Jews to Palestine in the twentieth century rather than their departure in the first century:

> But the most important sign in Matthew has to be the restoration of the Jews to the land in the rebirth of Israel. Even the figure of speech 'fig tree' has been a historic symbol of national Israel. When the Jewish people, after nearly 2,000 years of exile, under relentless persecution, became a nation again on 14 May 1948 the 'fig tree' put forth its first leaves.[190]

Nothing in Matthew 24, however, indicates that Jesus intended his hearers to understand that he was promising that Israel would become a nation state once more. The New Testament is silent on the question. Nevertheless, Lindsey has popularized the notion that the return of Jewish people to Palestine since 1948 is the fulfilment of biblical prophecy. Lindsey speaks repeatedly of the 'rebirth' of Israel, insisting, 'The nation of Israel cannot be ignored; we see the Jews as a miracle of history . . . all the unconditional covenants . . . were made only with the physical descendants of Abraham, Isaac and Jacob as a unique nation.'[191]

Nowhere, however, is a third re-gathering to the land explicitly mentioned in the Bible. Each passage quoted by Scofield or Lindsey refers either to the first or second re-gathering to the land, or, as in Amos 9, to Pentecost. It is significant that, following the rebuilding of Solomon's temple in 516 BC there are no further biblical references to any further return to the land. For example, when Paul lists the present benefits that still pertain to the Jewish people in Romans 9, he does not mention the land or kingdom as one of them.

More conclusive, however, are the categorical statements made by Jesus in which he specifically rules out any notion that Israel would enjoy a divinely mandated national identity as a kingdom in the future: 'Therefore I tell you that the kingdom of God will be taken away from you and given to a people who will produce its fruit' (Matt. 21:43). Indeed, Jesus insists that the subjects of the kingdom, that is, unbelieving Jews, will be 'thrown outside' (Matt. 8:10–12);

---

190. Lindsey, *Late Great Planet Earth*, p. 53.
191. Ibid., p. 45; Lindsey, *Road to Holocaust*, p. 186.

none of those who were originally invited 'will get a taste of my banquet' (Luke 14:15–24); that the vineyard will be rented 'to other tenants'; to 'a people who will produce its fruit'; to those who will come from the 'roads and country lanes'; from 'the east and west and will take their places at the feast with Abraham, Isaac, and Jacob in the kingdom of heaven'. Gerstner interprets this as signalling:

> the end of the nation of Israel as the chosen people of God. They have been tried and found wanting. God's patience has been exhausted. If there were any doubts about that being the obvious meaning of the words, the parable on which they are based would utterly eliminate any lingering procrastination.[192]

R. T. France argues that 'a people' (Greek *ethnos*) suggests not just a change of leadership, but that the very composition of the people of God was to change: a new community in which both Jews and Gentiles would find their place.[193] However, Ryrie appears to reverse the intention of the text to fit a dispensational framework. He asserts: 'The kingdom of God shall be taken from you (leaders of Israel), and given to a nation (Israel) bringing forth the fruits thereof.'[194] Schuyler English in *The New Scofield Study Bible* repeats this dubious interpretation (p. 1005).

Based on biblical passages such as these, covenantal theologians argue that there is no theological significance to the founding of the State of Israel in 1948.[195] This has, nevertheless, not hindered Christian Zionists from encouraging and facilitating the emigration of Jewish people to Israel from Russia and Eastern Europe.

Restorationism assessed

The nineteenth-century restorationist movement arose from the literal and futurist hermeneutic of the early dispensationalists who, having written off the church, believed the Old Testament predicted a spiritual revival among the

---

192. Gerstner, *Wrongly Dividing the Word of Truth*, pp. 190–191.

193. France, *Matthew*, p. 310.

194. Ryrie, *Basis of the Premillennial Faith*, p. 72.

195. See Chapman, *Whose Promised Land?*, p. 322; Robertson, *Israel of God*, p. 194; Gary Burge, *Who are God's People in the Middle East?* (Grand Rapids, MI: Zondervan, 1993), pp. 104ff.; Motyer, *Israel in the Plan of God*, p. 9; Walker, *Jesus and the Holy City*, pp. 286–287; William E. Cox, *Biblical Studies in Final Things* (Phillipsburg: Presbyterian and Reformed, 1966), p. 86; Wagner, *Dying in the Land of Promise*, pp. 129ff.

Jewish people, restored to their land in belief and associated with the return of the Lord. This would all occur, they believed, in their lifetime. Prophecies that had already been fulfilled in the return of the Jews from Babylonian exile were applied to their own generation.

While it is true that only 50,000 exiles had returned in around 538 BC, compared with the 603,550 men (excluding women and children) that had come out of Egypt a thousand years earlier (see Num. 1:46), and although they returned to only a small part of the original territory and built only a small replica of Solomon's temple, God's prophets nevertheless describe this restoration as so wonderful that it goes well beyond the limitations of any literal realization. Haggai and Zechariah, for example, describe a glorious future where Jerusalem becomes a great city surrounded by a wall of fire and into which the Gentile nations stream to worship. As Palmer Robertson explains, the imagery here metaphorically bursts the limitations of the old covenant wineskin.[196]

The New Testament describes how this vision found its fulfilment, as Peter quotes from Joel, Stephen from Isaiah and James from Amos, in the Pentecostal outpouring of God's Spirit on all people. This demonstrated that because of the death of Jesus, 'God does not show favouritism but accepts those from every nation who fear him and do what is right' (Acts 10:34–35, NIVI). Nevertheless, by re-erecting the wall of division between the church and Israel, restorationists see in the discovery of the lost tribes, the rise of the Zionist movement and the founding of the State of Israel in 1948, signs that God is apparently keeping his original promises to the Jewish people.

Political dispensationalists, especially, have distanced themselves from any linkage between the repentance and restoration which was expected by the prophets. Organizations such as the ICEJ and Exobus, for example, have worked ever more closely with the secular Jewish Agency to facilitate the return of Jewish people to Zion.

Eretz Israel: reclaiming Judea, Samaria and beyond

Since Christian Zionists believe the Jews remain God's 'chosen people' and that their final restoration is prophesied, it follows that the promises made to Abraham concerning their original inheritance in the land of Canaan must also still apply. An examination of the scriptural claim to the land will lead to an analysis of how the borders of Eretz Israel are defined.

---

196. Robertson, *Israel of God*, pp. 16–17.

Eretz Israel: in prophecy fulfilled

The claim to the land from Egypt to Iraq is based on the covenant God made with Abraham in Genesis 12, 13 and 15. The covenant is later confirmed to Isaac in Genesis 26 and Jacob in Genesis 28. Both Isaac and Jacob are promised that they and their descendants will possess the land. By the time of Moses, however, the Israelites are reminded that their residence in the land was conditional. They are warned that if they rebel against God, they will be 'scattered among the nations' (Lev. 26:33), but that if they confess their sins, 'I will remember my covenant with Jacob and my covenant with Isaac, and my covenant with Abraham, and I will remember the land' (Lev. 26:42). Invariably, however, Christian Zionists have minimized the conditionality of the covenants in favour of Israel's unconditional 'rights'. McNeile, for example, at the annual LJS conference of 1822, expressed the hope that the Jewish people would 'unite in claiming possession of that land which was given to them as a "heritage forever"'.[197]

With the rise of the Jewish Zionist movement in the nineteenth century, the founding of the State of Israel in 1948 and especially since the capture of East Jerusalem in 1967, the contemporary State of Israel has increasingly come to be seen as the realization of God's covenant promises. As Hal Lindsey has expressed it, 'To Israel as a nation were made unique promises . . . they were the only nation that was promised a specific plot of land, a city, and a kingdom.'[198] David Brickner reflects the views of contemporary Christian Zionists generally when he affirms, 'I believe the modern day State of Israel is a miracle of God and a fulfilment of Bible prophecy.'[199] Hagee and Walvoord both draw out the theological significance of these events. Hagee, for example, sees 1948 as a vindication of dispensationalism's distinction between Israel and the church: 'On May 15, 1948, a theological earthquake levelled replacement theology when the State of Israel was reborn after 2000 years of wandering.'[200] Similarly, Walvoord claims the events of 1967 have 'to a large extent revealed the premises and conclusions of both the amillenarians and postmillenarians to be in error'.[201] Neither deduction necessarily follows unless one accepts a priori a literal hermeneutic and futurist eschatology. Nevertheless, the

---

197. McNeile, Collected Works, vol. 2, p. 435.

198. Lindsey, Road to Holocaust, p. 197.

199. David Brickner, 'Don't Pass Over Israel's Jubilee', Jews for Jesus, Newsletter (April 1998).

200. Hagee, Final Dawn over Jerusalem, pp. 113–114.

201. John F. Walvoord, 'Will Israel Build a Temple in Jerusalem?', Bibliotheca Sacra 125 (April 1968), p. 102.

question being asked increasingly is not whether the Jewish people have a claim to the land of Canaan, for that is assumed, but rather, how much land?

Eretz Israel: its borders defined

To many Christian Zionists the present borders of Israel, even including the disputed Occupied Territories, are only a fraction of those God intends for the Jewish people. Darby is quite explicit in describing the methods and motives to be used as well as the extent of their legitimate territory:

> The first thing, then, which the Lord will do will be to purify His land (the land which belongs to the Jews) of the Tyrians, the Philistines, the Sidonians; of Edom and Moab, and Amon – of all the wicked, in short from the Nile to the Euphrates. It will be done by the power of Christ in favour of His people re-established by His goodness.[202]

Darby, therefore, sees the restoration of the Jewish people as a means to 'purify' the wicked from the land, in terms similar to those used in Joshua. Although Darby saw this 'ethnic cleansing' as an act of God, it is nevertheless clear he did not expect this would lead to a peaceful transition of ownership. It is rare to find contemporary Christian Zionists being as explicit. Surprisingly, however, it is largely among the writings of Messianic Zionists such as Arnold Fruchtenbaum, Louis Goldberg and David Brickner, all associated with Jews for Jesus, together with Randall Price, that the geographical extent of Eretz Israel is delineated most clearly.[203]

Fruchtenbaum explains that the 'exact' borders are 'from the river of Egypt to the great river, the Euphrates'. He clarifies that the former border refers to 'the most eastern branch of the Nile Delta, which now goes along the line of the modern-day Suez Canal'. Randall Price provides a map showing the boundaries to include parts of Egypt, Lebanon and Syria as well as the West Bank.[204] At no point in history have the Jews ever possessed all this land, even under King David or Solomon. So Fruchtenbaum deduces, 'Since God cannot lie, these things must yet come to pass . . . a Jewish State must be formed where they

---

202. Darby, 'The Hopes of the Church of God', in *Collected Writings*, vol. 2 Prophetic 1, p. 380.

203. Arnold G. Fruchtenbaum, 'This Land is Mine', *Issues* 2.4 (available online at <http://www.jfjonline.org/pub/issues/02-04/land.htm>); Fruchtenbaum, *Israelology*, p. 573; Louis Goldberg, 'Whose Land Is It?', *Issues* 4.2; Brickner, *Future Hope*, p. 90; Randall Price, *Jerusalem in Prophecy* (Eugene, OR: Harvest House, 1998), p. 98.

and their descendants can dwell ... there will be a time when the Jewish people will possess all of the Promised Land.'[205] While political dispensationalists encourage Israel to occupy this land by force, Fruchtenbaum believes this will be fulfilled only after the Messiah returns, when, presumably, according to their belief, the Middle East will have been considerably depopulated and subjugated following the battle of Armageddon.

Eretz Israel assessed

Lindsey and Fruchtenbaum, like virtually all Christian Zionists, insist that the Abrahamic covenant remains unconditional.[206] However, subsequent references to the land in Scripture stress that humility and meekness rather than 'chosenness' became a precondition for inheriting or remaining in the land, whereas arrogance or oppression were legitimate grounds for exile. For example, the psalmist explains, 'But the meek will inherit the land and enjoy great peace' (Ps. 37:11).[207] Zionists also downplay the repeated warnings in the Law as well as the Hebrew Prophets which stress that the land belongs to God and residence there is always conditional. For example, 'The land must not be sold permanently, because the land is mine and you are but aliens and my tenants' (Lev. 25:23). Because the land belongs to God, it cannot be permanently bought or sold, let alone stolen or confiscated, as has occurred in the Occupied Territories since 1967. The land is never at the disposal of Israel for its national purposes. Instead, it is Israel who are at the disposal of God's purposes. The Jews remain tenants in God's land. The ethical requirements for continued occupancy are clearly outlined in the Law. The prophet Ezekiel amplifies the same warnings:

> Thus says the Lord God of Israel: You shed blood, yet you would keep possession on the land? You rely on your sword, you do abominable things ... yet you would keep possession of the land? ... I will make the land a desolate waste, and her proud strength will come to an end, and the mountains of Israel will become desolate so that no one will cross them. Then they will know that I am the LORD, when I have made the land a desolate waste because of all the detestable things they have done. (Ezek. 33:25–29)

On the basis of sober warnings such as this, the question may legitimately be

---

205. Fruchtenbaum, 'This Land is Mine'.
206. Lindsey, *Road to Holocaust*, p. 186; Fruchtenbaum, *Israelology*, p. 573.
207. Jesus universalizes this promise: 'Blessed are the meek, for they will inherit the earth' (Matt. 5:5).

asked whether, due to its present expansionist policies, the State of Israel might not expect another exile rather than a restoration.

From a New Testament perspective, the contrast between contemporary Zionist expectations and the historic Christian hope could not be greater. Abraham's descendants, both Jewish and Gentile, are now promised not just Canaan but the entire world, indeed the cosmos itself.[208] Jesus, in the Sermon on the Mount, quotes and expands on Psalm 37, to promise that the meek will inherit much more than Palestine. Now they will inherit the earth. Paul explores this profound realization in Romans, where he concludes that 'Abraham and his offspring received the promise that he would be heir of the world' not through the Law but by faith (Rom. 4:13). It is no longer merely a portion of the earth that is the consummation of God's work of redeeming a fallen world, but one in which the entire cosmos participates. So paradise restored is not just a return to the land but a reconstructed cosmos, a new heaven and a new earth which becomes the home of the resurrected faithful remnant.[209] John Stott concludes,

> Instead, according to the apostles, the Old Testament promises are fulfilled in Christ and in the international community of Christ. A return to Jewish nationalism would seem incompatible with this New Testament perspective of the international community of Jesus.[210]

The tension over claims to the land are, however, even more polarized regarding the status of Jerusalem.

Jerusalem: the eternal and exclusive Jewish capital

The place and purpose of Jerusalem, or 'Zion' as it is sometimes called, are deeply felt within Christian Zionism. While Brearley accepts that neither land nor Jerusalem is intrinsically holy, she still insists that, 'Jerusalem is the place where the Lord has "chosen to place his name" (Deut. 14:23; 16:2, 6, 11; 26:2).' Lindsey also points out that,

---

208. See Eph. 1:1–23 which refers to our inheritance, 'in the heavenly realms'.
209. See O. Palmer Robertson, 'A new-covenant perspective on the land', in Johnston and Walker (eds.), *The Land of Promise*, pp. 121–141.
210. John Stott, 'Foreword', in Johnston and Walker (eds.), *The Land of Promise*, pp. 10–11.

Jerusalem's importance in history is infinitely beyond its size and economic significance. From ages past, Jerusalem has been the most important city on this planet . . . More prophecies have been made concerning Jerusalem than any other place on earth.[211]

The significance of Jerusalem within Christian Zionism will be examined in the context of the fulfilment of prophecy and how this shapes its eschatological future.

Jerusalem in history: the times of the Gentiles

The most frequently quoted biblical prophecy concerning the contemporary Jewish claim to Jerusalem is found in Luke 21:24 where Jesus said, 'Jerusalem will be trampled on by the Gentiles until the times of the Gentiles are fulfilled.' Revelation 11:2 says that the Gentile 'trampling' of Jerusalem would continue for only '42 months', so dating this event is problematic. Scofield suggests that the 'times of the Gentiles' began with the Babylonian captivity of Judah under Nebuchadnezzar and will be 'brought to an end by the destruction of Gentile world-power by the . . . coming of the Lord in glory (Rev. 19:11, 21), until which time Jerusalem is politically subject to Gentile rule".'[212] With hindsight, however, Schuyler English revises the last sentence to read more ambiguously, 'Until then Jerusalem will be, as Christ said, "trampled on by the Gentiles".'[213] He does this because Jerusalem is no longer 'subject to Gentile rule' but clearly not, as Scofield had predicted, as a result of the 'coming of the Lord in glory'.

Most Christian Zionists regard 1967 as the significant date when these prophecies were fulfilled. The Israeli capture of the Old City and East Jerusalem from Jordan in only six days was seen as nothing less than a miracle. For many it marked not only the end of the 'times of the Gentiles' but also signalled the imminent return of the Messiah.

Jan Willem van der Hoeven, whose book *Babylon or Jerusalem?* has a foreword written by Teddy Kollek, the former Mayor of Jerusalem, sees the prediction Jesus made in Luke 21:24 as now fulfilled: 'Finally, after nearly 2,000 long years, the Jewish people were reunited with their ancient city and capital. Jerusalem – literally trodden under foot by so many different nations – was back in the fold of her own people just as Christ had foretold' (p. 152). Wendell Stearns explains why the events of 1967 resulted in a 'reunification' of Jerusalem:

---

211. Lindsey, *Israel and the Last Days*, p. 20.
212. *Scofield Reference Bible*, fn. 1, p. 1345.
213. Schuyler English (ed.), *The New Scofield Reference Bible*, pp. 1330–1331.

The artificial boundary line that had divided Jerusalem was broken down in 1967 when Israel, in the miraculous Six-Day War, reunited the city which had been 'trodden down by the Gentiles' for nearly two thousand years. Jerusalem was again under Jewish jurisdiction.[214]

Lindsey, however, suggests the 'times' are not quite over. On the basis of the same verse, he believes attempts to negotiate a settlement of the Palestinian–Israeli conflict will always remain futile. This is because, he insists, the 'Bible tells us' that the dispute over Jerusalem and indeed Israel's borders will never be settled by any peace agreement, 'nor any whiz-bang diplomatic breakthrough'. Jerusalem will, he predicts, continue to be 'a stumbling block for the entire world . . . we are literally witnessing the end of the times of the Gentiles'.[215] A year later, in 1995, Lindsey rephrased the last sentence to give more emphasis to his timing: 'We are literally witnessing the last hours of the times of the Gentiles. God's focus is shifting back to His people Israel.'[216] By 'hours' it is assumed Lindsey was speaking metaphorically. If it is problematic trying to make sense of the past based on a futurist reading of prophecy, interpreting the future is even more controversial.

Jerusalem in eschatology: Ground Zero
It would be misleading to suggest that the future described for Jerusalem by Christian Zionists is anything but bleak. Hagee claims: 'Jerusalem the golden is caught in a supernatural crossfire . . . We are racing toward the end of time, and Israel lies in the eye of the storm.'[217] In Matthew 24 and Luke 21 Jesus describes events that were about to occur in Jerusalem. In Matthew the 'sign' for his hearers was the desecration of the temple, in Luke it would be the armies surrounding Jerusalem. The instructions Jesus gave in both accounts are the same: flee Judea for the mountains and escape.

Following his literalist hermeneutic, however, Scofield argues that whereas in Luke's account Jesus is predicting the destruction of Jerusalem by Titus in AD 70, in Matthew's account Jesus is referring to a still future crisis, 'after the manifestation of the "abomination"'. To explain why the instructions are virtually identical, Scofield claims, 'as the circumstances in both cases will be similar, so are the warnings. In the former case Jerusalem will be destroyed; in

---

214. Stearns, *Biblical Zionism*, p. 123.

215. Lindsey, *Planet Earth 2000 AD*, pp. 162, 164.

216. Lindsey, *Final Battle*, p. 95.

217. Hagee, *Final Dawn over Jerusalem*, p. 131.

the latter it will be delivered by divine interposition.'[218] Scofield's interpretation leaves unanswered the question, why, if the city will be delivered (as in Matthew's account), does Jesus still warn everyone to flee? It is also hard to imagine that those listening would have deduced anything other than that Jesus was speaking personally and directly to them.

Typical of other futurists, Lindsey believes that the prophecies in Zechariah 12 – 14 amplify the account in Matthew and describe events that are about to take place. The fearful siege of Jerusalem will, he claims, be conducted by the Soviet army.[219] He deduces that these chapters could only be describing contemporary events because it is clear that 'the Jews would have to be dwelling in and have possession of the ancient city of Jerusalem at the time of the Messiah's triumphant advent'.[220] He argues that Armageddon will be triggered by a dispute over Jerusalem; indeed, 'we've got that dispute right now' he discerns. Jerusalem's fate, he claims, and, by implication, the cause of the next world war, will be a direct result of the failure of the West to support Israel: 'As a matter of fact, the West helped guarantee the world a dispute over Jerusalem by forcing the Israelis into a pact with the Palestinians.'[221] How much of Jerusalem will be left standing when Jesus returns is a matter of conjecture, given Lindsey's terrifying description of the war of Armageddon:

> The Bible also makes clear that Jerusalem – the focal point of the end times fighting – will be vanquished by Israel's enemies in the hours just before the Lord comes. In fact, it seems that the destruction of the holy city is the final straw that angers God and provokes Jesus' return.[222]

If such an appalling prospect is imminent, as Lindsey suggests, it is surprising that he does not invoke Jesus' warnings in Matthew 24 to 'flee to the mountains' and encourage Jerusalemites today, as Jesus did then, to save themselves from the terrifying onslaught to come. Lindsey does, however, offer some comfort to the survivors. During the millennium, he promises, 'Jerusalem will be the spiritual centre of the entire world . . . all people of the earth will come annually to worship Jesus who will rule there', indeed he claims it will become something

218. *Scofield Reference Bible*, fn. 1, p. 1033.
219. Lindsey, *Late Great Planet Earth*, p. 54.
220. Ibid.
221. Lindsey, *Planet Earth 2000 AD*, p. 247.
222. Ibid., p. 262.

of a tourist attraction.[223] Lindsey's predictions highlight the contradiction, rarely admitted by Christian Zionists, that their futurist eschatology leads them to expect both the exaltation and destruction of most Jewish people.

Taking a stand against God's apocalyptic plans for Jerusalem, however, 'spells disaster', claims Jarvilehto of the ICEJ. Based on her interpretation of Zechariah 12:3 ('I will make Jerusalem an immovable rock for all the nations. All who try to move it will injure themselves'), she believes God is currently using the status of Jerusalem as a test of people's obedience to the Bible.[224] As with other prophecies previously cited, whether this particular text is intended to be interpreted in such a way is debatable since the next verse goes on to warn that God will strike every horse with panic and every rider with madness. Notwithstanding the inadvisability of using horses in contemporary warfare, most dispensational commentators understand this prophecy to be describing a future siege of Jerusalem preceding the battle of Armageddon.

Jerusalem assessed

For dispensationalists especially, Jerusalem appears as non-negotiable to Israel as Zion is to Zionism. The New Testament, however, knows nothing of a pre-occupation with a nationalistic and materialistic earthly Jerusalem, let alone Zionism as it exists today. Access to heaven no longer has anything to do with the earthly Jerusalem. Jesus had already made this clear to the woman of Samaria when he said, 'a time is coming when you will worship the Father neither on this mountain nor in Jerusalem'(John 4:21). At his trial Jesus explained further, saying, 'My kingdom is not of this world. If it were, my servants would fight to prevent my arrest by the Jews. But now my kingdom is from another place' (John 18:36). The turning point for the disciples comes with the resurrection encounters and Pentecost. Until this point they seemed to share the same understanding of the land as other first-century Jews. They had looked forward to God's intervention which would at last restore political sovereignty to the Jews in Israel.[225] This is reflected in the unfulfilled hopes of the disciples on the road to Emmaus who, unknowingly, confess to Jesus: 'we had hoped that he was the one who was going to redeem Israel' (Luke 24:21). This idea is also clearly still in the minds of the disciples even as Jesus is about

---

223. Lindsey, *Israel and the Last Days*, p. 165.

224. Ulla Jarvilehto, 'Political Action for Israel', *Christians and Israel: Essays in Biblical Zionism and on Islamic Fundamentalism* (Jerusalem: ICEJ, 1996), p. 58.

225. See Colin Chapman, 'Ten questions for a theology of the land', in Johnston and Walker (eds.), *The Land of Promise*, p. 179.

to ascend to heaven, for they ask, 'Lord, are you at this time going to restore the kingdom to Israel?' (Acts 1:6). John Calvin comments, 'There are as many mistakes in this question as there are words.'[226] Jesus' reply indicates that he has another agenda for his disciples: 'It is not for you to know the times or dates the Father has set by his own authority. But you will receive power when the Holy Spirit comes on you; and you will be my witnesses in Jerusalem, and in all Judea and Samaria, and to the ends of the earth' (Acts 1:7–8). Jesus redefines the boundaries of the kingdom of God and thereby the meaning of chosen-ness. The expansion of the kingdom of God throughout the world requires the exile of the apostles from the land.[227] They must turn their backs on Jerusalem and on their hopes of a materialistic kingdom. They are sent out into the world but never told to return. Subsequent to Pentecost, under the illumination of the Holy Spirit, the apostles begin to use old covenant language concerning the land in new ways. So, for example, Peter speaks of an inheritance which, unlike the land, '. . . can never perish, spoil or fade' (1 Pet. 1:4). Paul similarly asserts, 'Now I commit you to God and to the word of his grace, which can build you up and give you an inheritance among all those who are sanctified' (Acts 20:32).

Christians are told instead to inhabit Jerusalem by faith and look forward to the appearing of a heavenly Jerusalem: 'But you have come to Mount Zion, to the heavenly Jerusalem: the city of the living God. You have come to thousands upon thousands of angels in joyful assembly, to the church of the firstborn, whose names are written in heaven' (Heb. 12:22–23). Similarly, Paul announces, 'But the Jerusalem that is above is free, and she is our mother' (Gal. 4:26). In Galatians 4, Paul is at his most explicit in criticizing the 'Jerusalem-dependency'[228] of the legalists who were infecting the church in Galatia. They are in slavery, he insists. Quoting from Isaiah 54:1, Paul takes a promise origi-nally referring to the earthly Jerusalem and applies it to the Jerusalem above, which is the home of all who believe in Jesus Christ. Paul must have shocked fellow-Jews when he equated Jerusalem and its Christ-renouncing Judaism with Hagar and her slave children. As has been shown in the context of the relation-ship between Israel and the church, Jewish and Gentile believers in Galatia are now the children of Abraham and Sarah. Like Isaac, they are children of the promise. By making this equation, Paul nullifies any future exclusive Jewish claim to be the authentic children of Abraham, with all its covenantal privileges, apart from through faith in Jesus Christ. J. C. De Young adds:

---

226. John Calvin, *The Acts of the Apostles 1–13* (Edinburgh: St Andrew Press, 1965), p. 29.
227. See Robertson, 'A new-covenant perspective on the land', p. 136.
228. See Walker, *Jesus and the Holy City*, p. 129.

> Gal. 4:21ff. represents, perhaps, the sharpest polemic against Jerusalem in the New
> Testament . . . Far from being pre-occupied with hopes for a glorification of the
> earthly Jerusalem, Paul's thought represents a most emphatic repudiation of any
> eschatological hopes concerning the earthly city.[229]

As Palmer Robertson also observes, by the end of the Apostolic era, the focus of God's redemptive work in the world has shifted from Jerusalem to places like Antioch, Ephesus and Rome.[230] There is, therefore, no evidence that the apostles believed that the Jewish people still had a divine right to the land, or that the Jewish possession of the land would be important, let alone that Jerusalem would remain a central aspect of God's purposes for the world. On the contrary, in the Christological logic of Paul, Jerusalem as much as the land, has now been superseded. They have been made irrelevant in God's redemptive purposes.

The contradiction between the Jerusalem-based Christian Zionist agenda and the progressive revelation of Scripture is most controversially seen in the popular dispensational expectation of a rebuilt Jewish temple. This is also probably the most contentious issue uniting many Christian Zionists with Orthodox Jews.

The temple: rebuilding for desecration

Many Christian Zionists today believe passionately that another Jewish temple is not only mandated in Scripture but that its rebuilding is imminent. Therefore, they actively support those committed to achieving it. After considering the importance of the temple within Christian Zionism, we will explore the biblical basis of their claims, together with its theological purpose, and then go on to examine the practical issues associated with its rebuilding.

The importance of the temple to Christian Zionists
For the past nineteen centuries, religious Jews have prayed this prayer three times a day: 'May it be Thy will that the Temple be speedily rebuilt in our days.' Randall Price claims that the Torah 'obligates the Jewish nation to rebuild the Temple whenever it becomes possible to do so (Ex 25:8)'.[231] However, in August 1967, when Israeli Defence Force chaplain Rabbi Shlomo Goren blew

---

229. J. C. De Young, *Jerusalem in the New Testament* (Amsterdam: Kampen, 1961), p. 106, cited in Walker, *Jesus and the Holy City*, p. 131.

230. Robertson, 'A new-covenant perspective on the land', p. 138.

231. Randall Price, *Time for a Temple? Jewish Plans to Rebuild the Temple* (n.d.) [Internet],

the *shofar* and performed a religious ceremony near the Dome of the Rock just days after the capture of the Old City of Jerusalem, he was criticized by both the secular Israeli press and Orthodox Jews.[232] Some twenty years later, *Time* magazine reported the findings of a survey undertaken in 1989 which showed that 18% of Israelis thought it was time to rebuild the temple.[233] A similar Gallup poll conducted just seven years later in 1996, to assess opinion on Israeli sovereignty over the Temple Mount, found that 58% of Israelis support the Temple Mount Faithful and the rebuilding of the Jewish temple.[234] On the assumption that Muslim Arab Israelis would have opposed such a plan, the proportion of Jewish Israelis in favour must therefore have been significantly higher. Indeed, this was allegedly the largest show of support any organization has ever received in Israel on any subject. Significantly, the highest percentage of support came from young Israelis.[235]

Contemporary Christian Zionists who have written on the rebuilding of a Jewish temple include Thomas Ice and Randall Price, Grant Jeffrey, Hal Lindsey, Tim LaHaye and Dave Hunt.[236] Their combined published book-sales exceed 100 million and are available in more than fifty languages. Their views are, therefore, neither marginal or obscure, indeed, Grace Halsell speculates that 10% of Americans support this movement.[237] Other Christian Zionist leaders, including Peter Wagner, James DeLoach, Terry Reisenhoover and Doug Kreiger, have been influential in gathering significant American

---

Friends of Israel Gospel Ministry, <http://www.foigm.org/img/timetemp.htm>. [Accessed August 2004.]

232. See John F. Walvoord, 'Will Israel Build a Temple in Jerusalem?', *Bibliotheca Sacra* 125 (April 1968), p. 106.

233. Richard N. Ostling, 'Time for a New Temple?', *Time*, 16 October 1989, p. 64.

234. The Gallup Poll was conducted for Gershon Salomon and the Temple Mount Faithful and is cited on their website: <http://www.templemount.org/ftm/events.html>.

235. See Price, *Coming Last Days Temple*, p. 26.

236. See Ice and Price, *Ready to Rebuild*; David Dolan, *Israel in Crisis: What Lies Ahead?* (Grand Rapids, MI: Fleming Revell, 2001), pp. 103–124; Lindsey, *Planet Earth 2000 AD*, pp. 153–167; Tim LaHaye and Jerry B. Jenkins, *Are We Living in the End Times?*, pp. 121–129; Hunt, *Cup of Trembling*, pp. 343–367.

237. Grace Halsell, *Christian Fundamentalists and Jewish Orthodox Cults Plot Destruction of Al Aqsa Mosque* (n.d.) [Internet], Friends of Al-Aqsa website, <http://www.aqsa.org.uk/flyers/plots.html>. [Accessed August 2004]; see also, Grace Halsell, 'Shrine Under Siege', *The Link* (May/June 1992), vol. 25, issue 2.

financial and political support for extreme Jewish organizations such as Gush
Emunim and the Temple Mount Faithful.[238]

Hal Lindsey claims the Temple Mount is 'the most disputed 35 acres on the
Planet', and the single most important key to prophecies yet to be fulfilled.[239]
He writes, 'I know this sounds crazy, but I believe the fate of the world will be
determined by an ancient feud over 35 acres of land.'[240] Lindsey is emphatic:

> Obstacle or no obstacle, it is certain that the Temple will be rebuilt. Prophecy
> demands it . . . With the Jewish nation reborn in the land of Palestine, ancient
> Jerusalem once again under total Jewish control for the first time in 2600 years, and
> talk of rebuilding the great Temple, the most important sign of Jesus Christ's soon
> coming is before us . . . It is like the key piece of a jigsaw puzzle being found . . . For
> all those who trust in Jesus Christ, it is a time of electrifying excitement.[241]

He reminisces that twenty-five years ago the idea 'seemed quaint – even far
fetched. Today, nobody's laughing about the notion.'[242] Jews for Jesus also
endorses and sells The Coming Last Days Temple, by Randall Price, who advocates the rebuilding of the Jewish temple next to, if not in place of, the Dome
of the Rock:

> The Muslim Dome of the Rock currently sits on the Temple Mount. With Arab–Israeli
> conflict raging and the Temple Mount at the center of the controversy, what will the
> future bring? The Bible has answers – prophecies with predictions about the future
> Temple found in both Old and New Testaments. Some claim that these prophecies are
> merely symbolic, but are they? Does the Bible give evidence that we can expect a literal
> Temple and even a restored sacrificial system? What about the magnificent Temple
> prophesied by Ezekiel? Dr Price surveys the latest developments and offers a
> fascinating perspective on how they fit with Bible prophecies about the last days.[243]

238. See Halsell, Forcing God's Hand, pp. 63–73.

239. Lindsey, Planet Earth 2000 AD, p. 156.

240. Hal Lindsey, World's fate hangs on 35 acres (2001) [Internet], World Net Daily,
       <http://www.worldnetdaily.com/news/article.asp?ARTICLE_ID=21794>.
       [Accessed August 2004.]

241. Lindsey, Late Great Planet Earth, pp. 56–58.

242. Lindsey, Planet Earth 2000 AD, p. 156.

243. Jews for Jesus review of Randall Price, Coming Last Days Temple,
       <http://store.jwsforjesus.org/ppp/product.php?prodid=152>. [Accessed August
       2004.]

John Walvoord, formerly chancellor of Dallas Theological Seminary, claims in the foreword to *The Coming Last Days Temple*, 'It is doubtful whether there has ever been or ever will be another volume on the Temple as comprehensive and complete as this volume.' He goes on to extol the book not only among Christians but also among Orthodox Jews: 'The scholarly analysis of the doctrine of the Temple will prove to be of great benefit both to Christian theologians and to those of the Jewish faith, especially those who are part of the Orthodox movement. This volume is highly recommended as an integral part of the scholarly presentation of biblical truth.' Many Christian and Jewish Zionists are, therefore, united in the conviction that the Muslim Dome of the Rock must be destroyed, the third Jewish temple built, priests consecrated and sacrifices reinstituted in fulfilment of biblical prophecy and to hasten the coming of Messiah.

The origins of Christian support for the temple movement
The necessity of having a rebuilt temple to desecrate is a logical conclusion if a literal and futurist reading of passages such as Daniel 9 and Matthew 24 is accepted. However, it is rare to find such an expectation in Christian writings prior to the twentieth century.[244] Indeed, this contradicts the stance taken by the early church, for which the temple had ceased to hold any significance.[245]

   When the Church of the Holy Sepulchre was built opposite the then derelict site of the temple, it was deliberately designed to parallel the layout of Herod's temple.[246] Thomas Ice and Randall Price claim, 'By placing the church directly opposite and facing the Temple, and in fact on higher ground overlooking the Temple, Christians dramatically emphasized the claim of Christ in John 2:19 that He would destroy the Temple.'[247] During the Byzantine era, other churches were built and enhanced in Jerusalem, but the area of the

---

244. In his 732-page analysis of the future Jewish temple, *The Coming Last Days Temple*, Randall Price lists over forty books written in the last thirty years but only two written in the nineteenth century. See also, B. W. Newton, 'The Renewal of the Near East', in Fromow (ed.), *B. W. Newton and Dr S. P. Tregelles*, pp. 121–127; Blackstone, *Jesus is Coming*, p. 191; G. H. Pember, *The Great Prophecies of the Centuries Concerning Israel and the Gentiles* (5th edn, London: Hodder and Stoughton, 1902).

245. While Irenaeus, Hippolytus and Origen believed a literal temple would be rebuilt, in the *Epistle of Barnabas* and writings of Chrysostom and Jerome, the church itself is seen as the temple; cited in Frazier, *A Second Look at the Second Coming*, pp. 141–142.

246. *Egeria's Travels in the Holy Land*, translated by John Wilkinson (Jerusalem: Ariel, 1981), p. 167.

247. Ice and Price, *Ready to Rebuild*, p. 34.

temple was deliberately left desolate. Accounts of pilgrims describe wild animals prowling among the ruins. By the seventh-century reign of Emperor Heraclius, the temple area was being used as a rubbish tip, hence the naming of the Dung Gate which dates from about this time. The *Muthir al-Ghiram*, for example, reports of Muslims in Jerusalem who describe how local Christians offended the Jews by turning the site into a giant dung heap.[248] The conviction that the Jewish temple would never be rebuilt remained uncontested until the rise of premillennial dispensationalism in the early nineteenth century. Since then, belief in the imminent rebuilding of a Jewish temple has gradually grown in popularity. The Temple Mount now lies at the heart of the controversy concerning the Jewish claim to exclusive sovereignty over the Old City of Jerusalem.

Scofield was probably the first and most influential writer to popularize the idea of the necessity for rebuilding the Jewish temple. In his Bible notes, Scofield taught that it was God's intention, having restored the nation of Israel to Palestine, to build two more temples and reinstitute the priesthood and sacrificial system:

> In a sense all the Temples (i.e. Solomon's; Ezra's; Herod's); that which will be used by the unbelieving Jews under the covenant with the Beast (Dan. 9:27; Mt. 24:15; 2 Thes. 2:3, 4); and Ezekiel's future kingdom Temple (Ezk. 40 – 47), are treated as one house – the 'house of the Lord'.[249]

Scofield would probably, however, have been appalled to think Christians would ever want to support the building of another Jewish temple since, in his opinion, it would be associated with Satanic worship.

The biblical basis for the rebuilding of the Jewish temple

Soon after the capture of the Temple Mount in 1967, John Walvoord was already speculating about when the temple would be built. In an article published by Dallas Theological Seminary, he summarizes the position of dispensationalists who take the authors of the Bible 'to mean what they say':

> Orthodox Jews for many years have been praying daily for the rebuilding of the Temple. In this expectation, they have had the support of premillenarians who interpret Scriptural prophecies as meaning what they say when they refer to a

---

248. G. Le Strange, *Palestine Under the Moslems* (Beirut: Khayats, [1890] 1965), p. 139.
249. *Scofield Reference Bible*, fn. 2, p. 963.

future Temple in Jerusalem. The world as a whole, as well as the majority of the church, have tended to ignore this expectation as being too literal an interpretation of prophecy.[250]

The conviction that the temple must be rebuilt is based both on the assumption that certain Old Testament prophecies referring to the temple have not yet been fulfilled and on a few New Testament references which, when read using a futurist literal hermeneutic, imply the existence of a Jewish temple immediately prior to the return of Christ.

Unfulfilled Old Testament prophecies
One of the most frequently quoted Old Testament passages concerning the temple is Daniel 9:24–27. The sanctuary is destroyed in verse 26, yet sacrifices are brought to an end only when the 'abomination that causes desolation' desecrates the temple in verse 27. On the basis of a literal chronology, in which it is necessary to place a gap of nearly 2,000 years between the two verses, Lindsey confidently argues:

> This prophecy speaks of sacrifice and offerings which demand that the Jews rebuild the Temple for the third time upon its original site. At that point, Judaism and Islam will be placed on an inevitable course of war over the site, a war that will start Armageddon . . . any move toward that direction is a crucial clue to what hour it is on God's prophetic timetable.[251]

David Brickner reaches the same conclusion. Based on a futurist reading he also deduces that the temple must have been rebuilt, for 'Daniel tells us this ruler puts an end to sacrifice and sets up some kind of abomination (a loathsome horror that would be anathema to Jewish worship) right inside the Temple in Jerusalem.'[252] Similarly, Fruchtenbaum insists, 'As it was in the days of Antiochus Epiphanes, so it will be again in the future when a gentile ruler will abominate the temple by means of idolatry.'[253] As has already been shown,

---

250. John F. Walvoord, 'Will Israel Build a Temple in Jerusalem?', *Bibliotheca Sacra* 125 (April 1968), p. 100.

251. Lindsey, *Israel and the Last Days*, p. 23.

252. Brickner, *Future Hope*, p. 18.

253. Arnold G. Fruchtenbaum, 'The Messianic Time Table According to Daniel the Prophet', *Issues* 5.1 (available online at <http://www.jfjonline.org/pub/issues/05-01/messianictime.htm>).

there is nothing in the text of Daniel 9 that requires a futurist reading, or suggests a gap between the sixty-ninth and seventieth weeks, especially one spanning 2,000 years, or indeed predicts the rebuilding of a Jewish temple. The other important Old Testament passage used to support the rebuilding of the temple is Ezekiel 43. Moishe Rosen believes that,

> at some point in these stressful days, the ancient Jewish Temple will be rebuilt on the holy Temple Mount in Jerusalem . . . Prophecy foretells the rebuilding of the Jewish Temple and the reinstitution of the sacrifices prescribed in the law of Moses. In a vision of the future Temple, Ezekiel received this word . . . Some way, somehow, the Temple will be rebuilt, in spite of the fact that two Arab shrines now stand on the only site on earth where this Temple may stand.[254]

Such an interpretation is possible only by artificially imposing dispensational presuppositions and a futurist hermeneutic upon the text. The same assumptions are, however, used in the interpretation of references to the imminent destruction of the temple in the New Testament.

Unfulfilled New Testament prophecies

The most important New Testament passage used to support the belief in the rebuilding of the Jewish temple is Matthew 24. While dispensationalists agree that in the first two verses Jesus is warning of the imminent destruction of Jerusalem, they claim that by verse 15 Jesus is describing the desecration of another future temple which has yet to be built. This futurist interpretation of Matthew 24, like that of Daniel 9:24–27 requires a gap of some 2,000 years between these verses. So, for example, John Walvoord argues that it could not refer to AD 70 since it appears to describe an event immediately preceding the return of Christ: 'The abomination of desolation has reference to a future event paralleling to some extent "the abomination that maketh desolate" of Daniel 11:31.'[255] Hal Lindsey takes a similar if rather more dogmatic view:

> Of course, for Temple rites to be stopped in the last days, we know they must be restarted. The words of Jesus Himself in Matthew 24:15 require that a new holy

---

254. Rosen, *Overture to Armageddon?*, p. 114; see also, p. 166. For a critique of this view, see John B. Taylor, *Ezekiel: An Introduction and Commentary* (Leicester: IVP, 1969), pp. 250–254.

255. Walvoord, 'Will Israel Build a Temple in Jerusalem?', p. 103.

place be built and a complete sacrificial system re-instituted. And since only a consecrated Temple can be defiled, this prophecy shows that the physical Temple must not only be rebuilt, but a functioning priesthood must begin practising once again.[256]

While Lindsey and Walvoord believe Jesus was predicting a future desecration of a rebuilt temple, non-dispensationalist commentators observe that within a generation of Jesus' prediction, Josephus was recording how Jewish Zealots desecrated the temple, using it as a fortress against the Romans.

The first-century fulfilment

Eusebius, the fourth-century church historian, refers to the eyewitness accounts of Josephus to show how these predictions were understood as having been fulfilled by AD 70.[257] Writing in the *Jewish Wars*, Josephus links Daniel's prophecy to the desecration of the temple and destruction of Jerusalem in AD 66–70: 'In the very same manner Daniel also wrote concerning the Roman government, and that our country should be made desolate by them.'[258] Josephus specifically associates the desecration of the temple with the activities of Jewish Zealots who, between November of AD 67 and the spring of AD 68, used the temple as a military fortress, executed Jewish opponents inside it and even entered the holiest of holies.[259] He describes how those 'Jews do walk about in the midst of the holy places, at the very time when their hands are still warm with the slaughter of their own countrymen.'[260] Believing God would intervene and deliver them by force, he records how the Zealots invited the Idumean army of some 20,000 troops to help defend Jerusalem from the Romans. Instead, they took advantage of the city and plundered it, 'nor did the Idumeans spare anybody . . . and now the outer Temple was all of it overflowed with blood; and that day, as it came on, they saw eight thousand five-hundred dead bodies there'.[261] Josephus regarded the death of Ananus as the beginning of the

---

256. Lindsey, *Planet Earth 2000 AD*, p. 158.

257. Eusebius, 'On the Predictions of Christ', in *The Ecclesiastical History and the Martyrs of Palestine* (London: SPCK, 1927), 3.5.4, p. 69; 3.7, pp. 73–74.

258. Josephus, *Jewish Antiquities*, in *The New Complete Works of Josephus* (Grand Rapids: Kregal, 1999), 10.2.7 (276), p. 357.

259. Josephus, *Jewish Antiquities*, 4.5.4 (343), p. 823.

260. Ibid., 4.3.10 (162–163), pp. 813–814.

261. Ibid., 4.5.1 (313), p. 821.

destruction of Jerusalem, and it is possible that Christians saw in his murder and the appointment of apostate high priests like Phannias, the sacrilege Jesus had warned of in Matthew 24. Later, the temple was subsequently defiled once more by the invading Roman army. Josephus describes the scene: 'And now the Romans . . . brought their ensigns to the Temple and set them near to its eastern gate; and there did they offer sacrifices to them, and there they did make Titus Imperator with the greatest acclamations of joy.'[262]

As a credible first-century eyewitness and historian, Josephus shows conclusively, therefore, how the temple was desecrated on numerous occasions, first by Jewish Zealots, then by the marauding Idumeans and finally by Titus and his Roman army. Whether at the hands of Jews or pagans, with the destruction of Jerusalem in AD 70 the 'Abomination' had indeed brought desolation. John Calvin believed that God 'deserted his Temple, because it was only founded for a time, and was but a shadow, until the Jews so completely violated the whole covenant that no sanctity remained in either the Temple, the nation, or the land itself'.[263]

Dispensationalists ignore this historical evidence as well as the views of the Reformers, preferring to interpret Matthew 24, and passages such as 2 Thessalonians 2:1–4, as still awaiting fulfilment. While Jesus repeatedly warned of the destruction of the temple, and was known by his critics to have done so, he never promised that it would ever be rebuilt.[264] In Hebrews, the author describes the offering of sacrifices between the death of Christ and the destruction of the temple as an 'illustration' of, and 'copies' of, heavenly realities, a 'reminder of sins' but unable, unlike the finished work of Christ, to take sin away.[265] Peter uses the same terminology to describe the way Christians are being made into the new house of God, in which Jesus is the 'precious cornerstone':

> you also, like living stones, are being built into a spiritual house to be a holy priesthood, offering spiritual sacrifices acceptable to God through Jesus Christ. For in Scripture it says:

---

262. Josephus, *Jewish Wars*, in *The New Complete Works of Josephus* (Grand Rapids: Kregal, 1999), 6.6.1 (316), p. 900.

263. John Calvin, *Commentary on the Book of the Prophet Daniel*, translated by Thomas Myers, 2 vols. (Grand Rapids: Eerdmans, 1948), vol. 2, p. 390.

264. John 2:19; Matt. 26:61; 27:40; Mark 14:58; 15:29.

265. Heb. 9:9, 23; 10:1–3, 11.

'See, I lay a stone in Zion,
 a chosen and precious cornerstone,
and the one who trusts in him
 will never be put to shame.'

Now to you who believe, this stone is precious. But to those who do not believe,

'The stone the builders rejected
 has become the capstone.'
(1 Pet. 2:5–7)

Indeed, there is not a single verse in the New Testament which promises that the Jewish temple would be rebuilt or that a 2,000-year 'parenthesis' should be placed between references to its desecration and destruction. Christians favouring the rebuilding of the temple consistently ignore the way in which the temple is invested with new meaning in the New Testament as a 'type' for Jesus Christ and his church as did many of the Early Church Fathers.[266] Instead, they advocate a return to the very practices made redundant by the once-and-for-all atoning work of the Son of God.

The theological purpose for rebuilding the Jewish temple

Dispensationalists disagree on the reasons for rebuilding the temple. Most believe that the intention is to reintroduce the Levitical sacrificial system, but they disagree on what kind of sacrifice will be offered and its purpose. Based on his reading of Daniel 12:11, Walvoord, for example, insists temple sacrifices must be reintroduced because, 'Judging by scriptures, this is precisely what they will do as it would be impossible to cause sacrifices to cease if they were not already in operation.'[267] Scofield in his reference Bible claims that the sacrifices mentioned in Ezekiel 43:19 will, however, only be a 'memorial' offering: 'Doubtless these offerings will be memorial, looking back to the cross, as the offerings under the old covenant were anticipatory, looking forward to the cross. In neither case have animal sacrifices power to put away sin (Heb. 10.4; Rom. 3.25)' (p. 890). However, the verse quite explicitly refers to the sacrifice

---

266. See *Epistle of Barnabas*, in A. Roberts and J. Donaldson (eds.), *Ante-Nicene Fathers* (Peabody: Hendrikson, 1994), vol. 1, p. 147; Chrysostom, 'Homily 3 on 2 Thessalonians, 2:4', in P. Schaff (ed.), *Nicene & Post-Nicene Fathers* (Peabody: Hendrikson, 1994), vol. 13, pp. 332–338.

267. Walvoord, 'Will Israel Build a Temple in Jerusalem?', p. 104.

of a 'young bullock as a sin offering'. While Scofield compromises on the issue, *The New Scofield Reference Bible* goes further, undermining the entire hermeneutical foundation of dispensationalism:

> The reference to sacrifices is not to be taken literally, in view of the putting away of such offerings, but is rather to be regarded as a presentation of the worship of redeemed Israel, in her own land and in the millennial Temple, using the terms with which the Jews were familiar in Ezekiel's day (p. 864).

If this particular reference to sacrifice need not be taken literally, then the whole presuppositional base of dispensationalism is seriously weakened, flawed by its own internal inconsistency. Following a literal reading, the sacrifice of a young bullock cannot be synonymous with a memorial offering which consisted only of grain and oil.[268] The immediate context for Ezekiel's vision of a rebuilt temple is the promised return of the Jews from Babylonian exile, not some long-distant eschatological event. Furthermore, if Ezekiel were referring to some future millennial age, according to Mosaic Law, Jesus Christ could not serve in such a temple because he is not of the tribe of Levi.[269] But even if in some way he could, it would surely be incongruous for Jesus to offer animal sacrifices when the New Testament asserts he has replaced them by the shedding of his own blood. Such an interpretation undermines the New Testament emphasis that the sacrifice of Christ was sufficient, final and complete.[270] If religious Jews do indeed rebuild their temple and reinstitute sacrifices for the atonement of sin, it will simply demonstrate their rejection of the atoning work of Jesus Christ. However, for Christians to support the reinstitution of the sacrificial system is surely a sign of apostasy since they would be, in the words of the writer to the Hebrews, 'crucifying the Son of God all over again and subjecting him to public disgrace'.[271]

Several commentators even equate 'the blood of swine' referred to in Isaiah 66:3 with the temple sacrifices offered after the death of Christ, between AD 33 and AD 70, claiming it was these that desecrated the temple and fulfilled Daniel's prophecy about the abomination causing desolation.[272] Indeed,

---

268. Lev. 2:2, 9, 16.

269. Heb. 7:14. See Venema, *Promise of the Future*, p. 286.

270. Heb. 2:17; Rom. 3:25.

271. Heb. 6:4–6. See also, Heb. 9:25–26; 10:1–3.

272. See DeMar, *Last Days Madness*, p. 86; Edward J. Young, *The Book of Isaiah*, 3 vols. (Grand Rapids: Eerdmans, 1972), vol. 3, p. 520.

George Pember, an early dispensationalist, while taking a futurist view of prophecy nevertheless controversially applies the verse to the renewal of sacrifices in the rebuilt temple:

> Then, in reference to the sacrifices which are again being offered, the Lord adds: 'He that killeth the ox is as the slayer of a man: he that sacrificeth the sheep as one that breaketh the neck of a dog: he that offereth an oblation, it is swine's blood: he that causeth incense to rise up as a memorial is as one that blesseth an idol.' Nevertheless, the Jews, while they profess to sacrifice to Jehovah, will continue to delight in their abominations.[273]

Messianic dispensationalists take a diametrically opposed viewpoint to this, insisting that the reintroduction of temple sacrifices will be an essential and authentic aspect of future Jewish worship. Zhava Glaser, of Jews for Jesus, for example, describes how over the past 1,900 years the liturgy used in the synagogue has kept the memory of the temple alive in Jewish hearts and prayers. Therefore, she insists, 'when God instituted the sacrificial system, it was instituted for all time':

> What flour is to bread, the sacrificial system is to the religion revealed in the Jewish scriptures. It is not a garnish. It is not a flavoring. It is the very substance out of which the Jewish religion was constructed. We can forever design our own substitutes, but they cannot satisfy our yearnings the way God's own provision can. Though some rabbis might minimize the revealed system of worship and its requirements, can the individual Jew neglect what God says? Can there be a 'proper' Judaism without a priesthood, an altar, a sacrifice and a place on earth where God meets the individual?[274]

Glaser reflects the position of classic dispensationalists who hold that the temple will be rebuilt because the Jews have a separate covenant relationship with God, apart from the church. She, therefore, does not appear to see the high priesthood of Jesus as in any sense necessarily replacing or superseding the Jewish sacrificial system, but apparently perpetuating it during the millennium.

----

273. Pember, *Great Prophecies of the Centuries*, pp. 353–354.
274. Zhava Glaser, 'Today's Rituals: Reminders or Replacements?', *Issues* 8.3.

The temple movement assessed

It has been shown that the Christian support for the rebuilding of the Jewish temple, like the claim to Eretz Israel and Jerusalem, arises solely from a literal and futurist hermeneutic. On the basis of a few allegedly unfulfilled Old and New Testament prophecies, many Christian Zionists are convinced that a third temple will be built in place of, or near, the Dome of the Rock in Jerusalem and believe that a Jewish priesthood will once again offer sacrifices. They also believe this yet-to-be-built temple will then be desecrated by the Antichrist and replaced during the millennium by a much larger temple, as described by Ezekiel. This viewpoint is incompatible with the way the New Testament describes the temple as an illustration, a copy and shadow for the atoning work of Jesus Christ.

Covenantalists affirm that the movement in the progressive revelation of Scripture is always from the lesser to the greater. It is never reversed. The New Testament repeatedly sees such Old Testament concepts as the temple, high priest and sacrifice as 'types' pointing to and fulfilled in Jesus Christ. Typology in Scripture never typifies itself, nor is it ever greater than that which it typifies.[275] It is therefore argued that Christians who advocate the rebuilding of the temple are regressing to a pre-Christian sacrificial system, superseded and annulled by the finished work of Jesus Christ.[276] The New Testament portrays the temple as a temporary edifice, a shadow and type anticipating the day when God will dwell with people of all nations because of the atoning work of the true temple, Jesus Christ.

The purpose of the temple, therefore, finds its ultimate significance and fulfilment not in another man-made sanctuary but in Jesus Christ and his church. The writer of Hebrews assures Christ's followers: 'But you have come to Mount Zion, to the heavenly Jerusalem, the city of the living God. You have come to thousands upon thousands of angels in joyful assembly' (Heb. 12:22). The book of Revelation expressly says that in the future the Lord will dwell with his people without any need of a temple.[277] This is why the New Testament refuses to allow a return to the patterns of the old covenant. Regression to the older, shadowy forms of the old covenant, such as the temple, are forbidden to Christians. This transition within the progressive flow of biblical history is explained fully by the writer to the Hebrews. Hebrews 8:13

---

275. See John Noe, *The Israel Illusion* (Fishers, IA: Prophecy Reformation Institute, 2000), p. 16.
276. Robertson, *Israel of God*, pp. 53–83, 194.
277. Rev. 21:22.

provides not only the hermeneutical key to challenge Christian Zionism, but also explains Paul's vehemence at the Judaizing tendencies corrupting the church in Galatia:

> By calling this covenant 'new', he has made the first one obsolete; and what is obsolete and ageing will soon disappear . . . The law is only a shadow of the good things that are coming – not the realities themselves. For this reason it can never, by the same sacrifices repeated endlessly year after year, make perfect those who draw near to worship. (Heb. 8:13; 10:1)

The followers of Jesus, indwelt by the Holy Spirit have become temples in which his *shekinah* glory dwells. To suggest, therefore, that the *shekinah* is to return to a single local shrine in Jerusalem to which Jews and Christians must come to worship is to regress from the reality to the shadow, to re-erect the dividing curtain of the temple and to commit apostasy, since it impugns the finished atoning work of Christ.[278] The preoccupation, therefore, among Christian Zionists with locating the site of the temple, with training temple priests, with breeding red heifers and raising funds for the temple treasury is at best a distraction, and at worst a heresy. Christian support for the rebuilding of the Jewish temple is, however, also invariably linked to a belief in an imminent apocalyptic war, unparalleled in human history. Christian Zionists are, in the words of Don Wagner, intrinsically and pathologically, 'anxious for Armageddon'.

The future: the eschatology of Christian Zionism

Of the four main eschatological traditions: amillennial, premillennial, post-millennial and transmillennial, Christian Zionism is predominantly, if not exclusively, premillennial.[279] Both broad strands, covenantal and dispensational, are inherently pessimistic about the future, prior to the return of Christ. It is the latter, however, with its separate destinies for Israel and the church and its unique doctrine of the rapture and tribulation which has, especially since 1970, come to shape Christian Zionism through the apocalyptic and Messianic

---

278. See Robertson, *Israel of God*, p. 82.

279. For a specific examination of dispensational Christian Zionism, see Venema, *Promise of the Future*, pp. 205–218. See also, Grenz, *Millennial Maze*, and Clouse (ed.), *Meaning of the Millennium*.

dispensationalism associated with leaders like Hal Lindsey, Tim LaHaye, Moishe Rosen and David Brickner.[280] Lindsey claims, for example, that his book *The Late Great Planet Earth* 'has been instrumental all around the world in bringing tens of thousands of Jews to faith in Jesus as their Messiah. I run into them everywhere.' He also claims,

> The first Prime Minister of Israel, David Ben Gurion, was reading it shortly before he died. Since everything in his room has been kept the way it was before he died, a copy of *The Late Great Planet Earth* remains on his desk. A friend of mine who is one of Israel's top military commanders passed out hundreds of copies of the Hebrew translation to the Israeli Defence forces, even though he personally hasn't as yet believed in Jesus as the Messiah.[281]

Gary DeMar and Peter Leithart observe that 'If Lindsey had not intimated at dates, and used the regathering of unbelieving ethnic Israel to their land as the basis for his speculations, *The Late Great Planet Earth* would not have been an eschatological novelty. It was the predictions that sold the books.'[282] While they suggest that many who call themselves dispensationalists are really 'Lindseyite dispensationalists', in so far as dispensational writers such as John Walvoord and Tim LaHaye share Lindsey's approach to prophecy (and they in turn have been imitated by others such as Grant Jeffrey, Charles Dyer, Dave Hunt and Jack Van Impe), the generic term 'apocalyptic dispensationalism' is a more appropriate descriptive term for what has become the prevailing genre of dispensationalism today.

Apocalyptic dispensationalism has grown in popularity largely because of Lindsey's unconventional approach to prophecy and those who imitate him. Crucial to this pessimistic reading of biblical prophecy is the conviction that a period of tribulation is imminent along with the secret rapture of the church and the rebuilding of the Jewish temple on the Temple Mount. This will trigger the war of Armageddon in which large numbers of Jews will suffer and die. Jesus will return to rescue the remnant of believing Jews, restore the kingdom to Israel and rule from Jerusalem for a thousand years. An examination of Lindsey's novel prophetic style will lead to an analysis of the main features of Christian Zionist eschatology, namely: the signs of the

---

280. E.g. Hindson, *Approaching Armageddon*; Rosen, *Overture to Armageddon?*; Brickner, *Future Hope*.
281. Lindsey, *Road to Holocaust*, p. 195.
282. DeMar and Leithart, *Legacy of Hatred*, p. 17.

times; the rapture; the tribulation and Armageddon; the second advent and Day of Judgment.

Predicting the future: the prophet Hal

Hal Lindsey has been largely responsible for popularizing a rather controversial, if now widely held, approach to prophecy. Essentially, Lindsey is providing a teleology, that is an interpretation of history, rather than an eschatology, which is concerned primarily with the return of Christ and beyond.[283] Lindsey assumes, for example, that prophecy is pre-written history; is authenticated by predictive accuracy; is written in code and needs deciphering.

Prophecy: pre-written history

Charles Ryrie first described the Bible as 'history prewritten',[284] while Charles Dyer views the dispensations as 'providing us with a chronological map to guide us'.[285] Derek Prince amplifies this further by claiming, 'The central theme of biblical prophecy . . . revolves around the land and the people of Israel.'[286] Lindsey has popularized this idea that biblical prophecy is essentially futuristic and predictive, revealing God's future plans for earth and specifically concerning Israel. So he claims, 'The center of the entire prophetic forecast is the State of Israel. Certain events in that nation's recent history prove the accuracy of the prophets. They also force us to accept the fact that the "countdown" has begun.'[287] On the back cover of *The Late Great Planet Earth*, he asserts: 'Three millenniums of history are strewn with evidence of their prophetic marksmanship and to ignore their incredible predictions of man's destiny and the events which are soon to affect this planet will be perhaps the greatest folly of this generation.' In the introduction to *There's A New World Coming*, Lindsey also claims, 'The information in the book you're about to read is more up-to-date than tomorrow's newspaper . . . I think you will be surprised to see what kind of predictions were made almost two thousand years ago'

---

283. See Vernard Eller, 'Theology of Promise *v.* Theology of Hope', *The Christian Century*, 10 April 1968, available online at <http://hccentral.com/eller1/cco41068.html>; see also, Mick Broderick, 'Heroic Apocalypse, Mad Max, Mythology and the Millennium', in C. Sharrett (ed.), *Crisis Cinema: The Apocalyptic Idea in Postmodern Narrative Film* (Washington: Maissoneuvre Press, 1993), pp. 250–272.

284. Charles Ryrie, *The Living End* (Old Tappan, NJ: Revell, 1976), p. 80.

285. Dyer, *Rise of Babylon*, p. 189.

286. Prince, *Last Word on the Middle East*, p. 54.

287. Lindsey, *1980's: Countdown*, p. 11.

(p. 7). By 1980, Lindsey had become more dogmatic as to the veracity of his latest book: 'it is intended to analyze what *will* occur in the decade we have just entered' (emphasis added).[288] In *Planet Earth 2000 AD* (1996), Lindsey suggests that although the world is spinning out of control, 'as you will discover, everything is in order. God told us these things would happen – in advance' (p. 2). Lindsey claims the biblical prophets have simply recorded future events. So in *Planet Earth, The Final Chapter* (1998), Lindsey insists, 'These weapons are so new, so secret, and so deadly that few people outside of military circles even know such weapons exist. But God knew, and he told Zechariah all about them when he was given details of another, upcoming battle for Jerusalem' (p. 227). Lindsey does not explain how these weapons could remain secret if Zechariah wrote about them 2,400 years ago.

Treating prophecy as pre-written history, Lindsey detaches predictions concerning the future from the covenantal context within which the prophecies were originally given. His view is at variance with the Hebrew prophets themselves who consistently stress their mandate to call God's people to repent and return to their covenant relationship. It was not their stated intention primarily to reveal arbitrary and otherwise hidden facts about predestined future events thousands of years hence. Authentic biblical prophecy is always conditional rather than fatalistic. The promises and warnings of Scripture are conditional upon how people respond to God's instructions. Consequently, sometimes the prophecies did not come true. For example, when Micah predicted that Jerusalem would be 'ploughed like a field' and 'become a heap of rubble' (Mic. 3:12), his warnings led to repentance and revival under King Hezekiah (Jer. 26:17–19): 'As a result, the Lord held back his judgement He had in mind'.[289] The same principle is seen in the story of Jonah (Jon. 4:1–3, 10–11).

It is suggested, therefore, that Lindsey has more in common with the false prophets who flattered the people with promises of peace and prosperity without specifying the covenantal preconditions of repentance and faith.[290] By treating prophecy as deterministic and 'prewritten', Lindsey legitimatizes Israel's unilateral territorial claims while ignoring the conditional nature of the covenant relationship.

Prophecy: predictive accuracy
In his first work, *The Late Great Planet Earth*, Lindsey surveys the apparent

---

288. Ibid., p. 7 (*emphasis added*).

289. Lindsey, *Planet Earth, the Final Chapter*, pp. 52–53.

290. See Van der Waal, *Hal Lindsey and Biblical Prophecy*, p. 51.

revival of interest in astrology, spiritualism and clairvoyancy: 'The Bible makes fantastic claims; but these claims are no more startling than those of present day astrologers, prophets and seers. Furthermore, the claims of the Bible have a greater basis in historical evidence and fact' (pp. 17–18). In his third book, *There's A New World Coming: A Prophetic Odyssey*, written three years later, Lindsey continues to take a comparative approach to prophecy, comparing the claims of the Old Testament prophets to those of the druids of Stonehenge:

> Through these stones, 4000 years ago, priests could sight the sun, moon and stars and predict with exact accuracy the seasons, sun risings and eclipses of the sun and moon . . . There have been many, throughout the centuries of man's long history, who have sought to predict the course of human events, but none have had the incredible accuracy of the ancient Hebrew prophets.[291]

In 1994, looking back at the popularity of *The Late Great Planet Earth*, Lindsey challenges his critics, 'Not surprisingly, then, I'll confidently hold up my track record against that of any modern-day astrological charlatan or New Age clairvoyant.'[292] Ironically, the last chapter of *The Late Great Planet Earth* is entitled, 'Polishing the Crystal Ball' (p. 180),[293] while a paragraph-heading in *There's a New World Coming*, describing the book of Revelation, is entitled, 'John's Chain of ESP' (p. 12). In taking a comparative as well as cavalier approach to prophecy, Lindsey has been criticized for blurring the distinction between biblical and occult sources.[294] This is further exacerbated by Lindsey's belief that prophecy is also veiled and needs decoding.

Prophecy: in 'Bible code'

Lindsey claims to have unlocked prophetic puzzles throughout the Bible. Hidden away within these enigmas are specific predictions concerning the present and imminent future. In the wake of the 'Bible code' debate, Lindsey rewrote *There's a New World Coming* (1973) and renamed it *The Apocalypse Code* (1997), claiming to have deciphered 'long-hidden messages about man's future and the fate of the earth' (back cover). The back cover of *The Final Battle* also states: 'You couldn't get a better picture of what World War III will be like

---

291. Lindsey, *There's a New World Coming*, back page.
292. Lindsey, *Planet Earth 2000 AD*, p. 4.
293. See also DeMar, *Last Days Madness*, p. 197.
294. See Van der Waal, *Hal Lindsey and Biblical Prophecy*, p. 51.

without being bodily transported into the future. Hal Lindsey has done it again!' [295] Van der Waal writes, 'In his books, Hal Lindsey uses biblical prophecy to open a supermarket in which he sells the curious inside information about the near future, especially World War III.'[296] To do so, Lindsey has to perform 'acrobatic stunts', twisting biblical texts to fit his future scenario, propounding what some critics regard as a modern form of Gnosticism.[297] He claims that only those who read his books or subscribe to his online news service will be able to understand prophecy. Responding to criticism that he did not foresee the collapse of Soviet Communism, Lindsey carefully denies that he ever claimed to be a prophet. He does, however, confess to making 'a series of predictions' and is happy to quote others who believe he is 'The Jeremiah for this generation.'[298]

Lindsey's novel and controversial approach, frequently copied if rarely equalled, assumes therefore that prophecy is history pre-written, is authenticated by predictive accuracy and requires his own decoding. Such a pessimistic and determinist view of the future has certain profound implications for the Jewish people as well as for international relations in the Middle East. As will be explored in the next chapter, this futurist eschatology and the dispensational presuppositions which underpin it have been exploited to serve the interests of religious and political Zionism.

Signs of the end: times are changing

The rise of a literal and futurist premillennial reading of prophecy, associated with the Albury and Powerscourt conferences, led to much speculation as to how contemporary events, such as wars, famines and earthquakes, proved that the end of the world was imminent. In his book *The Last Days: A Discourse on the Evil Character of These our Times Proving them to be the 'Perilous Times' of the 'Last Days'* (published in 1828), Edward Irving sought to show that 'we are already entered upon the Last Days, and the ordinary life of a man will carry many of us to the end of them' (p. 10). Compared to the signs highlighted by contemporary apocalyptic dispensationalists, Irving's book, essentially an exposition of 2 Timothy 3:1–6, sounds rather tame. Irving includes chapters on trucebreakers, the fierce, despisers, traitors, and what he termed 'heady highminded' people (p. 5). Nevertheless, the degeneracy of British moral life

---

295. Lindsey, *Final Battle*, back cover.
296. Van der Waal, *Hal Lindsey and Biblical Prophecy*, p. 53.
297. Ibid., pp. 54–55.
298. Lindsey, *Planet Earth 2000 AD*, p. 191; *Final Battle*, back cover.

proved to Irving that his were the last days of the 'Jewish captivity and Gentile dispensation' (p. 10).

Seventy years later, Scofield was still expounding a bleak forecast when he spoke at the Niagara prophetic conference in 1897 on the 'Return of the Lord': 'The signs and portents of the end-time are now so many and so ominous that men of vision everywhere, and in every walk of life, are taking note of them; and this quite apart from the interpretation of them which prophecy gives.' Looking back at previous prophecy conferences, he reminded the audience that their message had not changed: 'We have risen from our study of the Word of God to come up here year by year to utter this warning – that the age ends in disaster, in ruin, in the great, final, world-catastrophe and for this we have been branded pessimists.'[299]

In 1908, in *Jesus is Coming*, Blackstone listed eight signs of Christ's 'speedy' coming. They were: the prevalence of travel and knowledge; perilous times; spiritualism; apostasy; world-wide evangelism; rich men; Israel; and significantly, Zionism (p. 10). Referring to Daniel's prophecy, Blackstone notes: 'It is significant that this first Zionist congress assembled just 1,260 years after the capture of Jerusalem by the Mohammedans in AD 637' (p. 241). The trauma of the First World War heightened speculation still further among dispensationalists. It also generated a good deal of cynicism regarding hopes for world peace, a pessimism that still persists today. In 1918, Scofield published *What Do The Prophets Say?*, a series of studies which included a chapter entitled, 'Does the Bible Throw Light on This War?' In it he writes:

> So far as the prophetic Word has spoken there is not the least warrant for the expectation that the nations engaged in the present gigantic struggle will or can make a permanent peace. It is fondly dreamed that out of all the suffering and carnage and destruction of this war will be born such a hatred of war as will bring to pass a federation of the nations – the United States of the World – in which will exist but one army, and that an international peace force, rather than an army. For once there is some correspondence between a popular dream and the prophetic Word. For that Word certainly points to a federated world-empire in the end-time of the age (pp. 18–19).

This fixation with a pessimistic assessment of the geo-political scene also affected attitudes towards the place of the Jews within this bleak scenario. Dispensationalists like Benjamin Newton, for example, took the view that the

---

299. Scofield, *Truth* 19 (1897), p. 385; cited in Canfield, *Incredible Scofield*, p. 125.

Jews would be part of a European political and religious alliance in league with the Antichrist:

> When the Papists, and the Greek church and Judaism, and Mohommedanism, and Anglicanism, shall re-echo this sentiment, and when it shall become governmentally adopted by the nations of the Roman world, we shall soon see the 'Ephah' and 'wickedness', its inmate, established in the land of Shinar.[300]

To Newton, the Jews were also consigned their allotted destiny with the Antichrist in a preordained prophetic scheme: 'the great majority of Israel, especially those in the Land, will have linked themselves with Antichrist, and will share his doom'.[301]

As has been shown, Newton's prophetic speculations reflect the way in which the focus of premillennial dispensationalism, by the end of the nineteenth century, had become more concerned with dating the 'signs of the times' than with proclaiming the Christian gospel. Gone was the passion for the lost that had fired postmillennial missionary expansion a century earlier. Those who identified more with covenantal premillennialism and remained committed to the established denominations, to Jewish evangelism as well as restorationism, tended to view the same signs differently. So, for example, the response of the London Jews' Society to the Balfour Declaration was optimistic, since it signalled the end of the 'Times of the Gentiles':

> In the light of prophetic scripture we recognise that such an action on the part of our government and on the part of the Allied Powers, in being united in their resolve to reinstate the Jew in his own land, is full of significance . . . Ever since AD 70 Jerusalem and Palestine have been under Gentile domination, and now we seem to be on the very verge of a literal fulfilment of the last prediction, and it is certainly a distinct warning to us that the Lord 'is near, even at the very doors' (St Matt. 24:32).[302]

---

300. Newton, *Babylon*, pp. 145, 150; 'Shinar' is the earliest Hebrew name for Babylon. It is interesting that Charles Dyer, a modern Dallas Seminary dispensationalist, similarly regards the apocalyptic references to Babylon in the book of Revelation as referring literally rather than figuratively to modern Iraq. See Dyer, *Rise of Babylon*, pp. 61–65.

301. B. W. Newton, 'A Statement of Doctrinal Belief', Article 32, in Fromow (ed.), *B. W. Newton and Dr S. P. Tregelles*, p. 60.

302. *Jewish Missionary Intelligence* (1917), pp. 129–130; cited in Crombie, *For the Love of Zion*, p. 160.

As has been shown, similar assertions were made in 1948 when the State of Israel was declared,[303] and again in 1967 with the capture of East Jerusalem.[304] Some thirty-five years later Lindsey was still insisting, 'Folks, the footsteps of our Lord and Savior, Jesus Christ, can already be heard as He approaches the doors of heaven to return.'[305]

Dwight Wilson observes how premillennial history is 'strewn with a mass of erroneous speculations which have undermined their credibility'. The supposed restoration of the Jewish people merely compounded disagreement as to whether the Jews were to be restored before or after the coming of Jesus, in faith or in unbelief. Similarly, he argues pessimistically that since 'The restoration . . . has been pinpointed to have begun in 1897, 1917, and 1948 . . . It is not likely that the situation will change greatly.'[306]

While covenantal and dispensational premillennialists agree that these are the 'Last Days', they disagree, however, over what will happen next. While dispensationalists disagree among themselves as to whether a secret rapture will remove Christians before, during or after the period known as the tribulation, covenantalists believe the church will remain on earth until Christ returns.

The rapture: the great escape

Dispensationalism, with its novel distinction between God's eternal purposes for Israel and the church, is also responsible for the doctrine of the rapture. Popularized by Darby[307] but probably originating with Irving,[308] dispensationalists believe there will be two stages to Christ's imminent return. First, there will be an invisible 'appearing' when Christians will be removed from the earth and meet Christ in the air, a process which came to be known as 'the rapture of the saints'. With the restraining presence of the Holy Spirit removed from the world, the Antichrist will arise, evil will prevail and unbelievers, including

---

303. CMJ, 'The State of Israel: Why should we support it?', *Always be Prepared to Give an Answer Resource* (St Albans: CMJ, 1996).

304. Van der Hoeven, *Babylon or Jerusalem?*, p. 151.

305. Lindsey, *Planet Earth 2000 AD*, p. 160; *Planet Earth, the Final Chapter*, p. 108.

306. Wilson, *Armageddon Now!*, pp. 216–218.

307. Darby, 'The Rapture of the Saints and the Character of the Jewish Remnant', in *Collected Writings*, vol. 2, Prophetic 1, pp. 153–155.

308. Bass, *Backgrounds to Dispensationalism*, p. 41; Dave MacPherson, *The Unbelievable Pre-Trib Origin* (Kansas City: Heart of America Bible Society, 1973); also, *The Incredible Cover-Up* (Medford, OR: Omega Publications, 1975). See also, Edward Irving, 'Signs of the Times in the Church', *Morning Watch* 2, March 1830, pp. 156–158.

the Jews now restored to Israel, will suffer for seven years during the tribulation. Satan's rule will finally be crushed by the public appearance of Jesus
Christ. Concerning the rapture, Darby argued that 'The Church's joining
Christ has nothing to do with Christ's appearing or coming to earth. Her place
is elsewhere. She sits in Him already in heavenly places. She has to be brought
there as to bodily presence.'[309] This hope in a secret rapture perhaps explains
why dispensationalists are either complacent or disinterested in what will
happen to the Jews during the tribulation. Blackstone, for example, says,

> The detail of the manner of their restoration, and of their repentance and acceptance
> of Christ, is not so important to us. For those who are of the Church are to be taken
> away first, in the Rapture, and escape all these things through which Israel must pass.[310]

This is perhaps why dispensationalists are unafraid of another imminent
holocaust. Whereas Israel has been described as the 'Fuse of Armageddon',[311]
Christians will be raptured safely to heaven just before Armageddon begins. So,
in a review of John Walvoord's *End Times*, Jews for Jesus promises reassuringly:

> The end times can be happy and rewarding for Christians. The key is understanding
> them. With clarity, logic and conviction, this book dramatically explores world events
> in light of biblical prophecy, outlining the precepts of our faith. Written by one of
> the field's top experts, it is the definitive work on prophecy.[312]

With heightened tension associated with Y2K, other dispensational writers
ventured to emulate Hal Lindsey and speculated about an imminent rapture
and tribulation.[313] For example, Jews for Jesus offers this description of
LaHaye's bestselling *Left Behind* series:

> The bestselling Christian fiction series of all time, with over 7 million sold! Thrilling end-

---

309. Darby, 'Rapture', in *Collected Writings*, pp. 153–155.

310. Blackstone, *Jesus is Coming*, p. 176.

311. Lindsey, *Late Great Planet Earth*, p. 44.

312. Jews for Jesus review, see http://store.jewsforjesus.org/books/products/
    BK232.htm>. [Accessed May 2002.]

313. E.g. John Walvoord, *The Blessed Hope and the Tribulation* (Grand Rapids: Zondervan,
    1975); Tim LaHaye, *No Fear of the Storm: Why Christians Will Escape All the Tribulation*
    (Sisters, OR: Multnomah, 1992); Finis Jennings Dake, *The Rapture and the Second
    Coming of Christ* (Lawrenceville, GA: Dake Bible Sales, 1977).

time adventure looks at life on Earth following the Rapture. In one cataclysmic moment, millions around the globe disappear, vehicles careen out of control, loved ones vanish before your eyes, global chaos ensues . . . You'll pick it up – but not put it down![314]

It is for the same reason that Lindsey cautioned Christians against getting involved in the millennium celebrations planned for 31 December 1999. Given the state of the world, he claimed he was not planning to be around:

I wouldn't make any long-term earthly plans. We may be caught up to meet Christ in the clouds, between now and then . . . Could I be wrong? Of course. The Rapture may not occur between now and the year 2000. But never before in the history of the planet have events and conditions so coincided as to set the stage for this history-stopping event . . . I want to spend the final pages of this book discussing what I expect to see happen in the hours and minutes we have left.[315]

Passages used by dispensationalists, such as 1 Thessalonians 4, actually say nothing about any secret rapture, still less that the church will be removed and later return to earth with Christ at his public appearing. Clarence Bass insists: 'Only by involved exegetical interpretation can the pre-Tribulation Rapture be supported.'[316] Nevertheless, with Christians removed, dispensationalists speculate on one of the more controversial aspects of their eschatology – the fate of the Jews during the tribulation and battle of Armageddon.

Armageddon: Jacob's trouble

In Matthew 24 Jesus warned his hearers to flee from the impending fall of Jerusalem to the Romans. Dispensationalists take such prophecies and apply them to future events. In so doing, they warn of dire consequences for Jewish people today. Early dispensational descriptions of the events surrounding the tribulation and Armageddon tend to be concise and almost clinical.[317] Scofield's notes, for example, describe how 'Armageddon is the appointed place for the beginning of the great battle in which the Lord, at his coming in

312. Jews for Jesus website, <http://store.jewsforjesus.org/ppp/product.php?prodid=130>. [Accessed August 2004.]

315. Lindsey, Planet Earth 2000 AD, p. 306.

316. Bass, Backgrounds to Dispensationalism, p. 39.

317. An exception to this was S. D. Baldwin who wrote Armageddon: Or the Overthrow of Romanism and Monarchy; the Existence of the United States Foretold in the Bible (Cincinnati: Applegate and Company, 1854).

glory, will deliver the Jewish remnant besieged by the Gentile world-powers under the Beast and False Prophet.'[318]

William Blackstone is more explicit about the suffering of the Jewish people during the tribulation. In his immensely influential book, *Jesus is Coming*, Blackstone asserts, 'Surely Israel shall be restored; but there is an awful time of trouble awaiting her. Their sins are mountain high. Upon them is the guilt of innocent blood, even the precious blood of Jesus Christ' (p. 174). Whether intentionally or otherwise, Blackstone perpetuated the claim that Jews remain guilty of deicide, a charge that has led to much anti-Semitism. He goes on to refer to 'Jacob's trouble' mentioned in Jeremiah 30:6–7 and warns, 'It is probable that "the times of the Gentiles" are near their end, and that the nations are soon to plunge into the mighty whirl of events connected with Israel's godless gathering' (p. 241). To Blackstone, therefore, while Zionism might indeed be a 'sign', it was certainly not one to be welcomed or associated with. Other dispensationalists such as James Gray and Arno Gaebelein, who contributed to the *Scofield Reference Bible*, have also been criticized for apparently expressing anti-Semitic sentiments.[319]

The Jewish people fare little better in the predictions of more contemporary dispensationalists, who provide even more graphic and detailed descriptions of the suffering that will take place in Israel during the tribulation and battle of Armageddon. Charles Ryrie, for example, predicts this will be 'the time of Israel's greatest bloodbath'.[320] Walvoord similarly predicts a holocaust in which at least 750 million people will perish.[321] LaHaye warns that 'Jacob's trouble', prophesied by Jeremiah 30:7, will certainly be far worse than the Spanish Inquisition . . . or even the Holocaust of Adolf Hitler.'[322]

While confident that Christians will escape Armageddon and witness the events from heaven, Lindsey was initially more ambivalent concerning the fate of the Jews.[323] In *There's a New World Coming* (1973), Lindsey claimed God will supernaturally deliver Messianic Jews who come to believe in Jesus during the tribulation: 'The fact that God redeems 144,000 literal Jews and ordains them His evangelists not only makes good sense but fits in with the counsel of God

318. *Scofield Reference Bible,* fn. 4, pp. 1348–1349.

319. Gaebelein, *Conflict of the Ages*; Weber, *Living in the Shadow*, p. 189.

320. Charles Ryrie, *The Living End* (Old Tappan, NJ: Revell, 1976), p. 81; ch. 8 is entitled 'A Bloodbath for Israel.'

321. Walvoord, *Israel in Prophecy*, p. 108.

322. LaHaye and Jenkins, *Are We Living in the End Times?*, p. 146.

323. Lindsey, *Late Great Planet Earth*, pp. 48, 165, 167.

... they are not Jehovah Witnesses, or Mormon elders, or some symbol of the Church; they are Jews, Jews, Jews!' (p. 121). In 1983, in *Israel and the Last Days*, Lindsey is still able to reassure Jewish people that during the tribulation, despite being at the 'vortex' of a world war involving hundreds of millions of soldiers and nuclear attack, in one of the greatest miracles of all time,

> Israel will be converted to faith in her true Messiah and then miraculously protected
> ... (Zechariah 12:8, 9). As promised, God will strengthen the Israelis to fight with a
> ferocity never seen before on this earth. He will also supernaturally protect them
> from being annihilated (pp. 45–46).

By 1994, however, Lindsey was offering a more pessimistic forecast: '... only a tiny fraction of the world's population will be left. Only a remnant will have survived. Many of the Jews would have been killed.'[324] In *The Final Battle* (1995), under the heading 'It will take a miracle to save Israel – Intelligence Digest', Lindsey claims, 'Israel is in for a very rough time. The Jewish State will be brought to the brink of destruction' (p. 184). In a later chapter, he clarifies what this will mean for the Jews:

> The land of Israel and the surrounding area will certainly be targeted for nuclear attack.
> Iran and all the Muslim nations around Israel have already been targeted with Israeli
> nukes ... All of Europe, the seat of power of the Antichrist, would surely be a nuclear
> battlefield, as would the United States ... Zechariah gives an unusual, detailed account
> of how hundreds of thousands of soldiers in the Israel battle zone will die. Their flesh
> will be consumed from their bones, their eyes from their sockets, and their tongues from
> their mouths while they stand on their feet (Zechariah 14:12). This is exactly the sort of
> thing that happens from the intense radiation of a neutron type bomb (pp. 255–257).

Lindsey claims that for a distance of 200 miles from the Valley of Jezreel near Megiddo across to the Jordan Valley then down to the Dead Sea and on to the Gulf of Aqaba, the entire valley will be filled with the debris of war and the bodies of animals and people, and, above all, blood. He writes:

> I have travelled the entire length of this valley ... It is almost impossible to imagine
> the valley covered with blood five feet high! Yet that is exactly what God predicts, and
> He always fulfils His Word. Some have asked, 'Wouldn't the blood coagulate and not
> flow?' Blood exposed to intense radiation doesn't coagulate ... Because of the

---

324. Lindsey, *Planet Earth 2000 AD*, p. 264.

intense radiation, blood will not coagulate. It will literally become a sea of blood five feet deep (pp. 251–252, 284).

But Lindsey believes God's power is stronger than nuclear weapons and that he will supernaturally protect the believing Israelis so that they will survive the worst holocaust the world will ever see. It is difficult to conceive how this will be possible, biologically or ecologically, or indeed how 144,000 Jewish evangelists will then have any ministry to perform in a post-nuclear winter, since half the world's population will have been annihilated already. Lindsey claims that the forces unleashed will be so destructive, they will be sufficient to modify the world's climate and topography, and to level every city.[325] It is difficult to imagine anyone still alive, let alone sane enough, who will want to listen, in his words, to '144,000 Hebrew Billy Grahams running round the world'.[326]

Lindsey's apocalyptic views are, however, shared by many other authors, including several associated with Jews for Jesus.[327] Reviewing *The Late Great Planet Earth*, the Jews for Jesus website promises: 'This book will undoubtedly help you decide where you fit in God's prophetic plan for the ages.'[328] David Brickner's own book, *Future Hope*, depicts an identical scenario to Lindsey's. His literalist exegesis similarly creates dissonance between biblical texts and contemporary events, with invading armies using Bronze Age military tactics while deploying twenty-first-century weaponry (pp. 71–72). While encouraging Jews to return to Israel, Brickner is pessimistic about their fate: 'The good news is, as the prophet said, that Israel will be delivered in the end. The bad news is that deliverance comes at enormous cost and through great conflict' (p. 35). Brickner is convinced Jerusalem will be the epicentre of the battle of Armageddon:

> There is terrible bloodshed as Jerusalem suffers horrible defeat . . . half of the people
> in the city are destroyed or taken into captivity. The destruction and devastation are

---

325. Lindsey, *Apocalypse Code*, p. 237.

326. Ibid., p. 118.

327. Rosen's book *Overture to Armageddon* was inspired by the Gulf War and Saddam Hussein's rise to power. See also, Brickner, *Future Hope*; Louis Goldberg, 'Haman, Hitler, and Now Hussein – Another Holocaust?', *Issues* 8.1 (available online at <http://www.jfjonline.org/pub/issues/08-01/hamanhitler.htm>. [Accessed August 2004.]).

328. Mitch Glaser, review of Hal Lindsey with C.C. Carson, *The Late Great Planet Earth*, in *Issues* 3.7 (available online at <http://www.jfjonline.org/pub/issues/03-07/bookreview0307.htm> [Accessed May 2002]).

hard to imagine. The nation of Israel is battered, broken and beaten. She is nearly destroyed . . . but it's not over yet (p. 74).

In an article entitled 'Haman, Hitler, and Now Hussein – Another Holocaust?', Louis Goldberg, the scholar-in-residence of Jews for Jesus, describes a similarly terrifying scenario awaiting Israel, based on his literal reading of Zechariah 13 – 14:

'So,' you might ask, 'with Israel once more on her ancient soil and enjoying freedom she has not known for 2,500 years, how in the world can we talk about another holocaust? How would nations and leaders permit such a situation ever to occur again?'[329]

Goldberg answers with a quotation from Zechariah 13 to prove that it will, in his calculations, lead to at least 2.5 million Jews dying in Israel alone. He claims that the suffering of survivors will be worse than at any other time in their history:

What horror! What destruction! How can we even talk about it? It should make every human being weep. With the ovens of Auschwitz and Bergen-Belsen still warm in the minds of the Holocaust survivors, how can we even begin to imagine another carnage?[330]

To corroborate his claim that Zechariah is referring to a future holocaust, Goldberg quotes the words of Shlomo Goren, a former senior intelligence officer who was the Coordinator of Government Operations in Judea, Samaria and the Gaza district: 'We are now entering the long, dark tunnel . . . We already hear the footsteps of Messiah as we begin our dark experiences!'[331] Rosen raises the apocalyptic temperature higher by claiming, 'The sure word of prophecy in the scripture promises that the dawn is nearing . . . Listen closely as the orchestra begins. Can you hear the themes? The piece they are playing is "The Overture to Armageddon".'[332]

Although Rosen, Brickner and Goldberg are all Jewish by birth, their writings could be construed as anti-Semitic for predicting with such certitude another holocaust as part of God's purposes, which in their own words, will be worse than anything experienced in history.

---

329. Goldberg, 'Haman, Hitler, and Now Hussein'.

330. Ibid.

331. Ibid.

332. Rosen, *Overture to Armageddon?*, p. 189.

Indeed, Rosen's *Overture to Armageddon* begins with a 'Warning to the Reader.' His purpose is clear: 'It is intended to shock the reader because the realities of life are often shocking' (p. 10). Lindsey's *The Final Battle* similarly begins with these instructions, 'Read this book. Learn from it. Pass it on to your friends. It may be the last chance some of them will ever have to avoid the horrible fate this book describes' (p. xxi). Messianic dispensationalists such as Rosen, Brickner and Goldberg, therefore, share with apocalyptic dispensationalists such as Lindsey and LaHaye, the conviction that a literal and futurist exposition of Old Testament prophecies will shock people into believing in Jesus, either before or during the tribulation, while believers themselves will escape the carnage through the rapture. They also remain confident that those same scriptures promise that most Jews will come to faith when Jesus returns, at least among those who survive long enough.

It is noteworthy that some Zionist agencies, such as the International Christian Embassy Jerusalem, while essentially dispensational in theology and believing that prophecies relating to the ingathering of the Jewish people to Israel are being fulfilled today, nevertheless dissociate themselves from the apocalyptic dispensationalism of Hal Lindsey and Tim LaHaye. In working closely at a political and humanitarian level with the Israeli government and Jewish agencies, their understanding of the future of Israel,

> does NOT include the distasteful belief that 'once all the Jews in the world emigrate to Israel, two-thirds of them will die in Armegeddon (sic) and one-third convert to Christianity'. There are some who call themselves Christian who subscribe to that teaching. We do not and have sought to refute it where possible.[333]

The ICEJ represents, therefore, a more optimistic, though non-evangelistic form of political dispensationalism. The uncharacteristic stance taken by the ICEJ nevertheless highlights a tension inherent within virtually all forms of dispensationalism. Because of their commitment to a literal futurist hermeneutic in which prophecy is pre-written history, dispensationalists predict both the persecution and salvation of the Jews.[334] They have, therefore, been criticized for acquiescing over crimes of anti-Semitism since they believe these awful acts may

---

333. Kern, *Blessing Israel? Christian Embassy Responds* (2 Nov. 1997) [Internet], Christian Peacemakers Team, <http://menno.org.cpt.news@mennolink.org> (*emphasis in original*). [Accessed May 2004.]

334. See Timothy P. Weber, 'A Reply to David Rausch's "Fundamentalism and the Jew",' *Journal of the Evangelical Theological Society* (March 1981), p. 70.

be the fulfilment of the prediction concerning 'Jacob's trouble'. Dwight Wilson's research into dispensationalism in the 1930s, for example, reveals that some premillennial writers placed part of the blame for anti-Semitism on the Jews themselves, that they were responsible for revolutions in continental Europe and even for the Great Depression in America. Wilson argues:

> Pleas from Europe for assistance for Jewish refugees fell on deaf ears and 'Hands Off' meant no helping hand. So in spite of being theologically more pro-Jewish than any other Christian group, the premillenarians also were apathetic – because of a residual anti-Semitism, because persecution was prophetically expected, because it would encourage immigration to Palestine, because it seemed the beginning of the Great Tribulation, and because it was a wonderful sign of the imminent blessed hope.[335]

This explains why, for example, Blackstone and Gaebelein could appear to use anti-Semitic rhetoric while supporting evangelistic initiatives among Jews, and why Lindsey, Brickner and Fruchtenbaum could envisage a bleak apocalyptic future for Israel while believing God will continue to bless America as long as it supports Israel. DeMar observes that within such an eschatology, 'Jews are always in jeopardy of being persecuted as long as dispensationalists push a false interpretation of prophecy that makes Jews the scapegoat for a distorted theological system.'[336] This leads inexorably to the most detrimental aspect of contemporary dispensationalism.

Aligning themselves with Jewish Zionists, they are implacably opposed to any peace-deal in the Middle East. While books by apocalyptic dispensationalists sell in their millions, few concern themselves with contemporary issues of peace and justice, other than to warn of a counterfeit peace which the Antichrist will offer Israel.[337] The various strands of dispensationalism are also united in the belief that God will judge the world on the basis of how people have treated the Jews.

Judgment Day: choosing sides and blessing Israel

The return of Christ is seen by all millennial traditions as the consummation of God's purposes on earth and synonymous with the Day of Judgment. Dispensationalism, with its rigid distinction between Israel and the church and its doctrine of a secret rapture and tribulation, is based on a rather more

---

335. Wilson, *Armageddon Now!*, pp. 96–97.
336. DeMar, *Last Days of Madness*, p. 451.
337. See, e.g., Hunt, *Global Peace and the Rise of Antichrist*.

complex eschatological chronology. There is a diversity of opinion as to the purpose of Christ's return as well as the basis of his judgment. Scofield, for example, having divided the world into three classes of people,[338] sees the return of Jesus Christ as having a 'threefold relation: to the church, to Israel, to the nations'.[339] He claims that after the Day of Judgment and the removal of the church there would still be 'a world-wide Gentile conversion and participation in the blessings of the kingdom', at least for those who survive Armageddon and are left on earth during the millennium. This is one reason why some dispensational organizations such as the ICEJ regard evangelism among Jewish people as inappropriate or unnecessary within this present dispensation.

Prior to the return of Christ and during the tribulation, classic and apocalyptic dispensationalism tend to associate unbelieving Israel with the devil. Scofield, for example, teaches that the Lord will return, after the secret rapture and removal of the saints to heaven, in order to 'deliver the Jewish remnant besieged by the Gentile world-powers under the Beast and False Prophet'.[340] Similarly, Blackstone places unbelieving Israel in league with the Antichrist, 'who will be received by the Jews'.[341] Lindsey also claims they will make a peace pact with the Antichrist, and a 'treaty with Hell',[342] while LaHaye has Israel sign 'a deal with the devil'.[343] Messianic and political dispensationalists, however, while disagreeing profoundly with each other as to whether Jews need to hear the gospel, nevertheless share a greater affinity with the Jewish people and place unbelieving Israel on God's side against the Antichrist and the Gentile nations. For example, Jan Willem van der Hoeven of the ICEJ claims that virtually the whole world will be against Israel:

> Nations will increasingly shut Israel out of their councils until they finally find themselves coming up against her at Armageddon (Zech. 14:2–3). Disaster will surely strike every nation that turns against Zion (Isa. 60:12) . . . Repeatedly the Bible states that the betrayal of Israel will be a major reason for the wrath of God being heaped upon the nations in the latter days.[344]

---

338. *Scofield Reference Bible*, p. 1221.

339. Ibid. p. 1148.

340. Ibid., fn. 4, pp. 1348–1349.

341. Blackstone, *Jesus is Coming*, p. 108.

342. Lindsey, *Planet Earth 2000 AD*, p. 254; *Late Great Planet Earth*, p. 151.

343. LaHaye and Jenkins, *Are We Living in the End Times?*, p. 159.

344. Jan Willem van der Hoeven, 'A Christian Response to Israel' (pamphlet), quoted in Wagner, *Anxious for Armageddon*, p. 102.

Brickner warns: 'Those who oppose the Messiah, who have aligned themselves with the Antichrist and against Israel, will be judged and delivered into "the abyss".'[345] Derek Prince goes further, insisting, 'When God comes to judge the nations, he will judge them on their response to the regathering of Israel. At that time, no nation will be able to plead ignorance of Israel's regathering, or of the fact that it represents the fulfilment of God's prophetic word.'[346] Writing in 1947, and based on radio programmes broadcast during the 1940s, DeHaan makes the return of the Jews to Palestine and the response of the nations to them, the basis for future world peace.

> The solution of this world's ills lies in this one formula: bring God's covenant people into God's Holy Land . . . there can be no peace in this world until the nation and the land, according to God's purposes are again wholly united . . . The key to lasting peace is the land of Israel and the Israel of the land . . . When Jerusalem is at peace the world will be at peace. Let us pray that the leaders of the nations will soon see that God is on the side of those who recognize his program.[347]

The implication is clear; while the historic churches, including covenantal-ists, believe that the judgment will be based on how people have responded to the claims of Jesus Christ, dispensationalists, whether implicitly or explicitly, appear to make Israel the decisive factor. How people and nations have responded to Israel's territorial claims and whether they have assisted or resisted Jewish emigration to Palestine will determine, in whole or in part, their eternal destiny. This deduction logically follows from the premise that Israel enjoys a separate and superior covenant, purpose and destiny on earth to the church; they remain God's 'chosen people'; are returning to their own land for ever through divine intervention; and the promise made to Abraham concern-ing those who blessed and cursed him now applies to his physical descendants. The distinction between Israel and the church and the literalist hermeneutic upon which it is based, inexorably leads to a reductionist eschatology in which Jesus is devalued, salvation and judgment redefined, and Israel sacralized. Indeed, it could be argued that if Israel is actually the measure for, and medi-ator of, ultimate justice and peace, then 'blessing' Israel has, for some Christian Zionists at least, become synonymous with believing in Jesus.

---

345. Brickner, *Future Hope*, p. 108.

346. Prince, *Last Word on the Middle East*, p. 118.

347. M. R. DeHaan, *Daniel the Prophet: 35 Simple Studies in the Book of Daniel* (Grand Rapids: Zondervan, 1947), pp. 168, 170.

The future assessed

Christian Zionism is inherently pessimistic regarding future world events. A speculative and futurist interpretation of ancient prophecies has led many to believe that the restoration of Jews and the founding of the State of Israel are signs of the end times. From its roots within classic dispensationalism, contemporary apocalyptic dispensationalism, in particular, contrasts the blessed hope of Christians with the fate of Jews during the last seven years before the return of Christ. While Christians will escape, Jews will suffer. Grace Halsell observes:

> Convinced that a nuclear Armageddon is an inevitable event within the divine scheme of things, many evangelical dispensationalists have committed themselves to a course for Israel that, by their own admission, will lead directly to a holocaust indescribably more savage and widespread than any vision of carnage that could have generated in Adolf Hitler's criminal mind.[348]

Such a fatalistic view of the future, with its pre-written script, will inevitably be predisposed to acquiesce in the face of anti-Semitism since this fulfils the prediction of 'Jacob's trouble'. Furthermore, because Christian Zionism is instinctively suspicious and pessimistic about anything international, ecumenical, involving the European Community or United Nations, efforts to achieve a lasting peace in the Middle East are spurned as counterfeit and a Satanic ploy to beguile Israel. The departure from the historic Christian faith is most clearly evident in the reductionist belief that God will judge the world on the basis of how individuals and nations have blessed or cursed Israel.

The distinctive theology of Christian Zionism: conclusions

This chapter has examined seven basic theological tenets which are accepted, in varying degrees, by evangelical Christian Zionists.

1. A literalist hermeneutic and futurist reading of prophecy is the foundation upon which the other six tenets are based. However, it has been argued that this method of interpretation is no more consistent or free of presuppositional influence than any other, and is at times inconsistent, contradictory and arbitrary.

---

348. Halsell, *Prophecy and Politics*, p. 195; see also, DeMar and Leithart, *Legacy of Hatred*, p. 26.

2. A belief that the Jews remain God's chosen people, and separate from the church, flows from this literalist hermeneutic. While covenantal and dispensational Christian Zionists view the relationship between the church and Israel somewhat differently, the consequences of both are essentially the same: Israel is elevated to a status above the church; for dispensationalists at least, Israel will replace the church on earth; while Christians, and indeed whole nations, will be blessed through their association with, and support of, Israel. This view is entirely at variance with the New Testament which universalizes the concept of the people of God and makes chosenness conditional on faith in Jesus Christ.

3. Belief in a final restoration of the Jews to Zion is also based on a literal and futurist reading of selective Old Testament prophecies. However, the texts themselves indicate that such a return occurred under Ezra and Nehemiah and that no further return is to be anticipated. It may be argued that Jesus repudiated any such expectation. New Testament writers apply such Old Testament promises to both believing Jews and Gentiles.

4. It is also an article of faith that Eretz or greater Israel, extending from the River of Egypt to the Euphrates, is the Jewish inheritance originally promised unconditionally to Abraham and his descendants for ever. The progressive revelation of Scripture shows that such promises were actually conditional and, from a New Testament perspective, have been universalized to embrace the entire cosmos.

5. Jerusalem, or Zion, lies at the heart of Christian Zionism. The city is seen as the eternal, undivided and exclusive Jewish capital. Nothing in the New Testament, however, substantiates this claim. Instead Christians are called to break with any dependency upon an earthly city and by faith to recognize that they are already citizens of the heavenly Jerusalem.

6. Most controversially, many believe the temple must be rebuilt and sacrifices re-instituted in order that it can be desecrated by the Antichrist before Jesus returns. The New Testament is emphatic that after the death of Christ, the temple, priestly caste and sacrificial system became obsolete and their perpetuation apostate.

7. For virtually all Christian Zionists, the immediate future is intrinsically pessimistic. The battle of Armageddon will, they claim, lead to the death of two-thirds of the Jewish people before Christ returns to save a remnant. He will judge the world on the basis of how the nations have treated the Jews. The next chapter will show that such fatalism has profound consequences for international diplomacy.

There are three inherent problems with Christian Zionism's distinctive theology. The promises of blessing made to the Jewish people are invariably detached from their covenantal context; the interpretation of those promises by Jesus and the New Testament writers is generally ignored; and the State of Israel is sacralized, the consummation of God's purposes on earth rather than the atoning work of Christ and his redeemed church.

Promises of blessing are isolated from their covenantal context

Christian Zionists detach the promises and warnings made to the Jewish people from their covenantal basis as well as their immediate historical context, imposing an artificial futurist interpretation. Such a view is at variance with the way in which the Hebrew prophets consistently stress their intention to call their contemporaries back to the terms of their covenantal relationship with God, not to reveal arbitrary and otherwise hidden facts about predestined future events thousands of years later. The truly prophetic element of the Hebrew Scriptures yearns for fidelity. God's message to his people is always two-edged, promising blessing but also warning of judgment. It was the false prophets who flattered the people with promises of peace and prosperity without specifying the covenantal preconditions of repentance and faith. The future, in biblical terms, is thereby in some sense conditional upon faith and obedience to God's revealed will.

The interpretation of Scripture by Jesus and the apostles is ignored

Their selective and dualistic hermeneutic leads Christian Zionists to ignore how Jesus and the apostles reinterpreted the Old Testament. It is instead made to speak dogmatically about present and future events with little or no reference to the way in which concepts such as land, city and temple are redefined in the New Testament. The implicit assumption is that the Old and New Testaments continue, in some sense parallel to each other, into the future, the former speaking of God's purposes for Israel and the latter of the church. This is not consistent with the way the New Testament interprets, fulfils, completes and at times annuls the Old. Under the old covenant, revelation from God came often in shadow, image, form and prophecy. In the new covenant that progressive revelation finds its consummation in reality, substance and fulfilment in Jesus Christ and his church.

The sacralizing of Zionism ultimately subordinates the cross

Set within the context of the wider fundamentalist movement, the distinctive eschatological focus of Christian Zionism is placed upon a restored Jewish kingdom rather than the body of Christ, and upon the contemporary State of

Israel rather than the cross of Christ.[349] In the atoning death of Christ, the temple with its sacrificial system was made obsolete. The destruction of the temple in AD 70 fulfilled this judgment. To suggest, therefore, that the temple must be rebuilt and sacrifices reintroduced in a restored Jewish kingdom centred on Jerusalem is to reverse the flow of biblical revelation and to suggest in some sense that the work of Christ was unfinished or incomplete. It may be argued that such a conclusion is implied by the writer of Hebrews who warns that to return to the shadows of the old covenant is apostasy for, 'to their loss they are crucifying the Son of God all over again and subjecting him to public disgrace' (Heb. 6:6).

Christian Zionism's particular reading of history and contemporary events, sustained by the dubious exegesis of selective biblical texts, sets Israel and the Jewish people apart from other peoples in the Middle East. In so doing, however unintentionally, it justifies the endemic racism intrinsic to Zionism, exacerbates tensions between Jews and Palestinians and undermines attempts to find a peaceful resolution of the Palestinian–Israeli conflict, all because 'the Bible tells them so.' The next chapter will examine the political consequences of this theological framework.

---

349. Bass, *Backgrounds to Dispensationalism*, p. 151.

3. THE POLITICAL IMPLICATIONS OF CHRISTIAN ZIONISM

Christian Zionism has profound political consequences. While some commentators have analysed the political involvement of Christians sympathetic to Zionism, especially prior to 1948,[1] few have examined the political activities of contemporary Christian Zionism.[2]

This chapter will examine six ways in which Christian Zionism has been translated into political action, namely: blessing Israel; facilitating Jewish emigration; supporting the settlement programme; lobbying for international recognition of Jerusalem as the capital of Israel; funding the rebuilding of the temple; and opposing the peace process, exacerbating relations with the Arab world and hastening Armageddon. Figure 6 illustrates the correlation between the distinctive doctrines and political activities of Christian Zionism (see p. 207).

---

1. See, e.g., Tuchman, *Bible and Sword*; Sharif, *Non Jewish Zionism*; Merkley, *Politics of Christian Zionism*; Prior, *Zionism and the State of Israel*.

2. See, e.g., Halsell, *Prophecy and Politics*; *Forcing God's Hand*; Wagner, *Anxious for Armageddon*; Merkley, *Christian Attitudes towards the State of Israel*; Burge, *Whose Land? Whose Promise?*

Doctrine	Practice
Chosen people	Standing with Israel
Restorationism	Facilitating the *aliyah* programme
Eretz Israel	Supporting West Bank settlements
Jerusalem	Lobbying for international recognition
Temple	Funding the rebuilding of the temple
The future	Opposing peace and hastening Armageddon

Figure 6. The correlation between Christian Zionist doctrine and practice

The chosen people: supporting Israeli colonialism

The conviction that the Jewish people remain God's 'chosen people' in some way separate from the church, is deeply rooted in Christian Zionism. A recent *Christianity Today* survey of evangelical opinion about Israel gives an indication of the strength of Christian Zionism in America. The survey revealed that 24% believe 'the biblical mandate for Christians is to support the State of Israel'.[3] This is expressed in a variety of ways: defending Israel against charges of racism and apartheid; lobbying Western governments on behalf of Israel; writing to the media when Israel receives adverse publicity; equating anti-Zionism with anti-Semitism;[4] promoting Israeli products; hosting pro-Israeli events; and participating in solidarity tours to Israel. The implications of this Christian support must first of all be examined within the context of how Zionism is viewed politically in the wider world.

---

3. Cited in Prior, *Zionism and the State of Israel,* p. 143.
4. Melanie Philips, 'Christians who hate the Jews', *Spectator* (February 2002);
   Philips has accused the author of anti-Semitism based on mis-quotations from
   S. Sizer, 'Justifying Apartheid in the Name of God', *Churchman* (Summer 2001),
   pp. 147–171.

Zionism and apartheid

Israel has been accused consistently of institutional racism and apartheid by the US government, the United Nations and the South African government, as well as by Israeli political activists and academics.[5]

The word 'apartheid' is a Dutch Afrikaans word derived from the root *apart*, meaning 'separate', and *heid*, meaning 'hood'. In the context of South Africa it was used to describe the legal and institutional segregation of inhabitants of European descent from those of non-European descent. In 1973, the UN defined apartheid as, 'inhuman acts committed for the purpose of establishing and maintaining domination by one racial group of persons over another racial group of persons and systematically oppressing them'.[6] Although subsequently revoked following pressure from the US, in 1975 the UN specifically applied that definition to Israel, condemning the ethnic exclusivism of Zionism as, 'a form of racism and racial discrimination'.[7]

The US State Department country reports on 'Israel and the Occupied Territories', provide an objective and accurate evaluation of the political consequences of Zionism. The 1989 report observed:

> Israel's Arab citizens have . . . not shared fully in the rights granted to Jewish citizens . . . The Department of State has observed that 'Israel welcomes Jewish immigrants . . . to whom it gives automatic citizenship and residence rights,' while it denies such citizenship and residence rights to Palestinians living in refugee camps in the West Bank and in Gaza who were born in Israel, and whose very lands Israel has expropriated and holds 'in trust for the Jewish people' . . . The fourth basic law is

---

5. Statement of the African National Congress concerning the Palestinian People, *World cannot ignore the plight of the Palestinian people* (25 August 2001) [Internet], Badil (Resouce Centre for Palestinian Residency and Refugee Rights), <http://www.badil.org/Resources/WCAR/ANC_Statement.htm>. [Accessed May 2003]; Jeff Halper, 'The 94 Percent Solution: A Matrix of Control', *Middle East Report* 216 (Autumn 2000), available online at <http://www.merip.org/mer/mer216/216_halper.html>. [Accessed May 2003.]

6. *International Convention on the Suppression and Punishment of the Crime of Apartheid* (1973) [Internet], United Nations, High Commissioner for Human Rights, <http://www.unhchr.ch/html/intlinst.htm>. [Accessed May 2003.]

7. *Elimination of all forms of racial discrimination*, 3379 (xxx) (10 Nov. 1975) [Internet], United Nations, General Assembly, <http://domino.un.org/unispal.nsf>. [Accessed May 2003.]

Israel's status law, which gives Israel's citizens with 'Jewish nationality' certain rights and privileges which are denied to Israel's citizens with 'Arab nationality'.[8]

The report for 1999 shows how little progress had been made in the preceding decade:

> The Government made little headway in reducing institutionalized legal and societal discrimination against Israel's Christian, Muslim, and Druze citizens, who constitute just over 20 percent of the population, but do not share fully the rights provided to . . . the country's Jewish citizens.[9]

The UN World Conference on Racism, held in Durban in August 2001, adopted the following declaration:

> For the purpose of the present Declaration and Programme of Action, the victims of racism, racial discrimination, xenophobia and related intolerance are individuals or groups of individuals who are or have been negatively affected by, subjected to, or targets of these scourges . . . We are concerned about the plight of the Palestinian people under foreign occupation. We recognize the inalienable right of the Palestinian people to self determination and to the establishment of an independent state . . . We recognize the right of refugees to return voluntarily to their homes and properties in dignity and safety, and urge all States to facilitate such return.[10]

The implementation of apartheid in South Africa was achieved through three Acts: the Population Registration Act, which defined nationality on the basis of race and thus designated what rights each race would enjoy; the Land Act, which reserved 87% of the land for whites only; and the Group Areas Act, which designated where different ethnic groups could live. Since 1948, successive Israeli

---

8. Cited in Shaw J. Dallal, 'Israel Is Not Comparable to "Advanced Western Democracies"', *Washington Report* (May 1990), p. 14; available online at: <http://www.geocities.com/CapitolHill/Senate/7891/dallal_isrl_dmcr.html>. [Accessed May 2003.]

9. *Country Report on Human Rights Practices: The Occupied Territories* (1999) [Internet], US Department of State, <http://www.state.gov/g/drl/rls/http/1999/417.htm>. [Accessed August 2004.]

10. United Nations, 'World Conference Against Racism, Racial Discrimination, Xenophobia and Related Intolerance Declaration', adopted on 8 September 2001, section 1, 62 and 64.

governments have implemented very similar legislation. The Israeli Population Registry Act (in tandem with the Law of Return) defines identity on the basis of race as well as religion; the Land Act reserves all land managed by the Jewish National Fund, now extending to 93% of the State of Israel, for exclusive Jewish residence while denying similar rights to Israeli Arabs.

Apart from in a few locations such as Haifa, Lod and Jaffa, most Israeli towns and villages are officially segregated. Professor Yvonne Haddad observes that Israel,

> not only bans the return of Palestinian Gentiles to their homeland, but also restricts its Christian and Muslim citizens to specified living areas and limits their access to resources which are monopolized and confiscated by the State (such as education, water, and land).[11]

In 1987, the Jewish academic Uri Davis published what is probably the most detailed work on racism in Israel: *Israel, An Apartheid State*.[12] In it Davis exposed the inherent apartheid in the official structures of the Jewish State which has, since 1948, like South Africa, defined the national status and citizenship rights of its population on racial grounds. He shows how, for example, 90% of the State of Israel has been legally defined as land which only Jews can lease or cultivate. In every aspect of Israeli society, whether in terms of educational provision, access to medical care, employment rights, or treatment under the judicial system, Arabs suffer systematic and institutional discrimination and racism. On Israeli birth certificates for Jewish children citizenship is given as 'Israeli'. In the case of Arabs this category is left blank. Arab children are thus stateless at birth, and must earn Israeli citizenship, whereas the Jewish child is born with it.

Arab villages falling outside Israeli 'zoning' plans are technically illegal and do not appear on Israeli maps, and thus cannot apply for water, electricity or telephones, and so on. Since 1948, over 500 such villages have been demolished and erased from maps of the State of Israel. While all Israelis receive child benefit for their first child, benefit for subsequent children is dependent on the parents completing their military service. Orthodox Jews are exempted from this requirement, while Arabs are not. Consequently, 99% of Jews apply, 99% of Arabs do not.

---

11. Yvonne Haddad, 'American Muslims and the Question of Identity', in Yvonne
     Haddad (ed.), *The Muslims of America* (New York: Oxford University Press, 1991),
     p. 224.

12. Davis, *Israel*, passim.

Numerous other well known Jewish figures have been critical of Israel's apartheid policies. For example, in 1991, Sir Yehudi Menuhin was awarded the prestigious Wolf Prize by the Israeli Government. In his acceptance speech before the Israeli Knesset he referred to Israel's continued occupation of the West Bank in these terms:

> This wasteful governing by fear, by contempt for the basic dignities of life, this steady asphyxiation of a dependent people, should be the very last means to be adopted by those who themselves know too well the awful significance, the unforgettable suffering of such an existence. It is unworthy of my great people, the Jews, who have striven to abide by a code of moral rectitude for some 5,000 years, who can create and achieve a society for themselves such as we see around us but can yet deny the sharing of its great qualities and benefits to those dwelling amongst them.[13]

Although Israel aspires to be a Western democracy, respecting and protecting the rights of ethnic and religious minorities, Jewish critics, especially, argue that institutionally, judicially and religiously the State of Israel continues to practise apartheid.

Standing with Israel
A CMJ resource pack produced in 1996, although later revised, originally included a section entitled 'The State of Israel: Why should we support it?' It expresses succinctly the reasons Christian Zionists identify with Israel: 'In the biblical worldview one cannot . . . divorce the issue of the people of Israel's relationship with God from their relationship to their delegated sovereignty in the land of Israel . . . It seems to us that God is undoubtedly behind the re-creation of the Jewish State in the modern world' and this is the reason why Christians are 'called to support the State of Israel'.[14]

However, as we have noted, Tony Higton, the current general director of CMJ, has stated that the society does not feel obliged to support the political State of Israel any more than it would any other secular state. Apart from the

---

13. Dan Izenberg, 'Wolf Prize winner raps government', *Jerusalem Post*, 6 May 1991.
14. CMJ, 'The State of Israel: Why should we support it?', in *Always be Prepared to Give an Answer*, resource pack (St Albans: CMJ, 1996). The present leadership of CMJ no longer agrees with this statement and it has been revised on their website.

support given by the United States government, Israel has been largely isolated within the international community. Hal Lindsey laments that,

> Twenty-six percent of all Security Council meetings between 1948 and the 1991 Madrid Conference dealt with the Arab–Israeli conflict. The U.N. Security Council passed a total of 175 resolutions. Seventy-four were neutral. Four were against the perceived interests of an Arab body. Ninety-seven were against Israel. In the U.N. General Assembly, the cumulative votes cast during this same period with or for Israel totaled 7,938. Those against Israel totaled 55,642.[15]

Based on Isaiah 40, Christian Zionists interpret the command to 'comfort, comfort my people, says your God' (v. 1) to mean supporting Israel financially and defending it when criticized or attacked.

In October 2000, for example, just days after Ariel Sharon's provocative visit to the Haram Al-Sharif, which appears to have been deliberately timed to undermine the government of Barak for negotiating with Arafat over a shared Jerusalem,[16] an advertisement appeared in the *New York Times* entitled 'Open Letter to Evangelical Christians from Jews for Jesus.' In it JFJ called upon evangelicals to show solidarity with the State of Israel at this critical time:

> Now is the time to stand with Israel. Dear Brothers and Sisters in Christ, our hearts are heavy as we watch the images of violence and bloodshed in the Middle East . . . Christian friends, 'The gifts and calling of God are irrevocable' (Romans 11:29). So

---

15. Hal Lindsey, *The hook-nosed Jew* (20 March 2002) [Internet], <http:www. worldnetdaily.com/news/article.asp?ARTICLE_ID=26892>. [Accessed May 2004.] See also, Morris B. Abram, *Anti-Semitism in the United Nations* (1997) [Internet], Christian Action for Israel website, <http://www.cdn-friends-icej.ca/un/antisem-un.html>. [Accessed August 2004.]

16. In July 2001 the Rabbinical Council of Judea, Samaria and Gaza called on all rabbis to bring their communities to visit the Temple Mount. This was the first time that a group of rabbis representing a significant proportion of the religious Jewish community had ruled that it was permissible for Jews to ascend the Temple Mount. Previously this had been forbidden to orthodox Jews. The rabbis also called upon the Yesha Council of Jewish settlements to organize mass visits to the Temple Mount from the settlements which comprise the more right-wing religious Jews. See N. Shragai, 'Rabbis call for mass visits to Temple Mount', *Ha'aretz*, 19 July 2001.

must our support for the survival of Israel in this dark hour be irrevocable. Now is the time for Christians to stand by Israel.[17]

The International Christian Zionist Center (ICZC) also expresses solidarity with Israel by organizing the annual Feast of Tabernacles celebration in Jerusalem, which brings thousands of Christian Zionists to the city with the intention of blessing Israel. They claim, 'This feast, according to the Word of God is a prophetic feast for the end-times, where all the nations of the earth are welcomed to celebrate this Feast with Israel.'[18] In January 2004, the Israeli Knesset formed the Christian Allies Caucus to coordinate activities with Christian Zionist supporters. The former Russian dissident Natan Sharansky, now the Israeli minister to the *diaspora* and for Jerusalem affairs, recently met with US evangelical leaders in Memphis to express appreciation for their 'steadfast support for the state of Israel'. Among the leaders attending were John Hagee, pastor of the 17,000-member Cornerstone Church in San Antonio, Adrian Rogers, past president of the Southern Baptist Convention, and Edward McAteer, friend of President Bush and chairman of the Religious Roundtable.[19] Many Christian Zionists are convinced that when the world turns against Israel and financial support from the United States falls away, the Jewish State will be able to rely on the economic support of Christian friends.

The Israeli lobby on Capitol Hill

Until the 1980s, US Middle-East policy was largely peripheral to the wider global threat posed by Soviet hegemony. The protection of Western Europe through NATO was a higher priority. The collapse of Communism, however, created a power vacuum in the Middle East which the US has filled. Following the Gulf War to liberate Kuwait and then, more recently, the war to liberate Afghanistan from the Taleban, the US has significantly increased its influence in the Middle East. At the same time there has been a significant increase in

---

17. 'Open Letter to Evangelical Christians from Jews for Jesus: Now is the Time to Stand with Israel', *New York Times*, 23 October 2000.

18. *About Us – Israel My Beloved: A summary of the goals and services of the ICZC* (2003) [Internet], International Christian Zionist Centre, <http://www.israelmybeloved.com>. [Accessed August 2004.]

19. Bill Broadway, 'The Evangelical-Israeli Connection: Many Christians Support Zionism Politically, Financially', *Northwest Arkansas News*, 24 April 2004, available online at <http://www.nwaonline.net/archive/2004/04/24/Religion/187897.html>. [Accessed May 2004.]

the impact of the pro-Israeli lobby. As a consequence, the Middle East, and Israel in particular, has become central to US foreign policy, not least because of the al Qaeda attacks on New York and Washington. In 2002, Dick Armey, the former US Republican House Majority Leader, linked Israel's conflict with the Palestinians with the US global war on terrorism: 'Let me be clear, Israel is fighting the same war on terrorism that we are fighting.'[20]

The Christian right came to influence US foreign policy largely through the election of Ronald Reagan in 1980. His victory over Jimmy Carter gave a considerable boost to the Christian Zionist cause. Donald Wagner outlines the issue:

> The election of Ronald Reagan ushered in not only the most pro-Israel administration in history but gave several Christian Zionists prominent political posts. In addition to the President, those who subscribed to a futurist premillennial theology and Christian Zionism included Attorney General Ed Meese, Secretary of Defence Casper Weinberger, and Secretary of the Interior James Watt.[21]

'White House Seminars' became a regular feature of Reagan's administration, bringing leading Christian Zionists like Jerry Falwell, Mike Evans and Hal Lindsey into direct personal contact with national and Congressional leaders. In 1982, for instance, Reagan invited Falwell to give a briefing to the National Security Council on the possibility of a nuclear war with Russia. Hal Lindsey also claimed Reagan invited him to speak on the subject of war with Russia to Pentagon officials.[22]

At the February 1991 National Prayer Breakfast, Ed McAteer, a right-wing political activist and president of the Religious Roundtable, launched the Christian Israel Public Affairs Committee (CIPAC), which was modelled on the powerful American Israel Political Affairs Committee (AIPAC), which for over twenty years has lobbied on behalf of the right-wing Israeli Likud Party. The board of directors of CIPAC includes Tom Dine, a director of AIPAC and Herbert Zweilbon, president of Americans for a Safe Israel. The executive

---

20. Quoted in Ali Abunimah, Nigel Parry and Laurie King-Irani, *Republican Party leader calls for ethnic cleansing of Palestinians on prime time talk show* (2 May 2002) [Internet], The Electronic Intifada, <http://electronicintifada.net/cgi-bin/artman/exec/view.cgi/4/569>. [Accessed May 2004.]

21. Donald Wagner, 'Beyond Armageddon', *The Link* (Americans for Middle East Understanding), vol. 25, no. 4, October–November 1992, p. 5.

22. See Halsell, *Prophecy and Politics*, p. 47.

director of CIPAC is Richard Hellman, a former aide to Senator Howard Baker and an ICEJ activist. The goals of CIPAC are identical to AIPAC but designed to galvanize Christian support for Israel. One of the first objectives of CIPAC was to lobby Congress to make $10 billion available in US loan guarantees to fund the resettlement of Jews from the former Soviet Union in Israel and the West Bank. The Bush administration linked the loan guarantees to the halting of Jewish settlements on the West Bank. Jan Willem van der Hoeven of the ICEJ told the *Jerusalem Post*: '[the] Christian community finds the Bush administration's policy on loan guarantees totally unacceptable'. He claims that 80% of America's evangelical Christians supported the loan guarantees.[23]

The Unity Coalition for Israel (UCFI) is probably the most recent network of Christian Zionists to be formed in the US yet it is already the largest and most powerful. The UCFI was founded by Esther Levens in Kansas in 1994 and now comprises a broad coalition of 200 different and autonomous Jewish and Christian organizations representing 40 million members who are 'dedicated to a secure Israel'.[24] Their principal strategy is to lobby the US media and political establishment, to challenge what they term 'disinformation and propaganda' and to express 'the truth about Israel'. The UCFI includes three of the largest Christian Zionist organizations: Bridges for Peace, the International Christian Embassy Jerusalem, and Christians for Israel.

This coalition has a major influence on both the Republican and Democratic parties by providing the bulk of campaign funding to both sides. Aluf Ben, a spokesman for Shimon Peres, was quoted in *Ha'aretz* as claiming '60 percent of all financial help to Democrats came from Jewish sources.'[25] According to the *Washington Report on Middle East Affairs*, 'most pro-Israel fund-raisers estimate that at least 60 to 90 percent of Democratic campaign funding comes from Jewish sources, which also supply perhaps 40 percent of Republican funding'.[26] Christian Zionists have also been influential in forging a closer relationship with Israel by facilitating solidarity pilgrimages and educational tours to the Holy Land.

---

23. *Jerusalem Post*, 11 October 1991, cited in Wagner, *Anxious for Armageddon*, p. 108.
24. See UCFI's homepage, <http://www.israelunitycoalition. org>.
25. See Israel Shahak, 'Ability of US Jewish Groups to set Clinton Agenda Depends on Media', *Washington Report* (June 1995), pp. 10, 94. This article is a translation by Dr Shahak of a former article by Aluf Ben, published in *Ha'aretz*, 17 March 1995.
26. Publisher's page, *Washington Report* (June 1995), p. 122; see also, Lenni Brenner, 'My people are American. My Time is Today: The Demographics of American Jews', *Counterpunch*, 24 October 2003; available online at <http://www. counterpunch.org/brenner10242003.html>.

Solidarity tours to Israel

Since 1967, following the capture of most of the important biblical sites associated with pilgrimages from Jordan and Syria, such as the Old City of Jerusalem, Bethlehem, Bethany, the Shepherds Fields of Beit Sahour, Hebron, Nablus, Sebaste, Jericho, Caesarea Philippi and Banias, Israel has systematically exploited what Shirley Eber describes as a lucrative 'touristic gold mine',[27] and made tourism a tool of propaganda.

Israel's greatest success, however, has been to enlist American evangelical leaders as allies in promoting pro-Israeli solidarity tours and pilgrimages. On 15 February 2004, Israeli tourism minister Benny Elon honoured Pat Robertson at the National Association of Broadcasters Convention in Charlotte, North Carolina.

> He praised Robertson's leadership of a movement that has 'saved Israel's tourism from bankruptcy' by promoting pilgrimages to the Holy Land despite U.S. government travel warnings after Sept. 11, 2001, terrorist attacks and renewed hostilities between Israelis and Palestinians.[28]

In his speech, Elon estimated that 400,000 evangelicals travelled to Israel in 2003, contributing millions of dollars to the Israeli economy. Jerry Falwell's Friendship Tour of Israel is not untypical of the kind of tour other Christian Zionist leaders organize. Falwell himself has led over thirty-two tours to Israel in the last thirty years. Taking upwards of 600 pilgrims at any one time, Falwell's itinerary has in the past included the following programme of events:

1. An Israeli American Friendship Banquet in Jerusalem with Dr Jerry Falwell and Prime Minister Menachem Begin.
2. Meetings with top Israeli Administration officials and Knesset Members.
3. Luncheon with Major Saad Haddad, Commander of Christian forces in Southern Lebanon.
4. Participating (particularly for pastors and other Christian laymen) in a transatlantic, live TV satellite program.
5. On-site tour of modern Israeli battlefields. (Hear military experts describe those battles and how they were decided.)
6. Official visit to an Israeli defence installation by a top military leader.

---

27. Shirley Eber, 'Getting Stoned on Holiday: Tourism on the Front Line', *In Focus: Tourism Concern* 2 (Autumn 1991), pp. 4–5.
28. Broadway, 'The Evangelical Israeli Connection'.

(This tour is rarely offered.) You will see strategic military positions, plus experience first-hand the battle Israel faces.
7. A Bibleland tour that avoids ancient Byzantine churches while emphasising the places where Jesus Himself, Moses, Abraham and other Bible Greats lived and walked.[29]

The order is significant – Falwell and Begin first, with Jesus and other 'Bible Greats' last. 'The International Christian Zionist Centre seeks to facilitate . . . Christian Zionist solidarity tours to Israel, preferably monthly, not just to visit the traditional tourist places, but also the settlements and other places and people who specifically need our support, comfort and love.'[30] According to Kamal Farah of the Anglican Pilgrimage Office, it is the policy of the Israeli government to ensure all tourists and pilgrims visit the three key sites of Yad Vashem, the Wailing Wall and Masada in order to perpetuate a favourable image of Israel, stifle criticism and reinforce their claim to the land:

> The Holocaust Museum reminds those who come that Christians are guilty of perpetrating the holocaust, and to represent Israel as a victim; The Wailing Wall is the religious place where they speak about waiting for the coming of the Messiah; and Masada represents a nation struggling for life and freedom. The whole story of how Masada should never fall again. This is the famous idea of being free, being independent and being ready to die for freedom rather than as slaves in their own country.[31]

Christian Zionist tours embrace this Israeli agenda. They focus on the religious and political significance of contemporary Israel with speakers from the Israeli government and visits to the settlements to reinforce Israel's claim to the land and place in prophecy. They invariably stay in Israeli hotels or Kibbutzim, use Israeli buses and guides and frequent Israeli tourist shops and restaurants. For example, to assist the settlements in becoming self-sustaining, Christian Friends of Israeli Communities (CFOIC) works closely with Lev Ha'Aretz, the tourism body for Jewish settlements in the West Bank and Gaza, to promote Christian tours to biblical sites now managed by the settlers.

Yigal Dilmoni, tourism director for the Samaria regional council claims the

29. Cited in Wagner, 'Beyond Armageddon', pp. 1–13.
30. Jan Willem van der Hoeven, *Christian Zionism Israel's last remaining ally?* (2003) [Internet], ICZC, <http://zionsake.tripod.com/Zionist_ally.htm>. [Accessed August 2004.]
31. Stephen Sizer, unpublished interview, May 2003.

area is getting around 40,000 Christian visitors annually. Tel Shiloh alone logged more than 20,000 visitors in 1999, more than 70% of them evangelicals from the US and Europe.

> Protestants feel they have a connection to the place . . . I get so excited when I hear them talking about the Tabernacle. They know it; they feel it. Some burst into song or prayer at the Tabernacle site, while others take its measurements to see if they correspond to those in Exodus 27.[32]

Sondra Baras, director of CFOIC, describes similar reactions: 'They're just spellbound. There's no other word . . . I've seen groups just pray and sing. It's a whole experience. They join hands in prayer – very spontaneously – because they are so moved by what they see.'[33]

Research into the pilgrimages has shown that because of the bias in favour of an Israeli tourist agenda approximately 95% of Western tour-groups visiting the Holy Land fail to make any contact with the indigenous Christian community.[34] While traditional pilgrimage groups are largely indifferent to the existence of an indigenous Christian community and focus on the biblical sites, pro-Israeli groups, drawn predominantly from American fundamentalist churches, visit the Holy Land with an apocalyptic agenda. They see themselves as active participants in what are the 'Last Days', showing solidarity with Israel. Kenneth Cragg, former Assistant Bishop of Jerusalem, has observed:

> Local Christians are caught in a degree of museumization. They are aware of tourists who come in great volume from the West to savour holy places but who are, for the most part, blithely disinterested in the people who indwell them. The pain of the indifference is not eased insofar as the same tourism is subtly manipulated to make the case for the entire legitimacy of the statehood that regulates it.[35]

The principal motivation among Christian Zionists for visiting the Holy Land is primarily to bring a blessing to the Jewish people, especially the settlers who are reclaiming Judea and Samaria. They seek to show solidarity with the State of Israel and witness the literal fulfilment of biblical prophecy. The presence

---

32. Doina Chiacu, 'Courting the Christians', *Jerusalem Post*, 24 March 2000.

33. Cited in ibid.

34. Stephen Sizer, *Visiting the Living Stones: Pilgrimages to the Un-Holy Land* (unpublished MTh thesis, Oxford University, 1994).

35. Cragg, *The Arab Christian*, p. 28.

of an indigenous Palestinian Christian community is an unwelcome complica-
tion either demonized as Muslim fundamentalists or cast as recent economic
migrants, drawn by the wealth of Israel. With greater contact occurring
between Western Christians and the State of Israel, Christian Zionists return
home galvanized in their support for agencies encouraging Jewish people to
make *aliyah* and claim their inheritance.

Restorationism: facilitating *aliyah* from Russia and Eastern Europe

Since the days of Joseph Wolff's expeditions to find the lost tribes of Israel in
the 1820s, Christian Zionists have been convinced that it is God's will for the
Jewish people to return to Israel as it was given in perpetuity to the descendants of Abraham. With the fall of Communism in the former Soviet Union
and Eastern Europe, Christian Zionists have become increasingly active in
facilitating Jewish émigrés to make *aliyah*.

A study of one agency, CMJ, illustrates the tension that restorationism
causes. Tony Higton states that today CMJ 'is not involved in actively encouraging Jewish people to move to Israel'.[36] Looking back to the early nineteenth
century, Kelvin Crombie believes the popularity of the London Jews' Society
was due in part to the conviction that 'God was going to use England to play
a leading role in helping to restore the Jewish people to their homeland and to
their Messiah'.[37] In 1992 the Council of CMJ reaffirmed, 'We see the return of
the Jewish people to the Land of Israel as a sign of God's faithfulness as
revealed in the scriptures.'[38] CMJ comments that their commitment 'recalls the
influence that the "Restoration of Israel" theology had on many of the
Society's founders'.[39] In the 1996 CMJ annual report, and in special editions of
Shalom in 1998, celebrating the 50th anniversary of the founding of the State
of Israel, Walter Riggans and Kelvin Crombie reaffirmed CMJ's commitment
to restorationism:

> In our day there seems to be in some Christian circles a restriction of interest to the
> State of Israel and to the significance of various events for the unfolding of biblical

---

36. Unpublished letter from Tony Higton, general director of CMJ, 8 July 2000.
37. Kelvin Crombie, *For the Love of Zion: Christian Witness and the Restoration of Israel*
    (London: Hodder & Stoughton, 1991), pp. 13–14.
38. 'CMJ Commitment', CMJ Council, 2 November 1992.
39. Ibid.

prophecies relating to the end times. CMJ has always been at the forefront of teaching about God's restoration of the Jewish people to and in Israel, and we are continually excited by, and watchful of all that is happening. We are humbled by what the Lord is doing among Israeli believers. In other words, our prayerful interest in the State of Israel is as constant and committed as ever.[40]

Crombie's claims are similar to those made in a pamphlet ITAC published in Israel in 1990:

ITAC (1990)	Crombie (1998)
ITAC, as the London Jews' Society is known today, has always believed, proclaimed and worked towards the return of the Jewish people to Zion. This policy is rooted in a firm belief in the message of biblical prophecy which has accurately foretold these things.[41]	In the 140 years leading to the formation of the State of Israel CMJ believed in, and worked towards, the restoration of the Jewish People to their own land. Our hope and prayer is that CMJ can continue in this commitment and that the society can uphold its unique heritage.[42]

Figure 7. A comparison between statements on restorationism by ITAC and Crombie

By land and sea: from restoration to transportation

Since 1980, a coalition of Christian Zionist agencies has taken the initiative in encouraging Jewish people to emigrate to Israel, seeing this as the fulfilment of prophecy.

Exobus was probably the first Christian Zionist agency to turn the doctrine of restorationism into a reality and assist Jews in the former Soviet Union to make *aliyah*. Exobus was founded in 1984 by Phil Hunter, director of the Good News Travels Bus Company, based in Hull, for the purpose of facilitating the transportation of Jews from the former Soviet Union to Israel. The first Exobus team was sent to the Ukraine in 1991 and since then they have assisted over 80,000 Jewish people to emigrate to Israel from the former Soviet Union

40. Walter Riggans, *General Director's Annual Report 1996* (St Albans: CMJ, 1996).

41. Israel Trust of the Anglican Church, *Immanuel House, Tel Aviv 1866–1990* (Tel Aviv: ITAC, 1990).

42. Kelvin Crombie, 'CMJ and the Restoration of Israel', *Shalom* 1 (1998).

in close cooperation with the Jewish Agency.[43] Exobus is now probably the largest Christian agency facilitating *aliyah*, comprising 60 team members, transporting over 250 émigrés a month.[44] The main financial support for Exobus comes from a sister agency, Christians for Israel International, that promotes Exobus in the US.[45]

Combining economic incentive with biblical argument, their 'fishing' teams visit Jewish communities and present concerts in Hebrew with song and dance. They explain from the Old Testament the biblical basis for making *aliyah*. Videos of émigrés from their own home town are shown, giving testimonies of how they have been blessed by moving to Israel. Exobus focuses its operations on the Ukraine which has the largest concentration of Jews, after New York and Israel.[46]

At the Third International Christian Zionist Congress held in Jerusalem in 1996, under the auspices of the ICEJ, a resolution was passed committing Christians to assist Jewish people make *aliyah*: 'Christian believers are instructed by Scripture to acknowledge the Hebraic roots of their faith and to actively assist and participate in the plan of God for the ingathering of the Jewish People and the restoration of the nation of Israel in our day.'[47]

The ICEJ asserts:

In no uncertain terms God has made known His intention to regather the scattered Jewish people and to plant them in the land with His 'whole heart and soul'

---

43. The Jewish Agency was established by the World Zionist Organization in 1929 as a partnership between the WZO and non-Zionist Jewish leaders. The Jewish Agency's role was paramount in setting up an economic and cultural infrastructure in the early years of the State. Later, it facilitated the *aliyah* of over one million new immigrants. Today it is a global partnership committed to assuring the future of the Jewish people. See <http://www.jafi.org.il>.

44. See Anne Dexter, 'The Eternal Covenant, Part 3: Exile and Restoration', *Shalom* (June 1989), pp. 10–11; also, Murray Dixon, 'Zionism and Christian Zionism after fifty years', *Shalom* 3 (1998). See also the Exobus website, <http://www.exobus. org/aboutexobus/whatis.html>.

45. See the website of Christians for Israel International, <http://www. christiansforisrael.org/>.

46. See *New Waves of Jews Flee to Israel* (n.d.) [Internet], Christians for Israel, <http://www.c4israel.org/ex/exwhoisex.htm>. [Accessed August 2004.]

47. 'International Christian Zionist Congress Proclamation', International Christian Embassy Jerusalem, 25–29 February 1996.

(Jeremiah 32:41). We believe that in the present massive wave of Soviet Jewish immigration to Israel (almost 400,000 since September 1989), the world is witnessing one of the most startling prophetic fulfilments of our time – one that should deeply touch the heart of every Bible-believing Christian and provoke him to action.[48]

Since 1991, the ICEJ has paid for the transportation of 40,000 émigrés, 15,000 of whom were taken to Israel on fifty-one ICEJ sponsored flights.[49] ICEJ Russian team-members are especially active in the more remote regions of the former Soviety Union. Like Exobus, the ICEJ and Bridges for Peace describe their ministry in terms of 'fishing' for Jews, based on Jeremiah 16:16. They locate Jews, persuade them to emigrate, help them obtain documents to prove their Jewish origins, distribute humanitarian packages and pay for exit permits, passports, debt repayment, transport and accommodation while their applications are processed by the Jewish Agency in the larger Russian cities. Once in Israel, the ICEJ, as well as BFP, assists émigrés with their resettlement costs, providing food, clothing, blankets, kitchen and school supplies as well as medical equipment, if needed.

Another organization active in transporting Jews to Israel is called the Ebenezer Emergency Fund. In December 1991, Gustav Scheller, a Swiss-born Englishman, sponsored a ship to bring Jews to Israel via the Black Sea port of Odessa. Inspired by Isaiah 60:9, '. . . in the lead are the ships of Tarshish, bringing your sons from afar, with their silver and gold', Scheller's 'Operation Exodus' has organized 135 sailings, bringing some 4,500 immigrants to Israel. Indeed, as a result of Scheller's vision, the first direct sea route since 1948 was opened from Russia to Israel. In order to gain the support of the Knesset and Jewish Agency, Scheller signed a charter stipulating that missionary activity by Ebenezer staff was forbidden before, during or after the voyages. Johannes Facius, chief executive of the Ebenezer Emergency Fund said, 'We felt we needed to let the authorities know that we would never initiate any kind of missionary activity. This is not our calling; our calling is to be part of the aliyah.'[50] Exobus also adhere to a 'non-missionising policy' but instead seek to share their faith in the God of Abraham, Isaac and Jacob, believing God's call upon their lives as believing Gentiles is to help the Jewish people home. There remains some ambiguity, neverthe-

---

48. *International Christian Embassy Jerusalem* (Jerusalem: ICEJ, 1993), p. 9.
49. Patricia Golan, 'On Wings of Faith', *Jerusalem Post*, 20 December 2001.
50. Ibid.

less, since Jews for Jesus, for example, encourages its supporters to send money 'to ministries that both rescue and witness to Jews, like Operation Exodus's Ebenezer Emergency Fund, Bridges for Peace and Blossoming Rose.'[51]

Fishermen and hunters: the incentives for making aliyah

Controversially, in 1992, the ICEJ recognized that the number of Russians emigrating to Israel was declining and therefore a new, more explicit strategy was devised to 'persuade' Jews to make *aliyah*. Believing that many Jews in the former Soviet Union were 'sitting on the fence concerning Israel', the ICEJ initiated the production of new material and videos to encourage Jews to leave before the window of opportunity was closed again. Using a double-decker bus equipped with a theatre and audio-visual exhibition about Israel, an ICEJ team toured the former Soviet Union claiming, 'The task of the fisher is to encourage them with a "good report" of the land like Joshua and Caleb, before God sends the hunters. The biblical fact is that in Israel, they have a "future and a hope."'[52] The implication is clear, as in pre-war Germany, the Jews should leave before 'God sends the hunters', the door closes and anti-Semitism increases. Jan Willem van der Hoeven is convinced that even Jews living in the United States will eventually emigrate to Palestine and that God may use anti-Semitism to achieve it. 'I pray that even if it takes anti-Semitism in America, God may use it to get his millions back to Israel. So we must have enough room there. So if we have six million American Jews coming we cannot give up the West Bank, can we?'[53] Anti-Semitism may, therefore, be tolerated or justified if it serves the higher end of persuading Jews to return to Zion.

Convinced that anti-Semitism is indeed on the rise in the former Soviet Union, Glen Haines has set up a worldwide network of boat and yacht owners who are willing to assist Jews escape. Called 'Operation Tarshish', it is also based on Isaiah 60:9. When needed, the 'boaters' will head for Russian ports to assist in a 'mass rescue operation'. Haines believes that when the doors close for Jewish people to leave the former Soviet Union, 'and persecution begins on a massive scale, that will be the time when "the ships of Tarshish" will be

---

51. Ibid.

52. *International Christian Embassy Jerusalem* (Jerusalem: ICEJ, 1993), p. 10.

53. Jan Willem van der Hoeven, from a talk given at Livets Ord (The Word of Life), Uppsala, Sweden, 2 December 1990, cited in Lester Wikstrom, 'The Return of the Jews and the Return of Jesus: Christian Zionism in the 1970s and 1980s', *Al-Liqa Journal* (May 1994), p. 76.

called upon by God, to bring his scattered children home'.[54] In line with his apocalyptic eschatology, Haines believes this will happen soon.

Probably the most influential way Christians participate in restorationism is by fundraising. John Hagee, for example, uses TV to solicit funds to facilitate Jews emigrating to Israel. He recently hosted a 'Tribute to Israel' service at his non-denominational Cornerstone Church in San Antonio, Texas, which was also syndicated as one of his daily nationwide TV programmes. The service included the church choir performing Hebrew songs and a guest appearance of the former Israeli Prime Minister Binyamin Netanyahu. During the pro-gramme a message appeared at the bottom of the screen promising '$300 will bring a Jew to Israel', and gave an 800-number to enable viewers to pledge money to support the *aliyah* effort from the former Soviet Union.[55] In December 2002, the Keren Hayesod Christian Fund was launched to attract financial support from evangelical churches and agencies especially in Scandinavia, Germany, Holland and the USA.[56] According to Micha Limor, head of the European desk of Keren Hayesod's 'United Israel Appeal', in Germany alone there are 50 different evangelical groups involved in encourag-ing, promoting and financing emigration of Jews to Israel.[57]

Over the last ten years, based on their apocalyptic eschatology and some-what dubious hermeneutic, Christian Zionists have facilitated one of the largest mass migrations of people since 1948. Raising tens of millions of dollars they have assisted many of the 700,000 Jewish émigrés from the former Soviet Union and Eastern Europe to make *aliyah*. It is uncertain how many have done so out of religious conviction, as economic migrants, or out of fear induced by the tactics used by Christian Zionist 'fishermen'.

Believing the West Bank forms an integral part of the land given by God to the Jewish people for ever, Christian Zionists have not only assisted Jews to emigrate from the former Soviet Union, they have also supported their re-settlement within the Occupied Territories.

---

54. See *More About Operation Tarshish* (n.d.) [Internet], Operation Tarshish website, <http://www-tarshish.org.il/about.htm>. [Accessed August 2004.]

55. Golan, 'On Wings of Faith'.

56. Keren Hayesod was founded in 1920 to raise £25 million for the colonization of Palestine. It quickly became the most important of the fundraising organizations, supplying the Jewish Agency with its operating budget. See <http://www.wzo. org.il/home/dev/karen.htm>. [Accessed June 2004.]

57. See 'New Keren Hayesod Christian Fund Launched', *Hotline*, <http://www.khuia. org.il/newhotline/eng/1612%zoenglish.htm>.

Eretz Israel: sustaining the West Bank settlements

For religious Zionists, the legitimate borders of Israel are considerably larger than those presently disputed with Syria, Jordan and the Palestinian authority. In 1917, the Balfour Declaration promised the Jewish people a homeland within Mandate Palestine, which then extended to both sides of the Jordan River. Zionists assumed that this would all be ceded to the new Jewish State. However, in 1922 Winston Churchill gave 78% of the territory to the Hashemite family to form what was initially called Transjordania. The termination of the British Mandate, due in large measure to Jewish terrorism, together with the unilateral declaration of the State of Israel, led to the war of 1948 as a peaceful agreement could not be reached through the 1947 UN partition proposal.

There are consequently three separate disputed borders of Israel: those recognized by the international community in 1949 but no longer by Israel; the borders following the war of 1967, including the Golan, Gaza and the West Bank, occupied by Israel and held in breach of numerous UN Security Council resolutions; and the much larger borders promised by God to Abraham which religious Zionists believe are Israel's legitimate inheritance. Following the war of 1948, the borders of Israel agreed at the 1949 Armistice were considerably larger than those offered to Israel in the 1947 Partition Plan. These nevertheless came to be recognized internationally as the *de facto* borders of the State of Israel. However, they were difficult to defend militarily and tensions led to the Suez Crisis with Egypt in 1956 and 'Six Day War' with its Arab neighbours in 1967. The 'Six Day War' resulted in Israel conquering the Golan Heights from Syria, the West Bank from Jordan and the Sinai Peninsula from Egypt. In 1977, when Menachim Begin and the Likud Party came to power, they began to utilize biblical imagery to justify the military occupation and settlement of the West Bank, renaming it 'Judea and Samaria'. They also gave Hebrew names to settlements located near ancient biblical towns and villages, reinforcing an historical claim stretching back 3,000 years.[58]

Christian Zionist involvement in the realization of Eretz Israel includes the military justification of these enlarged borders, the political adoption of the settlement programme and economic support for the settler movement.

Justifying Eretz Israel
David Allen Lewis, president of Christians United for Israel, puts the territorial claims of Israel into the wider context of the Middle East. He observes

---

58. See Martha Jacobs, 'The Key to Israel's Defense', *Issues* 4.2.

that, 'The Arabs already have 99.5 per cent of the land . . . this cannot be tolerated.'[59] Derek Prince also voices the common complaint among Christian
Zionists who lament that Israel 'has only 22% of the original inheritance
offered the Jews' by the British government in 1917.[60] Echoing the experience of the Israelites under Pharaoh, Jan Willem van der Hoeven offers a
theological rationalization for Israel's victory in 1948 and a justification for
its refusal to withdraw from what Lindsey describes as 'biblically Jewish
lands'.[61]

> God wanted to give His people that part of the land which they did not receive in
> 1948, and by hardening the hearts of the different Arab leaders – Presidents Nasser
> and Assad and King Hussein – He impelled Israel to react. The result of what
> became known as the Six Day War was that Judea and Samaria – heartland of biblical
> Israel – and the ancient city of Jerusalem – King David's capital – were returned to
> their original owner . . . Thus, the Lord, by hardening the hearts of the Arab leaders,
> caused His people Israel to inherit the rest of the land, especially their ancient city, in
> a war of self defense! Until then, since 1949, Jordan had illegally held and occupied
> the 'West Bank' and Jerusalem. Thus, when Israel recaptured Judea, Samaria and
> Jerusalem, they did not even take over a territory that legally belonged at that time to
> any nation! How few in the West have even realized this. God has His own sovereign
> way to fulfil His Word and promise.[62]

Bridges for Peace also asks the rhetorical question: 'What is so sacred about
the June 4th, 1967 line?' Nothing, they argue, since historically this was all part
of biblical Israel and 'squarely won in defensive battles in 1967 and 1973'.
Referring to the Golan, they claim that because it was legitimately annexed by
Israel in 1980, Christians should lobby their elected officials 'to protect Israel's
right to the Golan Heights and not pressure Israel into giving it away to the
Syrians'.[63]

At the First International Christian Zionist Conference held in 1985 and

---

59. David Allen Lewis, 'Christian Zionist Theses', in *Christians and Israel: Essays on
    Biblical Zionism and Islamic Fundamentalists* (Jerusalem: ICEJ, Jerusalem, 1996), p. 9.

60. Prince, *Destiny of Israel and the Church*, p. 71.

61. Lindsey, *Final Battle*, p. 122.

62. Jan Willem van der Hoeven, *Babylon or Jerusalem?* (Shippensburg, PA: Destiny Image
    Publishers, 1993), p. 151.

63. Bridges for Peace, 'The Golan Heights Déjà Vu', *Despatch from Jerusalem* (Sept.
    1999), pp. 10–11.

sponsored by the ICEJ, a resolution was passed calling upon the world to recognize this judaization of Palestine: 'All nations should recognize Judea and Samaria as belonging to Israel . . . This Congress declares that Judea and Samaria (inaccurately termed "the West Bank") are, and by biblical right as well as international law and practice ought to be, a part of Israel.'[64] At the Third International Christian Zionist Congress held in Jerusalem in February 1996, some 1,500 delegates from over 40 countries unanimously affirmed a more explicit declaration of Israeli sovereignty: 'The Land of Israel has been given to the Jewish People by God as an everlasting possession by an eternal covenant. The Jewish People have the absolute right to possess and dwell in the Land, including Judea, Samaria, Gaza and the Golan.'[65]

The purpose of Israel's occupation of the Golan, West Bank and Gaza goes well beyond the need for secure or defensible borders. Anne Dexter explains why negotiations involving 'land for peace' will never appease religious Zionists. Claiming that the question of ancient boundaries cannot be ignored, she insists that these biblical borders underlie the policies of many Israeli politicians, notably the right-wing Likud Party: 'It is the guiding principle in Israel's interpretation of West Bank autonomy, which insists that whatever the degree of self-determination allowed the people, the land itself belongs to Israel.'[66] In her view, therefore, Palestinians may be allowed limited autonomy but not statehood. She argues that Palestinian Christians, in particular, must accept Zionism and the settlements and learn to live with them: 'Arab Christians are squarely faced with the biblical election of the Jews, and their role throughout history, particularly in the present.'[67]

This conviction that the entire West Bank is integral to Israel has led many Christian Zionists to 'adopt' exclusive Jewish settlements to strengthen their claim to the land.

Adopting the settlements

Since 1967, using various economic and tax incentives as well as appealing to biblical rhetoric, Israel has encouraged over 400,000 Jews to colonize East Jerusalem, the West Bank, Gaza and the Golan Heights through 190 illegal

64. 'Declaration of the First International Christian Zionist Leadership Conference' (Jerusalem: ICEJ, 1985).

65. 'International Christian Zionist Congress Proclamation' (Jerusalem: ICEJ, 25–29 February 1996).

66. Anne Dexter, *View the Land* (South Plainfield, NJ: Bridge, 1986), pp. 214–215.

67. Ibid., p. 32.

settlements.[68] Several Christian Zionist organizations have given their full support to this judaization of the Occupied Territories. Jews for Jesus, for example, compares Israeli settlements in the Palestinian Territories with the settlement of Texas by the United States: 'Many might wish that the Israeli government could feel secure enough to withdraw the settlements on the West Bank. But on the same basis, the United States should seriously consider giving Texas back to Mexico and, indeed, should never have settled it in the first place.'[70]

The Christian Friends of Israeli Communities (CFOIC) was founded by Ted Beckett in 1995 in response to the Oslo Process which returned land to the Palestinian authority. The purpose of CFOIC was to forge links between illegal Jewish settlements in the Occupied Territories and churches and individual Christians internationally. It defines a settlement as:

> A piece of land where brave, Jewish pioneers have taken up residence. In most cases it is a barren rocky hilltop set up to establish a Jewish community where none had existed for thousands of years. In some cases, such as Shiloh, settlements are established on the original site of an ancient Jewish city. In others such as Hevron and Gush Etzion, a Jewish community is established on the site of a community destroyed by Arab armies during or prior to Israel's War of Independence.[70]

CFOIC encourages evangelical churches to participate in their 'Adopt-a-Settlement' programme to support the 'brave Jewish settlers' living in 'the heartland of biblical Israel'. It defines the Occupied Territories as 'Judea and Samaria' or 'the Mountains of Israel and the plains of Gaza'. It also insists it is 'not an evangelizing ministry, but rather aims to build bridges . . . between

---

68. 'Israeli Settlements in the Occupied Territories', Foundation for Middle East Peace (March 2002). FMEP lists 190 settlements with a total population of 213,672 in the West Bank and Gaza; 170,400 in East Jerusalem; and 17,000 in the Golan Heights, making a total of 401,072 settlers (based on 2001 figures).

69. *Do you approve of Zionism – that is, the reestablishment of the ancient state of Israel – when it involves so much force of arms and bloodshed?* (n.d.) [Internet], Jews for Jesus website, FAQ page, <http://www.jfjonline.org/witness/faq_zionism.htm>. [Accessed June 2004.]

70. *What are Israeli Communities?* (n.d.) [Internet], Christian Friends of Israel Communities, <http://www.cfoic.com/index.asp?mainpage=settlement>. [Accessed June 2004.]

Christians and Jews'.[71] Its mandate is 'to provide solidarity and aid to belea-guered Israeli settlers', and claims: 'CFOIC brings unconditional support to the Jewish communities and partners with the dedicated pioneers of Biblical Israel to fulfill Biblical prophecy.'[72]

In 1999, CFOIC claimed that thirty-nine illegal Jewish settlements had already been adopted by over fifty denominational as well as independent churches in the US, South Africa, Germany, Holland and the Philippines. For example, Faith Christian Center, Salem, Indiana, has adopted Har Bracha; Johnston Federated United Methodist Church, Johnston, Ohio, has adopted Itamar; Calvary Chapel, Nashville, Tennessee, has adopted Alei Zahav; and Shiloh Christian Fellowship, Oakland, California, has adopted Shiloh.

To strengthen the settlers' claim to the land, CFOIC publishes maps showing the few areas of the West Bank that had been transferred to the Palestinian authority as part of the Oslo Accord. They warn, however, that the withdrawals run counter to 'God's plan for the Jewish nation and . . . only weaken Israel in future confrontations with her enemies'.[73] Christian Zionists have not only made a clear stand in justifying Israel's illegal settlement of the West Bank, but their 'adoption' programme is also intended to be a means by which financial assistance as well as practical support for the settlers is delivered.

Funding the settlers

Besides facilitating the emigration of Jews to Israel, several Christian Zionist agencies are active in funding illegal Jewish settlements in the West Bank. During the 1991 ICEJ Feast of Tabernacles celebration, for example, represen-tatives from twelve countries presented cheques to the Israeli Prime Minister Yitshak Shamir to help finance the settlements.[74] Through its 'Social Assistance Programme', the ICEJ also provides financial support for projects in the Jewish settlements, including bullet-proof vests to strengthen the resolve of settlers living among what it describes as '3 million hostile Palestinians'.[75]

---

71. 'Adopt-a-Settlement' Program (n.d.) [Internet], Christian Friends of Israeli Communities, <http://www.cfoic.com/index.asp?mainpage= adoption>. [Accessed June 2004.]

72. Ibid.

73. Ibid.

74. See Wagner, Anxious for Armageddon, p. 108.

75. International Christian Embassy, <http://www.icej.org.il/about.html>; 'Life in the Settlements', Word from Jerusalem (May 2002), p. 7.

The ICEJ's 'Bulletproof Bus for Efrat' appeal, for example, is also raising $150,000 to purchase an armour-plated bus to transport settlers in and out of the West Bank from Efrat settlement.[76] Bridges for Peace (BFP) has a similar scheme called 'Operation Ezra' which funds over fifty otherwise unsustainable projects, such as the settlement farm, Sde Bar, near Beit Jala and the Herodian.[77] CFOIC aid for the settlements has also included medical equipment, computers, preschool supplies, library books and furniture.[78] Ray Sanders, director of Christian Friends of Israel, believes God raised up CFOIC at this strategic time as a response to the attempts to 'demoralise the residents of Judea, Samaria and Gaza and invalidate their rights to live in the land that God has given to them'.[79]

However tenuous, biblical mandate and divine imperative make for a powerful combination in the contemporary justification for the occupation and settlement of the rest of Eretz Israel. In order to achieve this vision it is imperative therefore that Israel retain, strengthen and expand its settlement programme in the Occupied Territories.

The effect of the pro-Israeli lobby on American foreign policy concerning the settlements appears to be working. Lind observes that during the Carter administration the settlements were regarded as 'illegal'; under Reagan they became an 'obstacle' to peace; while now they have simply become a 'complicating factor'.[80]

Christian Zionist organizations such as the ICEJ, BFP and CFOIC, as well as some of the leaders of CMJ and JFJ, are unequivocal not only in justifying Israel's present borders and defending the settlement programme, but also in offering practical and financial assistance to sustain and make permanent this annexation of Palestinian territory. Integral to this strategy is Jerusalem and the progressive Judaizing, occupation and settlement of Arab East Jerusalem and the Old City. For Zionism there can be no compromise, since controlling Jerusalem has always been a barometer of their existence as a nation.

---

76. International Christian Embassy, 'Bulletproof Bus for Efrat' appeal, *Word from Jerusalem* (May 2002).

77. Bridges for Peace, 'New Life on the Farm', *Despatch from Jerusalem* (January 2000), p. 5.

78. '*CFOIC: Standing in the Gap*' (n.d.) [Internet], Christian Friends of Israeli Communities, <http://www.cfoic.com/index.asp?mainpage=projfocus>. [Accessed June 2004.]

79. See <http://www.cfoic.org/010722_news.htm>.

80. Michael Lind, 'The Israel Lobby and American Power', *Prospect* (April 2002).

Jerusalem: lobbying for international recognition

At the core of Christian Zionist support for Israel's claim to the Occupied Territories lies the conviction that Jerusalem is, and must remain, the exclusive and undivided Jewish capital. Attempts to reach agreement in the wider Palestinian–Israeli conflict have so far stalled or stumbled over the final status of Jerusalem. Christian Zionists are strongly opposed to any proposal for joint sovereignty or the creation of a Palestinian capital in East Jerusalem.

The vital relationship between Jerusalem and Zionism is expressed most strongly by David Parsons. He even berates Jewish Zionists who define Zionism too loosely as simply 'support for a Zionist State', particularly those who considered an alternative location such as Uganda or South America. Parsons insists that it is 'disingenuous to separate the Jewish connection to Jerusalem from Zionism . . . and still contend that you are a Zionist'. What remains, he claims, 'is not worthy of the name'.[81] Jarvilehto similarly describes the decision of the UN to declare Jerusalem 'occupied territory' as a sign that the UN has been 'polluted with anti-Semitism'.[82]

Not only do Christian Zionists believe Jerusalem is integral to Zionism, they also believe God has mandated that it be the exclusive capital of the Jewish people and will bless or curse nations on the basis of how they respond on this issue. According to Clarence Wagner of Bridges for Peace,

> Despite the peace process, the idea of Jerusalem as the undivided capital of Israel is still far from accepted by the nations of the world or the Moslems . . . The nations can plot and plan what they will regarding the division of the land of Israel and the city of Jerusalem. Yet they will not succeed. In the end, God will be faithful to His prophetic word . . .[83]

The key, therefore, to securing this blessing is to gain international recognition of Jerusalem as Israel's capital. Christian Zionists recognize that the most dramatic and symbolic way to achieve this would be to persuade Western governments, and principally the US government, to move their embassies to Jerusalem.

---

81. David Parsons, 'Jerusalem, Thy Years are Determined', in *Christians and Israel*, pp. 46–47.

82. Ulla Jarvilehto, 'Political Action for Israel', in *Christians and Israel*, pp. 58–59.

83. Clarence Wagner, *Jerusalem 3000 Celebration* (n.d.) [Internet], Bridges for Peace, <http://www.bridgesforpeace.com/publications/dispatch/ commentary/Article-42.html>. [Accessed June 2004.]

In February 1984, therefore, the ICEJ sent a representative, Richard Hellman, to testify before the US Senate Committee on Foreign Relations in Washington to urge the US to move its embassy from Tel Aviv to Jerusalem and recognize the city as the capital of Israel. Jerry Falwell of Moral Majority and the AIPAC lobby also spoke in favour of such a move. Senator Bob Dole later introduced legislation in the American Senate which required the US embassy to be rebuilt in Jerusalem by 31 May 1999, and authorized $100 million for 'preliminary' spending.[84] Lamenting the failure of the US President to ratify the Senate decision, Dole insisted:

> Jerusalem is today . . . and should remain forever, the eternal and undivided capital of the State of Israel . . . The time has come . . . to move beyond letters, expressions of support, and sense of the Congress resolutions. The time has come to enact legislation that will get the job done.[85]

In 1992, the ICEJ sponsored various receptions marking the twenty-fifth anniversary of what they referred to as the 'Reunification of Jerusalem'. In 1996, at the International Christian Zionist Congress, this position was reiterated when the 1,500 participants signed a declaration insisting: 'Jerusalem must remain undivided, under Israeli sovereignty . . . the capital of Israel only, and all nations should so concur and place their embassies here.'[86]

In 1997 the ICEJ also gave support to a full-page advert placed in the *New York Times* entitled 'Christians Call for a United Jerusalem.' It was signed by ten evangelical leaders including Pat Robertson, chairman of Christian Broadcasting Network and president of the Christian Coalition; Oral Roberts, founder and chancellor of Oral Roberts University; Jerry Falwell, founder of Moral Majority; Ed McAteer, president of the Religious Roundtable; and David Allen Lewis, president of Christians United for Israel:

> We, the undersigned Christian spiritual leaders, communicating weekly to more than 100 million Christian Americans, are proud to join together in supporting the

---

84. *Bill to re-locate the United States Embassy from Tel Aviv to Jerusalem* (16 May 1995), US Department of Justice, Office of Legal Counsel, <http://www.usdoj.gov/olc/s770.16.htm>. [Accessed June 2004.]

85. See Donald Neff, 'Congress has been irresponsible on the issue of Jerusalem', *Washington Report* (Jan. 1998), pp. 90–91.

86. 'International Christian Zionist Congress Proclamation' (Jerusalem: IECJ, 25–29 February 1996).

continued sovereignty of the State of Israel over the holy city of Jerusalem. We support Israel's efforts to reach reconciliation with its Arab neighbors, but we believe that Jerusalem, or any portion of it, shall not be negotiable in the peace process. Jerusalem must remain undivided as the eternal capital of the Jewish people.[87]

Readers were invited to 'Join us in our holy mission to ensure that Jerusalem will remain the undivided, eternal capital of Israel.' They claimed, 'The battle for Jerusalem has begun, and it is time for believers in Christ to support our Jewish brethren and the State of Israel. The time for unity with the Jewish people is now.' In 1998, Hagee even insisted that the special status afforded the Jewish people by God superseded the rule of international law: 'A shared Jerusalem? Never! . . . God doesn't care what the United Nations thinks . . . He gave Jerusalem to the nation of Israel, and it is theirs.'[88]

The lobbying by Christian Zionists for the recognition of Jerusalem as the Israeli capital is unrelenting. In 2001, for example, the National Unity Coalition for Israel (NUCFI) published another resolution of solidarity with Israel, acknowledging Jerusalem as the undivided capital of the Jewish State and calling upon the US government to implement the Jerusalem Embassy Act, passed by the US Congress in 1995, to move the American embassy from Tel Aviv to Jerusalem. Signators included Hal Lindsey, Chuck Missler, Clarence Wagner and Elwood McQuaid.[89] In 2002, Falwell controversially linked the terrorist attacks on the World Trade Centre with Israel's exclusive claim to Jerusalem, calling upon his supporters to petition the US President to 'Keep Jerusalem Free.'[90] Christian Zionists have, therefore, been resolute in their efforts to get the international community to recognize Jerusalem as the *de facto* capital of Israel. Their efforts, so far unsuccessful, have focused on pressuring successive US presidents to authorize the transfer of the American embassy to Jerusalem, realizing that such a move would seal Israel's claim to the city as their undivided, eternal capital. However, even more critical to a Christian Zionist reading of prophecy is the necessity for the Jewish temple to be rebuilt.

---

87. 'Christians Call for a United Jerusalem', *New York Times*, 18 April 1997, available online at <http://www.cdn-friends-icej.ca/united.html>. [Accessed June 2004.]

88. Hagee, *Attack on America*, p. 42.

89. *Resolution of Solidarity with Israel* (2001) [Internet], Israel Unity Coalition, <http://www.israelunitycoalition.com>. [Accessed May 2002.]

90. Jerry Falwell Ministries, 'Keep Jerusalem Free Petition', <http://falwell.com/>. [Accessed May 2002.]

The temple: identifying with religious Zionism

Dispensational Christian Zionists, in particular, believe the Jewish temple must be rebuilt because their futurist eschatology leads them to believe that the Antichrist will desecrate it just prior to the return of Christ. Brickner claims that the preparations for rebuilding the temple began in 1967 with the capture of the Old City of Jerusalem.[91] Lindsey is equally sure that 'right now, as you read this, preparations are being made to rebuild the Third Temple'.[92] Contemporary Christian Zionists have been active in assisting Jewish organizations dedicated to rebuilding the Jewish temple by publicizing the Temple Mount organizations; searching for the temple site; facilitating the building programme; breeding the red heifers and funding the treasury.

Promoting the Temple Mount movement

Randall Price is the leading dispensational expert on the imminent plans to rebuild the Jewish temple. In his 735-page work, *The Coming Last Days Temple*, he provides comprehensive details and addresses of all the Jewish organizations involved in facilitating the rebuilding of the Jewish temple.[93] Together with Thomas Ice, their earlier book *Ready to Rebuild* demonstrates that this is not a theoretical or fringe subject but one in which significant numbers of Christians, together with religious Jews, are already actively participating, in the firm conviction that the temple will be rebuilt very soon. While Jews for Jesus insists that it does not endorse the activities of any particular Jewish group committed to rebuilding the Jewish temple, it nevertheless provides information on, and direct Internet links to, eight Jewish organizations, some of which have been implicated in attempts to seize the Temple Mount, destroy the Al Aqsa mosque and Dome of the Rock, rebuild the Jewish temple and re-institute temple worship, priesthood and sacrifices. These include the Temple Institute and Temple Mount Faithful.[94] Gershon Salomon is the controversial figurehead of the movement and founder of the Temple Mount Faithful. Zhava Glaser, of Jews for Jesus, praises Salomon for his courage to talk about 'the most important subject in the Jewish religion':

---

91. Brickner, *Future Hope*, p. 137.

92. Lindsey, *Planet Earth 2000 AD*, p. 156; *Final Battle*, p. 103.

93. Price, *Coming Last Days Temple*, pp. 616–644.

94. Rich Robinson, 'Israeli Groups Involved in Third Temple Activities', Jews for Jesus, Newsletter 10 (1993) [Internet], <http://www.jfjonline.org/pub/newsletters/5753-10/thirdtemple.htm>. [Accessed June 2004.]

His credentials as an Israeli patriot are impeccable, beginning at age eleven when he was arrested by the British authorities for putting up Zionist posters during their occupation of Israel. He has stood up for what he believes to be true ever since ... one must take Salomon seriously. Nine thousand people are on his 'Temple Mount Faithful' membership list.[95]

Speaking as a guest of the ICEJ, at the Christian Zionist Congress in 1998, Salomon insisted:

The mission of the present generation is to liberate the Temple Mount and to remove – I repeat, to remove – the defiling abomination there ... the Jewish people will not be stopped at the gates leading to the Temple Mount ... We will fly our Israeli flag over the Temple Mount, which will be minus its Dome of the Rock and its mosques and will have only our Israeli flag and our Temple. This is what our generation must accomplish.[96]

Sam Kiley writing in *The Times*, however, gives another perspective. He claims Salomon represents the 'almost acceptable face of millennial cults'. In an interview, Salomon insisted that the Islamic shrine must be destroyed:

The Israeli Government must do it. We must have a war. There will be many nations against us but God will be our general. I am sure this is a test, that God is expecting us to move the Dome with no fear from other nations. The Messiah will not come by himself; we should bring Him by fighting.[97]

Both the ICEJ and the ICZC promote Salomon's views.[98] Van der Hoeven further speculates that the Temple Mount is at the heart of the battle with Satan on earth. Israel's failure to destroy the Dome of the Rock gave him a

---

95. Zhava Glaser, 'Today's Rituals: Reminders or Replacements', *Issues* 8.3.

96. Nadav Shragai, 'Dreaming of a Third Temple', *Ha'aretz*, 17 September 1998, p. 3; cited in Price, *Coming Last Days Temple*, p. 417.

97. Sam Kiley, 'The righteous will survive and the rest will perish', in *The Times*, 13 December 1999, p. 39.

98. *The Hanukkah Event of the Temple Mount Faithful on the Temple Mount, Jerusalem and the Tomb of the Maccabbees* (27 Dec. 2000) [Internet], ICEJ, <http://www.cdn-friends-icej.ca/hanukkah.html>; Jan Willem van der Hoeven, *About the ICZC* (n.d.) [Internet], ICZC, <http://www.israelmybeloved.com/about/organization.htm>. [Accessed May 2002.]

temporary respite: 'Satan, who knows to always take seriously the things God takes seriously, kept his grip on the Temple Mount for hundreds of years, until he was almost unseated in the 1967 Six-Day War.'[99]

According to Grace Halsell, between 1967 and 1990 there were over 100 armed assaults on the Haram Al-Sharif by Jewish militants, often led by rabbis. She regrets that 'in no instance has any Israeli Prime Minister or the chief Sephardic rabbi or the chief Ashkenazi rabbi criticized these assaults'.[100] However, even if Jewish and Christian Zionists are successful in destroying the Al Aqsa mosque and Dome of the Rock, one of the unresolved difficulties they would still face is deciding where to rebuild the temple.

Searching for the temple site

It is critical to religious Zionists that any future temple is built on the same site as the temples of Solomon, Zerubbabel and Herod. There appears to have been continuity between them with each enclosing the protrusion of Mount Moriah, also known as the Foundation Stone, within the Holy of Holies. There are three alternative theories advocated by historians and archaeologists as to the exact site of the earlier temples.[101] The most commonly held, with both traditional support as well as a consensus among Israeli archaeologists today, is that the temple stood on the site of the Dome of the Rock.

In the 1970s, Lindsey insisted the Jewish temple would have to be built in place of the Dome of the Rock:

> There is one major problem barring the construction of a third Temple. That obstacle is the second holiest place of the Muslim faith, the Dome of the Rock. This is believed to be built squarely in the middle of the old Temple site. Obstacle or no obstacle, it is certain that the Temple will be rebuilt. Prophecy demands it.[102]

Lindsey appeared to know the exact location of the temple structure: 'Imagine my emotions as I stood under a sign at the Wall which read in Hebrew:

---

99. Van der Hoeven, *About the ICZC*.
100. Grace Halsell, 'The Hidden Hand of the Temple Mount Faithful', *Washington Report* (Jan. 1991), p. 8.
101. These are the Northern Theory, the Southern Theory and the Central Theory; see discussion in Price, *Coming Last Days Temple*, pp. 337–342.
102. Lindsey, *Late Great Planet Earth*, pp. 56–58. Lindsey is in error on this point; the Dome of the Rock is the *third* most holy shrine of Islam after Mecca and Medina.

"Holy of Holies, 10 Metres", with an arrow pointing towards a spot thirty feet behind the existing Wall in the direction of the Dome of the Rock!'[103] By 1983, however, Lindsey had changed his mind. Now favouring the northern theory, Lindsey believed this discovery 'has accelerated the countdown to the events that will bring the Messiah Jesus back to earth'. This was because 'the predicted Third Temple can now be built without disturbing the Dome of the Rock . . . the Temple and its immediate guard wall could be rebuilt and still be twenty-six meters away from the Dome of the Rock.'[104] Having discovered the true site of the Herodian temple, Lindsey proceeded to find scriptural verification for this new location based on clues as to its dimensions in Revelation 11: 'We are literally in the very last days of the Church Age. The Temple will be rebuilt soon!'[105] Brickner also favours the claims made by Randall Price that the Jewish temple could actually be rebuilt alongside the Dome of the Rock, although he concedes in something of an understatement, 'it remains a sensitive issue to say the least'.[106] To suggest that a Jewish temple could be erected next to the Dome of the Rock is rather naïve, as is Lindsey's claim that a new Jewish temple would enhance Israel's tourism revenue and become 'the greatest tourist attraction in the world'.[107] It is inconceivable that the Muslim authorities would countenance any Jewish construction within the confines of the Haram Al-Sharif. In any case, most orthodox Jews remain convinced that the Dome of the Rock is an abomination and must be removed before the temple can be rebuilt.

Facilitating the building programme

In order to sustain a fully functioning temple rather than simply create a tourist attraction or museum, it is also necessary to identify, train and consecrate priests to serve in the temple. The dilemma facing prospective priests is how to become ritually pure before they can offer sacrifices for others. According to Numbers 19:2, the ashes of a pure unblemished red heifer, itself previously offered by a ritually pure priest, must be mixed with water and sprinkled on both them and the temple furniture. With the destruction of the temple in AD 70 the ashes used in the ceremony were lost and the Jews of the *diaspora* have, therefore, been perpetually unclean ever since. The search for

---

103. Lindsey, *There's a New World Coming*, p. 163.
104. Lindsey, *Israel and the Last Days*, p. 29.
105. Ibid., p. 30.
106. Brickner, *Future Hope*, p. 61.
107. Lindsey, *Planet Earth 2000 AD*, p. 163.

the ashes of the last red heifer have so far proved unsuccessful. In 1998, however, Clyde Lott, a Pentecostal Mississippi rancher, formed Canaan Land Restoration of Israel, Inc., for the purpose of raising livestock suitable for temple sacrifice.[108]

According to *Newsweek*, in 1997, the first completely red heifer for 2,000 years was born at the Kfar Hassidim kibbutz near Haifa and named 'Melody'.[109] Unfortunately, she eventually grew white hairs on her tail and udder. Undaunted, Chaim Richman, an Orthodox rabbi and Clyde Lott, the Pentecostal cattleman, have teamed up to breed red heifers in the Jordan Valley, in the hope of saving Israel's cattle industry as well as producing a perfect specimen for sacrifice.[110]

The design and construction work, furnishings and utensils, the training of priests and breeding of sacrifices all require funds and, in large measure, like the red heifer, these are being provided by Christian Zionists. The Jerusalem Temple Foundation was founded by Stanley Goldfoot, a former terrorist member of the Stern Gang, together with Terry Reisenhoover and several other American evangelicals to facilitate the rebuilding of the temple.[111]

According to Grace Halsell, Goldfoot raises up to $100 million a year for the Jerusalem Temple Foundation through American Christian TV and radio stations and evangelical churches, including Chuck Smith's Calvary Chapel in Costa Mesa, California.[112] Goldfoot has also acknowledged receiving funds from the ICEJ. Jan Willem van der Hoeven admitted that 'when supporters volunteer to give money for building a Temple, he directs them to Goldfoot'. The ICEJ also sells an audio tape about plans to construct a Jewish temple on

---

108. Randall Price incorrectly attributes this story to *Time*. It actually appeared in *Newsweek*. He also misspells one of the contributor's names; Price, *Coming Last Days Temple*, p. 375.

109. Kendall Hamilton, Joseph Contreras and Mark Dennis, 'The Strange Case of Israel's Red Heifer', *Newsweek,* 19 May 1997.

110. Jeremy Shere, 'A Very Holy Cow', *Jerusalem Post*, 25 May 1997.

111. Louis Rapoport, 'Slouching towards Armageddon: Links with Evangelicals', *Jerusalem Post International Edition*, 17–24 June 1984; Halsell, *Forcing God's Hand* , p. 68. As a member of the Stern Gang and also Irgun (a notorious terrorist organization founded in 1931), Goldfoot was responsible for planting the bomb at the King David Hotel in Jerusalem on 22 July 1946 which killed 100 British soldiers and officials. In 1948 he was also convicted and jailed by an Israeli court for the murder of UN envoy Count Bernadotte.

112. See Halsell, *Prophecy and Politics*, p. 106; *Forcing God's Hand* , pp. 63–73.

Haram Al-Sharif.[113] Pat Robertson's Christian Broadcasting Network, Peter Wagner's World Prayer Center, as well as the ICEJ, have all raised funds for Gershon Salomon's Temple Mount Faithful.[114]

Gordon Welty explains the apparent contradiction of evangelical Christians supporting Jewish terrorists:

> Their power is to keep inconsistencies in airtight compartments, so that they themselves never recognize these inconsistencies . . . If the money a muscular Christian donates to the Jewish terrorists buys the dynamite that destroys the mosque, the muscular Christian will say simply, 'It was an act of God.'[115]

As Lawrence Wright has also observed, 'Jewish longing for the Temple, Christian hopes for the Rapture, and Muslim paranoia about the destruction of the mosques [are being] stirred to an apocalyptic boil.'[116] The implacable hostility Christian Zionists show towards any compromise over the competing claims to the land, the status of Jerusalem or plans to rebuild the Jewish temple, combined with their formidable influence in US Middle East policy makes for an ominous future, given the inherent pessimism of their eschatology.

The future: opposing peace and hastening Armageddon

Christian Zionism finds its consummation in the future hope of all Israel restored to their land and to their Lord, bringing blessing to the whole world. While Britain was the principal sponsor and protector of Zionism in the nineteenth century, the United States has fulfilled the role of benefactor and guardian in the twentieth century. While the United Nations is invariably viewed with mistrust, the special relationship between America and Israel ensures their

113. Halsell, *Prophecy and Politics*, p. 98.
114. See Jay Gary, 'The Temple Time Bomb', *Presence Magazine*, 30 May 2001, <http://www.presence.tv/cms/templebomb.shtml>; also, 'Unmasking Religious Terrorism', *Presence Magazine*, 30 March 2001, <http://www.presence.tv/cms/terrorism.shtml>. [Accessed June 2004.]
115. Cited in Halsell, *Forcing God's Hand*, p. 115.
116. Lawrence Wright, *Letter from Jerusalem: Forcing the End* (1999) [Internet], Frontline, <http://www.pbs.org/wgbh/pages/frontline/shows/apocalypse/readings/forcing.html>. [Accessed June 2002.]

mutual survival against global terrorism.[117] Antipathy for Arabs generally has led to the ethnic cleansing of Palestinians and the demonization of Islam, while Arab leaders such as Yasser Arafat and Saddam Hussein are cast for the role of Antichrist.[118] In such a dualistic and polarized world, Christian Zionists are at best sceptical and at worst hostile towards the Middle East peace process.

The US-Israeli alliance

Jerry Falwell offers a simple explanation for the close relationship between Israel and America. God has been kind to America because 'America had been kind to the Jew.'[119] Mike Evans, founder and president of Lovers of Israel, Inc., is representative of those who find a biblical basis for the special relationship between Israel and America:

> Only one nation, Israel, stands between . . . terrorist aggression and the complete decline of the United States as a democratic world power . . . Surely demonic pressure will endeavour to encourage her to betray Israel . . . Israel is the key to America's survival . . . As we stand with Israel, I believe we shall see God perform a mighty work in our day. God is going to bless America and Israel as well . . . If Israel falls, the United States can no longer remain a democracy . . . Arab money is being used to control and influence major US Corporations, making it economically more and more difficult for the United States to stand against world terrorism.[120]

For Christian Zionists such as Jerry Falwell and Mike Evans, America is seen as the great redeemer, her super-power role in the world predicted in Scripture and providentially ordained.[121] The two nations of America and Israel are like Siamese twins, linked not only by common self-interest but more significantly by similar religious foundations.

Senator Bob Dole summarizes this special relationship succinctly:

> American-Israeli friendship is no accident. It is a product of our shared values. We are both democracies. We are both pioneer states. We have both opened our doors to

---

117. See Simon, *Jerry Falwell and the Jews*, pp. 63–64.
118. See Dyer, *Rise of Babylon*, pp. 147–148; see also, Joseph Chambers, *A Palace for the Antichrist: Saddam Hussein's Drive to Rebuild Babylon and Its Place in Bible Prophecy* (Green Forest, AR: New Leaf Press, 1996).
119. Cited in Halsell, *Forcing God's Hand* , p. 100.
120. Evans, *Israel, America's Key to Survival*, p. xv and back cover.
121. See Lienesch, *Redeeming America*, p. 197.

THE POLITICAL IMPLICATIONS OF CHRISTIAN ZIONISM 241

the oppressed. We have both shown a passion for freedom and we have gone to war to protect it.[122]

Rosemary and Herman Ruether warn of the danger of this kind of logic for its 'dualistic, Manichaean view of global politics. America and Israel together against an evil world.'[123] The special relationship that dispensationalists accord to Israel underpins this conviction that Israel and 'Christian' America will stand together. They are perceived to be pitted against an evil world dominated by communist and Islamic totalitarian regimes antithetical to the Judeo-Christian democratic values of America and Israel.

Antipathy towards Arabs

Christian Zionists, while lovers of Israel, rarely show the same feelings towards Arabs, indeed their antipathy is often in inverse proportion to their empathy for Israel. Anti-Arab prejudices and orientalist stereotypes are common in their writings.[124] For the orientalist, the West is seen as liberal, peaceful, rational and capable of embracing 'real' values, whereas the Middle East is not. The perceptions of the Revd John Holmes illustrate this. Following a visit to Palestine in 1929 he wrote with admiration about the Jewish pioneer settlers he had encountered, comparing them with the English settlers who colonized North America:

> For this reason I was not surprised later, when I read Josiah Wedgewood's 'The Seventh Dominion' to find this distinguished Gentile Zionist of Britain speaking of these Jewish pioneers as 'the Pilgrim Fathers of Palestine'. Here is the same heroism dedicated to the same ends . . . It is obvious that the native Arabs while no less stubborn and savage than the American Indians, cannot be removed from the scene.[125]

Ramon Bennett illustrates how such prejudices remain common today, describing the modern Arab nations as 'barbarous': 'The customs of hospitality and

---

122. Bob Dole, *Near East Report,* vol. 21, no. 20, 18 May 1977, cited in Sharif, *Non-Jewish Zionism,* p. 136.

123. Rosemary and Herman J. Ruether, *The Wrath of Jonah: The Crisis of Religious Nationalism in the Israeli-Palestinian Conflict* (San Francisco: Harper, 1989), p. 176.

124. See, e.g., Said, *Orientalism,* passim; and Ramon Bennett, *Philistine: The Great Deception* (Jerusalem: Arm of Salvation, 1995); passim.

125. John Haynes Holmes, *Palestine Today and Tomorrow: A Gentile's Survey of Zionism* (New York: Macmillan, 1929), pp. 89, 248, cited in Sharif, *Non-Jewish Zionism,* p. 135.

generosity have changed little in 4,000 years,' he claims, 'nor have the customs of raiding (thieving, rustling), saving face or savagery.'[126] Citing John Laffin, Bennett argues that the Arab 'is neither a vicious nor, usually, a calculating liar but a natural one'.[127] Kenneth Cragg concurs with Edward Said's criticism of orientalism, for its 'crude stereotype imaging of the East' and for being:

> ... a gross form of Western superiority complex, expressed in a literature and a scholarship that imposed its own false portrayal on the East and refused to care sensitively for the East's own evaluation of itself. By distortion it had its own way with its eastern versions and made these the instrument of control and, indeed, of denigration ... 19th and 20th Century Western Orientalism is thus found uniformly culpable, and a conniver with misrepresentation.[128]

With the rise of Arab nationalism and especially Palestinian aspirations towards self-determination, the polemic against Arabs has grown. Comparisons between Hitler and the Arabs are now frequent in the writings of contemporary Christian Zionists.[129] Van der Hoeven of the ICEJ is typical: 'Just as there was a definite ideology behind the hatred and atrocities of Hitler and the Nazis, there is one behind the hatred and wars by the Arabs against the Jews and people of Israel.'[130] Citing Joseph Gunther and Samuel Katz, van der Hoeven claims:

> The greatest contemporary hero (in the Arab world) is Hitler ... Hitler's *Mein Kampf* is still required reading in various Arab capitals and universities ... The only reason that the Arabs have not yet done to the Israeli Jews what Hitler did to their forefathers in Europe is that they have thus far lacked the military means and weapons of mass destruction which were at Hitler's disposal, to do so. Had there not been an Israeli Defence Force to defend the remnant of European Jewry that immigrated to Israel, the Arabs would have gladly fulfilled Hitler's dream a long time ago by finishing off those of the Jews the Nazi megalomaniac had left alive.[131]

---

126. Bennett, *Philistine*, pp. 21, 23.

127. Ibid., p. 23; John Laffin, *The Arab Mind*, (London: Cassell, 1975), p. 70.

128. Said, *Orientalism*, cited in Cragg, *The Arab Christian*, p. 297.

129. See Jan Willem van der Hoeven, *Babylon or Jerusalem?* (Shippensburg, PA: Destiny Image Publishers, 1993), pp. 132–133; Bennett, *Philistine*, p. 134.

130. van der Hoeven, *Babylon or Jerusalem?*, pp. 132–133.

131. Jan Willem van der Hoeven, *Hitler and the Arabs* (2001) [Internet], the Freeman Centre, <http://www.freeman.org/m_online/apr01/hoeven.htm>. [Accessed June 2004.]

Hal Lindsey also insists, 'Long ago the psalmist predicted the final mad attempt of the confederated Arab armies to destroy the nation of Israel . . . The Palestinians are determined to trouble the world until they repossess what they feel is their land.'[132] Franklin Graham, president of the Billy Graham Evangelistic Association, made similar unguarded remarks in a newspaper interview in 2000: 'The Arabs will not be happy until every Jew is dead. They hate the State of Israel. They all hate the Jews. God gave the land to the Jews. The Arabs will never accept that.'[133]

Hatred of Arabs is personified in attitudes towards Yasser Arafat. For example, the ICEJ's antipathy towards Arafat is illustrated by its *Middle East Intelligence Digest*. The June 1997 edition included an article entitled 'Evil that will not die: Arafat shares Hitler's determination to wipe out the Jews.'[134] What is not so often mentioned is that in the 1930s the German Zionist Federation, the Stern Gang and Vladimir Jabotinsky, the founder of revisionist Zionism, were all sympathetic towards fascism, or collaborated with the Nazis.[135]

In February 1999, Arafat was invited to attend the forty-seventh annual Congress-sponsored National Prayer Breakfast in Washington. The breakfast is normally attended each year by more than 3,000 political and religious leaders and his invitation generated considerable controversy. For example, the Traditional Values Coalition, founded by Pat Robertson and representing 40,000 churches, urged congressmen to boycott the breakfast. Randy Tate, executive director of the Christian Coalition, described Arafat as an 'unrepentant terrorist'.[136] Other organizations that boycotted the breakfast included James Dobson's Focus on the Family, the National Unity Coalition for Israel and the International Christian Embassy Jerusalem. The ICEJ said that attending the breakfast with Arafat would be 'like praying with Satan himself'.[137] Despite considerable pressure from pro-Israeli groups, the invitation was not

---

132. Lindsey, *Israel and the Last Days*, pp. 38–39.

133. *Charlotte Observer*, 16 October 2000.

134. ICEJ, 'Evil that will not Die' (June 1997) [Internet], *Middle East Intelligence Digest*, <http://www.cdn-friends-icej.ca/medigest/june97/evil.html>. [Accessed May 2004.]

135. Lenni Brenner, *51 Documents – Zionist Collaboration with the Nazis* (Fort Lee, NJ: Barricade, 2002).

136. *Clinton prays for peace at annual breakfast* (4 February 1999) [Internet], CNN, <http://www.cnn.com/ALLPOLITICS/stories/1999/02/04/prayer.breakfast/>. [Accessed June 2004.]

137. Ibid.

withdrawn. It was left to the White House press secretary, Joe Lockhart, to defend the invitation. He lamented, 'It's done every year in the spirit of reconciliation. And it's unfortunate that there are some who don't fully understand the spirit of reconciliation and inclusion.'[138]

Antipathy for Arabs generally is also often associated, in particular, with racist attitudes towards Palestinians.

The ethnic cleansing of Palestine

Frequently, defending Israeli security leads Christian Zionists to deny Palestinians basic human rights. For example, Neil Cohen argues that equality or partnership between Jews and Arabs in Israel or the Occupied Territories is untenable because God gave the land to the Jewish people:

> We live in an age of political correctness which claims we live in a world where all people have equal rights. I don't agree with that because I don't think it squares with the biblical record . . . the search for peace in the Middle East, laudable though it is, is a wild goose chase.[139]

Rob Richards similarly justifies Israel's policy of segregation by designating Palestinians as 'alien' residents in Eretz Israel: 'Palestinians and Arabs who have made Israel their home come under that biblical word "alien".'[140] Brickner also uses the term 'sojourner' to describe the status of Palestinians in Eretz Israel,[141] while van der Hoeven describes as 'sick' the propaganda that 'Jews displaced Arab natives in Palestine'.[142] Such arguments ignore the fact that most Palestinians (at least those over the age of 55) did not choose to 'make their home in Israel' when the State of Israel was unilaterally imposed upon them in 1948. Indeed, many have been displaced twice, in 1948 and 1967. Today there are over 3.5 million Palestinians registered as refugees by the United Nations, constituting 25% of all refugees in the world.

Some, like Dave Hunt, go much further, questioning the very existence of Palestinians. He is typical of others like Ramon Bennett who equate

---

138. Ibid.
139. Neil Cohen, Paper delivered to the Guildford Diocesan Evangelical Fellowship, St John's, Woking. Surrey, 18 March 1997.
140. Richards, *Has God Finished with Israel?*, p. 159.
141. Brickner, 'Don't Pass Over Israel's Jubilee', Jews for Jesus Newsletter, April 1998.
142. van der Hoeven, *Hitler and the Arabs*.

Palestinians with the ancient Philistines and Amalakites using the term 'Palestinian' in an entirely pejorative sense:[143]

> Central to the Middle East conflict today is the issue of the so-called Palestinian people . . . Palestinians? There never was a Palestinian people, nation, language, culture, or religion. The claim of descent from a Palestinian people who lived for thousands of years in a land called Palestine is a hoax! That land was Canaan, inhabited by Canaanites, whom God destroyed because of their wickedness. Canaan became the land of Israel given by God to His people. Those who today call themselves Palestinians are Arabs by birth, language, and culture, and are close relatives to Arabs in surrounding countries from whence most of them came, attracted by Israel's prosperity.[144]

Hunt's logic could presumably be used to challenge the right to self-determination for citizens of the United States or indeed of dozens of European and Middle East nations founded in the twentieth century.

Dr Thomas McCall of Zola Levitt Ministries also suggests Palestinians are a less advanced race to the Jews. Referring to the limited Palestinian autonomy in Jericho he observes:

> I'm afraid the casino is an example of what the Palestinians do with the land when they acquire it. They are not an advanced culture, and they have never founded an indigenous economy. As a matter of fact, they are dependent on Israel for their livelihood.[145]

Nazi treatment of the Jews illustrates how easily the denigration of an 'inferior' people can lead to the denial of their human rights and the rationalization for their removal or eradication.

Jews for Jesus, for example, justifies Israel's use of military force to achieve and maintain control of the Occupied Territories. Comparing the present Israeli occupation with Joshua's conquest of Canaan, JFJ argues, 'In Moses' time the sons of Jacob did not traipse into the land of Canaan and find a welcoming-committee eager to greet them and congratulate them upon their arrival. God

---

143. Bennett, *Philistine*, passim.
144. Dave Hunt, *O Jerusalem, Jerusalem* (September 2000) [Internet], The Berean Call, <http://www.thebereancall.org/Newsletters/2000+Newsletters/4499.aspx>. [Accessed June 2004.]
145. Thomas McCall, 'Gershon Salomon & the Temple Mount Faithful: An Interview', *Levitt Letter*, Zola Levitt Ministries (July, 1977).

commanded that they take Canaan by force.' It claims the same principle applies today: 'There may be some who think that God has learned some new lessons since ancient times, but to our knowledge, God does not change. It is entirely possible that once again he might move Israel to resort to force.'[146]

Dick Armey, former Republican House Majority Leader in the House of Representatives, made ground-breaking news by justifying the ethnic cleansing of Palestinians from the Occupied Territories. In an interview with Chris Matthews on CNBC on 1 May 2002, Armey stated:

> Most of the people who now populate Israel were transported from all over the world to that land and they made it their home. The Palestinians can do the same and we are perfectly content to work with the Palestinians in doing that. We are not willing to sacrifice Israel for the notion of a Palestinian homeland . . . I'm content to have Israel grab the entire West Bank . . . There are many Arab nations that have many hundreds of thousands of acres of land, soil, and property and opportunity to create a Palestinian State.[147]

Matthews gave Armey several opportunities to clarify that he was not advocating the ethnic cleansing of all Palestinians from the West Bank, but Armey was unrepentant. When asked, 'Have you ever told George Bush, the President from your home State of Texas, that you think the Palestinians should get up and go and leave Palestine and that's the solution?', Armey replied, 'I'm probably telling him that right now . . . I am content to have Israel occupy that land that it now occupies and to have those people who have been aggressors against Israel retired to some other arena.'[148] Armey's view that Palestinians should be 'retired' is only the latest in a series of calls in the mainstream US and UK media for the ethnic cleansing of Palestinians from the Occupied Territories.[149]

---

146. *Do you approve of Zionism . . .?*, Jews for Jesus website, FAQ page.

147. See 'Rep. Dick Armey calls for Ethnic Cleansing of Palestinians', in Alexander Cockburn and Jeffrey St Clair (eds.), *Counterpunch* [Internet], <http://www. counterpunch.org/armey0502.html>. [Accessed May 2004.] Dick Armey and his family are members of Lewisville Bible Church, Lewisville, Texas.

148. Ibid.

149. See Charles Krauthammer, 'Mideast Violence: The Only Way Out', *Washington Post*, 15 May 2001. Emmanuel A. Winston called for the 'resettling the Palestinians in Jordan', *USA Today*, 22 February 2002. See also, John Derbyshire, 'Why don't I care about the Palestinians?', *National Review*, 9 May 2002; Clarence Wagner, 'Apples for Apples, Osama Bin Laden and Yasser Arafat', *Dispatch from Jerusalem* (May 2002), pp. 1, 6, 17.

While such racist attitudes are common among Christian Zionists towards Arabs, along with the stereotypes that Palestinians are terrorists and should find a home in Jordan, it is more especially Muslims who are demonized.

Demonizing Islam

Donald Bridge was for some while warden of the Garden Tomb, a focal point for evangelical pilgrims in Jerusalem. His views are illustrative of other Christian Zionist authors. In his guidebook, *Travelling Through the Promised Land*, Bridge repeatedly caricatures and slanders Muslims.[150] In describing the significance of Jerusalem to the three monotheistic faiths, he writes: 'Jews worldwide mark their calendars with events that took place here. Muslims worldwide are eager to engage in holy wars here.'[151] When describing the Temple Mount, Bridge writes, 'Arab feeling soon runs high here, and is expressed in anti-Christian and anti-Jewish frenzy. Mullahs shouting over the minarets' loudspeakers can turn a congregation into a rampaging mob within minutes.'[152] On a walk through the Old City of Jerusalem he contrasts the Muslim and Jewish Quarters:

> The Jewish Quarter basked in golden sunshine . . . Take a few steps out of the Jewish into the Arab Quarter and the contrast is dramatic. It is more colourful, more noisy, more crowded, more dirty. The sounds and smells are totally different. The (to us) alien chant, part moan, part yell, part gargle echoes hauntingly from a dozen minarets . . . Arab head-dresses splash the heaving crowds with black and white or red check, and about one in every fifteen looks uncomfortably like Yasser Arafat.[153]

Besides erroneously describing the Muslim Quarter as Arab (since all of the Old City is designated Arab in international law), the book would have probably been labelled anti-Semitic had Bridge actually written 'uncomfortably like Menachem Begin' or 'Yitzhak Shamir'.

Anti-Arab and Islamaphobic sentiments have become even more widely tolerated since 11 September 2001. For example, numerous dispensational authors have written about America's war against Islamic terrorism following

---

150. Donald Bridge, *Travelling Through the Promised Land* (Fearn: Christian Focus, 1998), p. 67.
151. Ibid., pp. 55–56.
152. Ibid., p. 70.
153. Ibid., p. 60.

the tragedy.[154] Lindsey's antipathy is evident when he claims, 'Islam considers it a sacred mission of religious honor to recapture Old Jerusalem.'[155] His books are replete with similarly dogmatic and stereotyped assertions:

> All Moslems see Israel as their enemy . . . The Arab nations are united in their fanatical obsession to destroy Israel . . . Agreements in the Arab nations don't mean the same thing they mean in the Judeo-Christian world. Islam not only has a track record of re-interpreting, denouncing and reversing settlements, such actions are actually encouraged if they further the cause of Allah . . . This movement seeks not only to destroy the State of Israel but also the overthrow of the Judeo-Christian culture – the very foundation of our western civilisation . . . They have, like the Communists, at their philosophic core the sworn duty to 'bury us'.[156]

Other Christian Zionist authors have made similar claims.[157] Such views have recently been described as a form of 'new McCarthyism'.[158] In February 2002, for example, Pat Robertson caused considerable controversy when he too described Islam as a violent religion bent on world domination. He also claimed American Muslims were forming terrorist cells in order to destroy the country. Robertson made the allegations on his Christian Broadcasting Network's *700 Club*. After clips showing Muslims in America, the announcer Lee Webb asked Robertson, 'As for the Muslim immigrants Pat, it makes you wonder, if they have such contempt for our foreign policy why they'd even want to live here?' Robertson replied:

> Well, as missionaries possibly to spread the doctrine of Islam . . . I have taken issue with our esteemed President in regard to his stand in saying Islam is a peaceful religion. It's just not. And the Koran makes it very clear, if you see an infidel, you are

---

154. See Hagee, *Attack on America*; Grant R. Jeffrey, *War on Terror: Unfolding Bible Prophecy* (Toronto: Frontier Research, 2002); Price, *Unholy War*; Ray Comfort, *Nostradamus: Attack on America and More Incredible Prophecies* (South Plainfield, NJ: Bridge Logos, 2002).

155. Lindsey, *Israel and the Last Days*, pp. 38–39.

156. Lindsey, *1980's: Countdown*, p. 45; *Israel and the Last Days*, p. 33; *Planet Earth 2000 AD*, p. 256; *Final Battle*, pp. 4–5.

157. See Mark Hitchcock, *The Coming Islamic Invasion of Israel* (Portland, OR: Multnomah, 2002); Price, *Unholy War*.

158. A term coined by William Safire, a former Nixon speechwriter and conservative Republican who thought George Bush, Sr, was insufficiently pro-Israel; cited in Lind, 'The Israel Lobby and American Power'.

to kill him . . . the fact is our immigration policies are now so skewed to the Middle East and away from Europe that we have introduced these people into our midst and undoubtedly there are terrorist cells all over them.[159]

At the 2002 Southern Baptist Convention[160] held in Florida, the former national convention leader, the Revd Jerry Vines, pastor of the 25,000-member First Baptist Church of Jacksonville, brought applause from several thousand participants of the pastors' conference when he described Muhammad as 'a demon-possessed paedophile'.[161]

Such antipathy towards Arabs, denigration of Palestinians and hatred of Islam invariably also leads Christian Zionists to oppose any peaceful resolution of the Palestinian–Israeli conflict which might require or coerce Israel to relinquish territory or compromise its security.

Opposing the peace process

While Christian Zionists invariably recognize Israel's unilateral claim to the Occupied Territories, they also oppose Palestinian aspirations to self-determination since the two are intrinsically incompatible. David Pileggi, for example, observes:

> Despite their widespread PR successes, the Palestinians have failed to convince most Israelis and Diaspora Jews that they have given up their dream of dismantling Israel in favour of a State in the West Bank and Gaza Strip . . . Palestinians cannot be trusted with a State at the heart of Israel.[162]

Walter Riggans also criticizes the Oslo and Wye Peace Accords because they threaten to legitimize Palestinian claims to Jerusalem and the West Bank.

---

159. Alan Cooperman, 'Robertson Calls Islam a Religion of Violence, Mayhem', *Washington Post*, 22 February 2002, p. 2.

160. The Southern Baptist Convention is a coalition of 42,000 churches with 16 million members. Since the 1980s it has become increasingly fundamentalist. See <http://www.sbcannualmeeting.org/sbc02/>.

161. See Richard Vara, 'Texas secession rumor, attacks on Islam mark Baptist meeting', *Houston Chronicle*, 10 June 2002; Alan Cooperman, 'Anti-Muslim Remarks Stir Tempest', *Washington Post*, 19 June 2002. According to Cooperman, the newly elected president of the Southern Baptists, the Revd Jack Graham, defended Vine's speech as 'accurate'.

162. David Pileggi, 'Letter from Jersualem', *Shalom* (July 1991).

Identifying with Israelis, he claims, 'Many Jewish people are quite devastated, and feel they have been betrayed into the hands of cunning and ruthless Palestinians who are exploiting the accords as a first step towards the elimination of Israel.' Indeed, Riggans claims that the peace accords have been a betrayal of God's intentions for the Jewish people: 'The peace . . . is a false one and there are those who believe its roots are from the evil one.'[163] Clarence Wagner of BFP shares this perspective. He is equally dismissive of the peace negotiations:

> We need to encourage others to understand God's plans, not the man-inspired plans of the UN, the US, the EEC, Oslo, Wye, etc. God is not in any plan that would wrestle the Old City of Jerusalem, including the Temple Mount area and the Mount of Olives, and give it to the Moslem world. Messiah is not coming back to a Moslem city called Al-Quds, but to the regathered, restored Jewish city of Jerusalem.[164]

The biblical literalism of Christian Zionism leads many to demonize Arabs and Palestinians as Satanic enemies of the Jewish people; their futurist reading of prophecy demands that much of the Middle East belongs to the Jewish people; and their eschatology predicts a pessimistic and apocalyptic end to the world. Peace talks are, therefore, not only a waste of time, they demonstrate at best a lack of faith and at worst a rebellious defiance towards God's plans. Such infallible certitudes lead some Christian Zionists to anathematize those who do not share their presuppositions.

Forcing God's hand

Christian Zionists often attempt to silence critics with the threat of divine retribution. For example, Brickner even warns other evangelicals who do not share a Zionist perspective that they are fighting against God:

> Peril awaits those who presume to say that God is finished with His chosen people . . . Just as God judged the nation of Egypt for her ill treatment of His people, so will He judge nations today. Evangelicals who would understand the Middle East must pay close attention to the teaching of Scripture, and take note of the cosmic forces that now do battle in the heavens but will soon do battle on earth. They must choose carefully which side to uphold.[165]

---

163. Walter Riggans, 'The Messianic Community and the Hand Shake', *Shalom* 1 (1995), including a quote from Benjamin Berger, elder at Kehilat HaMashiach, Jerusalem.

164. C. Wagner, 'Driving the Nations Crazy', p. 9.

165. Brickner, 'Don't Pass Over Israel's Jubilee'.

Christians are left in no doubt which side to 'uphold'. Pat Robertson warned recently:

> If the United States takes a role in ripping half of Jerusalem away from Israel and giving it to Yasser Arafat and a group of terrorists, we are going to see the wrath of God fall on this nation that will make tornadoes look like a Sunday school picnic.[166]

Robertson even suggests that Rabin's assassination was an act of God, a judgment for his betrayal of his own people: 'This is God's land and God has strong words about someone who parts and divides His land. The rabbis put a curse on Yitzhak Rabin when he began cutting up the land.'[167]

Such pronouncements coming from highly influential Christian leaders appear little different from those of Muslim fundamentalists who call for a 'holy war' against the West. Dave MacPherson has noted that the danger of such Armageddon theology is not so much that it is fatalistic, but that it is so contagious.[168] Karen Armstrong traces within Western Christian Zionism evidence of the legacy of the Crusades. Such fundamentalists have, she claims, 'returned to a classical and extreme religious crusading'.[169]

Christian Zionists recognize that since 1948 Israel's most strategic ally has been the United States, in vetoing censure at the United Nations, guaranteeing loans to fund the settlements, providing the latest military hardware to maintain their military occupation of the West Bank, taking Israel's side in negotiations with the Arab world and Palestinians, and, most recently, recognizing they share in a common war against global terrorism.[170] Christian Zionists have, therefore, sanctified this relationship while demonizing Arabs and Islam; they have defended Israel's right to live within secure and expanded borders while encouraging the ethnic cleansing of Palestinians from their land;

---

166. Pat Robertson, *On Israel and the Road Map to Peace* (n.d.) [Internet], the Official Site of Pat Robertson, <http://www.patrobertson.com/Teaching/TeachingonRoadMap.asp>. [Accessed June 2004.]

167. Pat Robertson, *Pat answers your questions on Israel* (12 February 2002) [Internet], *700 Club*, Christian Broadcasting Network, <http://cbn.org/700club>. [Accessed June 2004.]

168. Dave MacPherson, cited in Halsell, *Forcing God's Hand*, p. 10.

169. Armstrong, *Holy War*, p. 377.

170. For allegations of Israeli complicity in the 9/11 tragedy, see 'Five Israelis were seen filming as jet liners ploughed into the Twin Towers on September 11, 2001', *Sunday Herald*, 2 November 2003, <http://ww1.sundayherald.com/37707>.

and they have opposed the peace process where it threatens to partition Jerusalem or dismantle the vision of Eretz Israel. The implacable conviction that God has mandated in Scripture exclusive and sovereign Jewish rule over Eretz Israel, the entire city of Jerusalem and the Temple Mount, leads Christian Zionist leaders to invoke God's wrath on those who oppose them, even fellow evangelicals.

The political implications of Christian Zionism: conclusions

This chapter has argued that Christian Zionism as a movement has profound and lasting political consequences. Christian Zionists have shown varying degrees of enthusiasm for implementing six basic theological convictions that arise from their literal and futurist reading of the Bible:

1. The belief that the Jews remain God's chosen people leads Christian Zionists to seek to bless Israel in material ways. However, this also invariably results in the uncritical endorsement of and justification for Israel's racist and apartheid policies, in the media, among politicians and through solidarity tours to Israel.
2. As God's chosen people, the final restoration of the Jews to Israel is, therefore, actively encouraged and facilitated through partnerships between Christian organizations and the Jewish Agency.
3. Eretz Israel, as delineated in Scripture, belongs exclusively to the Jewish people, therefore the land must be annexed and the settlements adopted and strengthened.
4. Jerusalem is regarded as the eternal and exclusive capital of the Jews, and cannot be shared with the Palestinians. Therefore, strategically, Western governments are placed under pressure by Christian Zionists to relocate their embassies to Jerusalem and thereby recognize the fact.
5. The third temple has yet to be built, the priesthood consecrated and sacrifices reinstituted. As dispensational Christian Zionists, in particular, believe this is prophesied, they offer varying degrees of support to the Jewish Temple Mount organizations committed to achieving it.
6. Since Christian Zionists are convinced there will be an apocalyptic war between good and evil in the near future, there is no prospect for lasting peace between Jews and Arabs. Indeed, to advocate that Israel compromise with Islam or coexist with Palestinians is to identify with those destined to oppose God and Israel in the imminent battle of Armageddon.

Clearly, not all Christian Zionists embrace each of these six tenets, or with the same degree of conviction or involvement. Nevertheless, as has been argued, the overall consequences of such uncritical support for the State of Israel, especially among American evangelicals who identify with Christian Zionism in larger numbers than in Britain, are inherently and pathologically destructive.

4. CONCLUSIONS

This chapter will summarize the main factors in the development of Christian Zionism since 1800; it will distinguish between its variant forms; delineate between its constructive and destructive aspects; offer a critical summary; and propose an alternative.

Observations on the development of Christian Zionism

Seven observations can be made concerning the development and contemporary significance of this movement:

1. Christian Zionism, through its active and public support for Jewish restoration to Palestine, predated the rise of Jewish Zionism by at least sixty years.
2. Its origins lie within nineteenth-century British premillennial sectarianism. By the early twentieth century it had become a predominantly American dispensational movement and pervasive within all main evangelical denominations.
3. While the strategic value of a Jewish homeland in Palestine was a factor in British foreign policy during the nineteenth century, it became a feature of American foreign policy by the end of the twentieth century.

4. Without the initiative and commitment of British Christians (clergy, politicians and statesman) during the nineteenth century, it is questionable whether the Jewish Zionist dream of a national homeland in Palestine would have been realized.

5. Without the sustained political support of Christian Zionists in America, and significant government funding, it is doubtful whether the State of Israel would have remained in existence since 1948, let alone continued to occupy and settle the West Bank since 1967.

6. Conservative estimates would suggest that the Christian Zionist movement is at least ten times larger than the Jewish Zionist movement and has become a dominant lobby within contemporary American politics.

7. Underpinning Christian Zionism is a novel theological system based on an ultra-literal and futurist reading of the Bible which, while its origins are rooted in the Reformation and Puritanism, is essentially the product of early nineteenth-century millennialist sectarianism.

Variant forms of Christian Zionism

Four distinct strands of contemporary evangelical Christian Zionism emerge based on their theological understanding of the relationship between the church and Israel, their approach towards evangelism, restorationism, Eretz Israel and the settlements, Jerusalem, the temple and Armageddon.

These are: covenantal premillennialism, Messianic dispensationalism, apocalyptic dispensationalism and political dispensationalism. Figure 8 summarizes their unique characteristics (p. 256).

Covenantal premillennialism and Messianic dispensationalism share a common commitment to evangelize Jewish people before the second advent. Messianic dispensationalism, by virtue of its two-covenant theology, is also committed to reviving Jewish worship, including temple practices. It shares with apocalyptic dispensationalism a strong emphasis on end-times prophecy as well as a pessimism regarding peace in the Middle East. Apocalyptic dispensationalism also shares with political dispensationalism a commitment to maintaining strong US military and political ties with Israel. Political dispensationalism may be distinguished by its disavowal of evangelism, its optimistic eschatology and reinterpretation of the Christian gospel. For political dispensationalism the purpose of the church is to support and bless Israel since the Jews are accepted by God on the basis of their own covenant and will recognize their Messiah when he returns. If covenantal premillennialism may be regarded as the most orthodox and benign form of Christian Zionism,

Doctrine	Covenantal premillennial	Messianic dispensational	Apocalyptic dispensational	Political dispensational
Relationship to church	Part	Separate	Separate	Separate
Evangelism	Essential	Essential	Optional	Unnecessary
Restorationism	Prophesied	Prophesied	Prophesied	Implemented
Eretz Israel and settlements	Negotiable	Millennium	Non-negotiable	Solidarity
Jerusalem exclusive capital	Negotiable	Millennium	Non-negotiable	Lobbying for
Temple rebuilt	Irrelevant	Millennium	Imminent	Irrelevant
Armageddon	Optional	Inevitable	Inevitable	Repudiated
Representatives	Higton and Riggans	Rosen, Brickner and Fruchtenbaum	Lindsey, Evans and LaHaye	Robertson and Falwell
Organizations	CMJ and CWI	JFJ and AMFI	DTS	ICEJ & BFP

Figure 8. A taxonomy of the variant types of Christian Zionism[1]

political dispensationalism appears to be the most problematic. Figure 9 below summarizes the distinctive elements of each.

---

1. It is recognized that these variant forms of Christian Zionism are not entirely discreet and that there is a degree of overlap, especially in their theological perspectives. Furthermore, some Christian Zionist agencies are circumspect in their official doctrinal statements on controversial subjects such as the settlements or temple. This study has therefore relied on the published views of leaders and representatives of these agencies, recognizing that their views remain their own and do not necessarily reflect those of their organization as a whole.

Type of Christian Zionism	Distinctive elements
1. Covenantal premillennial	Evangelism and restorationism
2. Messianic dispensational	Evangelism and the Jewish temple
3. Apocalyptic dispensational	Prophecy and Armageddon
4. Political dispensational	Defending and blessing Israel

Figure 9. A summary of the variant types of Christian Zionism

The constructive and destructive aspects of Christian Zionism

A balanced and objective assessment of Christian Zionism is difficult given that its supporters and critics use emotive language to defend or condemn Zionism. At the same time, opinions as to the causes and solutions to the Middle East crisis are deeply polarized. It is possible, nevertheless, to summarize the constructive and destructive features of Christian Zionism and assess in what ways it may be regarded as a blessing or a curse on the Jewish people. The chart in figure 10 summarizes the constructive and destructive aspects of Christian Zionism highlighted by this book (see p. 258).

It may be observed that none of the constructive aspects are intrinsic or exclusive to Christian Zionism but are shared by other philo-Semitic evangelical agencies that work among Jewish people and yet do not support Zionism.[2]

A critical assessment of Christian Zionism

The fundamental question Christian Zionists must answer is this: What difference did the coming of the kingdom of God in the person of Jesus Christ make to the traditional Jewish hopes and expectations concerning the

---

2. Based on interviews with representatives. These agencies would include InterVarsity Christian Fellowship (USA), the YMCA, World Vision and Youth for Christ.

Constructive	Destructive
1. Encouragement of dialogue between Jews and Christians	1. Justification of apartheid within an exclusive Jewish State
2. Commitment to share the gospel with Jewish people (except political dispensationalism)	2. Undermining Christian witness in the Middle East by partisan support for Israel
3. Stand against anti-Semitism	3. Encouragement of religious intolerance and Islamaphobia
4. Education of the Gentile church in the Jewish origins of the Christian faith	4. Tacit acceptance of the ethnic-cleansing of Palestinians by their support for the Jewish Settlements
5. Compassion for and humanitarian work among Jewish refugees	5. Denigration of moderate Jews willing to negotiate a land-for-peace deal
	6. Incitement of religious fanaticism by supporting the rebuilding of the Jewish temple on Haram Al-Sharif
	7. Apocalyptic eschatology in danger of becoming a self-fulfilling prophecy.

Figure 10. The constructive and destructive consequences of Christian Zionism[3]

land and people?[4] Clarence Bass crystallizes the issue with a series of more specific rhetorical questions:

> It is legitimate to ask whether Dispensationalism is not orientated more from the Abrahamic Covenant than from the Cross. Is not its focus centred more on the

---

3. Stephen Sizer, 'Justifying Apartheid in the Name of God', *Churchman* (Summer 2001), pp. 147–171.

4. See Colin Chapman, 'Ten questions for a theology of the land', in Johnston and Walker (eds.), *The Land of Promise*, pp. 172–187.

Jewish kingdom than on the Body of Christ? Does it not interpret the New Testament in the light of Old Testament prophecies, instead of interpreting those prophecies in the light of the more complete revelation of the New Testament?[5]

Christian Zionists believe that the coming of Jesus Christ made little or no difference to the nationalistic and territorial aspirations of first-century Judaism. They appear to read the Old Testament in the same way that the first disciples did before Pentecost, believing the coming of the kingdom of Jesus meant a postponement of Jewish hopes for restoration rather than the fulfilment of those hopes in the Messiah and his new and inclusive Messianic community.

As a result, the Middle East Council of Churches (MECC), representing the indigenous and ancient Oriental and Eastern Churches, regards Christian Zionism as a deviant heresy. It asserts, for instance, that Christian Zionists have aggressively imposed an aberrant expression of the Christian faith and an erroneous interpretation of the Bible which is subservient to the political agenda of the modern State of Israel. It claims the movement represents a tendency to:

> force the Zionist model of theocratic and ethnocentric nationalism on the Middle East ... (rejecting) ... the movement of Christian unity and inter-religious understanding which is promoted by the (indigenous) churches in the region. The Christian Zionist programme, with its elevation of modern political Zionism, provides the Christian with a world view where the gospel is identified with the ideology of success and militarism. It places its emphasis on events leading up to the end of history rather than living Christ's love and justice today.[6]

In its apocalyptic and political forms especially, Christian Zionism distorts the Bible and marginalizes the universal imperative of the Christian message of equal grace and common justice. Kenneth Cragg summarizes the implications of its intrinsic ethnic exclusivity:

> It is so; God chose the Jews; the land is theirs by divine gift. These dicta cannot be questioned or resisted. They are final. Such verdicts come infallibly from Christian biblicists for whom Israel can do no wrong – thus fortified. But can such positivism, this unquestioning finality, be compatible with the integrity of the Prophets themselves? It certainly cannot square with the open peoplehood under God which is

---

5. Bass, *Backgrounds to Dispensationalism*, p. 151.
6. MECC, *What is Western Fundamentalist Christian Zionism?*, p. 13.

the crux of New Testament faith. Nor can it well be reconciled with the ethical demands central to law and election alike.[7]

Such literalist assumptions preclude any possibility of an alternative reading of the Bible, history or a just and lasting outcome to the Middle East peace-negotiations. Instead, Christian Zionism shows an uncritical tolerance of Rabbinic Judaism and an endorsement of the Israeli political right. At the same time it demonstrates an inexcusable lack of compassion for the Palestinian tragedy and the plight of the indigenous Christian community. In doing so, whether intentionally or otherwise, it has legitimized their oppression in the name of the gospel while committing the Jewish people themselves to an apocalyptic future far more horrifying than even the Shoah.

Christian Zionism only thrives on a literal and futurist hermeneutic in which ancient Old Testament promises of blessing to the Jewish people are applied to the contemporary State of Israel. To do so it is necessary to ignore or marginalize the New Testament which reinterprets, annuls, fulfils and expands these promises in and through Jesus Christ. Palmer Robertson has summarized this progressive revelation of the purposes of God:

> In the process of redemptive history, a dramatic movement has been made from type to reality, from shadow to substance. The land which once was the specific locale of God's redemptive working served well within the old covenant as a picture of Paradise lost and promised. Now, however, in the era of new-covenant fulfilment, the land has been expanded to encompass the cosmos . . . In this age of fulfilment, therefore, a retrogression to the limited forms of the old covenant must be neither expected or promoted. Reality must not give way to shadow.[8]

Ultimately, therefore, the choice is between two theologies: one based primarily on the shadows of the old covenant; the other on the reality of the new covenant. In identifying with the former, Christian Zionism is an exclusive theology that focuses on the Jews in the land rather than an inclusive theology that centres on Jesus Christ, the Saviour of the world. It consequently provides a theological endorsement for racial segregation, apartheid and war. This is diametrically opposed to the inclusive theology of justice, peace and reconciliation which lie at the heart of the new covenant.

---

7. Cragg, *The Arab Christian*, p. 238.

8. O. Palmer Robertson, 'A new-covenant perspective on the land', in Johnston and Walker (eds.), *Land of Promise*, p. 140.

To suggest, therefore, that the Jewish people continue to have a special relationship with God, apart from faith in Jesus, or have exclusive rights to land, a city and temple is, in the words of John Stott, 'biblically anathema'.[9] Paul's warning to the church in Galatia concerning the nationalistic and legalistic Christian Judaizers infecting the church of his own day is perhaps an appropriate description of and response to contemporary Christian Zionism: 'Get rid of the slave woman and her son' (Gal. 4:30).

Biblical Zionism: a covenantal alternative

This study has sought to repudiate not only anti-Semitism but also nationalistic Zionism. The choice does not have to be between Christian Zionism and 'replacement' theology, the idea that the spiritual church, as the 'new Israel', has in some sense replaced physical Israel within God's purposes.

Other writers such as David Holwerda, Steve Motyer, O. Palmer Robertson and Cornelius Venema have already very ably presented the case for covenantalism.[10] The purpose of this book has been to make a case for a covenantalist approach to the Palestinian–Israeli conflict by focusing on and critiquing its antithesis, namely dispensational Christian Zionism.

A covenantalist recognizes, for example, that the Bible consistently teaches that God has only ever had one people throughout history – those who share the faith of Abraham, whether Jews or Gentiles – and one means of atonement, the sacrifice of the Lord Jesus Christ in our place. Based on passages such as Romans 9 – 11, covenantalists recognize the Jewish people are loved by God, have fulfilled a unique role in history leading to the birth of Christianity and pray that one day all Jews will come to recognize Jesus as their Messiah.

Covenantalism affirms that the church is Israel renewed and restored in Christ but now enlarged to embrace people of all nations. The following comparison between covenantalism and dispensationalism highlights their differing approach to doctrines relating to Israel and the future.

Based on covenantal presuppositions, it is contended that a biblical approach to the Palestinian–Israeli conflict will work and pray for the peace and security of the Jewish and Palestinian people because they are created in the image and likeness of God with intrinsic meaning, value and dignity. It will

---

9. John Stott, cited in Wagner, *Anxious for Armageddon*, p. 80.
10. Holwerda, *Jesus and Israel*; Motyer, *Israel in the Plan of God*; O. P. Robertson, *Israel of God*; Venema, *Promise of the Future*.

Doctrine	Covenantalism	Dispensationalism
Biblical hermeneutic	Literal – typological and contextualized	Ultra-literal
Old Testament prophecy	Largely fulfilled	Largely futurist
Basis of salvation	New covenant by grace through faith	7 dispensations in which mankind tested
Israel's national promises	Spiritualized and universalized in church	Awaiting future fulfilment in Israel
Unbelieving Jewish people	Loved by God but cut off from God's people	Unconditionally the chosen people
Zionism	Secular substitute for faith in the Messiah	Preceding revival and a Jewish kingdom
Relationship of Israel to the church	One people of God	Two separate peoples of God
Ecclesiology	Church began with Israel	Church began at Pentecost
View of the church	Victorious Bride of Christ	Parenthesis that has failed
Eretz Israel	Fulfilled and annulled	Unconditional inheritance of the Jews
Jerusalem	Historical role no longer significant	Capital of the Jewish kingdom
Temple	Fulfilled in Jesus now redundant	To be rebuilt and desecrated
View of future	Expectant	Apocalyptic

Figure 11. A comparison between covenantalism and dispensationalism *continued overleaf*

Doctrine	Covenantalism	Dispensationalism
Eschatology	Largely amillennial, postmillennial or preterist	Premillennial
Armageddon	Figurative battle between good and evil	Literal and imminent battle at Megiddo
Return of Jesus	One visible event	Two-stage rapture: invisible and visible
Kingdom of God	Not of this world	Soon to be made visible centred on Jerusalem
Millennium	Figurative	Literal 1,000-year reign of Christ on earth

Figure 11 *continued*

acknowledge that Jews and Palestinians, like all other races, have the right to self-determination and to live within secure and internationally recognized borders. It will support international peace efforts based on biblical principles of justice and peace, on mutual recognition and reconciliation. Unlike Christian Zionism, covenantalism finds it unnecessary to justify or sacralize the State of Israel through tenuous biblical or theological arguments. It also distances itself from those who seek to impose a predetermined and apocalyptic agenda on the people of the Middle East.[11]

With the repudiation of the destructive elements of Christian Zionism, Jews and Arabs, like Isaac's children, Jacob and Esau, can be assisted by Christians to stop fighting over their birthright and start sharing the blessings.[12]

Garth Hewitt, a peacemaker and friend of all three faith communities, has expressed the hope of this author in a song based on words taken from the Jewish Talmud: 'Ten measures of beauty God gave to the world, nine to Jerusalem, one to the remainder. Ten measures of sorrow God gave to the

---

11. See Chapman, *Whose Promised Land?*, p. 274.

12. Yeheskel Landau, an illustration given in an unpublished talk at St George's Cathedral, Jerusalem (Dec. 1998).

world, nine to Jerusalem, one to the remainder'.[13] The words of Garth's chorus are offered as a valedictory prayer.

> May the justice of God fall down like fire
> and bring a home for the Palestinian.
>
> May the mercy of God pour down like rain
> and protect the Jewish people.
> And may the beautiful eyes of a Holy God
> Who weeps for his children
> Bring his healing hope for his wounded ones
> For the Jew and the Palestinian.[14]

---

13. Talmud, Kiddushin 49b.
14. Garth Hewitt, 'Ten measures of beauty'.

aliyah A Hebrew word meaning 'going up' used in a general sense to describe going up to Jerusalem on pilgrimage. In the context of Zionism it refers to the ingathering of the Jewish people returning to their homeland.

amillennialism There will be no literal or physical kingdom on earth when Christ returns. The kingdom of God is present in the world now as Christ rules the church through his Word and the Spirit. Revelation 20 is metaphorical.

Antichrist A human or supernatural figure who opposes God and the church and will reign on earth prior to his defeat at Christ's return. Usually associated with premillennialism.

apartheid A Dutch Afrikaans word derived from the root *apart* meaning 'separate', and *heid* meaning 'hood'. It describes the legal and institutional segregation of people on the basis of their race or colour.

apocalyptic Derived from Revelation 1:1 and meaning 'unveiling', it refers to biblical or extra-biblical literature that reveals the mystery of God's end-time purposes prior to the return of Jesus Christ.

apostasy A deliberate falling away or repudiation of the Christian faith by professing Christians; one of the predicted signs of the times indicating the imminent return of Christ.

Armageddon From the Hebrew for 'Mountain of Megiddo' it is mentioned in Revelation 16:16 as the place where the final battle on earth will take place. Others understand it as a symbol of the final overthrow of evil by God.

chiliasm From the Greek *chilias* meaning 'a thousand', it is a synonym for millennialism. It is used as a general term to describe either the literal 1,000-year kingdom of premillennialism or the extensive era of postmillennialism.

classical dispensationalism The original dispensational position of Scofield and Chafer. God has two peoples, eternally separate: an earthly people (the Jews) and a heavenly people (the church). Two ways to salvation: law and grace.

covenant A solemn and binding commitment between God and his people. Based on Jeremiah 31 and the New Testament, the 'new' covenant is a synonym for God's grace revealed in the redemption of Christ resulting in a church of Jews and Gentiles.

covenant theology Scripture delineates God's plan of salvation under two covenants. The promise was life, the proviso obedience, the penalty death. Under the first, Adam failed, under the second, Jesus triumphed in our place.

covenantal premillennialism A literal 1,000-year kingdom on earth following the sudden return of Christ. The Jewish people will have a place of prominence but as part of the universal church. Synonymous with historic premillennialism.

dispensationalism Seven periods of time during which humanity has or will be tested according to some specific revelation of God. Israel and the church are separate. The millennium will be the culmination of God's purposes for Israel.

end times Synonymous with the 'last days' and used in Scripture to describe the period of history from the death of Christ to his return. More particularly used by premillennialists and dispensationalists to describe the present era.

Eretz Israel This is 'Greater' Israel as delineated in Genesis, the land God promised Abraham and his descendents on both sides of the River Jordan from the River of Egypt in the south to the Euphrates in the north.

eschatology From the Greek *eschatos* meaning 'last' and *logos* meaning 'word'; the doctrine of the future and specifically the events preceding the return of Christ. Variants include futurist, idealist, historicist and realized.

evangelicalism A movement within Protestant Christianity that emphasizes a personal relationship with God through Jesus Christ, a commitment to the Bible as the infallible Word of God and the sharing of the gospel with unbelievers.

fundamentalism The name originally derives from a series of pamphlets called *The Fundamentals* published between 1910–1915. Broadly, the term often refers to any evangelical conservatism that has a high view of the Bible.

futurism Biblical prophecies, especially those relating to Israel, are interpreted as referring to still future events because they have not been fulfilled literally. These include, for example, the rebuilding of the Jewish temple.

hermeneutics The Greek word *hermeneia* (meaning 'interpretation') denotes the principles used in biblical interpretation. Historically these include allegorical (Roman Catholic), typological (Reformed) and literalist (fundamentalist).

historic premillennialism A literal 1,000-year kingdom on earth following the sudden return of Christ. The Jewish people will have a place of prominence but as part of the universal church. Synonymous with covenantal premillennialism.

historicism The book of Revelation is interpreted by historicists as describing leaders, movements and major events in history from the birth of the church until the return of Christ.

hyper-dispensationalism This sees the 'church age' commencing in Acts 13 when the Jewish people rejected the gospel and Paul turns to the Gentiles, instead of in Acts 2 at Pentecost.

idealism The symbolic interpretation of Revelation describing the conflict between good and evil through history. Unlike the preterist or historicist, the idealist does not link the interpretation to specific historic events.

literalism The interpretation of Scripture, especially prophecy, based upon the plain meaning of the words of the text. Usually distinguished from grammatical-historical interpretation, literalism is associated most frequently with futurism.

Messianic dispensationalism A movement of Jews who believe Jesus to be their Messiah. Invariably dispensational, evangelistic and pro-Zionist, they are convinced the temple will be rebuilt and Jewish worship reinstituted.

mid-tribulationism The church will be raptured secretly to heaven half-way through the seven-year tribulation on earth when unbelievers and the Jews will suffer and have to endure the battle of Armageddon before Christ returns visibly.

millennium A 1,000-year reign on earth based on Revelation 20 when Satan is bound and Christ reigns on earth. Usually associated with covenantal premillennialism, dispensational premillennialism or postmillennialism.

neo-dispensationalism Israel and the church, although separate people of God, will be united in the millennium. There is only one covenant and one way to God, through faith in Jesus Christ. Espoused by Ryrie and Walvoord.

postmillennialism An extended period of peace and prosperity on earth prior to the return of Christ. The gospel will be proclaimed to all nations and Christian values will be universally embraced. Revelation 20 is symbolic.

post-tribulationism The church will be raptured secretly to heaven *after* the seven-year tribulation on earth, during which time they will suffer persecution and the battle of Armageddon before Christ returns visibly to rescue his elect.

premillennialism A literal 1,000-year kingdom on earth following the sudden return of Christ. There are two variants, covenantal and dispensational, depending on whether Israel and the church will share eternity together.

preterism The events prophesied by Jesus prior to his death and the book of Revelation either occurred by AD 70 when Jerusalem and the temple were destroyed or by the fall of the Roman Empire in the fifth century AD.

pre-tribulationism The church will be raptured secretly to heaven before the seven-year tribulation begins on earth when unbelievers and the Jews will suffer persecution and the battle of Armageddon before Christ returns visibly.

progressive dispensationalism The church is not a parenthesis but foretaste of God's kingdom. God has one purpose for Israel and the church, although Old Testament prophecies regarding Israel will still be fulfilled in the millennium by ethnic Jews.

rapture Covenantalism teaches that believers will be united with Christ when he returns. Dispensationalists divide the event into two parts. A secret rapture will remove believers during the tribulation after which they will appear with Christ.

replacement theology A term often used by Christian Zionists to caricature covenantalists as affirming that the spiritual church, as the 'new Israel', has replaced physical Israel within God's purposes.

restorationism The conviction that the Bible predicts and mandates a final and complete restoration of the Jewish people to Israel.

signs of the times These are specific signs which Jesus predicted would occur before his return. These include an increase in apostasy, wars, famines and earthquakes as well as a marked increase in Jewish people believing in Jesus.

tribulation A period of seven years of suffering on earth immediately prior to the return of Christ. Popular within dispensationalism especially. There are three variants depending on when the church is raptured – pre-, mid- or post-tribulation.

typology A method of interpretation in which Old Testament 'types' are seen as fulfilled in the New Testament. These include people (David), places (Zion) and events (Passover) which are prefigurements or shadows of New Testament realities.

ultra-dispensationalism Also known as Bullingerism after E. W. Bullinger. The 'church age' begins in Acts 28. Therefore, only a few of the Pauline epistles are for the church. The rest of the New Testament is for the Jewish dispensation.

Zion The land of Israel or, more specifically, Jerusalem. It is at the heart of the Zionist dream, where land, city and temple are once more restored to the Jewish people, either inaugurated by the Messiah or brought about by human effort.

Zionism The movement for the return of the Jewish people to their ancient homeland and the resumption of Jewish political sovereignty in the land of Israel centred on Jerusalem as their eternal and undivided capital.

APPENDIX

Challenging Christian Zionism

A statement produced and affirmed at the Fifth International Conference of the Sabeel Ecumenical Palestinian Liberation Theology Center, Jerusalem, 14–18 April 2004.

'Blessed are the peacemakers, for they will be called children of God' (Matt. 5:9).
Christian Zionism is a modern theological and political movement that embraces the most extreme ideological positions of Zionism, thereby becoming detrimental to a just peace within Palestine and Israel. The Christian Zionist programme provides a world-view where the gospel is identified with the ideology of empire, colonialism and militarism. In its extreme form, it places an emphasis on apocalyptic events leading to the end of history rather than living Christ's love and justice today. We also repudiate the more insidious form of Christian Zionism pervasive in the mainline churches that remains silent in the face of the Israeli occupation of Palestine. Therefore, we categorically reject Christian Zionist doctrines as a false teaching that undermines the biblical message of love, mercy and justice.

We further reject the contemporary alliance of Christian Zionist leaders and organizations with extremist elements in the governments of Israel and the United States that are presently seeking to impose their unilateral pre-emptive strategies and militaristic rule over others, including Palestine and Iraq. As a result of the 14 April 2004 Bush-Sharon memorandum of understanding, the crisis in Israel and Palestine has moved into a new phase of oppression of the Palestinian people. This will inevitably lead to unending cycles of violence and counter-violence that are already spreading throughout the Middle East and other parts of the world. We reject the heretical teachings of Christian Zionism that facilitate and support these extremist policies as they advance a form of racial exclusivity and perpetual war rather than the gospel of universal love, redemption and reconciliation taught by Jesus Christ.

Rather than condemn the world to the doom of Armageddon, we call upon everyone to liberate themselves from ideologies of militarism and occupation and instead to pursue the healing of the world. We call upon Christians in churches on every continent to prayerfully remember the suffering of the Palestinian and Israeli people, both of whom are victims of policies of occupation and militarism. These policies are reviving a system of apartheid that is turning Palestinian cities, towns and villages into impoverished ghettos surrounded by exclusively Jewish colonies. The recent construction of the Israeli wall on Palestinian land precludes a viable Palestinian state.

Therefore, we commit ourselves to the following principles as an alternative way (Sabeel):

- We affirm that all people are created in the image of God and called to honor the dignity and respect the equal rights of every human being.
- We call upon people of good will everywhere to reject the theology of Christian Zionism and all parallel religious and ideological fundamentalisms that privilege particular people at the expense of others.
- We are committed to the power of non-violent resistance to defeat the occupation and attain a just and lasting peace.
- With renewed urgency we warn that the theology of Christian Zionism is leading to the moral justification of empire, colonization, apartheid and oppression.
  Moreover, we affirm that a just and lasting peace in Palestine and Israel must be based on the Jerusalem Sabeel Document: Principles for a Just Peace in Palestine-Israel (2004) [see <http://www.sabeel.org>].

Sabeel's vision embraces two sovereign states, Palestine and Israel, which will enter into confederation or even a federation, possibly with other neighboring countries, where Jerusalem becomes the federal capital. Indeed, the ideal and best solution has always been to envisage ultimately a bi-national state in Palestine-Israel where people are free and equal, living under a constitutional democracy that protects and guarantees all their rights, responsibilities and duties without racism or discrimination – one state for two nations and three religions.

This is where Sabeel takes its stand. We will stand for justice. We can do no other. Justice alone guarantees a peace that will lead to reconciliation and a life of security and prosperity for all the peoples of our land. By standing on the side of justice, we open ourselves to the work of peace – and working for peace makes us children of God.

God demands that justice be done. No enduring peace, security or reconciliation is possible without the foundation of justice. The demands of justice will not disappear. The struggle for justice must be pursued diligently and persistently but non-violently.

> *And what does the LORD require of you?*
> *To act justly and to love mercy,*
>   *and to walk humbly with your God.*
> (Micah 6:8)

BIBLIOGRAPHY

ABANES, RICHARD (1998), *End-Times Vision: The Doomsday Obsession*, Nashville: Broadman & Holman.

ALLIS, OSWALD T. (1945), *Prophecy and the Church*, Philadelphia: Presbyterian & Reformed.

ALNOR, WILLIAM M. (1989), *Soothsayers of the Second Coming*, Old Tappan, NJ: Fleming H. Revell.

ARMERDING, CARL E. and W. WARD GASQUE (1989), *A Guide to Biblical Prophecy*, Peabody, MA: Hendrikson.

ARMSTRONG, KAREN (1988), *Holy War: The Crusades and Their Impact on Today's World*, London: Macmillan.

ATEEK, NAIM S. (1990), *Justice and Only Justice: A Palestinian Theology of Liberation*, Maryknoll: Orbis.

BALMER, RANDALL (1993), *Mine Eyes Have Seen the Glory: A Journey into the Evangelical Subculture in America*, rev. edn, Oxford: Oxford University Press.

BASS, CLARENCE (1960), *Backgrounds to Dispensationalism*, Grand Rapids: Eerdmans.

BEBBINGTON, D. W. (1989), *Evangelicalism in Modern Britain: A History from the 1730s to the 1980s*, London: Unwin Hyman.

BLACKSTONE, W. E. (1916), *Jesus is Coming*, 3rd edn, Chicago: Fleming H. Revell.

BLAISING, CRAIG A. and DARRELL L. BOCK (eds.) (1992), *Dispensationalism, Israel and the Church: The Search for Definition*, Grand Rapids: Zondervan.

— (1993), *Progressive Dispensationalism*, Wheaton: Victor.

BOETTNER, LORAINE (1958), *The Millennium*, Grand Rapids: Baker.

BOONE, KATHLEEN C. (1989), *The Bible Tells Them So: The Discourse of Protestant Fundamentalism*, London: SCM.

BOSTON, ROBERT (1996), *The Most Dangerous Man in America? Pat Robertson and the Rise of the Christian Coalition*, New York: Prometheus.

BOYER, PAUL (1992), *When Time Shall Be No More: Prophecy Belief in Modern American Culture*, Cambridge, MA: Harvard University Press.

BRICKNER, DAVID (1999), *Future Hope: A Jewish Christian Look at the End of the World*, San Francisco: Purple Pomegranate.

BROOKES, JAMES H. (1895), *Till He Come*, 2nd edn, New York: Fleming H. Revell.

BRUCE, STEVE (1988), *The Rise and Fall of the New Christian Right: Conservative Protestant Politics in America 1978–1988*, Oxford: Clarendon.

BRUGGEMANN, WALTER (1977), *The Land*, Philadelphia: Fortress.

BURGE, GARY (2003), *Whose Land? Whose Promise?*, Carlisle: Paternoster.

BUTT, GERALD (1994), *A Rock and a Hard Place: Origins of Arab–Western Conflict in the Middle East*, London: Harper Collins.

—(1995), *The Lion in the Sand: The British in the Middle East*, London: Bloomsbury.

CANFIELD, JOSEPH M. (1988), *The Incredible Scofield and his Book*, Vallecito, CA: Ross House Books.

CAPLAN, LIONEL (ed.) (1987), *Studies in Religious Fundamentalism*, London: Macmillan.

CARSON, D. A. and JOHN D. WOODBRIDGE (eds.) (1986), *Hermeneutics, Authority and Canon*, Leicester: IVP.

CARTER, JIMMY (1985), *The Blood of Abraham*, London: Sidgwick & Jackson.

CHACOUR, ELIAS (1984), *Blood Brothers: A Palestinian's Struggle for Reconciliation in the Middle East*, Eastbourne: Kingsway.

—(1990), *We Belong to the Land*, London: Marshall Pickering.

CHAFER, LEWIS S. (1936), *Dispensationalism*, Dallas: Dallas Seminary Press.

—(1947), *Systematic Theology*, 8 vols., Dallas: Dallas Seminary Press.

CHAPMAN, COLIN (2002), *Whose Promised Land, Israel or Palestine?*, rev. edn, Oxford: Lion.

CHILTON, DAVID (1985), *Paradise Restored: A Biblical Theology of Dominion*, Tyler, TX, Dominion.

—(1987), *The Days of Vengeance: An Exposition of the Book of Revelation*, Tyler, TX: Dominion.

CHOMSKY, NOAM (1993), *The Fateful Triangle: The United States, Israel and the Palestinians*, London: Pluto.

CLOUSE, ROBERT G. (ed.) (1977), *The Meaning of the Millennium*, Downers Grove, IL: IVP.

CLOUSE, ROBERT G., ROBERT N. HOSACK and RICHARD V. PIERARD (1999), *The New Millennium Manual*, Grand Rapids: Baker.

COAD, ROY (1968), *A History of the Brethren Movement*, Exeter: Paternoster.

COHEN, NORMAN J. (ed.) (1990), *The Fundamentalist Phenomenon*, Grand Rapids: Eerdmans.

COX, WILLIAM E. (n.d.), *Why I Left Scofieldism*, Phillipsburg, NJ: Presbyterian & Reformed.

—(1974), *An Examination of Dispensationalism*, Philadelphia: Presbyterian & Reformed.

COXE, A. CLEVELAND (1994), *Anti-Nicene Fathers*, Peabody, MA: Hendrikson.

CRAGG, KENNETH (1992), *The Arab Christian: A History in the Middle East*, London: Mowbray.

—(1997), *Palestine, the Prize and Price of Zion*, London: Cassell.

CULVER, DOUGLAS J. (1995), *Albion and Ariel: British Puritanism and the Birth of Political Zionism*, New York: Peter Lang.

DALLIMORE, ARNOLD (1983), *The Life of Edward Irving, The Fore-runner of the Charismatic Movement*, Edinburgh: Banner of Truth.

DARBY, JOHN NELSON (1962), *The Collected Writings of J. N. Darby*, ed. William Kelly, 34 vols., Kingston on Thames: Stow Hill Bible and Trust Depot.

DAVENPORT, ROWLAND A. (1970), *Albury Apostles*, London: Free Society.

DAVIES, W. D. (1974), *The Gospel and the Land: Early Christianity and Jewish Territorial Doctrine*, Berkeley: University of California.

DAVIS, URI (1987), *Israel, An Apartheid State*, London: Zed.

DEMAR, GARY (1997), *Last Days Madness: Obsession of the Modern Church*, Atlanta, GA: American Vision.

DEMAR, GARY and PETER LEITHART (1989), *The Legacy of Hatred Continues: A response to Hal Lindsey's The Road to Holocaust*, Tyler, TX: Institute of Christian Economics.

DOLAN, DAVID (1991), *Holy War for the Promised Land: Israel's Struggle to Survive*, London: Hodder & Stoughton.

DOYLE, ROBERT (1999), *Eschatology and the Shape of Christian Belief*, Carlisle: Paternoster.

DRUMMOND, ANDREW L. (n.d.), *Edward Irving and His Circle*, London: James Clarke.

DYER, CHARLES H. (1991), *The Rise of Babylon: Signs of the End Times*, Wheaton, IL: Tyndale House.

EL ASSAL, RIAH ABU (1999), *Caught in Between*, London: SPCK.

ELLIOT, ELISABETH (1969), *Furnace of the Lord: Reflections on the Redemption of the Holy City*, London: Hodder & Stoughton.

ELLIS, MARC H. (1988), *Toward a Jewish Theology of Liberation*, London: SCM.

ELLISON, HENRY L. (1968), *The Mystery of Israel: An Exposition of Romans 9–11*, Exeter: Paternoster.

EVANS, MIKE (1980), *Israel, America's Key to Survival*, Plainfield, NJ: Logos.

FABER, GEORGE STANLEY (1804), *A Dissertation on the Prophecies that have been fulfilled, are now fulfilling or will hereafter be fulfilled relative to the Great Period of 1260 years, the Papal and Mohammedan (sic) Apostasies, the Tyranical Reign of the Antichrist or the Infidel Power and the Restoration of the Jews*, London: F. C. and J. Rivington.

—(1809), *A General and Connected View of the Prophecies Relative to the Conversion, Restoration, Union and Future Glory of the Houses of Judah and Israel. The Progress and Final Overthrow of the Antichristian Confederacy in the Land of Palestine and the Ultimate General Diffusion of Christianity*, London: F. C. and J. Rivington.

FALWELL, JERRY (1981), *The Fundamentalist Phenomenon*, New York: Doubleday.

FAIRBAIRN, PATRICK (1975), *The Typology of Scripture Viewed in Connection with the Whole Series of The Divine Dispensations*, vol. 1, Welwyn: Evangelical Press; 1st edn 1900.

FINKELSTEIN, NORMAN G. (2000), *The Holocaust Industry: Reflections of the Exploitation of Jewish Suffering*, London: Verso.

FLAPAN, SIMHA (1979), *Zionism and the Palestinians*, London: Croom Helm.

FLEGG, COLUMBA GRAHAM (1992), *Gathered under Apostles: A Study of the Catholic Apostolic Church*, Oxford: Clarendon.

FRANCE, RICHARD T. (1989), *Matthew*, TNTC, Leicester: IVP.

FRAZIER, T. L. (1999), *A Second Look at the Second Coming*, Ben Lomond, CA: Conciliar Press.

FRERE, J. HATLEY (1850), *Notes Forming a Brief Interpretation of the Apocalypse intended to be read in connection with the combined view of the prophecies of Daniel, Edras and St John showing that all prophetic writings are formed upon one plan*, London, J. Hatchard & Sons; 1st edn 1815.

FROMOW, GEORGE H. (ed.) (n.d.), *B. W. Newton and Dr. S. P. Tregelles, Teachers of the Faith and the Future*, Taunton: Phoenix.

FRUCHTENBAUM, ARNOLD G. (1992), *Israelology: The Missing Link in Systematic Theology*, rev. edn, Tustin, CA: Ariel Ministries Press; 1st edn 1989.

FULLER, DANIEL P. (1980), *Gospel and Law, Contrast or Continuum?: The Hermeneutics of Dispensational and Covenant Theology*, Grand Rapids: Eerdmans.

GAEBELEIN, ARNO C. (1933), *The Conflict of the Ages*, New York: Our Hope.

—(1991), *The History of the Scofield Reference Bible*, Spokane, WA: Living Words Foundation.

GERSTNER, JOHN H. (1982), *A Primer on Dispensationalism*, Phillipsburg, NJ, Presbyterian & Reformed.

— (1991), *Wrongly Dividing the Word of Truth*, 1st edn, Brentwood, TN: Wolgemuth & Hyatt; 2nd edn Morgan, PA: Soli Deo Gloria, 2000.

GLOCK, CHARLES Y. and RODNEY STARK (1966), *Christian Beliefs and Anti-Semitism*, New York: Harper & Row.

GOLDINGAY, JOHN E. (1981), *Approaches to Old Testament Interpretation*, Leicester: IVP.

—(1995), *Models for the Interpretation of Scripture*, Grand Rapids: Eerdmans.

GOLDSWORTHY, GRAEME (1981), *Gospel and Kingdom: A Christian Interpretation of the Old Testament*, Exeter: Paternoster.

—(1991) *According to Plan: The Unfolding Revelation of God in the Bible*, Leicester: IVP.

GORENBERG, GERSHOM (2000), *The End of Days: Fundamentalism and the Struggle for the Temple Mount*, Oxford: Oxford University Press.

GRAHAM, BILLY (1983), *Approaching Hoofbeats: The Four Horsemen of the Apocalypse*, Waco: Word.

GREEN, JOEL B. (1984), *How to Read Prophecy*, Leicester: IVP.

GRENZ, STANLEY J. (1992), *The Millennial Maze: Sorting out Evangelical Options*, Downers Grove, IL: IVP.

GRIER, W. J. (1970), *The Momentous Event: A discussion of Scripture teaching of the Second Advent*, London: Banner of Truth.

HADDAD, HASSAN and DONALD WAGNER (1986), *All in the Name of the Bible: Selected Essays on Israel and American Christian Fundamentalism*, Brattelboro, VT: Amana Books.

HAGEE, JOHN (2001), *Attack on America*, Nashville: Nelson.

HALSELL, GRACE (1981), *Journey to Jerusalem*, New York: Macmillan.

—(1986), *Prophecy and Politics: Militant Evangelists on the Road to Nuclear War*, Westport: Lawrence Hill.

—(1999), *Forcing God's Hand: Why Millions Pray for a Quick Rapture – and Destruction of Planet Earth*, Washington: Crossroads International.

HARRISON, JOHN FLETCHER CLEWS (1979), *The Second Coming: Popular Millenarianism 1780–1850*, London: Routledge & Kegan Paul.

HENDRIKSON, WILLIAM (1940), *More than Conquerors: An Interpretation of the Book of Revelation*, London: IVP.

——(1968), *Israel in Prophecy*, Grand Rapids: Baker.

HENGSTENBERG, ERNST WILHELM (1869), *The Prophecies of the Prophet Ezekiel*, trans. A. C. Murphy and J. G. Murphy, Edinburgh: T. & T. Clark.

HERZL, THEODOR (1896), *The Jewish State*, London: David Nutt.

——(1956), *The Diaries of Theodor Herzl*, New York.

HEWITT, GARTH (1995), *Pilgrims & Peacemakers: A Journey towards Jerusalem*, Oxford: Bible Reading Fellowship.

HINDSON, EDWARD (1997), *Approaching Armageddon: The World Prepares for War with God*, Eugene, OR: Harvest House.

HITCHCOCK, MARK (2002), *Is America in Prophecy?*, Portland, OR: Multnomah.

HODGES, JESSE WILSON (1957), *Christ's Kingdom and Coming with an Analysis of Dispensationalism*, Grand Rapids: Eerdmans.

HOLWERDA, DAVID E. (1995), *Jesus and Israel: One Covenant or Two?*, Leicester: IVP.

HOUSE, H. WAYNE (ed.) (1998), *Israel The Land and the People*, Grand Rapids, MI: Kregel.

HOUSE, H. WAYNE and THOMAS ICE (1988), *Dominion Theology: Blessing or Curse?*, Portland: OR: Multnomah.

HULSE, ERROL (1982), *The Restoration of Israel*, 3rd edn, Worthing: Henry Walter.

HUNT, DAVE (1983), *Peace, Prosperity and the Coming Holocaust*, Eugene, OR: Harvest House.

——(1990), *Global Peace and the Rise of Antichrist*, Eugene, OR: Harvest House.

——(1995), *A Cup of Trembling: Jerusalem and Bible Prophecy*, Eugene, OR: Harvest House.

ICE, THOMAS and RANDALL PRICE (1992), *Ready to Rebuild: The Imminent Plan to Rebuild the Last Days Temple*, Eugene, OR: Harvest House.

INTERNATIONAL CHRISTIAN EMBASSY JERUSALEM (1996), *Christians and Israel: Essays in Biblical Zionism and on Islamic Fundamentalism*, Jerusalem: ICEJ.

IRVING, EDWARD (1827), *The Coming of Messiah in Glory and Majesty, by Juan Josafat Ben-Ezra a converted Jew, Translated from the Spanish, with a Preliminary Discourse*, London: L. B. Seeley & Sons.

——(1828), *Babylon and Infidelity Foredoomed by God: A Discourse on the Prophecies of Daniel and the Apocalypse which relate to these Latter Times, and until the Second Advent*, 2nd edn, Glasgow: William Collins.

——(1828), *The Last Days: A Discourse on the Evil Character of These Our Times Proving Them to be the 'Perilous Times' of the 'Last Days'*, London: James Nisbet.

JEFFREY, GRANT R. (1991), *Messiah: War in the Middle East & Road to Armageddon*, Toronto: Frontier Research Publications.

JOHNSTON, PHILIP and PETER WALKER (eds.) (2000), *The Land of Promise: Biblical, Theological and Contemporary Perspectives*, Leicester: Apollos.

JORSTAD, ERLING (1970), *The Politics of Doomsday: Fundamentalists of the Far Right*, Nashville: Abingdon.

KAC, ARTHUR (1958), *The Rebirth of the State of Israel, Is it of God or of men?*, London: Marshall, Morgan & Scott.

KAPLAN, ROBERT D. (1993), *The Arabists: The Romance of an American Elite*, New York: Macmillan.

KRAUS, C. NORMAN (1958), *Dispensationalism in America*, Richmond: John Knox.

KYLE, RICHARD (1998), *The Last Days are Here Again*, Grand Rapids: Baker.

LADD, GEORGE ELDON (1956), *The Blessed Hope: A Biblical Study of the Second Advent and the Rapture*, Grand Rapids: Eerdmans.

LAHAYE, TIM and JERRY B. JENKINS (1995), *Left Behind*, Wheaton: Tyndale House.

—(1999), *Are We Living in the End Times?*, Wheaton: Tyndale House.

LAHAYE, TIM and THOMAS ICE (eds.) (2003), *The End Times Controversy: The Second Coming Under Attack*, Eugene, OR: Harvest House.

LAMBERT, LANCE (1975), *The Battle for Israel*, Eastbourne: Kingsway.

LAWRENCE, BRUCE B. (1989), *Defenders of God: The Fundamentalist Revolt Against the Modern Age*, San Francisco: Harper & Row.

LESHEM, MOSHE (1989), *Balaam's Curse: How Israel Lost Its Way And How It Can Find It Again*, New York: Simon & Schuster.

LIEBMAN, ROBERT C. and ROBERT WUTHNOW (eds.) (1983), *The New Christian Right: Mobilization and Legitimation*, New York: Aldine.

LIENESCH, MICHAEL (1993), *Redeeming America: Piety & Politics in the New Christian Right*, Chapel Hill, NC: University of North Carolina Press.

LINDBERG, BETH M. (n.d.), *A God-Filled Life: The Story of William E. Blackstone*, Chicago: American Messianic Fellowship.

LINDSEY, HAL (1970), *The Late Great Planet Earth*, London: Lakeland.

—(1973), *There's a New World Coming*, New York: Vision House.

—(1981), *The 1980's: Countdown to Armageddon*, New York: Bantam.

—(1983), *Israel and the Last Days*, Eugene, OR: Harvest House.

—(1989), *The Road to Holocaust*, New York: Bantam.

—(1994), *Planet Earth 2000 AD*, Palos Verdes, CA: Western Front.

—(1995), *The Final Battle*, Palos Verdes, CA: Western Front.

—(1997), *The Apocalypse Code*, Palos Verdes, CA: Western Front.

—(2003), *The Everlasting Hatred: The Roots Of Jihad*, Murrieta, CA: Oracle House.

LIPSET, SEYMOUR MARTIN and EARL RAAB (1971), *The Politics of Unreason: Right-Wing Extremism in America 1790–1970*, London: Heinemann.

MACPHERSON, DAVE (1983), *The Great Rapture Hoax*, Fletcher, NC: New Puritan Library.

MARSDEN, GEORGE M. (1980), *Fundamentalism and American Culture: The Shaping of Twentieth Century Evangelicalism 1870–1925*, New York: Oxford University Press.

—(1991), *Understanding Fundamentalism and Evangelicalism*, Grand Rapids: Eerdmans.

MARSHALL, I. HOWARD (ed.) (1977), *New Testament Interpretation: Essays in Principles and Methods*, Exeter: Paternoster.

MARTENS, E. A. (1981), *Plot and Purpose in the Old Testament*, Leicester: IVP.

MARTY, MARTIN E. (1970), *Righteous Empire: The Protestant Experience in America*, New York: Harper & Row.

MARTY, MARTIN and R. SCOTT APPLEBY (eds.) (1991), *Fundamentalism Observed*, Chicago: University Chicago Press.

MATHISON, KEITH A. (1995), *Dispensationalism: Rightly Dividing the People of God?* Phillipsburg, NJ: Presbyterian & Reformed.

MERKLEY, PAUL (1998), *The Politics of Christian Zionism 1891–1948*, London: Frank Cass.

—(2001), *Christian Attitudes towards the State of Israel*, Kingston and London: McGill-Queen's University Press.

MIDDLE EAST COUNCIL OF CHURCHES (1988), *What is Western Fundamentalist Christian Zionism?*, rev. edn, Limassol, Cyprus: MECC.

MOODY, WILLIAM R. (1900), *The Life of Dwight L. Moody*, Murfreesboro, TN: Sword of the Lord.

MORRIS, LEON (1973), *Apocalyptic*, London: IVP.

MOTYER, ALEC (1996), *Look to the Rock: An Old Testament Background to our Understanding of Christ*, Leicester: IVP.

MOTYER, STEVE (1989), *Israel in the Plan of God: Light on Today's Debate*, Leicester: IVP.

MURRAY, IAN (1971), *The Puritan Hope: Revival and the Interpretation of Prophecy*, Edinburgh: Banner of Truth.

NEWTON, BENJAMIN WILLS (1859), *Antichrist, Europe and the Middle East: The Antichrist Future*, London: Houlston & Sons.

—(1863), *Map of Ten Kingdoms of Roman Empire*, London: Lucus Collins.

—(1890), *Babylon: Its Future History and Doom with remarks on the Future of Egypt and Other Eastern Countries*, 3rd edn, London: Houlston & Sons.

NOE, JOHN (1999), *Beyond the End Times: The Rest of the Greatest Story Ever Told*, Bradford, PA: International Preterist Association.

—(2000), *Shattering the 'Left Behind' Delusion*, Bradford, PA: International Preterist Association.

NOLL, MARK A. (1994), *The Scandal of the Evangelical Mind*, Leicester: IVP.

O'NEILL, DAN and DON WAGNER (1993), *Peace or Armageddon?: The Unfolding Drama of the Middle East Peace Accord*, Grand Rapids: Zondervan.

PACKER, J. I. (1958), *'Fundamentalism' and the Word of God*, London: IVP.

—(1980), *Beyond the Battle for the Bible*, Westchester, IL: Cornerstone.

PALMER, H. P. (1935), *Joseph Wolff, His Romantic Life and Travels*, London: Heath Cranton.

PATE, C. MARVIN (ed.) (1998), *Four Views of the Book of Revelation*, Grand Rapids: Zondervan.

PATE, C. MARVIN and CALVIN B. HAINES (1995), *Doomsday Delusions: What's Wrong with Predictions about the End of the World*, Downers Grove, IL: IVP.

PAYNE, J. BARTON (1973), *Encyclopaedia of Biblical Prophecy: The Complete Guide to Scriptural Predictions and Their Fulfilment*, London: Hodder & Stoughton.

PENTECOST, DWIGHT (1958), *Things to Come: A Study in Biblical Eschatology*, 1st edn, Grand Rapids: Zondervan; 2nd edn, 1964.

PETERS, JOAN (1984), *From Time Immemorial: The Origins of the Arab–Jewish Conflict Over Palestine*, London: Michael Joseph.

PIETERS, ALBERTUS (n.d.), *A Candid Examination of the Scofield Bible*, Grand Rapids: Douma Publications.

PRAGAI, M. J. (1985), *Faith and Fulfilment: Christians and the Return to the Promised Land*, London: Vallentine, Mitchell.

PRICE, RANDALL (1999), *The Coming Last Days Temple*, Eugene, OR: Harvest House.

—(2002), *Unholy War: America, Israel and Radical Islam*, Eugene, OR: Harvest House.

PRINCE, DEREK (1982), *The Last Word on the Middle East*, Fort Lauderdale: Derek Prince Ministries International.

—(1992), *The Destiny of Israel and the Church*, Milton Keynes: Word.

PRIOR, MICHAEL (1997), *The Bible and Colonialism: A Moral Critique*, Sheffield: Sheffield Academic Press.

—(1999), *Zionism and the State of Israel: A Moral Inquiry*, London: Routledge.

RAMM, BERNARD (1970), *Protestant Biblical Interpretation: A Textbook of Hermeneutics*, 3rd edn, Grand Rapids: Baker.

—(1983), *After Fundamentalism: The Future of Evangelical Theology*, San Francisco: Harper & Row.

RANTISI, AUDEH (2003), *Blessed are the Peacemakers: A Palestinian Christian in the West Bank*, Swindon: Eagle.

RAUSCH, DAVID A. (1979), *Zionism within early American Fundamentalism, 1878–1918: a convergence of two traditions*, New York: Mellen Press.

—(1991), *Communities in Conflict: Evangelicals and Jews*, Valley Forge, PA: Trinity Press International.

—(1993), *Fundamentalists, Evangelicals and Anti-Semitism*, Valley Forge, PA: Trinity Press International.

RICHARDS, ROB (1994), *Has God Finished with Israel?*, Crowborough: Monarch Olive.

RIGGANS, WALTER (1988), *Israel and Zionism*, London, Handsell.

ROBERTSON, O. PALMER (1980), *The Christ of the Covenants*, Phillipsburg, NJ: Presbyterian & Reformed.

— (2000), *The Israel of God*, Phillipsburg, NJ: Presbyterian & Reformed.

ROBERTSON, PAT (1992), *The Secret Kingdom: Your Path to Peace, Love and Financial Security*, rev. edn, Dallas: Word.

ROSEN, MOISHE (1991), *Overture to Armageddon? Beyond the Gulf War*, San Bernardino, CA: Here's Life Publishers.

RUETHER, ROSEMARY RADFORD and HERMAN J. RUETHER (1989), *The Wrath of Jonah: The Crisis of Religious Nationalism in the Israeli–Palestinian Conflict*, San Francisco: Harper.

RUSSELL, D. S. (1994), *Prophecy and the Apocalyptic Dream: Protest and Promise*, Peabody, MA: Hendrikson.

RYRIE, CHARLES C. (1953), *The Basis of the Premillennial Faith*, Neptune, NJ: Loizeaux Brothers.

—(1995), *Dispensationalism*, Chicago: Moody Press.

SAID, EDWARD W. (1978), *Orientalism*, New York: Vintage.

—(1992), *The Question of Palestine*, rev. edn, London: Vintage.

—(1993), *Culture and Imperialism*, London: Chatto & Windus.

—(1995), *The Politics of Dispossession: The Struggle for Palestinian Self Determination 1969–1994*, London: Vintage.

SANDEEN, ERNEST ROBERT (1970), *The Roots of Fundamentalism: British & American Millenarianism 1800–1930*, Chicago: University Chicago Press.

SARDAR, ZIAUDDIN and MERRYL WYN DAVIES (2002), *Why do People Hate America?*, Cambridge: Icon.

SAUCY, ROBERT L. (1993), *The Case for Progressive Dispensationalism: The Interface Between Dispensational and Non-Dispensational Theology*, Grand Rapids: Zondervan.

SCHLINK, BASILEA M. (1987), *Israel, My Chosen People*, rev. edn, Basingstoke: Marshall Pickering.

SCHLISSEL, STEVE and DAVID BROWN (1990), *Hal Lindsey and the Restoration of the Jews*, Edmonton, Alberta: Still Waters Revival Books.

SCHUYLER ENGLISH E. (ed.) (1984), *The New Scofield Study Bible*, New York: Oxford University Press.

SCOFIELD, CYRUS INGERSON (1888), *Rightly Dividing the Word of Truth*, New York: Loizeaux Brothers.

—(1917), *The Scofield Reference Bible*, London: Oxford University Press.

—(1918), *What do the Prophets say?*, London: Marshall Bros.

SHARIF, REGINA (1983), *Non-Jewish Zionism: Its Roots in Western History*, London: Zed.

SHEPHERD, NAOMI (1987), *The Zealous Intruders: The Western Rediscovery of Palestine*, London: Douve.

SIMEON, CHARLES (1832–1855), *Horae Homileticae: Discourses on the Old and New Testament*, 21 vols., London: Samuel Holdsworth.

SIMON, MERRILL (1984), *Jerry Falwell and the Jews*, Middle Village, NY: Jonathan David.

SIZER, STEPHEN (1999), 'Christian Zionism: A British Perspective', in Naim Ateek and Michael Prior (eds.), *Holy Land – Hollow Jubilee*, London: Melisende, pp. 189–198.

—(2000), 'The Premised Land, Palestine and Israel', in Michael Prior (ed.), *They Came and They Saw*, London: Melisende, pp. 144–161.

—(2000), 'A Survey of Guidebooks on the Holy Land', in Duncan Macpherson (ed.), *A Third Millennium Guide to Pilgrimages to the Holy Land*, London: Melisende, pp. 71–83.

—(2000), 'Dispensational Approaches to the Land', in Johston and Walker (eds.), *The Land of Promise*, pp. 142–171.

—(2003), *In the Steps of Jesus and the Apostles*, Swindon: Eagle.

STEARNS, WENDELL (1994), *Biblical Zionism*, Hilversum, Holland: Moriah Foundation.

STEVENS, GEORGE H. (1959), *Go, Tell My Brethren: A Short Popular History of Church Missions to Jews*, London: Olive.

STEWART, DON and CHUCK MISSLER (1991), *The Coming Temple*, Orange, CA: Dart.

STRAUB, GERARD THOMAS (1988), *Salvation for Sale: An Insider's View of Pat Robertson*, Buffalo, NY: Prometheus.

STROZIER, CHARLES B. (1994), *Apocalypse: On the Psychology of Fundamentalism in America*, Boston: Beacon.

TOON, PETER (ed.) (1970), *Puritans, the Millennium and the Future of Israel: Puritan Eschatology 1600–1660*, Cambridge: James Clarke.

TRAVIS, STEPHEN (1988), *I Believe in the Second Coming of Jesus*, rev. edn, London: Hodder.

TREGALLES, S. P. (1886), *Hope of Christ's Second Coming*, London: Hunt, Barnard & Co.

TUCHMAN, BARBARA W. (1957), *Bible and Sword: How the British came to Palestine*, London: Macmillan.

TUCKER, RUTH (1999), *Not Ashamed: The Story of Jews for Jesus*, Sisters, OR: Multnomah.

VAN DER HOEVEN, JAN WILLEM (1993), *Babylon or Jerusalem?* Shippensburg: Destiny Image.

VAN DER WAAL, C. (1991), *Hal Lindsey and Biblical Prophecy*, Neerlandia, Alberta: Inheritance Publications.

VENEMA, CORNELIS P. (2000), *The Promise of the Future*, Edinburgh: Banner of Truth.

WAGNER, DONALD E. (1995), *Anxious for Armageddon*, Scottdale, PA: Herald Press.

—(2001), *Dying in the Land of Promise*, London: Melisende.

WAGNER, DONALD E. and DAN O'NEILL (1993), *Peace or Armageddon?: The Unfolding Drama of the Middle East Peace Accord*, Grand Rapids: Zondervan.

WALKER, ANDREW (1985), *Restoring the Kingdom: The Radical Christianity of the House Church Movement*, London: Hodder & Stoughton.

WALKER, PETER W. L. (1996), *Jesus and the Holy City: New Testament Perspectives on Jerusalem*, Grand Rapids: Eerdmans.

— (ed.) (1992), *Jerusalem, Past & Present in the Purpose of God*, rev. edn, Cambridge: Tyndale House.

WALVOORD, JOHN F. (1957), *The Rapture Question*, Findlay, OH: Dunham.

—(1962), *Israel in Prophecy*, Grand Rapids: Zondervan.

—(1990), *The Prophecy Knowledge Handbook*, Wheaton, IL: Victor.

—(1990), *Armageddon, Oil and the Middle East Crisis*, Grand Rapids: Zondervan.

—(1993), *The Final Drama*, Grand Rapids: Kregal.

—(1998), *End Times: Understanding Today's World Events in Biblical Prophecy*, Waco, TX: Word.

WAY, LEWIS (1821), *The Latter Rain*, 2nd edn, London.

WEBER, TIMOTHY P. (1979), *Living in the Shadow of the Second Coming: American Premillennialism 1875–1982*, New York: Oxford University Press.

WHISENANT, EDGAR (1988), *88 Reasons Why the Rapture Will Be in 1988*, Nashville: World Bible Society.

WHITE, JOHN WESLEY (1992), *Thinking the Unthinkable: Armageddon – are all the pieces in place?*, Milton Keynes: Word.

WILCOCK, MICHAEL (1975), *I Saw Heaven Opened: The Message of Revelation*, BST, Leicester: IVP.

WILKEN, ROBERT L. (1992), *The Land Called Holy: Palestine in Christian History and Thought*, New Haven: Yale University Press.

WILKINSON, JOHN (1978), *God's Plan for the Jews*, London: Messianic Testimony.

WILLS, GARRY (1990), *Under God: Religion and American Politics*, New York: Simon & Schuster.

WILSON, DWIGHT (1977), *Armageddon Now! The Premillenarian Response to Russia and Israel since 1917*, Grand Rapids: Baker.

WYNGAARDEN, MARTIN J. (1955), *The Future of the Kingdom in Prophecy and Fulfillment*, Grand Rapids: Baker.

YAMAUCHI, EDWIN (1982), *Foes from the Northern Frontier*, Grand Rapids: Baker.

YOUSSEF, MICHAEL (1991), *America, Oil & the Islamic Mind: The Real Crisis Is the Gulf Between Our Ways of Thinking*, Grand Rapids: Zondervan.

INDEX OF PEOPLE

INDEX OF SUBJECTS

INDEX OF BIBLICAL REFERENCES